Oxford Studies in the History of Art and Architecture

General Editors
Anthony Blunt   Francis Haskell   Charles Mitchell

THE
PRE-RAPHAELITE
LANDSCAPE

ALLEN STALEY

CLARENDON PRESS · OXFORD

1973

Oxford University Press, Ely House, London W.1

GLASGOW NEW YORK TORONTO MELBOURNE WELLINGTON
CAPE TOWN SALISBURY IBADAN NAIROBI DAR ES SALAAM LUSAKA ADDIS ABABA
BOMBAY CALCUTTA MADRAS KARACHI LAHORE DACCA
KUALA LUMPUR SINGAPORE HONG KONG TOKYO

PRINTED IN GREAT BRITAIN BY LUND HUMPHRIES

For

Etheleen and Oliver

Preface

THE BEST-KNOWN artists belonging to or associated with the Pre-Raphaelite Brotherhood were not primarily landscape painters, and their best-known pictures are not landscape paintings. This book is not a history of the movement, but a one-sided look at the work of some of these artists during the 1850s and 1860s, and the reader should bear in mind that there were other facets of the movement which are here ignored. The name of Dante Gabriel Rossetti is conspicuously absent from most of the following pages, and I have made no effort to discuss his central contribution to the history of the Pre-Raphaelite Brotherhood and to nineteenth-century art in general. On the other hand, I hope that the reader will be able to see the activities of these artists in a perspective not unlike that of the exhibition-going public of the 1850s, for whom Rossetti's work was unknown and Pre-Raphaelitism was what Ruskin said it was. The book is not just about Pre-Raphaelite landscape painting, but also about the Pre-Raphaelite approach to the natural world, which did lead eventually to the emergence of a school of landscape painting as an integral but distinctive part of the Pre-Raphaelite movement.

If Rossetti's name is missing, that of John Ruskin appears more frequently than that of any single artist, and this is how it should be. Ruskin dominated the contemporary art world of the 1850s. He provided the underlying ideas; he patronized the artists; he was their chosen advocate; and he remains the one mid-Victorian writer on art whose critical opinions are of more than documentary or curiosity value. Ruskin loomed large in the consciousness of most of the artists discussed in this book, and he must inevitably loom large in our awareness of their art. I have quoted and discussed his opinions abundantly, but I have tried to do so in a fashion that illuminates the pictures, rather than using the pictures to illustrate his ideas. Although I hope that this examination of activities with which he was involved in myriad ways will reflect some light, this is not a book about Ruskin.

I began this study in London in 1960 and submitted it in considerably different form as a doctoral dissertation at Yale University in 1965. I am indebted to Michael Kitson and to Robert Herbert, who gave me much assistance at the beginning of my investigations, and I owe a particular debt to George Heard Hamilton, who supervised the writing of my dissertation. Since 1965, the general re-awakening of interest in Victorian art has brought to light large numbers of works by the less well-known artists, and our knowledge of the major figures has been considerably expanded, particularly by Mary Bennett's exhibitions of John Everett Millais and Holman Hunt, and by books on Millais, Hunt, and Rossetti by Mary Lutyens, Diana Holman-Hunt, and Virginia Surtees. Incorporating what I have learned since 1965 has meant writing what is essentially a new book. I am grateful to John Gere, who has given me advice and encouragement from the beginning; indeed, a footnote in his catalogue for the Phaidon Press *Pre-Raphaelite Painters* of 1948 was my initial point of departure. Mary Bennett has throughout generously shared the results of her investigations with me, and only she can know how deeply I am in her debt. In addition, the invariable hospitality and helpfulness of collectors, dealers, scholars, and museum officials have made my work easier and pleasanter than I ever deserved, and I can never properly acknowledge all the assistance I have received or my debts for suggestions and bits of information. However, I would like to record my gratitude to the following people: Keith Andrews, Patrick J. Brett, Charles Carter, James Coats, Malcolm Cormack, Peter Fitzgerald, M. A. Ford, Mrs. Robert Frank, Robin Gibson, the late Charles Handley-Read, M. S. Hickox, the Reverend Gerald Hollis, Nerys Johnson, Elizabeth Johnston, Dr. Gilbert Leathart, Ian Lowe, Jeremy Maas, Hugh Macandrew, Ronald Marshall, Richard Morphet, Armide Oppé, Richard Ormond, Andrew McIntosh Patrick, William Plomer, Graham Reynolds, Ian Robertson, Robert Rosenblum, Miranda Strickland-Constable, Colin Thompson, Mrs. Warwick Tompkin, William Vaughan, Mrs. C. D. Wales, Ellis K. Waterhouse, Catherine Williams, and John Woodward. My employers since 1962, the Frick Collection, the Philadelphia Museum of Art, and Columbia University, have all been generous with time, facilities, and financial support; in 1970 I was the recipient of a grant from the Columbia University Council for Research in the Humanities. Finally, I am grateful to the staff of the Clarendon Press for proposing that I make this study into a book and for subsequent supervision of its production.

New York
October 1972

Contents

List of Plates

COLOUR

MONOCHROME

34a William Holman Hunt
Helston, Cornwall
1860
Watercolour
$7\frac{5}{8} \times 10\frac{1}{8}$ in.
Whitworth Art Gallery, University of
Manchester

34b William Holman Hunt
Festa at Fiesole (True Merit Overlooked)
1868
Watercolour
$13\frac{3}{4} \times 19\frac{7}{8}$ in.
Collection of Mrs. E. M. S. C. Tompkin

35a William Holman Hunt
Sunset at Chimalditi
1868
Watercolour
$14 \times 20\frac{1}{8}$ in.
Private collection, Great Britain

35b William Holman Hunt
Sunset in the Val d'Arno
1868
Watercolour
$14 \times 19\frac{3}{4}$ in.
The Johannesburg Art Gallery

36a William Holman Hunt
The Ponte Vecchio, Florence
between 1866 and 1869
Watercolour
$10 \times 21\frac{1}{2}$ in.
Victoria and Albert Museum, London

36b William Holman Hunt
The Festival of St. Swithin
dated 1866–75
Oil on canvas
$28\frac{3}{4} \times 35\frac{7}{8}$ in.
Ashmolean Museum, Oxford

37a William Holman Hunt
*London Bridge on the Night of the Marriage of the
Prince and Princess of Wales*
1863
Oil on canvas
$25\frac{5}{8} \times 38\frac{5}{8}$ in.
Ashmolean Museum, Oxford

37b William Holman Hunt
The Ship
1875
Oil on linen
$29\frac{1}{2} \times 38$ in.
Tate Gallery, London

38a James Collinson
*Mother and Daughter: Culver Cliff, Isle of
Wight, in the Distance*
c.1855
Oil on panel
$20\frac{3}{4} \times 16\frac{5}{8}$ in.
Collection of Mr. and Mrs. Paul Mellon

38b Dante Gabriel Rossetti
The Bower Meadow
1850–72
Oil on canvas
$33\frac{1}{2} \times 26\frac{1}{2}$ in.
City Art Gallery, Manchester

39a Edward Hopley
Puck and the Moth
exhibited 1853
Oil on board
$10\frac{1}{8} \times 6\frac{1}{4}$ in.
Collection of Lady Clark

39b Edward Hopley
Puck and the Moth
exhibited 1853
Oil on board
$10\frac{1}{8} \times 6\frac{1}{4}$ in.
Collection of Lady Clark

40a John Everett Millais
*A Huguenot, on St. Bartholomew's Day, Refusing
to Shield Himself from Danger by Wearing the
Roman Catholic Badge*
1851–2
Oil on canvas
$36\frac{7}{8} \times 25\frac{5}{8}$ in.
Private collection, Great Britain

40b Charles Allston Collins
The Good Harvest of 1854
exhibited 1855
Oil on canvas
$17\frac{1}{4} \times 13\frac{3}{4}$ in.
Victoria and Albert Museum, London

41a Arthur Hughes
The Young Poet
c.1849
Oil on canvas
25×36 in.
City Museum and Art Gallery, Birmingham

41b Arthur Hughes
Ophelia
exhibited 1852
Oil on canvas
$27 \times 48\frac{3}{4}$ in.
City Art Gallery, Manchester

41c Arthur Hughes
The Long Engagement
1853–9
Oil on canvas
$41\frac{1}{2} \times 20\frac{1}{2}$ in.
City Museum and Art Gallery, Birmingham

42a Arthur Hughes
Home from Sea
1856–63
Oil on panel
$20 \times 25\frac{3}{4}$ in.
Ashmolean Museum, Oxford

51b   Thomas Seddon
Jerusalem and the Valley of Jehoshaphat from the
Hill of Evil Counsel
1854–5
Oil on canvas
$26\frac{1}{2} \times 32\frac{3}{4}$ in.
Tate Gallery, London

52a   Thomas Seddon
The Well of Enrogel
1854
Watercolour
$9\frac{3}{4} \times 13\frac{3}{4}$ in.
Harris Museum and Art Gallery, Preston

52b   Thomas Seddon
The Mountains of Moab
1854
Watercolour
$9\frac{15}{16} \times 13\frac{7}{8}$ in.
Ashmolean Museum, Oxford

53a   Thomas Seddon
Arabs at Prayer in the Desert
begun 1855
Oil on canvas
$25\frac{3}{8} \times 44\frac{1}{8}$ in.
Private collection, U.S.A.

53b   Thomas Seddon
View on the Nile
dated 1855
Oil on canvas
8×12 in.
Ashmolean Museum, Oxford

54a   George Price Boyce
Near the Public Gardens, Venice
1854
Watercolour
$7\frac{3}{8} \times 10\frac{5}{8}$ in.
Collection of Mrs. John Gere

54b   George Price Boyce
Tomb of Cangrande della Scala, S. Maria Antica,
Verona
1854
Watercolour
15×11 in.
J. S. Maas & Co. Ltd., London

55a   George Price Boyce
The Mill on the Thames at Mapledurham
1860
Watercolour
$10\frac{1}{2} \times 22$ in.
Reproduced by permission of the Syndics of
the Fitzwilliam Museum, Cambridge

55b   George Price Boyce
At Binsey, near Oxford
1862
Watercolour
$12\frac{1}{2} \times 21\frac{1}{8}$ in.
Cecil Higgins Art Gallery, Bedford

56a   George Price Boyce
Red Barn at Whitchurch
1863
Watercolour
$8\frac{1}{16} \times 11\frac{5}{16}$ in.
Ashmolean Museum, Oxford

56b   George Price Boyce
Landscape: Wootton, Autumn
1864–5
Watercolour
$9\frac{3}{4} \times 13\frac{3}{4}$ in.
Tate Gallery, London

57a   George Price Boyce
The Thames by Night from the Adelphi
exhibited 1866
Watercolour
$8\frac{3}{4} \times 13\frac{1}{8}$ in.
Tate Gallery, London

57b   George Price Boyce
From a Window at Ludlow
1871
Watercolour
$5\frac{1}{2} \times 7\frac{7}{8}$ in.
National Gallery of Scotland, Edinburgh

58a   John William Inchbold
Flamborough Head
1849
Watercolour
$9\frac{1}{2} \times 12\frac{1}{4}$ in.
Collection of M. Hailparn

58b   John William Inchbold
Thames, Early Morning
c.1849
Watercolour
10×14 in.
Collection of Mr. and Mrs. Paul Mellon

59a   John William Inchbold
The Chapel, Bolton
1853
Oil on canvas
$25\frac{1}{2} \times 33$ in.
Northampton Art Gallery

59b   John William Inchbold
The Moorland (Dewar-Stone, Dartmoor)
1854
Oil on canvas
$13\frac{3}{4} \times 20\frac{1}{2}$ in.
Tate Gallery, London

60a   John William Inchbold
At Bolton (The White Doe of Rylstone)
1855
Oil on canvas
27×20 in.
City Art Gallery, Leeds

70 John Brett
Val d'Aosta
1858
Oil on canvas
$34\frac{1}{2} \times 26\frac{7}{8}$ in.
Collection of Sir Francis Cooper, Bt.

71a John Brett
Florence from Bellosguardo
1862–3
Oil on canvas
$23\frac{1}{2} \times 39\frac{1}{2}$ in.
Tate Gallery, London

71b John Brett
Massa, Bay of Naples
1864
Oil on canvas
$25\frac{1}{4} \times 40\frac{1}{4}$ in.
Herron Museum of Art, Indianapolis

72a John Brett
Morants Court in May
1864
Oil on canvas
$17\frac{1}{2} \times 27\frac{1}{2}$ in.
Collection of Mr. and Mrs. Allen Staley

72b John Brett
Study for *The Hedger*
*c.*1860
Monochrome wash and bodycolour
$9\frac{3}{4} \times 7\frac{1}{8}$ in.
Private collection, Great Britain

72c John Brett
Near Goring-on-Thames
1865
Watercolour
12×16 in.
Whitworth Art Gallery, University of
Manchester

73a John Brett
Etna from the Heights of Taormina
1870–1
Oil on canvas
$33 \times 48\frac{1}{2}$ in.
Mappin Art Gallery, Sheffield

73b John Brett
*The British Channel Seen from the Dorsetshire
Cliffs*
1871
Oil on canvas
$41\frac{3}{4} \times 83\frac{3}{4}$ in.
Tate Gallery, London

74a Robert Tonge
Cheshire Landscape
1853
Oil on canvas
$20 \times 34\frac{1}{8}$ in.
Walker Art Gallery, Liverpool

74b William Davis
Bidston Marsh at Wallasey
1853
Oil on board
$11\frac{7}{8} \times 17\frac{7}{8}$ in.
Walker Art Gallery, Liverpool

75 William Davis
Old Mill and Pool at Ditton, Lancashire
Oil on canvas
$20\frac{7}{8} \times 14\frac{1}{8}$ in.
Walker Art Gallery, Liverpool

76a William Davis
At Hale, Lancashire
Oil on canvas
$13 \times 19\frac{3}{4}$ in.
Walker Art Gallery, Liverpool

76b William Davis
A Field of Green Corn
Oil on panel
12×15 in.
Collection of John Gillum

77a William Davis
A Grass Field
Oil on canvas
9×13 in.
Collection of John Gillum

77b William Davis
Harrowing
*c.*1859
Oil on canvas
$17\frac{1}{4} \times 26$ in.
Private collection, Great Britain

78a Alfred William Hunt
Gwm Trifaen – The Track of an Ancient Glacier
*c.*1858
Oil on canvas
$23\frac{3}{4} \times 35\frac{3}{4}$ in.
Tate Gallery, London

78b Alfred William Hunt
Welsh Landscape
1858
Watercolour
$9\frac{7}{8} \times 14\frac{1}{4}$ in.
Ashmolean Museum, Oxford

79a Alfred William Hunt
Brignal Banks
*c.*1859
Oil on canvas
$11\frac{1}{4} \times 18\frac{1}{8}$ in.
Walker Art Gallery, Liverpool

79b Alfred William Hunt
*A November Rainbow – Dolwyddelan Valley,
1865*
Watercolour
$19\frac{1}{2} \times 29\frac{3}{4}$ in.
Ashmolean Museum, Oxford

80a John Edward Newton
Gresford Mill
c.1861
Oil on canvas
12 × 14$\frac{1}{2}$ in.
Walker Art Gallery, Liverpool

80b Daniel Alexander Williamson
Peckham Common – Milking Time
c.1855–60
Watercolour
11$\frac{1}{2}$ × 15$\frac{1}{3}$ in.
Walker Art Gallery, Liverpool

81a Daniel Alexander Williamson
Morecambe Bay from Warton Crag
1862
Oil on board
9$\frac{15}{16}$ × 13$\frac{1}{4}$ in.
Walker Art Gallery, Liverpool

81b Daniel Alexander Williamson
Spring: Arnside Knot and Coniston Range of Hills from Warton Crag
1863
Oil on canvas
10$\frac{5}{8}$ × 16 in.
Walker Art Gallery, Liverpool

82a Daniel Alexander Williamson
Near the Duddon
1864
Oil on board
8$\frac{1}{2}$ × 14 in.
Williamson Art Gallery, Birkenhead

82b William Lindsay Windus
The Stray Lamb
1864
Oil on board
8$\frac{3}{4}$ × 12$\frac{1}{2}$ in.
Walker Art Gallery, Liverpool

83a William Millais
Hayes Common
1852–3
Oil on canvas
21$\frac{1}{2}$ × 33$\frac{1}{2}$ in.
Collection of Mr. and Mrs. Paul Mellon

83b William Millais
Glenfinlas
1853
Oil on canvas
17$\frac{1}{2}$ × 25$\frac{1}{2}$ in.
Collection of Lord Sherfield

84a Edward Lear
The Quarries of Syracuse
1847
Pen and watercolour
13$\frac{7}{8}$ × 19$\frac{7}{8}$ in.
Walker Art Gallery, Liverpool

84b Edward Lear
Venosa
1852
Oil on canvas
19$\frac{3}{4}$ × 32$\frac{3}{8}$ in.
Toledo Museum of Art, Toledo, Ohio

85a James Smetham
Naboth's Vineyard
1856
Oil on panel
8$\frac{3}{4}$ × 6$\frac{3}{4}$ in.
Tate Gallery, London

85b James Smetham
Going Home
c.1877
Watercolour
14$\frac{1}{2}$ × 20$\frac{1}{2}$ in.
Walker Art Gallery, Liverpool

86a John Bunney
Landscape from Fiesole
1867
Watercolour
19$\frac{1}{4}$ × 29$\frac{1}{2}$ in.
Collection of Mrs. E. M. S. C. Tompkin

86b John Bunney
The West Front of St. Mark's
1876–82
Oil on canvas
57 × 89 in.
Collection of the Guild of St. George, University of Reading

87a Frank Randal
Piazza delle Erbe Looking South
1884
Watercolour
13$\frac{7}{8}$ × 9$\frac{3}{4}$ in.
Ashmolean Museum, Oxford

87b Frank Randal
Verona from the Garden of the Palazzo Giusti
1884
Watercolour
8$\frac{1}{2}$ × 5$\frac{1}{4}$ in.
Collection of the Guild of St. George, University of Reading

87c Thomas Matthews Rooke
Laon: View of the Town and Cathedral from the Northeast
1886
Watercolour
9 × 11$\frac{3}{4}$ in.
Collection of the Guild of St. George, University of Reading

88a Thomas Matthews Rooke
Old Chalet at Sierre
1884
Watercolour
$13\frac{1}{4} \times 9\frac{5}{8}$ in.
Collection of the Guild of St. George,
University of Reading

88b Albert Goodwin
St. Anthony's Works, Newcastle upon Tyne
1864
Watercolour
$9\frac{1}{2} \times 13\frac{3}{4}$ in.
Private collection, Great Britain

89a Charles Napier Hemy
Among the Shingle at Clovelly
1864
Oil on canvas
$17\frac{1}{4} \times 28\frac{1}{4}$ in.
Collection of Mrs. Charlotte Frank

89b Atkinson Grimshaw
The Old Mill: Audby
1869
Oil on panel
$24\frac{1}{2} \times 34\frac{1}{2}$ in.
City Art Gallery, Leeds

90a William Dyce
Fisherfolk near a Wreck
1830
Oil on canvas
36×46 in.
Collection of Henry J. Hurst

90b William Dyce
The Rhône at Avignon
1832
Watercolour
$7\frac{1}{4} \times 12$ in.
British Museum, London

91a William Dyce
The Flight into Egypt
Oil on board
$11\frac{1}{4} \times 15\frac{1}{2}$ in.
By permission of the owner, from a private
collection

91b William Dyce
George Herbert at Bemerton
exhibited 1861
Oil on canvas
34×44 in.
Guildhall Art Gallery, London

92a William Dyce
Madonna and Child
1845
Oil on canvas
$31\frac{1}{2} \times 25$ in.
Reproduced by Gracious Permission of Her
Majesty the Queen

92b William Dyce
Christabel
exhibited 1855
Oil on panel
$21\frac{1}{4} \times 17\frac{5}{8}$ in.
Museum and Art Gallery, Glasgow

93a William Dyce
Gethsemane
Oil on board
$16\frac{1}{2} \times 12\frac{3}{8}$ in.
Walker Art Gallery, Liverpool

93b William Dyce
*Titian Preparing to Make His First Essay in
Colouring*
exhibited 1857
Oil on canvas
$36 \times 26\frac{1}{2}$ in.
Art Gallery and Regional Museum, Aberdeen

94a William Dyce
David in the Wilderness
c.1859
Oil on board
$13\frac{7}{8} \times 19\frac{13}{16}$ in.
By permission of the owner, from a private
collection

94b William Dyce
The Man of Sorrows
c.1859
Oil on board
$13\frac{7}{8} \times 19\frac{13}{16}$ in.
By permission of the owner, from a private
collection

95a William Dyce
A Scene in Arran
1859
Oil on board
$13\frac{3}{4} \times 19\frac{3}{4}$ in.
Art Gallery and Regional Museum, Aberdeen

95b William Dyce
Welsh Landscape with Figures
1860
Oil on board
$13\frac{7}{8} \times 19\frac{7}{8}$ in.
Collection of Sir David Scott

96a William Dyce
*Pegwell Bay, Kent – a Recollection of October 5th,
1858*
exhibited 1860
Oil on canvas
$24\frac{1}{2} \times 34\frac{1}{2}$ in.
Tate Gallery, London

96b William Dyce
Pegwell Bay
c.1858
Watercolour
$9\frac{3}{4} \times 13\frac{3}{4}$ in.
Private collection, Great Britain

97a William Mulready
The Mall, Kensington Gravel Pits
c.1811
Oil on canvas
14 × 19¼ in.
Victoria and Albert Museum, London

97b William Mulready
Blackheath Park
exhibited 1852
Oil on panel
13½ × 24 in.
Victoria and Albert Museum, London

98a Myles Birket Foster
The Milk-maid
1860
Watercolour
11¾ × 17½ in.
Victoria and Albert Museum, London

98b Mark Anthony
Thinking of the Future: an Irish Sketch
exhibited 1845
Oil on canvas
21 × 32½ in.
Location unknown.

99a George Hemming Mason
The Gander
exhibited 1865
Oil on canvas
18 × 32 in.
The Trustees of the Lady Lever Art Gallery,
Port Sunlight

99b Frederick Walker
The Plough
1869–70
Oil on canvas
56½ × 83¾ in.
Tate Gallery, London

100a Albert Moore
Study of an Ash Trunk
1857
Watercolour
12 × 9 in.
Ashmolean Museum, Oxford

100b Frederic Leighton
The Lemon Tree
1859
Pencil
21 × 15½ in.
Collection of E. W. Huddart

Abbreviations

Andrews, 1964
Andrews, Keith, *The Nazarenes: A Brotherhood of German Painters in Rome* (Oxford, 1964).

Bennett, 1963
Bennett, Mary, "A Check List of Pre-Raphaelite Pictures Exhibited at Liverpool, and Some of Their Northern Collectors", *Burlington Magazine*, CV, 1963, pp. 486–95.

Bennett, 1964
[Bennett, Mary], *Ford Madox Brown: 1821–1893* (catalogue of an exhibition organized by the Walker Art Gallery, Liverpool), (Liverpool, 1964).

Bennett, 1967
[Bennett, Mary], *PRB: Millais: PRA* (catalogue of an exhibition organized by the Walker Art Gallery, Liverpool, and the Royal Academy of Arts, London), (London, 1967).

Bennett, 1969
[Bennett, Mary], *William Holman Hunt* (catalogue of an exhibition organized by the Walker Art Gallery, Liverpool, and shown also at the Victoria and Albert Museum, London), (Liverpool, 1969).

Boyce, 1941
[Boyce, George Price], "Extracts from Boyce's Diaries: 1851–1875", *The Old Water-Colour Society's Club: Nineteenth Annual Volume: 1941*, edited by Randall Davies (London, 1941) pp. 9–71.

Bradley, 1955
Bradley, John Lewis, *Ruskin's Letters from Venice: 1851–1852* (New Haven, 1955).

Brett, 1886
Three Months on the Scottish Coast: A Series of Sketches and Pictures Painted During the Summer of the Present Year, Accompanied by an Introductory Essay by John Brett (exhibition catalogue), (Fine Art Society, London, 1886).

Brett, 1895
Brett, John, "Landscape at the National Gallery", *Fortnightly Review*, LVII, 1 April 1895, pp. 623–39.

Brown, 1865
The Exhibition of Work and Other Paintings by Ford Madox Brown at the Gallery, 191 Piccadilly (exhibition catalogue), (London, 1865).

Burne-Jones, 1904
Burne-Jones, Georgiana, *Memorials of Edward Burne-Jones*, 2 vols. (London, 1904).

Dafforne, 1860
Dafforne, James, "British Artists: Their Style and Character: No. LI — William Dyce, R.A.", *Art Journal*, 1860, pp. 293–6.

Davies, 1936
Davies, Randall, ed., "William Holman-Hunt, O.M. (1827–1910): Contemporary Notices of His Exhibits in Water Colour", *The Old Water-Colour Society's Club: Thirteenth Annual Volume: 1935–1936* (London, 1936) pp. 12–36.

Doughty and Wahl, 1965–7

Doughty, Oswald, and Wahl, John Robert, *Letters of Dante Gabriel Rossetti*, 4 vols. (incomplete) (Oxford, 1965–7).

Du Maurier, 1951

Du Maurier, Daphne, ed., *The Young George Du Maurier: A Selection of His Letters, 1860–1867* (London, 1951).

Dyce, Mss.

Dyce, James Stirling, "The Life, Correspondence, and Writings of William Dyce, R.A., 1806–64: Painter, Musician, and Scholar", unpublished typescript in the Aberdeen Art Gallery.

Fredeman, 1965

Fredeman, William E., *Pre-Raphaelitism: A Bibliocritical Study* (Cambridge, Mass., 1965).

Gage, 1969

[Gage, John], *A Decade of English Naturalism: 1810–1820* (catalogue of an exhibition at the Norwich Castle Museum and the Victoria and Albert Museum, London, 1969–70), (Norwich, 1969).

Gibson, 1970

Gibson, Robin, "Arthur Hughes: Arthurian and related subjects of the early 1860s", *Burlington Magazine*, CXII, 1970, pp. 451–6.

Gombrich, 1960

Gombrich, E. H., *Art and Illusion: A Study in the Psychology of Pictorial Representation* (Princeton, 1960).

Goodwin, 1934

The Diary of Albert Goodwin, R.W.S. 1883–1927, privately published (1934).

Gosse, 1884

Notes by Mr. Edmund Gosse on the Pictures and Drawings by Mr. Alfred W. Hunt (exhibition catalogue), (Fine Art Society, London, 1884)

Grigson, 1948

Grigson, Geoffrey, "Gordale Scar to the Pre-Raphaelites", *The Listener*, XXXIX, 1948, pp. 24–5.

Grylls, 1957

Grylls, R. Glynn, "The Correspondence of F. G. Stephens", *Times Literary Supplement*, 5 and 12 April 1957, pp. 216 and 232.

Hamerton, 1874

Hamerton, Philip Gilbert, *Thoughts about Art*, new edition, revised (Boston, 1874).

Holman-Hunt, 1969

Holman-Hunt, Diana, *My Grandfather, His Wives and Loves* (London, 1969).

Hueffer, 1896

Hueffer, Ford Madox, *Ford Madox Brown: A Record of His Life and Work* (London, 1896).

Hunt, 1905

Hunt, William Holman, *Pre-Raphaelitism and the Pre-Raphaelite Brotherhood*, 2 vols. (London, 1905).

Ironside and Gere, 1948

Ironside, Robin, and Gere, John, *Pre-Raphaelite Painters* (London, 1948).

James, 1948

James, Admiral Sir William, *The Order of Release: the Story of John Ruskin, Effie Gray and John Everett Millais Told for the First Time in Their Unpublished Letters* (London, 1948).

Lang, 1959–62

    Lang, Cecil Y., ed., *The Swinburne Letters*, 6 vols. (New Haven, 1959–62).

Lutyens, 1967

    Lutyens, Mary, *Millais and the Ruskins* (London, 1967).

Marillier, 1904

    Marillier, H. C., *The Liverpool School of Painters: An Account of the Liverpool Academy from 1810 to 1867. With Memoirs of the Principal Artists* (London, 1904).

Millais, 1899

    Millais, John Guille, *The Life and Letters of Sir John Everett Millais*. 2 vols. (London, 1899).

Noakes, 1968

    Noakes, Vivien, *Edward Lear: The Life of a Wanderer* (London, 1968).

Roget, 1891

    Roget, John Lewis, *A History of the "Old Water-Colour" Society*, 2 vols. (London, 1891).

Rossetti, 1867

    Rossetti, William Michael, *Fine Art, Chiefly Contemporary: Notices Reprinted, with Revisions* (London, 1867).

Rossetti, 1899

    Rossetti, William Michael, ed., *Ruskin: Rossetti: Pre-Raphaelitism: Papers, 1854 to 1862* (London, 1899).

Rossetti, 1900

    Rossetti, William Michael, ed., *Praeraphaelite Diaries and Letters* (London, 1900).

Rossetti, 1903

    Rossetti, William Michael, ed., *Rossetti Papers, 1862 to 1870* (London, 1903).

Rossetti, 1906

    Rossetti, William Michael, *Some Reminiscences*, 2 vols. (London, 1906).

Rossetti, 1911

    Rossetti, William Michael, ed., *The Works of Dante Gabriel Rossetti* (London, 1911).

Ruskin, 1903–12

    Ruskin, John, *The Works of John Ruskin*, edited by E. T. Cook and Alexander Wedderburn, 39 vols. (London, 1903–12).

Scott, 1892

    Scott, William Bell, *Autobiographical Notes, and Notices of His Artistic and Poetic Circle of Friends, 1830–1882*, edited by W. Minto, 2 vols. (London, 1892).

Seddon, 1858

    [Seddon, John Pollard], *Memoir and Letters of the Late Thomas Seddon, Artist, By His Brother* (London, 1858).

Smetham and Davies, 1891

    Smetham, Sarah, and Davies, William, eds., *Letters of James Smetham, with an Introductory Memoir* (London, 1891).

Smith, n.d.

    [Smith, James], *Two Liverpool Artists: In Memoriam: D. A. Williamson, Born 24th September, 1823, Died 12th February, 1903; W. L. Windus, Born 1823, Died October, 1907* [Liverpool], n.d.

Sotheby, 1970

    Catalogue of 19th Century and Modern First Editions, Presentation Copies, Autograph Letters and Literary Manuscripts, sale catalogue (Sotheby & Co., London, 14–15 Dec., 1970).

Spielmann, 1898

Spielmann, M. H., *Millais and His Works* (Edinburgh and London, 1898).

Staley, 1963

Staley, Allen, "William Dyce and Outdoor Naturalism", *Burlington Magazine*, CV, 1963, pp. 470–76.

Stephens, 1850

Seward, John [Stephens, Frederick George], "The Purpose and Tendency of Early Italian Art", *The Germ*, no. 2, Feb., 1850, pp. 58–64.

Stephens, 1860

[Stephens, Frederick George], *William Holman Hunt and His Works: A Memoir of the Artist's Life, with Descriptions of His Pictures* (London, 1860).

Stephens, 1884

Stephens, Frederick George, "William Davis, Landscape Painter, of Liverpool", *Art Journal*, 1884, pp. 325–8.

Troxell, 1937

Troxell, Janet Camp, ed., *Three Rossettis: Unpublished Letters to and from Dante Gabriel, Christina, William* (Cambridge, Mass., 1937).

I

The Pre-Raphaelite Brotherhood from 1848 to 1851

WHEN THE Pre-Raphaelite Brotherhood was formed in the autumn of 1848, no manifesto was issued. Although the members of the Brotherhood and their immediate associates did make statements about the nature and purpose of art at various times, notably in the four issues of their short-lived periodical, *The Germ*, none of these statements can be taken as a clear-cut assertion of the beliefs of the group at the moment of their decision to join together in a Brotherhood. Probably, even at the moment of their greatest unity, they never agreed entirely upon a common purpose. This is certainly implied in Holman Hunt's memoirs, *Pre-Raphaelitism and the Pre-Raphaelite Brotherhood*, published in 1905, where he describes his laborious efforts to educate his friend Dante Gabriel Rossetti as to the true meaning of their movement.[1]

The extreme youth of all the figures involved is perhaps the most important single factor to remember when trying to assay what the artists were attempting when they chose to give themselves a corporate unity. In the autumn of 1848, William Holman Hunt was twenty-one years old; Dante Gabriel Rossetti was twenty; John Everett Millais was only nineteen. Of their four associates in the Brotherhood, William Michael Rossetti, Frederick George Stephens, Thomas Woolner, and James Collinson, none was older than twenty-three. Whatever they may have been, or wanted to be, in 1848, all of them were to change considerably in the next few years. It is with Pre-Raphaelitism as it took shape in the 1850s – or with one aspect of the movement which only came to the forefront in 1851 – that this study is concerned. Nonetheless, the movement was born in the 1840s, and some attention must be paid to its formative years.

Beyond the bonds of youthful conviviality and fellowship, which were of substantial importance, the members of the Brotherhood were probably most strongly united in their dislike of the conventionality and insipidity of most of the painting they saw being produced and exhibited around them. Holman Hunt's account of the movement's formation describes their 'determination ever to do battle against the frivolous art of the day, which had for its ambition "Monkeyana" ideas, "Books of Beauty", Chorister Boys, whose forms were those of melted wax with drapery of no tangible texture'.[2] In particular, the Pre-Raphaelites disliked the rising young associate members of the Royal Academy, whose pictures Dante Gabriel Rossetti described in 1850 as 'so closely resembling each other (though from different hands) as hardly to establish a separate recollection'.[3] In the review in which this comment appeared, Rossetti specifically cited William Powell Frith, Frederick Goodall, and Frank Stone; later, in 1865, William Michael Rossetti wrote 'Praeraphaelitism aimed at suppressing such styles of painting as were exemplified by Messrs. Elmore, Goodall, and Stone, at the time of its starting; and it did suppress them.'[4] But, if

[1]Hunt, 1905, I, 131, 140–41, 149–50, 174–6.
[2]*Ibid.*, p. 142.

[3]Rossetti, 1911, p. 571.
[4]Rossetti, 1867, p. 189.

the Pre-Raphaelites were reacting against what they considered the low state of some of the art around them, the form their reaction took depended heavily on other developments in English painting during the 1840s. The most obvious sign of this dependence is the name which the young artists chose to give to their movement.

The name 'Pre-Raphaelite Brotherhood' suggests a conscious emulation of early Italian art, and even before the meaning of the initials 'PRB' was made public in the spring of 1850, the first exhibited products of the Pre-Raphaelite Brotherhood were seen as imitations of early art. The first picture to be exhibited bearing the initials 'PRB' was Rossetti's *Girlhood of Mary Virgin* (Tate Gallery), which he sent to the Free Exhibition in Hyde Park in the spring of 1849. In May 1849, the *Art Journal* described Rossetti's picture as 'the most successful as a pure imitation of early Florentine art that we have seen in this country', and in his brief mention the reviewer managed to suggest similarities with the Giotteschi, Piero della Francesca, and Paolo Uccello.[5] In the following month, when the *Art Journal* reviewed the Royal Academy exhibition, Millais's *Isabella* (Walker Art Gallery, Liverpool) and Holman Hunt's *Rienzi* (Pl. 1a) were described in similar terms. The Millais was 'a pure aspiration in the feeling of the early Florentine school', while Hunt's picture provoked the comment, 'We have this year seen more essays in the manner of early Art than we have ever before remarked in the country within so short a period.'[6]

The Pre-Raphaelites' attachment to early Italian art, which the movement's name implied, and which the pictures demonstrated to contemporary viewers, was a product of the growing awareness of early art in England during the 1840s. This growth of interest is manifested by the number of books that appeared during the decade. Charles Eastlake's translation of Kugler's *Handbook of the History of Painting* appeared in 1842. It was followed by Mrs. Merrifield's translation of Cennino Cennini in 1844, Mrs. Jameson's *Memoirs of the Early Italian Painters, and of the Progress of Painting in Italy: From Cimabue to Bassano* in 1845, the second volume of Ruskin's *Modern Painters* in 1846, and Lord Lindsay's *Sketches of the History of Christian Art* in 1847. The extraordinary redirection of English taste which these works reflect is most evident in Ruskin. In 1843, in the first volume of *Modern Painters*, the seventeenth century provided the sole standard by which Ruskin set out to prove the superiority of Turner and other nineteenth-century landscape painters. In the second volume, published three years later, even Turner was set aside for eloquent passages describing Giotto, Fra Angelico, and Tintoretto.[7]

The growth of an art-historical interest in Quattrocento and earlier Italian painting went hand-in-hand with actual developments in English art during the decade. This was what at least some of the writers wanted; for example, in 1847 Lord Lindsay concluded his two volumes with an exhortation to English painters to study Italian art before Raphael and Michelangelo.[8] But at the centre of the new developments in painting was also the practical need of decorating the new Palace of Westminster, Sir Charles Barry's great building which replaced the Houses of Parliament destroyed by the fire of 1834. In 1841 a Commission, headed by Prince Albert, was appointed by Parliament to supervise the decoration of the new building. The Commission decided that the interior should be decorated with monumental frescoes, an undertaking without precedent in England, and sponsored a series of competitions to select the artists. The project was partly inspired by the example of the frescoes painted in Rome and Munich by the German Nazarenes, who

[5] *Art Journal*, 1849, p. 147.
[6] *Ibid.*, p. 171.
[7] See John Steegman, *Consort of Taste: 1830–1870* (London, 1950) pp. 49–74, and J. R. Hale, *England and the Italian Renaissance* (London, 1954) pp. 108–26 and 149–68.
[8] Lord Lindsay, *Sketches of the History of Christian Art*, 2nd edn. (London, 1885) II, 390.

earlier in the century had undertaken their own revival of early Italian art. Two German painters, Peter Cornelius and Julius Schnorr von Carolsfeld, gave advice, and at various times the Commissioners considered actually employing German artists.[9] In addition to following the German lead, the English also took a very practical interest in early Italian fresco-painting. The government sent abroad several representatives, including Mrs. Merrifield, Charles Eastlake, and William Dyce to study techniques. Eastlake's *Materials for a History of Oil Painting*, published in 1847, and Mrs. Merrifield's *Original Treatises, dating from the XIIth to XVIIIth Centuries on the Arts of Painting*, published in 1849, both resulted from this officially sponsored research. Dyce's report appeared as an appendix to the *Sixth Report of the Commissioners on the Fine Arts* in 1846.

This activity naturally led to a greater general awareness of early art among English artists. It also brought into prominence a number of artists who had some background of continental experience or training, the most important of them being William Dyce. Born in Aberdeen in 1806, Dyce visited Rome twice during the 1820s. On his second visit, in 1827–8, he came into contact with the Nazarene group, forming a friendship with Friedrich Overbeck which he maintained over the following twenty years.[10] To what extent his painting of the 1820s was influenced either by the Nazarenes or by early Italian art is unclear. His work done in Italy, notably a *Madonna and Child*, which the Germans took up a subscription to purchase, has all disappeared, and after he returned to Scotland, he turned to painting portraits in a fairly conventional style reminiscent of Raeburn and Lawrence. In 1837 he was appointed Master of the Trustee's Academy in Edinburgh, the chief art school in Scotland, and in the same year he travelled abroad on behalf of the newly formed Schools of Design in London to study methods of education in France and Germany. In 1838 he was appointed Superintendent of the Schools of Design, a position which he held until 1843.[11]

Dyce's appointment as a teacher seems to have ended his activity as a professional portrait painter and to have allowed him to follow a more adventurous path. At the Royal Academy in 1838 he exhibited a *Madonna and Child*; this was probably the picture in oil on gesso on stone now in Nottingham, which recalls both early Italian and Nazarene prototypes. In the following year he exhibited *St. Dunstan Separating Edwy and Elgiva* with the accompanying explanation in the catalogue: 'Design for the façade of a Chapel, in the style practised by the scholars of Giotto in upper Italy, intended to illustrate the polychromatic decoration of the end of the fourteenth century.' Reviewing the Royal Academy exhibition of 1839, the *Art Union* called Dyce's ideas 'peculiarly his own' and declared 'his course is not a wise one'.[12] However, in the following few years, Dyce's position was to shift rapidly from that of an educator with eccentric ideas to one of prominence among English artists, and even to that of leader of an acknowledged revolution. In 1841 he was one of the first witnesses to appear before the Commission responsible for the Parliament decorations. In 1845 he received the first actual commission for a fresco in the new House of Lords, and in the following winter he was sent abroad on behalf of the government. He was elected an associate member of the Royal Academy in 1844 and a full member in 1848. He received several commissions from Prince Albert during the 1840s, and, following the completion of his fresco in the House of Lords, he received in 1847 an additional commission for the Palace of West-

[9]Andrews, 1964, pp. 84–5. See also T. S. R. Boase, 'The Decoration of the New Palace of Westminster, 1841–63', *Journal of the Warburg and Courtauld Institutes*, XVII, 1954, pp. 319–24.
[10]Andrews, 1964, pp. 81–2.

[11]See Quentin Bell, *The Schools of Design* (London, 1963) pp. 77–153.
[12]*Art Union*, 1839, p. 170. The *Art Union* and the *Art Journal* are the same periodical; the name was changed in 1849.

minster: to paint a cycle of frescoes in the Queen's Robing Room, a project which was to occupy him for the rest of his life.

Dyce was the most eminent, but he was only one among several artists brought into prominence by the new activities and interests of the 1840s. One of the most significant results of the Parliament competitions was that, in addition to causing artists to look abroad and to the past for models of fresco-painting, they also attracted back to England a number of artists who had been trained or had lived on the continent. Among these artists was one figure who was to play a central role in the Pre-Raphaelite movement: Ford Madox Brown. Born in Calais of English parents, Brown studied painting first in Belgium; then from 1840 to 1844 he lived in Paris. In 1844 he submitted two cartoons for frescoes to the competitions for the Houses of Parliament, and he came to London to live. The style Brown brought with him, as represented by his cartoon of *The Body of Harold Brought before William the Conqueror* (South London Art Gallery), reflects the influence of French Romantic painting; specifically, it echoes Delacroix's *Crusaders Entering Constantinople* (Louvre, but painted for the Gallery of Battles at Versailles, in its way a French prototype for the Parliament decorations), which Brown would have seen exhibited in the Salon of 1841. Brown spent the winter of 1845–6 in Rome. There he visited the studios of Cornelius and Overbeck and was much impressed by both artists.[13] He was also exposed to early art, both in Italy and *en route*. In a letter written twenty years later he listed among his strongest memories the Holbeins in the museum at Basle.[14] Among the pictures he painted after his return, he described one, a *Portrait of James Bamford* (location unknown) as 'a Holbein of the 19th Century.'[15] Another work, a cartoon of the Madonna and Christ child with attendant angels, *Oure Ladye of Good Children* (Tate Gallery), was 'little more than the pouring out of the emotions and remembrances still within me of Italian Art';[16] and Brown's larger pictures from this period, *Chaucer at the Court of Edward III*, begun in Rome and finished in 1851 (Pl. 6), and *Wickliffe Reading his Translation of the Bible to John of Gaunt*, painted in the winter of 1847–8 (City Art Gallery, Bradford), both show strong Nazarene influence.[17]

In March 1848, Dante Gabriel Rossetti wrote a letter to Ford Madox Brown introducing himself as a student in the Royal Academy schools, professing admiration for Brown's works, and asking to become his pupil.[18] Rossetti did work under Brown very briefly, but, apparently because he found the kind of disciplined routine expected by Brown too irksome, he soon left and began to work instead in the studio of Holman Hunt. Nonetheless, Rossetti and Brown remained close friends for the rest of their lives, and Rossetti's *Girlhood of Mary Virgin*, although painted in Hunt's studio, shows a direct and heavy dependence on Brown's *Oure Ladye of Good Children*.[19] Either Brown was invited and declined to become a member of the Pre-Raphaelite Brotherhood, or an invitation to him was framed and never delivered.[20] In either case, although Holman Hunt later tried to minimize Brown's importance, he was intimately and significantly involved with the Brotherhood's formation and with most of its members' activities in the following years.

---

[13]Hueffer, 1896, pp. 44–5.

[14]*Ibid.*, p. 41.

[15]Brown, 1865, p. 16.

[16]*Ibid.*, p. 4. He also exhibited *A Reminiscence of the Early Masters* at the British Institution in 1847. This work, measuring twenty-four by seventeen inches, including frame, was too small to be identified as *Oure Ladye of Good Children*.

[17]For a somewhat unsympathetic discussion of Brown's debt to the Nazarenes see Hunt, 1905, I, 121–6.

[18]Hueffer, 1896, pp. 50–51.

[19]Hunt called the composition 'Overbeckian,' 1905, I, 174.

[20]Hueffer, 1896, pp. 62–6.

Hunt's attempt in *Pre-Raphaelitism and the Pre-Raphaelite Brotherhood* to belittle Ford Madox Brown's role in the formation of the Brotherhood was only part of a larger effort to deny Pre-Raphaelite emulation of either early Italian art or the German Nazarenes. According to Hunt's account, the first principle of Pre-Raphaelitism from the beginning was 'a child-like reversion from existing schools to Nature herself'.[21] Although what Hunt says must be respected as the most cogent first-hand account of Pre-Raphaelitism that we possess, the evidence of the name the artists chose to give to their Brotherhood, the critical reaction to their first pictures, cited above, and the pictures themselves all suggest that Hunt's arguments, published over half a century later, place a one-sided interpretation upon his own and his colleagues' activities in 1848. Nonetheless, unless we take Hunt's memoirs as total fabrications, which they certainly are not, truth to nature was an over-riding concern of Hunt's from well before the actual formation of the Pre-Raphaelite Brotherhood.

Realism or naturalism of one sort or another were interests widespread throughout Europe during the middle years of the nineteenth century, and it was perhaps inevitable that a would-be revolutionary movement whose first works appeared in the same year as Courbet's *Stonebreakers* would reflect them. However, if we compare Courbet's *Stonebreakers* with Rossetti's *Girlhood of Mary Virgin*, Millais's *Isabella*, or Hunt's *Rienzi*, it is apparent that whatever naturalistic or realistic urges lay behind the first Pre-Raphaelite pictures, they were not only very different from those present in Courbet's painting, but also mixed with other, even contradictory tendencies.[22] The inherent contradictions in the first Pre-Raphaelite pictures were soon reflected in a split between Rossetti on one hand and Hunt and Millais on the other. Whereas the archaizing and revivalist elements in Rossetti's art remained and became more important, Hunt and Millais both moved rapidly towards greater naturalism, divesting themselves of any obvious dependence on early art.

The two most conspicuous components of Pre-Raphaelite naturalism, which were present from the start, were minute detail and bright colour with a minimum of shadow. The artists considered both to be more true and less conventional than breadth of handling and the composition of a picture primarily in terms of contrasts of light and shade. For both their detailed handling and their bright colour, the Pre-Raphaelites had numerous fore-runners among English artists active in the 1830s and 1840s. Of most obvious significance for them were probably William Mulready and the watercolourist William Henry Hunt, both of whom, in addition to a finical delicacy in handling, developed in their different media unprecedented brightness of colour by glazing transparent broken colours over a white ground.

But, of course, bright colours were not foreign to the artists who lived before Raphael. The English painters in 1848 saw in early art not only quaintness, grace, and charm, but also an honesty and a freedom from the conventions which these later artists were trying to escape. In this, they shared the attitudes of Ford Madox Brown and William Dyce, the painters whose interest in early art anticipated their own. The most significant single change in Brown's art following his trip to Italy in 1845–6 was a lightening of his palette. This can be seen, for example, in the difference between his *Prisoner of Chillon* of 1843 (City Art Gallery, Manchester) and the large *Chaucer at the Court of Edward III* (Pl. 6) begun in Rome in 1845. Brown later ascribed the change to the impact of Italy: 'During

[21]Hunt, 1905, I, 125.
[22]The Courbet was destroyed in 1945. For a reproduc- tion see *Encylopedia of World Art* (New York, 1961) IV, Pl. 36.

my sojourn, Italian art had made a deep, and as it proved, lasting impression on me, for I never afterwards returned to the sombre Rembrandtesque style, I had formerly worked in'.[23] Although Brown's change from Rembrandtesque to Italianate light and colour could be interpreted simply as the substitution of one set of conventions for another, he saw it as part of an attempt to gain more exact truth. He described the *Chaucer* as the first work in which he endeavoured to treat light and shade 'absolutely, as it exists at any one moment, instead of approximately, or in generalized style'.[24] It should be noted, however, that although Brown began the *Chaucer* in Rome in 1845, he only completed and exhibited it in 1851, three years after the formation of the Pre-Raphaelite Brotherhood. Holman Hunt claimed that in completing the picture Brown was influenced by the Pre-Raphaelites' example.[25] The work which Brown claimed gave 'first evidence of an entirely new direction of thought and feeling' was his *Portrait of James Bamford* of 1846. It is now lost, but we do have Brown's statement of what he was trying to do and how it contrasted with his earlier work:

To those who value facile completeness and handling, above painstaking research into nature, the change must appear inexplicable and provoking. Even to myself at this distance of time [written in 1865], *this instinctive turning back to get round by another road*, seems remarkable. But in reality it was only the inevitable result of the want of principle, or rather confliction of many jarring principles under which the student had to begin in those days. Wishing to substitute simple imitation for *scenic effectiveness*, and purity of natural colour for scholastic depth of tone, I found no better way of doing so than to paint what I called a *Holbein of the 19th century*. I might, perhaps, have done so more effectively, but *stepping backwards* is stumbling work at best.[26]

No clearer statement exists of the link made by the Pre-Raphaelite group in the late 1840s between their aims toward a new naturalism free from inherited conventions and their awareness of early art. 'Simple imitation' and 'purity of natural colour' would become and remain essential ingredients of Pre-Raphaelite naturalism through the 1850s.

William Dyce's easel paintings of the 1840s, for example his *Madonna and Child* at Osborne House, painted for Prince Albert in 1845 (Pl. 92a), are much more obviously Italianate than any of Brown's pictures or those of the Pre-Raphaelites, and they do not appear to be based on the same naturalistic urges which Brown and his younger friends asserted lay behind their works. Nevertheless Dyce was concerned with the naturalness of effect of the Quattrocento works he admired. When he was in Italy in the winter of 1845–6 (at the same time as Ford Madox Brown), Dyce kept a notebook of his observations. This was the basis of his technical recommendations for fresco-painting published in 1846 (see above, p.3), but the full notes, which were not published, contain much more than the material of the report.[27] Dyce's greatest admiration was for Pinturicchio, who attracted him primarily because of his decorative richness; the Piccolomini Library in Siena was for Dyce 'a most magnificent piece of decorative art in which mere brilliancy and harmony of effect exceeds any other production I am acquainted with.' But Dyce also admired Pinturicchio for truth of local colour, and he was puzzled how Pinturicchio achieved his effects. He concluded that they depended on opposition of colour, rather than on chiaroscuro, but he remained at a loss to explain such methods as shading lake-coloured draperies with lake and nothing else:

I suspect that we modern painters do not study nature enough in the open air, or in broad daylight, or we should be better able to understand how the old painters obtained truth by such apparently

[23]Brown, 1865, p. 4.
[24] *Ibid.*
[25]Hunt, 1905, I, 225–6.
[26]Brown, 1865, p. 16.

[27]They are transcribed in Dyce, MSS., chapter XXI, 'Notes of Frescoes in Italy by William Dyce, R.A.' See also Staley, 1963.

anomalous means. In sunlight, shadows partake largely of the local colour of the objects, and still more so in the shade, viz: seen by the diffused light of the sky; indeed in the open air I have observed that peculiar indefiniteness of the shadows and darkening of the receding and undercut parts which is so characteristic of the older painters, and which nobody doubts is more effective for mural painting on a large scale than the sort of painter's studio shadowing, which from habit and prejudice one can hardly nowadays avoid. The Germans such as Cornelius attempt to follow the old painters in their method of darkening rather than shadowing: but without success, simply because they learn the method from old art rather than from nature ....

Of this I am quite convinced that no degree of study in the painting room with a small confined light will ever enable one to make any approach to the kind of open daylight reality obtained by the early painters.

Although Dyce was not as intimately involved with the Pre-Raphaelites as Ford Madox Brown, during the 1840s he was known and admired by them. He seems to have taken a special interest in Holman Hunt. According to Hunt's memoirs, they often talked together when Hunt was a student in the Life School of the Royal Academy. Later, Dyce commissioned Hunt to paint a copy of his *Meeting of Jacob and Rachel* exhibited at the Royal Academy in 1850, and he also procured for Hunt a commission to restore the frescoes by John Francis Rigaud in Trinity House. Hunt records one conversation in which they contrasted Dyce's art with the 'asphaltum indefiniteness' of Wilkie and Hilton.[28]

In addition to helping Holman Hunt, Dyce also gave the Pre-Raphaelites support in one other way which was to have vast consequences: he made John Ruskin look at their pictures. According to Ruskin,

My real introduction to the whole school was by Mr. Dyce, R.A., who dragged me, literally, up to the Millais picture of the *Carpenter's Shop* [the painting in the Tate Gallery usually called *Christ in the House of His Parents;* exhibited at the Royal Academy in 1850] which I had passed disdainfully, and forced me to look for its merits.[29]

Ruskin's editors cite this letter as proof that Ruskin did not inspire Pre-Raphaelitism,[30] and similar denials of Ruskin's importance for the origins of the movement have also been made in various accounts of the movement, notably in the life of Millais by his son, John Guille Millais.[31] But the denials are misleading. Although Ruskin may not have been aware of the young artists until 1850, and although they had no personal contact for another year, the Pre-Raphaelites had certainly been exposed to Ruskin and to his preaching through his books. For Holman Hunt, Ruskin was of seminal importance; in the summer of 1847 a friend lent Hunt Ruskin's *Modern Painters*, of which by then the first two volumes had been published. Its impact was immediate: 'of all its readers none could have felt more strongly than myself that it was written expressly for him. When it had gone, the echo of its words stayed with me, and they gained a further value and meaning whenever my more solemn feelings were touched.'[32]

The two volumes of *Modern Painters* which were available to Hunt embody a similar combination of interests in nature and in Italian art to that which we have seen in Ford Madox Brown and William Dyce. In Ruskin's case, the link seems accidental, or rather the outgrowth of his evolving sensibility. *Modern Painters* began as a defence of Turner. The seeds lay as far back as 1836 when Ruskin, then seventeen years old, wrote a reply to *Blackwood's Magazine* protesting at its hostile criticism of Turner.[33] The reply was not published, and by 1843, when the first volume of *Modern Painters* appeared, Ruskin's defence of

[28]Hunt, 1905, I, 206–07, 228–9. In 1851 Dyce also offered Hunt a job as his studio assistant, *ibid.*, p. 261.
[29]Ruskin, 1903–12, XXXVII, 427–8.
[30]*Ibid.*, XII, p. xlv.
[31]Millais, 1899, I, 61.

[32]Hunt, 1905, I, 73.
[33]Ruskin, 1903–12, III, 635–40. The five volumes of *Modern Painters* are *ibid.*, III–VII. The introductions to these volumes contain the essential background information.

Turner had grown into a projected three-volume treatise on landscape art. Ultimately *Modern Painters* was to consist of five volumes with chapters on almost everything under the sun, but in 1843 the defence of Turner was still very much to the fore. Ruskin originally wanted to call the book *Turner and the Ancients*, but the publishers changed it to *Modern Painters: Their Superiority in the Art of Landscape Painting to All the Ancient Masters: Proved by Examples of the True, the Beautiful, and the Intellectual, From the Works of Modern Artists, Especially from those of J. M. W Turner, Esq. R.A.: By a Graduate of Oxford*. The three classes of the True, the Beautiful, and the Intellectual cited in the title were intended to be the subjects of the three separate volumes, and in the first Ruskin set out vigorously to prove Turner's superiority in truth to all other artists, both ancient and modern. Following a fairly involved theoretical preamble, Ruskin's method of argument was simple. By long descriptive passages he attempted to demonstrate the objective facts of nature; he then compared the work of all other artists unfavourably to his own descriptions and concluded by demonstrating how only Turner achieved the truth. Although truth was to be only one aspect of Ruskin's three-volume attack, he made it abundantly clear that it was the most essential quality in art, and his fundamental criterion of evaluation.

The second volume of *Modern Painters*, published in 1846, does not contradict the first, but it is a very different book. Not only is it about beauty rather than truth, as Ruskin had intended from the start, but it has a different cast of characters. In the first volume, the 'Ancient Masters' to whom Ruskin compared Turner were mainly the landscape and seascape painters of the seventeenth century. His frame of reference was limited to the picture collections available to him in London at the Dulwich Gallery and the then young National Gallery. A trip to Italy in 1845 was for Ruskin something of a revelation. As a result, he turned his back on landscape painting and began to establish himself as England's most eloquent advocate of Italian art. In the subsequent volumes of *Modern Painters* Ruskin returned to the subject of landscape and to Turner, but as the third and fourth volumes appeared only in 1856, and the fifth in 1860, they were too late to have had any influence in shaping the initial goals of Pre-Raphaelitism.

For the formation of the Pre-Raphaelite Brotherhood in 1848, Ruskin's second volume probably had the greater immediate importance, helping to nourish the urge that led the Brotherhood to call itself Pre-Raphaelite. But in 1851, when Ruskin published a pamphlet entitled *Pre-Raphaelitism*, he claimed in his preface that the Pre-Raphaelites were putting into practice what he had called for in the concluding pages of the first volume of *Modern Painters*.[34] There Ruskin had turned the book's insistence upon Turner's truth to nature into an exhortation to the young artists of England:

They . . . should go to Nature in all singleness of heart, and walk with her laboriously and trustingly, having no other thoughts but how best to penetrate her meaning, and remember her instruction; rejecting nothing, selecting nothing, and scorning nothing; believing all things to be right and good, and rejoicing always in the truth.[35]

This passage was assumed by many contemporary critics to be the basic proposition underlying the detailed naturalism of the Pre-Raphaelites. It was, however, only one eminently quotable bit lifted out of a long and involved book which argues consistently for the kind of painting which Pre-Raphaelite art was to become. Truth to nature, Ruskin's battle-cry in 1843 and Holman Hunt's in 1848, was, of course, not a new idea; concepts of natural truth have motivated so many artists, at so many times, painting in so many different manners, that the phrase is virtually meaningless. But Ruskin presented his demands in

[34]*Ibid.*, XII, 339.   [35]*Ibid.*, III, 623–4.

specific and idiosyncratic terms which define a very different path than that of, say, Constable (who set out to be a 'natural painter' and whom Ruskin detested). The most repeated of Ruskin's principles, and the one which most distinguishes him from most earlier English theorists, notably Reynolds, is his preference for particular truths over general ones, those which are the most informative about the individual qualities of a subject rather than about what the subject has in common with everything else.[36] Of particular truths, the most valuable are the most 'historical', 'which tell us the most about the past and future states of the object to which they belong'.[37] Thus, for Ruskin truth of tone, as seen in a landscape by Claude, is of little value because it is characteristic only of a single moment, whereas the detailed delineation of a tree's branches tells us what the tree has been and what it will become.

These principles lead directly to another *leit-motiv* of the book: insistence upon detail and finish. This concern may seem out of place in a book about Turner, but Ruskin argued that Turner's breadth was based on a fine control over the details of nature, which the artist had developed in his earlier works. Thus Turner became a model for the young artist, who should only be allowed to indulge in broader effects after a faithfully minute study of natural forms.[38] In his concluding advice, Ruskin emphatically repeated his demand for detail. He criticized the public preference for brilliancy and rapidity of execution as a taste for glitter and claptrap. Artists should make and exhibit sketches, but these should be distinct from finished works. A picture should have the wholeness and effect of nature, but it would be incomplete unless it also contained 'the inexhaustible perfection of nature's details'. After satisfying himself on the first requirement, the painter should always ask himself, 'Can my details be added to? Is there a single space in the picture where I can crowd in another thought?'[39]

Despite its different focus, the second volume of *Modern Painters* repeats the emphasis on detail and finish. Now, instead of Turner's, it is the 'divine finish' of Perugino, the young Raphael, Fra Angelico, Pinturicchio, Giovanni Bellini, 'and all such serious and loving men', which is praised and contrasted to the coarse and slurred painting of Ribera, Salvator Rosa, and Murillo.[40] Ruskin praised the backgrounds of Perugino for their exquisite refinement of natural detail, but he did not urge their imitation: 'the only safe mode of following in such steps is to attain perfect knowledge of Nature herself'.[41]

The Pre-Raphaelites set out to follow this advice to the letter. In Holman Hunt's account, the real moment of genesis of Pre-Raphaelitism was a conversation between Hunt and Millais – or, more accurately, a lecture Hunt gave to Millais – that took place in February 1848.[42] After railing against the lack of discipline and lack of purpose among present-day artists, Hunt brought in *Modern Painters* as his chief weapon: 'By Jove! passages in it made my heart thrill. He feels the power and responsibility of art more than any author I have ever read.' Hunt described the book at some length to Millais because of the contrast of the men 'of such high purpose and vigour', which it described, to 'the un-inspired men of today'. It demonstrated a need for young artists to consider what course to follow, and it helped one 'to see the difference between dead art and living art at a critical juncture'. Bursting with revolutionary enthusiasm, Hunt and Millais agreed to paint their next pictures according to new principles. Although in his harangue Hunt had described the second volume of *Modern Painters*, his resolution was more in accord with the advice

[36]*Ibid.*, pp. 149–54
[37]*Ibid.*, p. 163.
[38]*Ibid.*, pp. 623–4.
[39]*Ibid.*, p. 622.

[40]*Ibid.*, IV, 137–8.
[41]*Ibid.*, pp. 321–3
[42]Hunt, 1905, I, 81–91.

which concluded volume one. He could not alter his present picture, *The Flight of Madeleine and Porphyro* (Guildhall Art Gallery, London), which was an interior, night scene, but he declared: 'I purpose after this to paint an out-of-door picture, with a foreground and background, abjuring altogether brown foliage, smoky clouds, and dark corners, painting the whole out of doors, direct on the canvas itself, with every detail I can see, and with the sunlight brightness of the day itself.'

The next picture, in which Hunt put this resolution into practice, was *Rienzi Vowing to Obtain Justice for the Death of His Younger Brother Slain in a Skirmish between the Colonna and Orsini Factions* (Pl. 1a). *The Flight of Madelaine and Porphyro* had been most original in being based on a poem, 'The Eve of St. Agnes', by Keats, who was still little known. Otherwise, it is not too unlike the theatrically staged and elaborately costumed scenes from history and literature being painted by those associate members of the Royal Academy of whom the the Pre-Raphaelites so disapproved. *Rienzi* is still a painting of a literary subject in historical costume, but it is a much more individual, and indeed revolutionary work, as Hunt intended it to be. Based on Bulwer-Lytton's novel *Rienzi: The Last of the Roman Tribunes*, Hunt's picture manifests the new Pre-Raphaelite ambitions in several ways. It shows Cola di Rienzi swearing an oath over the body of his dead brother; Rienzi's fulfilment of that oath by leading a popular revolution, which overthrows the Roman nobility, forms the substance of the novel. In 1848 the novel had an obvious message, which Bulwer-Lytton pointed out in the preface to a new edition published that year. Hunt also saw the message: 'Like most young men, I was stirred by the spirit of the passing revolutionary time. The appeal to Heaven against the tyranny exercised over the poor and helpless seemed well fitted for pictorial treatment'.[43] Hunt's embodiment of his subject in a lucid, four-square figural composition seems to relate the picture to a series of Neo-classic depictions of fervent patriotic oaths, harking back to and beyond Jacques Louis David's *Oath of the Horatii*. But the delicate drawing and bright colours, as well as Hunt's choice of a subject from fourteenth-century Italy, point to other sources. As we have seen, the *Art Journal* classified *Rienzi* among the 'essays in the manner of early art', and it described Hunt's picture as 'perhaps more austere in its denials than any of the others.'[44]

To put into practice his resolution of February, Hunt had begun his picture in the summer of 1848 by attempting to paint each part from nature. He took his canvas to Lambeth to paint directly in the sunlight a fig-tree in the garden of F. G. Stephens's father. He also painted there a patch of grass and dandelions. He painted the background and trees at Hampstead. Later, for the shields and spears he took his canvas to the Tower of London, and he painted the figures in the studio during the following winter. His work from nature was done with what Hunt describes as unprecedented exactness. He painted 'directly and frankly, not merely for the charm of minute finish, but as a means of studying more deeply Nature's principles of design, and to escape the conventional treatment of landscape backgrounds'.[45]

Unfortunately, an assessment of *Rienzi* must depend as much on Hunt's statement of what he did as on the picture itself. In 1886 he discovered that it had been covered with a heavy and harmful varnish which was affecting the pigments. In removing this he found the background so severely damaged that he extensively repainted it.[46] The foregound parts were apparently not repainted, but their present condition suggests that they suffered from the scraping required to remove the varnish. As the picture now stands, the handling

[43]*Ibid.*, p. 114.
[44]*Art Journal*, 1849, p. 171.
[45]Hunt, 1905, I, 111–12.
[46]*Ibid.*, p. 183n2.

in the foregound is much thinner than that in Hunt's works of the following years, and the detail is less abundant. Hunt describes the 'gravelly variations and pebbles, all diverse in tints and shapes as found in Nature', which he painted 'instead of the meaningless spread of whitey brown which usually served for the near ground',[47] but the variations and pebbles are now barely noticeable. Whether detail has actually disappeared is open to question. If we accept the probability that the picture no longer possesses its original appearance, we should also note that in their reviews neither the *Athenaeum* nor the *Art Journal* made any mention of the picture's natural detail when it appeared at the Royal Academy in 1849.[48] Despite Hunt's assertions to the contrary, it is perhaps appropriate to discern in his treatment of foreground details some of that archaizing spirit which the contemporary reviewers saw as the picture's dominant quality. It is difficult not to see the charm of minute finish in the foreground dandelions and, behind it, a desire to emulate the foreground flowers of Quattrocento paintings.

In his next two major pictures, *A Converted British Family Sheltering a Christian Priest from the Persecution of the Druids*, exhibited at the Royal Academy in 1850 (Pl. 26b), and *Valentine Rescuing Sylvia from Proteus*, from Shakespeare's *Two Gentlemen of Verona*, exhibited in 1851 (Pl. 1b), Hunt followed the path he laid down in *Rienzi*. Both pictures are elaborate compositions of several figures, and both are historical reconstructions. As in *Rienzi*, landscape elements are limited to subordinate parts of the pictures, but Hunt began each picture by painting those parts directly from nature. For the earlier picture he worked during August and early September 1849 on the Lea Marshes in Essex. He painted the background of the other in Knole Park in Kent in the latter part of October and early November of 1850. Although the landscapes seem relatively insignificant in terms of the over-all compositions of the pictures, Hunt seems to have considered them of essential importance. He chose the subject of the *Druids* because it would allow him to compete in the Academy's Gold Medal contest, which required the illustration of 'An Act of Mercy'; however, as he worked out the composition he realized that the specified size of canvas for the competition would not leave 'a margin, most precious in my eyes', on which to paint a landscape setting. He included the landscape and did not enter the competition.[49]

In the *Druids* the chief figures are seen in a hut. The landscape setting consists of a strip of water to which the hut is open along the foreground, a view of a Stonehenge-like monument through an opening underneath the hut's roof, and a narrow strip of landscape running from bottom to top of the picture along its right side. Hunt had projected all these elements in a drawing dating from May 1849 which is reproduced in his memoirs as the 'First Design' for the picture (Art Gallery of Johannesburg).[50] The landscape background contains figures – a mob of Druids pursuing a priest – which contribute to the picture's story, and on the right side is a cultivated garden which Hunt intended to symbolize the influence of Christianity. Correspondingly the background of *Valentine Rescuing Sylvia* is supposed to represent the Forest of Mantua, through which are seen approaching the Duke of Milan and his retinue.

In both pictures the elaboration of foreground detail is much more pronounced than in *Rienzi*, and, in both, separately delineated leaves and other botanical details are the chief elements thus elaborated. The distant parts of the pictures do not share this precision. The trees along the horizon of the *Druids* are quite fuzzy, in sharp contrast to the leaves along the top of the hut to which they are juxtaposed. In the 1851 painting not only are the

[47] *Ibid.*, p. 112.
[48] The *Athenaeum* review is quoted *ibid.*, p. 178 n1.
[49] *Ibid.*, p. 173.
[50] *Ibid.*, p. 175.

landscape elements of the background less precise and elaborate than the foreground leaves and grass, but the group around the Duke of Milan appears to be unfinished. Although Hunt's account of his work on this picture describes his usual difficulties in completing it in time for the Academy exhibition, he does not say that he was forced to leave the background unfinished.[51] As the background figures in the small oil sketch of the subject, which he began earlier but completed and sold as a replica in 1852 (collection of Mrs. E. M. S. C. Tompkin), show a similar treatment, it appears intentional, as if Hunt was avoiding carrying the sharp focus of his foreground into the depth of the picture, but had no better way of achieving breadth than to leave his work unfinished.

In *Valentine Rescuing Sylvia* Hunt for the first time made extensive use of a new technique, as did Millais in his pictures of the same year. This was painting over a wet white ground.[52] Previously, to gain brilliant colours they had painted over a white ground, following the lead of older artists such as William Mulready. They apparently developed independently the use of a wet ground applied fresh each day, probably by attempting to emulate in oil paint the methods of fresco painting. Thus, their practice, which would become a cornerstone of subsequent Pre-Raphaelite painting, was ultimately a product of the interest in early technical processes generated by the programme for decorating the new Palace of Westminster. Exactly when Hunt and Millais began to develop the technique is unrecorded. In his picture exhibited in 1851 Hunt used it for the heads and hands of Valentine and Proteus and for the brighter costumes. The result was much greater brilliance in colour, and this development in the work of both Hunt and Millais was noted by contemporary observers.[53]

In Hunt's account of his career, his pictures of 1850 and 1851 continued the study of nature which he had first put into practice in *Rienzi*. Both were painted 'with unprecedented care for their landscapes'.[54] This is the view taken also in the first substantial review of Hunt's early activities, a pamphlet, *William Holman Hunt and His Works*, published anonymously in 1860, but written by Frederick George Stephens. Stephens was an erstwhile pupil of Hunt's and one of the founding members of the Pre-Raphaelite Brotherhood, who gave up painting to become a critic. In his pamphlet Stephens defined Pre-Raphaelitism as basically concerned with minute truth to nature.[55] According to Stephens, *Rienzi* was 'anything but perfect' as a Pre-Raphaelite picture, but Hunt progressed in the *Druids* – 'Above all, this picture showed the partially successful representation of the natural effect of sunlight' – and he made in *Valentine Rescuing Sylvia* 'an enormous advance in execution, in potency, and fidelity of treatment'.[56] Contemporary critics outside the immediate Pre-Raphaelite circle still saw Hunt's and his colleagues' pictures in terms of imitation of early art, but now they had a reason other than the evidence of the pictures themselves. In the spring of 1850 the world learned the meaning of the initials PRB which the artists had put on their pictures exhibited the year before. This information seems to have acted as a red rag, and in place of the general approval which met the pictures exhibited in 1849, came an almost unanimous castigation of the return to 'all the objectionable peculiarities of the infancy of art'.[57] Largely as a result of such criticism Dante Gabriel Rossetti ceased to exhibit his work publicly in London after 1850. Millais continued to share with Hunt the critical vicissitudes, and his work achieved even greater notoriety.

Although Millais was the most naturally gifted member of the original Pre-Raphaelite

[51]*Ibid.*, p. 246.
[52]*Ibid.*, pp. 275–7.
[53]See for example: Hueffer, 1896, p. 77; Rossetti, 1911, p. 586; *Art Journal*, 1851, pp. 157–61.
[54]Hunt, 1905, I, 277.
[55]Stephens, 1860, pp. 8–9.
[56]*Ibid.*, pp. 17–18.
[57]*Art Journal*, 1850, p. 176.

group, who rapidly attracted the most attention to his works, he was less important in shaping its outlook than either Hunt or Rossetti. Intellectually he was a disciple of Hunt's. He was the companion to whom Hunt expressed his resolution in February 1848 to paint his out-of-door picture, and a year later than Hunt he also put the resolution into practice. Millais's first Pre-Raphaelite picture, *Isabella*, begun in 1848 and exhibited in 1849, shows, like Hunt's picture of the preceding year, a subject from Keats in an interior setting. But in 1850 Millais exhibited three pictures at the Royal Academy, one of which, *Ferdinand Lured by Ariel* (Pl. 2a, and Col. Pl. 1a), is set in the open air. This is a small picture, only $25\frac{1}{2}$ by 20 inches, and it consists essentially of a standing figure before a foliate background. This background rises directly behind the figure of Ferdinand to approximately four fifths of the height of the painting; there is no depth of space. The entire background, except for the open sky at the top, is delineated with a thoroughness comparable to – or even surpassing – that of the foreground foliage in Hunt's *Druids* of the same year. Because of the suppression of space, of the sheer variety of plant forms delineated, and of Millais's extreme minuteness of handling, this natural detail did receive attention from contemporary critics. The *Art Journal*, which still took no notice of any naturalistic elements in Hunt's *Druids*, described *Ferdinand Lured by Ariel* as 'quattro-cento' and eccentric, but it saw something else: 'The emphasis of the picture is in its botany, which is made out with a microscopic elaboration, insomuch as to seem to have been painted from a collection of grasses, since we recognize upwards of twenty varieties; there may be more; and such is the minute description of even one leaf, that the ravages of an insect are observable upon it.'[58] This microscopic natural detail appears at the expense of space, atmosphere, or any feeling of light and shade. It fills a substantial part of the picture, but, allied to the fairy subject from Shakespeare's *Tempest*, it seems to belong to a world of dreams and enchantment rather than to the world as we normally know it. The hyper-real clarity of delineation does not contradict, but enhances the sense of fantasy.

In 1851 Millais again exhibited three pictures at the Royal Academy, one of which was of an outdoor subject. This was *The Woodman's Daughter* (Pl. 2b), based on Coventry Patmore's poem 'The Tale of Poor Maud'. It shows two children, Maud and the rich squire's son, in the immediate foreground, Maud's father at work slightly beyond them, and a wooded landscape stretching into the distance. Millais painted the background near Oxford in the summer of 1850. As the figures are of a smaller scale than those in Millais's and Hunt's previous pictures, the background is proportionately the most extensive of any Pre-Raphaelite picture to date. The foreground grass and leaves are painted with the same precision as the botanical detail in *Ferdinand Lured by Ariel*, but the microscopic treatment does not extend into the depth of the picture much beyond the figures. As in Hunt's *Valentine Rescuing Sylvia from Proteus*, the distant forest is painted with relative breadth. Unlike the autumnal colours of Hunt's picture, which indeed was begun in late October, Millais's are of a startling green, which is maintained with little diminution throughout the landscape.

The points of view in both Hunt's *Valentine Rescuing Sylvia from Proteus* and Millais's *Woodman's Daughter* are from slightly above the figures so that the background spaces seem to rise sharply. The arched top of Hunt's picture slices through the trunks of the distant trees, and there is no open sky. In Millais's, although the horizon is well above the heads of the figures, the trees in the distance are seen in their entire height, and there is a substantial area of open sky above them. We can also see underneath the foliage, between

[58] *Ibid.*, p. 175.

the trunks of the trees, to open sky along the horizon in the distance. The effect of recession through the tree trunks, marshalled in an almost one-point-perspective arrangement, recalls that of Uccello's *Hunt in a Forest* in the Ashmolean Museum. This similarity may not be coincidental; the Uccello was presented to the University Galleries in Oxford in 1850, the year that Millais painted the background of his picture while staying in the city.[59] As late as 1850–51, Pre-Raphaelite naturalism seems still to have been leavened by the example of Quattrocento painting. According to the critic for the *Art Journal*, *The Woodman's Daughter* not only displayed, but exaggerated 'every infirmity of early art'. This same critic singled out the high horizons and, by implication, faulty perspective in both Millais's and Hunt's pictures as particularly offensive.[60]

Although Rossetti defected in 1850 following Pre-Raphaelitism's first critical drubbing, by 1851 Hunt and Millais had gained other allies. Ford Madox Brown completed and exhibited his *Chaucer at the Court of Edward III* in 1851. As we have seen, Holman Hunt thought that in its completed state it showed Pre-Raphaelite influence. Most critics in 1851 still did not class Brown among the Pre-Raphaelites, although he suspected that they had begun 'to smell a rat'.[61] An artist whom the critics did look upon as another Pre-Raphaelite, and whom they attacked as mercilessly as either Hunt or Millais, was Charles Allston Collins, the son of the painter William Collins and brother of the writer Wilkie Collins. As a painter Charles Collins did little more than caricature Millais. His *Berengaria's Alarm for the Safety of Her Husband Richard Coeur de Lion* (City Art Gallery, Manchester), exhibited at the Royal Academy in 1850, is a weak reflection of Millais's *Isabella* of 1849. His *Convent Thoughts* (Pl. 3a) of 1851 seems equally dependent on *Ferdinand Lured by Ariel*, which it also followed by a year. The composition is essentially the same as Millais's, but the mass of greenery in *Ferdinand Lured by Ariel* has been separated into an ivy-covered wall in the background and a lily pond and two beds of flowers in the foreground. The tangle of vegetation has become a row of flowers, each rigidly distinct upon its own stalk. Lacking Millais's gifts as a draughtsman, Collins could not forge the elements of his picture into a comparable synthesis; the painting remains both dry and awkward, providing an object demonstration of mechanical accumulation of detail. It also seems very much a product of its time. The subject, a nun, reflects the obsessive mid-Victorian religiosity;[62] the style is palpably a product of the growth of interest in the Quattrocento during the previous decade. *Convent Thoughts* is hardly auspicious as an omen of anything, Yet, Collins's nun has turned aside from her missal to examine a withered blossom; she has gone directly to nature. Exhibited with a quotation from *Psalms*, 'I meditate on all Thy works; I muse on the work of Thy hands', this stiff little painting epitomizes what was to be the dominant interest in progressive English painting for the next decade.

[59]The exact date when the Uccello was first visible at Oxford is not recorded. It came as part of a gift from the Hon. William Fox-Strangways, most of which was in Oxford by March 1850, but part of the gift was not sent until the following October. I am indebted to Mr. Ian Lowe for this information.

[60]*Art Journal*, 1851, pp. 160–61.

[61]Hueffer, 1896, p. 73.

[62]Collins began the picture as an illustration of Shelley's 'Sensitive Plant', showing a girl emptying rainwater out of blossoms. He changed the subject to a nun when he became a high-church man; see Hunt, 1905, I, 294.

II

1851

IN PRACTICAL terms, the most note-worthy achievement of the Pre-Raphaelites in the first three years of their Brotherhood's existence was their success in turning almost the entire critical establishment in England against them. The reasons for this were complex and not entirely related to the stylistic qualities of the Pre-Raphaelite pictures. The religious subjects of Rossetti's *Ecce Ancilla Domini* (Tate Gallery), Hunt's *Druids*, and particularly Millais's *Christ in the House of His Parents*, all exhibited in 1850, provoked violent anti-Tractarian and anti-Catholic sentiments which were further outraged in 1851 by Collins's *Convent Thoughts*. The name Pre-Raphaelite Brotherhood also had in itself a capacity to arouse ire; in addition to keeping alive a firm belief that the pictures were painted in imitation of early art, it seems to have raised the spectre of the Roman Catholic and monastic inclinations of the German Nazarenes. In the extremely hostile comments in *The Times* in 1851, the Pre-Raphaelite pictures were called 'monkish follies'. *The Times* also noted the pictures' minute natural detail, but saw this as part of the 'mere servile imitation of the cramped style, false perspective, and crude colour of remote antiquity'.[1]

The near unanimity of the hostile criticism in 1851, following that of 1850, led the Brothers to take steps. Millais asked Coventry Patmore to seek the aid of Ruskin. Patmore approached Ruskin, and Ruskin complied with the request by writing a letter that appeared in *The Times* of 13 May, 1851. He followed it with a second letter in the issue of 30 May and a pamphlet entitled *Pre-Raphaelitism*, published in August 1851.

Ruskin announced in his first letter[2] that he had no acquaintance with the artists and 'very imperfect sympathy with them'. He carefully disassociated himself from their 'Romanist and Tractarian tendencies', and he deplored the cloistered sympathies of Collins's nun. 'But', he added about *Convent Thoughts*:

I happen to have a special acquaintance with the water plant, *Alisma Plantago* . . . and as I never saw it so thoroughly or so well drawn, I must take leave to remonstrate with you, when you say sweepingly that these men 'sacrifice *truth* as well as feeling to eccentricity.' For as a mere botanical study of the water lily and *Alisma*, as well as of the common lily and several other garden flowers, this picture would be invaluable to me, and I heartily wish it were mine.

He denied *The Times's* allegations of false perspective, with one small exception, and for that he offered to show worse errors in any twelve pictures containing architecture, chosen at random from the Royal Academy exhibition.

The most positive part of the letter had to do with the movement's name. Ruskin criticized the artists' lack of common sense in choosing to call themselves Pre-Raphaelites, but, nonetheless, he set out to say why they did so. Their paintings did not resemble ancient works, and critics who accused the Pre-Raphaelites of imitating early art were only revealing their own ignorance.

As far as I can judge of their aim—for, as I said, I do not know the men themselves – the Pre-Raphaelites intend to surrender no advantage which the knowledge or inventions of the present time

[1] *The Times*, 7 May 1851, p. 8.   [2] Ruskin, 1903-12, XII, 319-23.

can afford to their art. They intend to return to early days in this one point only – that, as far as in them lies, they will draw either what they see, or what they suppose might have been the actual facts of the scene they desire to represent, irrespective of any conventional rules of picture-making; and they have chosen their unfortunate though not inaccurate name because all artists did this before Raphael's time, and after Raphael's time did *not* this, but sought to paint fair pictures, rather than represent stern facts; of which the consequence has been that, from Raphael's time to this day, historical art has been in acknowledged decadence.

Thus, asserting that the purpose of Pre-Raphaelitism was not a return to 'archaic art', but to 'archaic honesty', Ruskin claimed the painters deserved respect simply for the indisputable labour and fidelity to a certain kind of truth displayed in their pictures. He concluded with the pronouncement 'there has been nothing in art so earnest or so complete as these pictures since the days of Albert Durer', and promised a second letter devoted to more special criticism.

What Ruskin originally intended his special criticism to be, we do not know, for under his father's advice he rewrote the second letter.[3] Even as it appeared it was critical enough.[4] Half of it was spent deprecating the homeliness of the Pre-Raphaelite figures. Ruskin then complained about defects in the colouring of flesh; Millais's flesh tints were 'wrought out of crude purples and dusky yellows', which Ruskin thought possibly came from attempting to gain too much transparency. He suggested that close study of minor detail was incompatible with flesh painting, and he noticed a similar weakness in the watercolour exhibited in 1850 by John Frederick Lewis, who in treatment of detail, Ruskin claimed, should be classed with the Pre-Raphaelites. But the fault which Ruskin thought most offended the public was an apparent want of shade. Here he took the offensive and laid the blame upon the other pictures at the Academy. Although he admitted some weaknesses, such as Hunt's tendency to exaggerate reflected lights, he wrote 'for the most part the pictures are rashly condemned because the only light which we are accustomed to see represented is that which falls on the artist's model in his dim painting-room, not that of sunshine in the fields'. Collins's nun suffered under a few more witticisms, although Ruskin said he had been informed that he was wrong in accusing the painters of Romanizing tendencies. Finally, the letter ended with another glowing conclusion: the Pre-Raphaelites 'may, as they gain experience, lay in our England the foundations of a school of art nobler than the world has seen for three hundred years.'

To the content of the two letters, the pamphlet, *Pre-Raphaelitism*, although much longer, added little about the movement. Beginning with generalities about the nature of work, Ruskin defined the proper work of the artist as, 'the faithful representation of all objects of historical interest, or of natural beauty existent at the period'.[5] However, modern artists were occupying themselves instead with 'drawing dances of naked women from academy models, or idealities of chivalry fitted out with Wardour Street armour, or eternal scenes from *Gil Blas*, *Don Quixote*, and the *Vicar of Wakefield*, or mountain sceneries with young idiots of Londoners wearing Highland bonnets and brandishing rifles in the foregrounds'. This 'inexpressible imbecility' Ruskin implicitly suggested was the result of the false and harmful teaching of the Royal Academy. He caricatured its 'Raphaelesque rules' – a principal light and shade of set proportions, an elaborate variety of poses, and the highest ideal beauty, consisting 'partly in Greek outline of nose, partly in proportions expressible in decimal fractions between the lip and chin; but mostly in that degree of improvement which the youth of sixteen is to bestow upon God's work in general' – whose purpose was

[3]Bradley, 1955, p. 262. [5]*Ibid.*, p. 349.
[4]Ruskin, 1903–12, XII, 324–7.

'the pursuit of beauty at the expense of manliness and truth'. This was what the Pre-Raphaelites were opposing. Their pictures, 'painted in a temper of resistance', by young men 'with little natural perception of beauty' were hardly likely to win the viewer from works 'enriched by plagiarism, polished by convention, invested with all the attractiveness of artificial grace, and recommended to our respect by established authority'.[6] Still, Ruskin found the violence of the attacks and the absence of support for the pictures strange. He again defended their perspective. Then, he launched into a comparison of Turner and Millais. This led to a discussion of several other contemporary artists and ultimately to the meat of the pamphlet, a description of the Turners in the Fawkes collection at Farnley Hall, which Ruskin had visited the previous April.[7]

Ruskin's justification for a pamphlet about Turner under the name *Pre-Raphaelitism* was that it would allay the accusations of inconsistency between his defence of the younger artists and his previous writings.[8] In his comparison of Millais and Turner, he tried to reconcile their differences, and ascribed to them a common defiance of false teaching.[9] He claimed that Turner's greatness lay in 'his taking possession of everything that he sees, – on his forgetting himself, and forgetting nothing else', and that all greatness in any artist lay in an intense sense of fact.

And thus Pre-Raphaelitism and Raphaelitism, and Turnerism, are all one and the same, so far as education can influence them. They are different in their choice, different in their faculties, but all the same in this, that Raphael himself, as far as he was great, and all who preceded or followed him who ever were great, became so by painting the truths around them as they appeared to each man's own mind, not as he had been taught to see them, except by the God who made both him and them.[10]

Into the pages on Turner Ruskin inserted an aside that the Pre-Raphaelites were overworking their pictures, a criticism which both Ruskin and the painters seem to have forgotten in the following years.[11] For the rest, the Pre-Raphaelites had to be content with a footnote, where Ruskin again rebutted their critics and elaborated the defence of their light which had appeared in his second letter: 'their system of light and shade is exactly the same as the Sun's; which is, I believe, likely to outlast that of the Renaissance, however brilliant'. He repeated his hopes of their founding a new and noble school, but added qualifications; it depended upon their painting nature, 'as it is around them, with the help of modern science', and if they were led into Romanism or mediaevalism they would come to nothing.[12]

In addition to his direct defence of the Pre-Raphaelites in the two letters and the pamphlet, Ruskin also inserted remarks about Hunt and Millais into the fifth edition of the first volume of *Modern Painters*, which appeared in September 1851. Then his militancy seemed to abate. Ten days before the publication of the pamphlet, he set off for Italy to work on *The Stones of Venice*. Returning to London only in July of 1852, Ruskin missed the critical storms of that year's exhibitions. His next public utterance about the Pre-Raphaelites was a defence of the aerial perspective in Millais's *Huguenot* (Pl. 40a) in the third volume of *The Stones of Venice*, published in October 1853.[13]

In May 1851 Ruskin was thirty-two years old. He had published two volumes of

[6]*Ibid.*, pp. 353–5.
[7]The pamphlet was dedicated to Francis Hawkesworth Fawkes. The other artists discussed were William Henry Hunt, Samuel Prout, John Frederick Lewis, William Mulready, and Edwin Landseer. For Ruskin's comparison of Turner and Millais, see below, p. 50

[8]Ruskin, 1903–12, XII, p. li.
[9]*Ibid.*, p. 361.
[10]*Ibid.*, p. 385.
[11]*Ibid.*, pp. 388–9.
[12]*Ibid.*, pp. 357–8n.
[13]*Ibid.*, III, 599, 621; XI, 59–60; and see below, p. 47

Modern Painters, *The Seven Lamps of Architecture*, and one volume of *The Stones of Venice*. His defence of Pre-Raphaelitism did not turn the tide of hostile criticism; in fact, it broadened the target for the attackers. But it was a godsend to the young painters. Praise by a writer of Ruskin's stature forced the critics to take them seriously. Still, in the next round of criticism, the pictures tended again to be lost sight of as the attackers levelled on Ruskin's theories. This meant that from 1851 through 1859 Pre-Raphaelitism was seen by most contemporary observers almost solely in terms of the naturalistic orientation proclaimed for the movement by Ruskin. His differentiation between 'archaic art' and 'archaic honesty', coinciding with the disappearance of Rossetti's works from public exhibition, seemed to settle the conflict within the movement between the goals of revivalism and naturalism definitely on the side of the latter.

Why did the Pre-Raphaelites turn to Ruskin in 1851? He had not seen the exhibitions of 1849, where the first Pre-Raphaelite pictures were exhibited, and, as we have seen, he only took notice of the Pre-Raphaelite pictures in 1850 when forced to by William Dyce, but the artists seem to have expected that he would respond favourably to their work. In the summer of 1850 when an anonymous article praising them appeared in *The Guardian* they erroneously thought that it might have been written by Ruskin.[14] In 1851 they had considered writing to Ruskin themselves. When Patmore, reporting Ruskin's response to his request, added that Ruskin was interested in buying Millais's *Return of the Dove to the Ark* (Ashmolean Museum, Oxford), William Michael Rossetti wrote that it was evident from this that Ruskin admired the Brotherhood, adding parenthetically 'were it from nothing else'.[15] This ambiguous 'nothing else' may have meant no more than that the artists, believing themselves to be working along lines recommended by Ruskin, thought that he should recognize this community of interest and that he should approve of and defend their work.

If Ruskin initially did see a relation between the activities of the young artists and what he had preached in *Modern Painters*, he kept it masked. Only after he had met and spent some time with Millais (and had prepared new editions of the first two volumes of *Modern Painters*) did he publicly acknowledge what they had in common, which suggests that it even may have been pointed out to him by Millais. Whatever the cause, the 'no acquaintance' and 'very imperfect sympathy' with the artists, professed in the first letter to *The Times* in May, were superseded by the preface to his pamphlet *Pre-Raphaelitism*, in August:

Eight years ago, in the close of the first volume of *Modern Painters*, I ventured to give the following advice to the young artists of England:

'They should go to nature in all singleness of heart, and walk with her laboriously and trustingly, having no other thought but how best to penetrate her meaning; rejecting nothing, selecting nothing, and scorning nothing.' Advice which, whether bad or good, involved infinite labour and humiliation in the following it, and was therefore, for the most part, rejected.

It has, however, at last been carried out, to the very letter, by a group of men who, for their reward, have been assailed with the most scurrilous abuse which I ever recollect seeing issue from the public press. I have, therefore, thought it due to them to contradict the directly false statements which have been made respecting their works; and to point out the kind of merit which, however deficient in some respects, those works possess beyond the possibility of dispute.[16]

This preface was not to go unquestioned. William Michael Rossetti immediately wrote in the *Spectator* that he did not think 'strict non-selection' was either desirable or possible, but he did not deny the implied genesis of Pre-Raphaelitism out of Ruskin's theorizing.[17]

[14]Rossetti, 1900, p. 288.   [16]Ruskin, 1903–12, XII, 339.
[15]*Ibid.*, p. 299.   [17]*Spectator*, 4 Oct. 1851, p. 956.

Ruskin himself was not to remain faithful to the dogma of 'rejecting nothing, selecting nothing', but for the rest of the 1850s his attitude towards the Pre-Raphaelites was to be that of an involved associate rather than of a detached observer, as it had been in May, 1851.

Following the appearance of Ruskin's second letter in *The Times*, Hunt and Millais wrote him a letter of appreciation. Ruskin then drove to Millais's studio and introduced himself. Holman Hunt says that Ruskin carried Millais off for a week's stay at his home at Denmark Hill,[18] but no other source mentions the stay. Nonetheless, Ruskin and Millais did become immediate friends. On 2 July, 1851, Millais wrote to his friend and patron in Oxford, Mrs. Thomas Combe: 'I have dined and taken breakfast with Ruskin, and we are such good friends that he wishes me to accompany him to Switzerland this summer . . . We are as yet singularly at variance in our opinions upon Art.' As an example of this variance, Millais cited their different opinions of Turner.[19] Ruskin's didactic inclinations – most recently made evident in his letters to *The Times* – must also have guaranteed that Millais heard plenty about his own art and what it should become.

Millais's letter to Mrs. Combe was written from Kingston-on-Thames in Surrey, where he and Hunt had gone to paint the landscape backgrounds of their next paintings. These paintings were Hunt's *Hireling Shepherd* (Pl. 5) and Millais's *Ophelia* (Pl. 4), and they display far more radically than any of the artists' previous works that careful attention to the appearance of nature which henceforth would be regarded as the essential Pre-Raphaelite quality. Along with Ford Madox Brown's *Pretty Baa-Lambs* (Pl. 8), which was begun separately during the same summer, they would establish the path which Pre-Raphaelitism would follow through the rest of the 1850s. As Ruskin had done in print, Hunt, Millais, and Brown settled in practice, in their work of this summer, the chief contradictions contained in their pictures from the previous three years. Hunt in his memoirs assesses the significance of Millais's *Ophelia*:

The landscape of *The Woodman's Daughter*, painted in 1850, might not be so conclusive in the testimony it offers of a new *evangel*, but the charm throughout the background of the *Ophelia*, and the pathetic grace of the lovewrapt maiden, are enough to proclaim that not in one feature alone, but in the whole picture, a new art was born.[20]

The outdoor paintings of the Pre-Raphaelite circle from 1851 and subsequent years indeed do constitute a 'new art'; and Brown and Hunt, as well as Millais, were present at its birth.

In subject, Millais's *Ophelia* is still a picture derived from a literary source. It does not, however, show an event that actually takes place in *Hamlet*, and it does not show a reconstructed scene as if it might be taking place on the stage. Thus, although there are earlier nineteenth-century depictions of the demise of Ophelia, notably Delacroix's painting of 1844 (Louvre), Millais's picture departs from the usual *tableaux-vivants* of most earlier and contemporary English paintings of Shakespearean subjects, even those of his friends, such as Ford Madox Brown's *Lear and Cordelia* of 1849 (Tate Gallery) or Holman Hunt's *Valentine Rescuing Sylvia from Proteus*. What is most distinctive in *Ophelia* is the degree to which everything theatrical is subordinated to the depiction of the natural world. The picture is based on Gertrude's description of Ophelia's death in the fourth act of *Hamlet*:

> There is a willow grows aslant the brook
> That shows his hoar leaves in the glassy stream;
> Therewith fantastic garlands did she make
> Of crowflowers, nettles, daisies, and long purples
> That liberal shepherds give a grosser name,

[18]Hunt, 1905, I, 257.
[19]Millais, 1899, I, 116–19.

[20]Hunt, 1905, II, 399.

Ophelia is shown floating in the stream, buoyed up by her clothes spread wide, and still singing snatches of old songs. Above and around her are the willow aslant the brook and the flowers enumerated in Gertrude's description.

Hunt's *Hireling Shepherd* also stems in part from Shakespearean inspiration. Hunt exhibited the painting at the Royal Academy in 1852 accompanied in the catalogue with the following quotation from one of Edgar's songs in *King Lear*:

> Sleepest or wakest thou, jolly shepherd?
> Thy sheep be in the corn;
> And, for one blast of thy minikin mouth,
> Thy sheep shall take no harm.

However, Hunt's picture does not illustrate *Lear* in the way that Millais's *Ophelia* does illustrate a passage from *Hamlet*. It shows a scene of rustic dalliance in which the figures are not in period costume but belong to the contemporary agricultural world. The incident of a shepherd neglecting his flock to show his shepherdess companion a death's head moth seems to be entirely of Hunt's invention. If we must ascribe a literary source to the picture it should be biblical rather than Shakespearean. The ancestry of Hunt's shepherd and sheep is in the parables of the New Testament and in Christian symbolism of the pastoral flock. When the Manchester City Art Gallery acquired *The Hireling Shepherd* in 1897, Hunt wrote a letter describing Shakespeare's shepherd as 'a type of other muddle-headed pastors, who, instead of performing their services to the flock – which is in constant peril – discuss vain questions of no value to any human soul.'[21] In his letter Hunt pointed out the foolishness of his shepherd's concern with the death's head moth, while his sheep are doomed to destruction from eating wheat and the lamb on the shepherdess's lap is being poisoned with sour apples.

For his implicit pastoral symbolism Hunt had both artistic and literary precedents. In 1850 Sir Edwin Landseer exhibited at the Royal Academy a painting of a shepherd carrying a sheep in the snow entitled *The Lost Sheep* and accompanied in the catalogue with a quotation from *Luke* XV.[22] In March 1851, Ruskin published a pamphlet on church organization which he called *Notes on the Construction of Sheepfolds*. To this, William Dyce, who was an active high-church man, replied with another pamphlet, *Notes on Shepherds and Sheep*. Hunt read both in the summer of 1851.[23]

Thus, there is abundant evidence that Hunt intended the picture to have a symbolic, moralizing message. In recent years, *The Hireling Shepherd* has been looked upon as a forerunner of Hunt's later religious pictures packed with heavy-handed symbolism. On the other hand, we should remember that Hunt wrote his letter explaining the picture forty-five years after he painted it, and after he had secured himself a position as a Great Victorian on the basis of his later religious works. Even then, in his letter of 1897, Hunt wrote:

I did not wish to force the moral, and I never explained it till now. For this meaning was only in reserve for those who might be led to work it out. My first object as an artist was to paint, not Dresden china *bergers*, but a real shepherd, and a real shepherdess, and a landscape in full sunlight, with all the colour of luscious summer, without the faintest fear of the precedents of any landscape painters who had rendered Nature before.

In a fragmentary manuscript in the John Rylands Library in Manchester, possibly a first draft for the letter of 1897, Hunt makes a similar statement but one in which he denies that he had originally intended the picture to have any religious message:

[21]This letter is printed in *The Art of William Holman Hunt*, O.M., D.C.L., exhibition catalogue, (Walker Art Gallery, Liverpool, 1907), p. 24, no. 35.

[22]Illustrated in the catalogue of the Pender sale (Christie's, London, 29 May 1897) no. 46.

[23]Millais, 1899, I, 122.

The Hireling Shepherd was not painted with any distinctly symbolic and allegorical view altho' I can understand how the work as it stands may be regarded as such. . . . It may of course bear application to religious as to other pursuits. And I am grateful to have it so solemnly used, but I must confess that [by] doing it my first object was to portray a real [Shepherd] and Shepherdess...[24]

When *The Hireling Shepherd* was exhibited in 1852, none of the critics seemed interested in delving into its deeper symbolic meaning. Even a friend who would have known Hunt's intentions first-hand, William Michael Rossetti, writing in the *Spectator*, only mentioned the 'moral suggestiveness' of the subject and declared that the most striking quality of the work was 'its peculiar manliness, and spirit of healthful enjoyment'.[25] The anonymous author of a long and thoughtful article about the Pre-Raphaelites which appeared in the *British Quarterly Review* wrote that there might be some allusion to the scriptural idea of a hireling shepherd,

but on the whole, the picture is a piece of broad rural reality, with none of the fantastic circumstance implied in the lines quoted, and with no attempt to bring out the scriptural allusion, if it exists, by deviating from what is English and modern ... There is certainly no attempt at poetry here; for a fellow more capable than the shepherd of drinking a great quantity of beer, or a more sunburnt slut than the shepherdess, we never saw in a picture.[26]

A less sympathetic critic, the reviewer for the *Athenaeum*, saw the picture in similar terms:

Mr. Hunt . . . carries anti-eclecticism to the absurd. Like Swift, he revels in the repulsive. These rustics are of the coarsest breed, – ill favoured, ill fed, ill washed. Not to dwell on cutaneous and other minutiae, – they are literal transcripts of stout, sunburnt, out-of-door labourers.[27].

In his pamphlet of 1860, F. G. Stephens, whose perspective was affected by a knowledge of Hunt's later religious paintings, *The Light of the World* (Pl. 27a), *The Scapegoat* (Pl. 29a), and *The Finding of the Saviour in the Temple* (City Art Gallery, Birmingham), still made no mention of any allegorical reference to the pastoral flock. He described the picture as a naturalistically rendered rural scene in which the moral interest went no further than the unfortunate fate of the neglected sheep.[28]

The general composition of *The Hireling Shepherd* – a couple embracing in the foreground, sheep in the background – recalls representations of *The Meeting of Jacob and Rachel*. Of the renderings of this subject which Hunt was likely to have known, the closest in composition to his picture is a Spanish seventeenth-century painting in the Dulwich College Picture Gallery, which Hunt says he haunted as a youth (Pl. 3c). This picture shows the couple kneeling and embracing before the sheep in a wide landscape. On the right, a sheep is partly hidden by a tree, a motif that possibly suggested the sheep emerging from behind the trees in the centre of Hunt's picture. Closer in time, he also knew *The Meeting of Jacob and Rachel* by William Dyce, of which Hunt had painted a copy when it was exhibited at the Royal Academy in 1850.[29] Hunt's composition is closer to that of the Dulwich picture than it is to Dyce's, which depicts three-quarter-length standing figures in biblical costume before a biblical landscape. But the manner in which Hunt's shepherd reaches around the shepherdess seems related to the gesture of Dyce's Jacob putting his hand around the neck of a reticent Rachel. Some smaller details such as Hunt's shepherd's beer keg and the wine flask of Dyce's Jacob also show similarities.

[24]John Rylands Library, Manchester, Rylands Eng. MS. 1216, f. 31.
[25]Rossetti, 1867, p. 235.
[26]*British Quarterly Review*, XVI, 1852, pp. 215–16.
[27]*Athenaeum*, 22 May 1852, p. 581.
[28]Stephens, 1860, pp. 19–21.
[29]For an engraving of Dyce's picture see Dafforne,

1860, p. 296. Variants are in the Leicester Art Gallery; the church of St. Lawrence, Knodishall, Suffolk; and the Hamburger Kunsthalle. The last named has full-length figures. It was exhibited at the Royal Academy in 1853 and is reproduced in Andrews, 1964, pl. 74b. Hunt's copy has disappeared.

Hunt's comments about the picture quoted above indicate his awareness of other earlier paintings of pastoral scenes. His phrase 'Dresden china *bergers*' has an eighteenth-century sound, suggesting Boucher's rural confections or Gainsborough's fancy pictures. However, Hunt's choice of words also anticipates a passage in *Pre-Raphaelitism and the Pre-Raphaelite Brotherhood* in which he criticizes William Mulready's 'taste for Dresden-china prettiness'.[30] There are several rural amatory scenes by Mulready to which *The Hireling Shepherd* might be compared: *The Sonnet* (Victoria and Albert Museum), and *Open Your Mouth and Shut Your Eyes* (Pl. 3b), both exhibited at the Royal Academy in 1839 and also included in an exhibition of Mulready's work at the Society of Arts in 1848, and *Burchell and Sophia in the Hayfield*, exhibited in 1847 (collection of Lord Northbrook). This latter picture, based on one of Mulready's illustrations to *The Vicar of Wakefield* published in 1843, depicts Burchell reaching around Sophia on the pretext of assisting her with her work. Like *The Hireling Shepherd* it shows a kind of non-embrace, and there is in both works a similar closeness of the figures without any feeling of real physical contact between them.

Dyce and Mulready were probably the two older, established artists most admired by Hunt at the beginning of his career. We have already discussed Hunt's relations with Dyce. His remark about Mulready's taste for prettiness is a qualification in a discussion in which he declared Mulready the most appropriate model for the young artist to follow in the 1840s. Mulready did provide not only a lead for the Pre-Raphaelites' bright colours but also compositional hints; Millais borrowed from Mulready's *Vicar of Wakefield* illustrations on at least two occasions: in *Isabella*, exhibited in 1849, and in *The Rescue* of 1855 (National Gallery of Victoria, Melbourne).[31] Hence it is plausible to see awareness of both Dyce's and Mulready's pictures behind *The Hireling Shepherd*. Yet, if we compare the works, the differences are more striking than the similarities. The Italianate, Raphaelesque refinement of Dyce, and the sugary delicacy of Mulready have given way to a more robust concern with actuality, which appears both in Hunt's unidealized figures and in their setting. The critical response to the picture cited above shows that contemporary observers could no longer respond within a frame of reference established by Dyce, as they had for Hunt's pictures of the previous years. If the comparison which was made in the first chapter between Hunt's *Rienzi*, or the other Pre-Raphaelite pictures exhibited in 1849, and Courbet's *Stonebreakers* seems almost laughable because of the pictures' manifest dissimilarities, it is transformed if we substitute *The Hireling Shepherd* for *Rienzi*. There are still important differences, but now there are equally important elements in common. Visiting Paris in 1849, Hunt had found paintings of the 'new Realistic school . . . coarse and ugly'. Three years later the critic for the *Athenaeum* used the adjectives 'coarsest' and 'repulsive' for Hunt's picture. During these years, Hunt's art, as well as Millais's, had changed more profoundly than he admits in *Pre-Raphaelitism and the Pre-Raphaelite Brotherhood*. It is now time to examine the manifestation of this change in the landscape elements of the pictures.

Hunt and Millais painted their landscape backgrounds near the village of Ewell, between Kingston-upon-Thames and Epsom in Surrey, some fourteen miles from Charing Cross. Both artists knew the area from visits to relatives and family friends during the 1840s. Late in June 1851 they took lodgings in a cottage on Surbiton Hill in Kingston; later in the summer they moved to Worcester Park Farm, a seventeenth-century hunting lodge near Cheam, where they remained until 6 Dec. They painted every day except Sunday, and

[30]Hunt, 1905, I, 49.
[31]For *Isabella* see Mulready's illustrations *Dispute between Moses and Thornhill* (p. 43) and *Conviction of Thornhill* (p. 278). For *The Rescue* see *The Fire* (p. 181).

their normal painting day lasted from eight o'clock in the morning until seven in the evening. Eleven hours a day, six days a week, for twenty-three weeks amounts to more than fifteen-hundred hours of work apiece. Even after that figure is reduced substantially to allow for lunches, bad weather, and miscellaneous distractions, the two painters still spent a staggering amount of time painting landscape backgrounds. During this period each started a second work. Hunt began the background of *The Light of the World* (Pl. 27a) on 7 Nov., and he worked on it at night while continuing *The Hireling Shepherd* by day. Millais painted the background of *A Huguenot, on St. Bartholomew's Day, Refusing to Shield Himself from Danger by Wearing the Roman Catholic Badge* (Pl. 40a). For all these pictures Hunt and Millais painted only the landscape settings in the country; the figural painting remained to be done after they returned to their London studios. As the deadline for submitting pictures for the Royal Academy exhibition was 1 April, the amount of time (under four months) which Hunt and Millais allowed for the figures was substantially less than that (over five) which they devoted to the landscapes. Three of the four pictures did appear at the Royal Academy in 1852; the exception was *The Light of the World*, which Hunt completed in 1853 and exhibited in 1854.

Each of the landscape backgrounds was apparently painted from a single location. Millais worked on the banks of the Ewell River; Hunt in a field two miles away. Each picture appears to be a faithful transcript of the appearance of the place at a certain time. However, the specific conditions of a certain time do not remain constant over a period involving hundreds of hours and running from June to December. The effects of light, weather, even of verdure, could not all have been copied directly from what was before the artists' eyes. During those long hours of working directly from nature, Hunt and Millais must constantly have had to adjust what they saw to accord with what they had already represented in their paintings. In *Ophelia* Millais had the lesser problem. By taking a myopic view of his subject, he bypassed temporal and meteorological concerns. There are shadows in the depth of the greenery, but they do not suggest the fall of light at a specific time. Questions of atmosphere or weather do not exist; Millais ignored them to concentrate his energies upon botanical fact. On the other hand, Hunt set out to paint his landscape 'in full sunlight, with all the colour of luscious summer'. He thus had to cope with more complications of changing conditions than Millais. Still, the conditions shown are those of a typical summer day. The sun shines and cumulus clouds drift across the sky. The mood is of the ripeness of full summer when days are long and time moves slowly. The shepherd and shepherdess are idling away the hours. Some sheep drift toward the corn, but most stand placidly in the shade or lie dozing in the sun. The time is specific, but it is hardly a 'fleeting moment' which must be seized rapidly before it passes.

The most obvious result of the many hours that Millais and Hunt spent painting directly from nature is the sheer quantity of detail that their pictures contain. Although natural detail had been an increasingly prominent element in Hunt's previous pictures, the advance from the foreground of *Valentine Rescuing Sylvia* to the abundance of the grass and flowers in *The Hireling Shepherd* (Col. Pl. 2a) is still substantial. A comparison of that grass and those flowers with the dandelions in *Rienzi* shows that an attempt to encompass the almost infinite complexity and multiplicity of nature has replaced the delineation of separate and isolated natural details. In *Ophelia* the abundance of plant life is even more striking than in *The Hireling Shepherd*. Millais had established a precedent in *Ferdinand Lured by Ariel* of treating nature as botanic detail and little else, but the foliate detail in *Ophelia* is still more prominent. It now rises to the top of the picture, and, instead of being distinctly behind the figure as in *Ferdinand Lured by Ariel*, it remains on the surface of the canvas. The brook is wide enough for Ophelia to float in, but the willows and the plants on the further bank bend over the stream so that the leaves and flowers at the top of the picture seem as near to us as those at the bottom. Perspective space has been abandoned for a direct, even primitive insistence on literal botanic detail. Background has become foreground covered inch by inch with microscopically observed detail in which the critic for the *Athenaeum* saw 'the botanical study of a Linnaeus.'[32]

In *The Hireling Shepherd*, foreground detail is combined with a spacious landscape background, one much more extensive and important in the composition of the picture than any that Hunt had previously painted. It includes the sheep, the field of wheat into which their leaders are straying, and beyond the sheep distant tree rows and fields. The elaboration of the immediate foreground is not maintained throughout the entire picture, but there is not as conspicuous a difference between the handling of the foreground and distance as in *The Druids* or *Valentine Rescuing Sylvia from Proteus*. In the wheatfield, which is well back from the foreground figures, the separate stalks are still clearly delineated one by one. However, what is most remarkable about the background, and what contemporary observers praised, was not its quantity of detail but its truth, or at least its novelty of effect. William Michael Rossetti wrote 'there is a feeling of the country – its sunny shadow-varied openness – such as we do not remember to have seen ever before so completely expressed.'[33] In 1860, F. G. Stephens declared that the representation of sunlight was 'an entirely new thing in art', and he explained:

For the painter first put into practice, in an historical picture, based upon his own observations, the scientific elucidation of that peculiar effect which, having been hinted at by Leonardo da Vinci, in one of his wonderful world-guesses, was partly explained by Newton, and fully developed by Davy and Brewster. He was absolutely the first figure-painter who gave the true colour to sun-shadows, made them partake of the tint of the object on which they were cast, and deepened such shadows to pure blue where he found them to be so, painted trees like trees, and far-off hedgerows standing clearly in pure summer air.[34]

This explanation may provide a rather muddled assessment of the place of Hunt's picture in the histories of science and art, but it does indicate what a contemporary and friend saw as revolutionary in Hunt's work: in two words, coloured shadows.

Hunt was not concerned with recording changing atmospheric effects; indeed, by his method of working, he was not prepared to record them. But, as we have seen, he expressed as early as 1848 his intention of painting 'the sunlight brightness of the day itself.'[35] To do this, he had to free himself from conventional schemata of light and shade, the 'brown foliage, smoky clouds, and dark corners' against which he had directed his resolution of 1848. What this meant was that the relation of light and dark areas, which had provided the main organizational structure of a picture from Claude through Constable ('I was always determined that my pictures should have chiaroscuro, if they had nothing else'), would be replaced by the relation of colours, without the tonal range of earlier works. Of course, Hunt was not the first artist to be interested in this redirection, nor was *The Hireling Shepherd* the first picture to show it. We can see behind Hunt's painting the spectrum of interests and activities discussed in the first chapter, and, as we have seen, Ruskin defended the Pre-Raphaelite pictures exhibited in 1851 against the criticism that they lacked shade. But it was the sunlight in *The Hireling Shepherd* which Stephens declared 'an entirely new thing in art'.

Despite all that has happened in art since *The Hireling Shepherd* was painted, its impact is

[32]*Athenaeum*, 22 May 1852, p. 581.
[33]*Spectator*, 15 May 1852, p. 472.
[34]Stephens, 1860, pp. 19–20.
[35]See above, p. 10

still startling. Hunt freed himself from what he considered conventional to such a degree that to eyes accustomed to Claude or Constable his greens still seem raw and garish. But these presumably were the colours which he saw before him while working in the country and which he recorded directly without allowing considerations of pictorial values to intervene. As Stephens observed, the colours are primarily the local colours, both in sunlight and shadow. Stephens also wrote that Hunt deepened the shadows 'to pure blue where he found them to be so'. The blue in the shadows is the reflected colour of the sky. Although Hunt's use of blue is not as marked as in some of his later works or as Brown's in *The Pretty Baa-Lambs* of the same year, it can be seen in the shadows under the distant hedgerow, for example, and, more prominently and perhaps less explicably, in the bare branches on the upper left which are drawn in pure blue at their further extremities. More complex reflections are seen in the clouds and in the stippled flesh tones of the figures. The brightness of *The Hireling Shepherd*, however, is not due to reflected colours, but to the primacy of local colours and to Hunt's refusal to modify them for the sake of tonal harmony.

Hunt's and Millais's technical methods also contributed to the brightness. Hunt says that in the country he and Millais used the wet white ground mainly for the blossoms of flowers.[36] They did not use it throughout their pictures, but as the areas in which they used the wet ground could not be retouched, the only way they could bring other parts of a picture into harmony with them would be to heighten their colours correspondingly. In *Valentine Rescuing Sylvia* the brightly coloured costumes, painted over a wet white ground, stand out from the relatively subdued colours of the forest beyond, but in *The Hireling Shepherd* a new luminosity is evident throughout the landscape, not only in the figures and flowers.

The technique of the wet white ground required an entirely fresh start, beginning with laying the ground, for each day's work. It thus forced concentration upon the local colour at the expense of consideration of the picture as a whole. Even where Hunt and Millais were not using this technique, however, their method seems to have been to work on a single area at a time, finishing it in detail while other parts of the canvas were still bare. Later, when painting his portrait of Ruskin (Pl. 20), Millais described a day's work as about the size of a five-shilling piece.[37] Despite any over-all conceptions of the picture that the artists may initially have had, in working from nature they observed and recorded in terms of local colour and specific detail.

If their working methods precluded the traditional organization of a picture, behind those methods lay a widespread dissatisfaction with that kind of organization, a dissatisfaction reflected, for example, in Ruskin's criticisms of Claude as well as in Hunt's determination to escape convention.[38] Truth to nature was to be paramount, and whatever stood in its way could be sacrificed. Therefore, that the pictures would lack traditional harmonies was inevitable as well as intentional. That they have any formal coherence at all is perhaps more surprising. But a new kind of organization based on relationships of colour and a consistency of handling over the entire surface is beginning to appear, replacing the traditional relationship of light and dark and the subordination of parts in an illusion of three-dimensional space. In Millais's *Ophelia*, where there is no spatial depth, the emergence of two-dimensional relationships is most obvious. It is worth noting that the *Athenaeum*, which disapproved of the 'misdirected observation and imitation of everything',

[36]Hunt, 1905, I, 276.   [38]Hunt, 1905, I, 86–8.
[37]Lutyens, 1967, p. 99.

25

nonetheless did see a kind of harmony in the *Ophelia* and advised its readers: 'Rightly to appreciate the general chromatic effect, this picture should be looked at from a little distance – when it becomes quite luminous.'[39] At a distance, the natural details lose interest as observed details and become part of an overall surface design. Although in *The Hireling Shepherd* there is still an extensive landscape background, we need only recall the spaciousness of pictures by Claude or Constable to see how, in contrast, everything in Hunt's picture crowds towards the surface. This is not only the result of the effect of the bright colours upon the landscape space. The figures are not conceived in depth but in a thin triangular silhouette on the surface of the picture. If we contrast them with the figures in a Raphael *Holy Family*, for example, or Mulready's figures in *Open Your Mouth and Shut Your Eyes* (Pl. 3b), their two-dimensionality is evident.

Another result of Hunt's and Millais's working method was that they tended to think of their figures separately from the rest of the pictures. The pictures were made up of parts which the artists could worry about at different times. Millais did not decide upon the subject of his second picture, the *Huguenot*, until well after he had set to work on its background. When Charles Collins joined Hunt and Millais at Worcester Park Farm, he laboured away at a background of a broken-down shed, while constantly changing his mind about what he should put in it.[40] For *The Hireling Shepherd* and *Ophelia*, Hunt and Millais apparently had fairly complete conceptions from the start, but their canvases still contained areas of white canvas for the figures when they took them back to London.

For *Ophelia*, Elizabeth Siddal, Rossetti's future wife, posed in Millais's studio in a bathtub filled with tinted water. It is, therefore, not surprising that the water does not have the same convincing verisimilitude as the surrounding greenery. William Michael Rossetti wrote that its purple colour was, 'we will not venture to say untruthful, but scarcely familiar to the eye, and the flow is so slight as hardly to enhance the appearance of liquidity.'[41] Hunt also painted his figures in the studio and imported a country girl to pose as the shepherdess. He had evident difficulties in fitting the figures into their space, most obviously in the lower right corner, where the feet of the shepherdess dangle precariously over a ditch. In contrast to his work out of doors on the background, Hunt's figure painting followed a more conventional pattern, beginning with making studies of the models posed in the nude. The flesh tones have a livid coppery redness, apparently the result of Hunt's attempt to impart to them the outdoor, sunlight effect of the rest of the picture. At least, so William Michael Rossetti explained. To the critic of the *Athenaeum* they looked as though they had drunk too much beer.

The figures have a more integral importance in the third revolutionary Pre-Raphaelite picture begun in 1851, Ford Madox Brown's *Pretty Baa-Lambs*. In April, Brown, Hunt, and Mark Anthony, a landscape painter and friend of Brown's, took a three-day trip to the Isle of Wight. After their return Brown, at his home in the south London suburb of Stockwell, began to paint *The Pretty Baa-Lambs*. According to an entry in his diary written three years later, in 1854, the painting occupied him for five months during the summer of 1851.[42] He completed it by the end of September. If Brown's memory was accurate, he began the painting before the first of May – two months before Hunt and Millais went off to Ewell to begin their pictures, and even before Ruskin wrote his letters in defence of the Pre-Raphaelites. This is Brown's description of his work, from his diary entry of 1854:

The *Baa Lamb* picture was painted almost entirely in sunlight, which twice gave me a fever while painting. I used to take the lay figure out every morning, and bring it in at night or if it rained . . .

[39]*Athenaeum*, 22 May 1852, p. 581.
[40]See below, p. 83

[41] Rossetti, 1867, p. 211.
[42]Rossetti, 1900, p. 108.

My painting-room being on a level with the garden, Emma [Brown's wife] sat for the lady, and Kate [his daughter] for the child. The lambs and sheep used to be brought every morning from Clapham Common in a truck: one of them ate up all the flowers one morning in the garden, where they used to behave very ill. The background was painted on the Common. The medium I used was Roberson's undrying copal (flake white).[43]

Brown had admired the brilliance of Hunt's and Millais's pictures exhibited at the Royal Academy in 1851, and in May he wrote to Lowes Dickinson in Rome advising him to adopt the pure white ground at once, in emulation.[44] However, his use of the undrying medium does not mean that he was employing Hunt's and Millais's technique of the *wet* white ground. He did visit them in Surrey during the summer of 1851 and learned the secret of the technique from Millais, but in Brown's diary the first reference to his use of the wet white ground is for the flesh tones of his *Christ Washing Peter's Feet* (Tate Gallery), which he began in the following winter.[45]

Brown continued to work on *The Pretty Baa-Lambs* after the summer of 1851. He altered the head of the woman in the spring of 1852 before sending the picture to the Royal Academy. He worked on it further in the autumn of 1852 and in the spring of 1853 before sending it to an exhibition in Glasgow. In 1852 he made a small copy (Pl. 12a) which he sold in 1854. The large picture remained unsold until 1859, when Brown worked on it once again before it was finally bought by his patron James Leathart of Newcastle. This later work resulted in the addition of a panoramic landscape background. According to Holman Hunt's description,[46] and according to the evidence of the copy made in 1852, the picture originally had a low horizon. The background painted on Clapham Common stopped at the cottage and trees on the fringe of the open land where the figures stand. Brown apparently added the further landscape to lessen the stark contrast between the vertical figures and the low horizontal landscape. The distant view of a wide estuary may be based on a lost landscape of *Southend*, which showed the Isle of Sheppey and the Nore lightship in the mouth of the Thames.[47] Brown began *Southend* in 1846, but completed it only in 1858.

The meaning of *The Pretty Baa-Lambs* is as ambiguous as that of *The Hireling Shepherd*. When the picture was exhibited at the Royal Academy in 1852, it seems to have puzzled most of the reviewers who took any notice of it. William Michael Rossetti described it as an eighteenth-century subject showing a pretty touch of domestic sentiment.[48] Other critics suspected a religious meaning, and the *Art Journal* concluded that it was a 'facetious experiment upon the public intelligence'.[49] Brown in the catalogue of his retrospective exhibition in 1865 acknowledged the confusion and wrote a statement in which he tried to set things straight:

This picture was painted in 1851, and exhibited the following year, at a time when discussion was very rife on certain ideas and principles in art, very much in harmony with my own, but more sedulously promulgated by friends of mine. Hung in a false light, and viewed through the medium of extraneous ideas, the painting was, I think, much misunderstood. I was told that it was impossible to make out what *meaning* I had in the picture. At the present moment, few people I trust will seek for any meaning beyond the obvious one, that is – a lady, a baby, two lambs, a servant maid and some grass. In all cases pictures must be judged first as pictures – a deep philosophical intention will not make a fine picture, such being rather given in excess of the bargain; and though all epic works of art have this excess, yet I should be much inclined to doubt the genuineness of that artist's ideas, who never painted from love of the mere look of things, whose mind was always on the stretch for a moral. This picture was painted out in the sunlight; the only

[43]*Ibid.*, p. 109.
[44]Hueffer, 1896, p. 77.
[45]Rossetti, 1900, p. 109.
[46]Hunt, 1905, II, 96.

[47]Brown, 1865, p. 11.
[48]*Spectator*, 15 May 1852, p. 472.
[49]*Art Journal*, 1852, p. 175.

intention being to render that effect as well as my powers in a first attempt of this kind would allow.[50]

Brown's denial of any meaning except the obvious one seems slightly disingenuous. His *oeuvre* of the 1840s and 1850s contains a number of other pictures of mothers or nurses with children: *Oure Ladye of Good Children* (Tate Gallery), *Out of Town* (City Art Gallery, Manchester), *Waiting* (private collection), *The Last of England* (City Art Gallery, Birmingham), and *Take Your Son, Sir!* (Tate Gallery). The first of these is of a *Madonna and Child*, and in all the others, as in *The Pretty Baa-Lambs*, there are reminiscences of the *Madonna* image. Also, the sheep, which Brown went to the trouble and expense of importing from Clapham Common, are not unlike those in *The Hireling Shepherd*, which Hunt later allowed to bear a weighty load of symbolism. Although Brown may not have intended his sheep as a pastoral flock, it is understandable that contemporary viewers expected them to have some meaning. It is ironic, however, that the critics were more ready to search for a hidden meaning in Brown's work than in Hunt's. Brown's assertion of the purely visual motivation of his work provides a significant antidote to the usual view of Pre-Raphaelitism as an excessively literary phenomenon. His statement also points to the importance which the study of nature directly out of doors had for the Pre-Raphaelites at this time. The friends Brown refers to are certainly the members of the Pre-Raphaelite Brotherhood. In the context of a statement about a picture in which the 'only intention' was to render the effect of sunlight, the 'certain ideas and principles in art' being sedulously promulgated by those friends could only be the ideas and principles lying behind the outdoor study of natural appearances, to which Brown, Hunt, and Millais all devoted themselves in the summer of 1851.

The landscape in *The Pretty Baa-Lambs*, especially as it originally stood, is less elaborate than the landscape in *The Hireling Shepherd*. If we compare areas of the foreground grass in the two pictures, we can see that Brown's delineation is less precisely detailed (Col. Pl. 2). His picture does not display an exploration of the botanical world comparable to that of Hunt's, much less to that of Millais's. What is of greater importance in Brown's work is his attention to the figures, which he, unlike Hunt and Millais, also painted out of doors in the sunlight. The figures are seen under the same light as the landscape surrounding them, and thus, unlike Hunt's figures, they belong to the landscape and are part of it. The result is not only that the picture, painted as more of a piece, has a greater unity than *The Hireling Shepherd*, but also that Brown's study of outdoor light on the human figure produced a more precocious vision of light and shadow than that achieved by Hunt. Stephens praised the blue shadows in *The Hireling Shepherd*, but those in *The Pretty Baa-Lambs* are much more prominent. Where precise shadows are cast across a white background – the baby's garment or the maid's bodice – they are of a strong blue. In flesh areas, where the shadows are softer, they are more violet or purple. On the grass, which has a strong colour of its own, the shadows show more darkening of the local colour without being noticeably bluer. The effect of the light on the modelling of the figures is also more pronounced in *The Pretty Baa-Lambs* than in *The Hireling Shepherd*. In Hunt's picture, despite the amount of colour in the flesh tones, the heads of the shepherd and shepherdess are modelled by subtle gradations from highlight to shadow. We still feel behind them the methods of modelling learned from drawing from casts and the controlled source of light of the painter's studio. In Brown's picture the contrast between highlight and shadow is harsher. Broad areas of flesh exposed to the full sunlight are blankly light, without modelling in light and shade.

[50]Brown, 1865, pp. 6–7.

Intermediary gradations have begun to disappear, and with them the volumetric modelling of three-dimensional form.

The Pre-Raphaelites were not the first artists to paint out of doors. Painters had sketched directly from nature at least as early as the seventeenth century, and, although painting finished pictures out of doors was not as common as sketching, there are examples predating the Pre-Raphaelites. In English art, the best-known is Constable's *Boatbuilding Near Flatford Mill* (Victoria and Albert Museum), which according to C. R. Leslie's *Memoir* of Constable was painted entirely in the open air.[51] But, as Graham Reynolds and John Gage have pointed out, for Constable this was primarily an exercise in finishing out of doors, and to prepare for it he made a study of Claude Lorraine.[52] The picture is based on sketches, and in general effect it does not differ markedly from works painted in the studio. From written descriptions, a more unusual example of early out-of-door painting was the now lost *Christ Giving Sight to the Blind* by Henry Richter.[53] A contemporary complained of the bluish hue of Richter's draperies and of the 'alabaster transparency and copper-coloured surface' of the areas of flesh. Richter published in 1817 a pamphlet entitled *Day-light: A Recent Discovery in the Art of Painting* in which he urged artists to paint and exhibit studies made directly out of doors, but he exhibited little, and his dicta on colour were mixed up with some rather odd metaphysics. He seems to have had little impact except possibly upon William Blake, who was a friend. Although studying nature out of doors was an important factor in the great achievements of English landscape painting in the first third of the nineteenth century, painting finished pictures out of doors was by and large not a concomitant. When it was practised by Constable it did not produce results different from what he was doing otherwise. The Pre-Raphaelites, on the other hand, did not paint studies from nature; they worked directly out of doors on pictures which they intended to exhibit. Their observations were not modified in the studio in the process of being transferred from the sketch to the finished picture. Although it can be said that each generation saw in nature what it wanted to see, it can also be said that the Pre-Raphaelite method encouraged a more immediate transformation of their art than the more pondered methods of their predecessors. Whether the transformation was achieved at too great a cost is still open to question.

The Pre-Raphaelites' painting out of doors, and in particular Ford Madox Brown's painting an entire figural picture in the sunlight anticipate interests of the French Impressionists in the 1860s. The stark lighting of Brown's figures and the coloured shadows have more in common with early examples of French *plein-aireism* such as Monet's *Women in the Garden* of 1866–67 (Louvre) than with previous English art. Although there is no evidence of any historical influence, at least one nineteenth-century critic proclaimed it. When R. A. M. Stevenson, who had studied in France, saw *The Pretty Baa-Lambs* in 1896, he exclaimed to Ford Madox Hueffer with appealing overstatement: 'By God! the whole history of modern art begins with that picture. Corot, Manet, the Marises, all the Fontainebleau School, all the Impressionists, never did anything but imitate that picture.'[54]

What does all this owe to Ruskin? Ultimately, even in Brown's case, a great deal. We have seen in Brown's comments about *The Pretty Baa-Lambs* the implied importance of the

[51]C. R. Leslie, R.A., *Memoirs of the Life of John Constable, R.A.*, ed. Jonathan Mayne, London, 1951, p.49.
[52]Graham Reynolds, *Catalogue of the Constable Collection in the Victoria and Albert Museum*, London, 1960, pp. 103–04, and *Constable: The Natural Painter*, London, 1965, pp. 55–6. Gage, 1969, p. 30 *et passim*.

[53]Gage, 1969, pp. 18–22. See also Roget 1891, I, 383–8.
[54]Ford Madox Hueffer, *Ancient Lights and Certain New Reflections: Being the Memoirs of a Young Man* (London, 1911) p. 207. For the Pre-Raphaelites and Impressionism, see also below, pp. 64 and 181.

'ideas and principles' of his Pre-Raphaelite friends, and we know the importance that *Modern Painters* had for Holman Hunt when he was formulating his ideas. More immediately, Ruskin could have been of little or no importance for Brown. The two had no personal contact in 1851, and Brown began *The Pretty Baa-Lambs* before Ruskin wrote his letters to *The Times*. On the other hand, Hunt and Millais had sought Ruskin's support. They probably would not even have started ambitious pictures in the summer of 1851 without his assertion of their right to respectful treatment. Ruskin's intervention came at a moment when Hunt was considering abandoning his career as an artist.[55] Hunt apparently did not meet Ruskin in 1851, when Millais did, but he was certainly re-exposed to Ruskin's influence through the medium of Millais. The two artists set off to the country with Millais full of excitement about his new friendship with the famous man.[56] After meeting Millais, Ruskin wrote that the Pre-Raphaelites had carried out his advice to the young artists of England about going to nature 'in all singleness of heart . . . rejecting nothing, selecting nothing'. Meanwhile, Hunt and Millais were doing what he said they had done with a dedicated thoroughness unmatched in any of their previous work.

Ruskin, absent in Venice until July 1852, made no public comment about the Royal Academy exhibition of that year. He never publicly mentioned *The Pretty Baa-Lambs* or *The Hireling Shepherd*. Probably he considered both of them ugly because of their subjects, an opinion he expressed about Brown's later work. He did approve of Millais's *Ophelia*. When the Royal Academy exhibition opened in May, Ruskin's father sent a report, consisting largely of praise of the picture, to Ruskin and a report of that letter to Millais.[57] In Ruskin's acknowledgment of his father's account of the exhibition, he expressed particular interest in the reception of *Ophelia*, in terms almost of a collaborator: 'I am *very* glad you like the *Ophelia* [as opposed to the press] – We will make the *Times* change its note, yet'.[58] When Ruskin returned to London, he wrote to Millais calling both *Ophelia* and the *Huguenot* exquisite, but also giving criticism. The pictures were spoilt by the shadows, which 'are all chilled and want varnishing or something'. He disliked Millais's flesh painting, and he disapproved of Millais's and Hunt's choice of the Surrey landscape for their backgrounds: 'When you do paint nature why the mischief should you not paint pure nature and not that rascally wirefenced garden-rolled-nursery-maid's paradise?'[59] However, these remarks were for private consumption; in 1854, in his first public reference to *Ophelia*, Ruskin wondered how anyone could criticize this 'loveliest English landscape, haunted by sorrow'.[60]

Ophelia was not as immediately popular as the *Huguenot*, which Millais also exhibited in 1852, but since the 1850s it has been perhaps the most widely admired of all Pre-Raphaelite pictures. Nonetheless – and despite Ruskin – it has had its critics: A. P. Oppé claimed it fulfilled Constable's prophecy, made in 1822, that art would die in England in thirty years.[61] In the artist's own century, the most appropriate criticism came from Tennyson. According to William Allingham's diary entry for Saturday, 25 August 1888:

While looking at a drawing with daffodils [by Mrs. Allingham], T. said 'Millais put daffodils along with wild-roses in his *Ophelia* picture. I pointed this out to him. He said he had painted the rosebush from nature; and some time after when he was finishing he wanted a bit of yellow and sent to Covent Garden and got the daffodils. I told him it was quite wrong.'[62]

[55]Hunt, 1905, I, 253–4, 261–2.
[56]In a letter to Thomas Combe, dated 9 May 1851, Millais called Ruskin 'the famous critic', Millais, 1899, I, 101.
[57]James, 1948, p. 176.
[58]Bradley, 1955, p. 275.
[59]James, 1948, p. 176.

[60]Ruskin, 1903–12, XII, 161 (in the Addenda to his Edinburgh lectures given in 1853, but not published until 1854).
[61]A. P. Oppé, 'Art', in G. M. Young, ed., *Early Victorian England: 1830–1865* (Oxford, 1934) II, 167.
[62]Helen Allingham and D. Radford, eds., *William Allingham: A Diary* (London, 1907) p. 379.

III

Ford Madox Brown

FORD MADOX BROWN'S 'first though not very recognizable attempt at an out-door effect of light' was *Manfred on the Jungfrau* (City Art Gallery, Manchester), which he painted in Paris in 1840–1.[1] In later years, he did not think highly of the depiction of the natural world in the picture, 'glaciers not having formed part of my scheme of study in those days'. He retouched the painting in 1861, and, according to his own account, he obliterated the original scheme of colour. As the picture now stands it does have a much lighter palette than other works from Brown's Paris period such as *The Prisoner of Chillon* of 1843 (City Art Gallery, Manchester).

We have seen that after his Italian trip Brown attempted to reform his art along naturalistic lines, substituting 'simple imitation for scenic effectiveness, and purity of natural colour for scholastic depth of tone'.[2] In his *Chaucer at the Court of Edward III* (Pl. 6), begun in 1845 and completed in 1851, he tried to treat the light and shade 'absolutely, as it exists at any one moment, instead of approximately or in generalized style'. He described the light as 'sunlight, not too bright, such as it is pleasant to sit in out-of-doors'.[3] The effect of light is not the result of work out of doors, which Brown commenced only in the summer of 1851 with *The Pretty Baa-Lambs*. The size of *Chaucer* – 146½ by 116½ inches – would have made such direct work on it impossible. The bright colours of the costumes of the foreground figures were probably a result of Brown's admiration for the brilliance of Hunt's and Millais's early pictures.[4]

The landscape background of *Chaucer*, which forms a relatively small part of the painting, is mainly characterized by the linear pattern of the distant hedgerows. It is based on a study Brown painted in 1849, *View from Shorn Ridgeway* (Pl. 7a), which shows the Essex landscape and the estuary of the Thames and Medway. The background of the large painting reproduces the study closely, but in reverse and with the colours somewhat heightened. Stylistically, the *View from Shorn Ridgeway* is close to the work of a friend of Brown's, Mark Anthony, a landscape painter who, like Brown, had spent several years working in France. *The Severn Valley* by Anthony (Pl. 7b) shows a similar view from a high vantage-point over a landscape broken by hedgerows to a broad body of water. Both Brown's and Anthony's foregrounds consist of massive dark areas of foliage which provide a contrast to the lighter, patterned areas of the further landscapes, and both contain genre figures. In Brown's landscape the foreground is rather clumsy, but he probably did not consider it important, as he reproduced only the distant landscape in *Chaucer*. His handling is broader than that of any of his work of the 1850s. The colours stay within a range of subdued greens and yellowish browns with a marked tonal diminution to an almost monochrome horizon. Brown began the *View from Shorn Ridgeway* on the spot on 2 July 1849.[5] He completed it in the summer of 1851, after finishing *Chaucer*, and gave it to Thomas Seddon. In 1873 he bought it back from Seddon's widow and retouched it.

[1]Brown, 1865, p. 18; reproduced in Bennett, 1964, pl. 1.
[2]See above, p. 6

[3]Brown, 1865, p. 3.
[4]See Hunt, 1905, I, 225–6, and Hueffer, 1896, p. 77.
[5]Rossetti, 1900, p. 104.

Another Essex landscape from the 1840s, also looking out over the estuary of the Thames, was *Southend*, now lost. Brown began it in 1846 and returned to Essex to complete it in 1858. He exhibited it at the Hogarth Club in 1858 and at the Liverpool Academy in 1860, and, according to Hueffer, he retouched it in 1861. The background which Brown added to *The Pretty Baa-Lambs* shows fields and the estuary of a river. As Brown added it in 1859, shortly after he completed *Southend*, it may be based on this picture.

Several versions exist of *Windermere*, or *Winandermere*, Brown's third landscape begun in the 1840s. The first version is an oil painting in the Lady Lever Art Gallery in Port Sunlight (Pl. 10a). Brown began it on 25 September 1848, while on a trip to the Lake District. He spent six days, four hours a day, painting from nature, the last day in the rain under an umbrella. Back in London he continued to work on the picture, and he also started another version.[6] He submitted one of these to the Royal Academy in 1849. It was rejected, but Brown did exhibit a *Windermere* the following year at the North London School of Design and in 1851 at the British Institution. The picture he exhibited was probably the second version, as in 1854 he wrote in his diary that he was 'making a picture' of the study of *Windermere* painted in the Lakes. At this time he cut down the sky so that this version (Pl. 10a) has an appearance and proportions quite different from the others.[7] The painted canvas is rectangular, but it is framed as a horizontal oval, a shape Brown used earlier in *An English Autumn Afternoon* (Pl. 9), which he began in 1852.

Another *Windermere*, or *Winandermere* as Brown distinguished it in 1865, is a smaller work in watercolour and heavy bodycolour in the William Morris Gallery in Walthamstow (Pl. 10b). In 1865 Brown dated this version 1859.[8] In composition it is practically identical to a lithograph made in the winter of 1853–4 (private collection) and to what is apparently another lithograph which Brown coloured in 1858 (City Art Gallery, Carlisle). The only noteworthy difference between the Walthamstow and Carlisle versions is that the former has a small rainbow on the left. The earlier duplicate, which Brown began in 1848 and sold in 1854 (unlocated), he also called *Winandermere*, so it is probable that the Walthamstow picture and its mates are based on it. These three all have elaborate cloud effects which Brown eliminated in the Port Sunlight version.

The view over the lake, the same in all four known versions, is a straightforward view from the north end of Windermere looking south, still easily recognizable today. As Brown mentioned in his diary that he spent the last day in the rain, the clouds in the Walthamstow version apparently reflect the weather he actually experienced. The Lake District subject and the meteorological interest bring Brown's view closer to the mainstream of English landscape painting than any of his other works. His composition, based on a dark foreground and lighter distances and framed by a series of *coulisses*, is also relatively conventional. Most of the elements of Brown's view are standard features in the watercolours of an older artist such as Copley Fielding; an example is Fielding's *Loch Lomond* of 1847 in the City Art Gallery, Manchester.[9] Brown's view over a lake to distant mountains and clouds is also prefigured in a picture of 1845 by Brown's friend Mark Anthony: *Killarney; the Lower Lake*, which was bought by Prince Albert (Pl. 10c). As Brown's *View from Shorn Ridgeway* of 1849 seems related to Anthony, a connection here seems likely as well. Brown repeats Anthony's low vantage-point, so that the expanse of water is extremly foreshortened, and his firmly modelled distant clouds are also reminiscent of Anthony's.

[6]*Ibid.*, pp. 95–102.
[7]*Ibid.*, pp. 113–15.
[8]Brown, 1865, p. 5.

[9]Reproduced in Martin Hardie, *Water-colour Painting in Britain* (London ,1967), II, pl. 211.

Compared to Anthony's clouds, however, Brown's are much more obtrusive. They dominate the picture, and they are so laboriously modelled that they seem as solid as the hills below them. Brown must have been doubtful of their success, for when he made his original study into a picture he altered it radically. He cut it down, thus raising the horizon; he eliminated the clouds except for a few wispy streaks; and he also eliminated a group of trees to the right whose foliage had balanced the stormy sky.[10] Brown was working on this picture in August 1854, a few days before he started his small landscapes, *The Brent at Hendon* and *Carrying Corn* (Pls. 12b and 14), and the elimination of the romantically exuberant sky is in accord with the style of these later works. Brown's landscapes from the 1850s show his concern with the 'simple imitation' of the physical world, not with elaborate effects of atmosphere and weather. However, atmosphere and weather are the main subjects of the other versions, and by eliminating them Brown eliminated the picture's *raison d'être*. But none of the versions is a real success. They constitute Brown's most important attempts at landscape before coming into the Pre-Raphaelite milieu, and they show him working rather uncomfortably within a frame of fairly conventional ambitions.

Brown was a figural painter, who only painted landscapes on the side. But all his major paintings begun in the 1850s, with the exception of *Christ Washing Peter's Feet* (Tate Gallery), have outdoor settings. We have already discussed *The Pretty Baa-Lambs*, begun in 1851 and painted entirely in the sunlight. In the following year Brown began three more paintings in which painting out of doors was of prime importance: *Work* (Pl. 11a), *The Last of England* (City Art Gallery, Birmingham), and *An English Autumn Afternoon* (Pl. 9). In June 1852 Brown moved from Stockwell, where he had painted *The Pretty Baa-Lambs*, to Hampstead, where he set to work in the main street. Writing in his diary two years later, Brown described his activity of 1852 (when he had neglected to keep up the diary):

The first work I undertook at Hampstead was the design for my picture of *Work*, still unfinished save the background . . . I began the background for *Work* in the Streets of Hampstead, painting there all day for two months, having spent much time in inventing and making an apparatus.[11]

Holman Hunt has described the operation in greater detail:

To follow our method more religiously he had taken a lodging near his chosen background. For an easel he constructed a rack on the tray of a costermonger's barrow, above the canvas were rods with curtains suspended, which could be turned on a hinge, so that they shrouded the artist while painting. When all was prepared, Brown himself wheeled the barrow to the desired post; and forthwith worked the whole day, surrounded of course by a little mob of idlers and patient children, who wondered when the real performance was going to begin.[12]

From all evidence, Brown seems to have begun directly on the background of the large picture. Nonetheless, he also made a smaller study of the site. In his diary for 6 Jan. 1855, we find: 'In the evening copied in the background from the *Study at Hampstead* into the design of *Work*, so as to get all quite correct.'[13] The *Study at Hampstead* is probably the small oil sketch with a single figure which Brown completed in December 1855 and gave to Thomas Woolner (Pl. 11b); the 'design' may have been an earlier version of a watercolour sketch in Manchester which shows several variants in the figures. The finished painting is from a slightly lower point of view than the oil sketch. Both show the short rise of The Mount, just to the west of Heath Street, which runs off on the right. The site today still looks almost exactly as it does in Brown's picture.

---

[10]He also eliminated two cows (whose *pentimenti* are still visible), and noted the fact in a letter to Thomas Seddon; see Sotheby, 1970, no. 702.

[11]Rossetti, 1900, p. 111.
[12]Hunt, 1905, II, 96–7.
[13]Rossetti, 1900, p. 154

This is not the place to follow the history of the painting, which Brown only completed and exhibited in 1865. However, we should remember that before the figural composition was completely decided, Brown had painted an elaborate and rigorously literal landscape setting.[14] Although the figures dominate the picture, their positions were dictated by the landscape which Brown did not alter in any way to suit the needs of his composition.

Work is usually looked upon as a symbolic statement of social comment. Brown's long explanation of the picture and the sonnet which he wrote to go with it make clear that he intended it as such. However, according to Brown's explanation, the symbolic overtones came later. His initial inspiration was the sight of actual labourers at work.

At that time extensive excavations were going on in the neighbourhood, and seeing and studying daily as I did the British excavator, or *navvy*, as he designates himself, in the full swing of his activity (with his manly and picturesque costume, and with the rich glow of colour, which exercise under a hot sun will impart), it appeared to me that he was at least as worthy of the powers of an English painter, as the fisherman of the Adriatic, the peasant of the Campagna, or the Neapolitan lazzarone. Gradually this idea developed itself into that of *Work* as it now exists, with the British excavator for a central group, as the outward and visible type of *Work*.[15]

In the thirteen years between the picture's commencement and its exhibition in 1865 it became much more than a northern version of picturesque Italian genre. It acquired an elaborately structured social message and an equally elaborately worked-out figural composition based on the rectangular opening of the excavation which provides the picture's focus. It also acquired a vast amount of observed detail, and, of course, the main part of the time Brown spent working on the picture was not devoted to developing its symbolism or its composition, but on the careful rendering of all the elements of the visible world.

Brown had previously spent several years working on his *Chaucer at the Court of Edward III*, which he completed a year before beginning *Work*. The difference in their subjects demonstrates the redirection of Brown's art resulting from his involvement with the Pre-Raphaelite Brotherhood. The realistic subject with symbolic significance, which we might compare to Hunt's *Hireling Shepherd*, is accompanied by a literalness both in details and in larger effect. Brown had attempted to show sunlight in *Chaucer*, but since completing it he had had the experience of painting *The Pretty Baa-Lambs* out of doors. He did not paint a picture of the size and complexity of *Work* entirely in the sunlight, but he did incorporate what he had learned about outdoor light. At the end of his statement explaining the picture Brown did not make claims for its social message; rather, he pointed to the light:

I have only to observe in conclusion, that the effect of hot July sunlight attempted in this picture, has been introduced, because it seems peculiarly fitted to display *work* in all its severity, and not from any predilection for this kind of light over any other. Subjects, according to their nature, require different effects of light. Some years ago, when one of the critics was commenting on certain works then exhibiting, he used words to the effect that the system of light of those artists was precisely that of the sun itself – a system that would probably outlast, etc., etc. He might have added, aye, and not of the sun only, but of the moon, and of the stars, and, when necessary, of so lowly a domestic luminary as a tallow candle! ...

For the imperfections in these paintings I submit myself to our great master, the public, and its authorised interpreters, pleading only that first attempts are often incomplete. For though certainly not solitary, attempts of this kind have not yet been so frequent as to have arrived at being mapped out in academic plans. But in this country, at least, the thing is done, 'la cosa

[14]The background was apparently completed by November 1856, when Thomas Plint saw it and commissioned Brown to finish the picture; Hueffer, 1896, p. 141.

[15]Brown, 1865, p. 27

muove,' and never again will the younger generation revert to the old system of making one kind of light serve for all the beautiful varieties under the heaven, no more than we shall light our streets with oil, or journey by stage-coach and sailing-packet.[16]

The critic commenting on certain works some years ago was Ruskin; the passage about the system of light being that of the sun itself appeared in his pamphlet *Pre-Raphaelitism*.[17]

Brown's additional remark that hot sunlight was only one kind of light, and that different subjects require different kinds of light is of pertinence not only to *Work*, but also to *The Last of England*, which he began four months after *Work*. This picture does not show sunlight, but Brown, nevertheless, painted it out of doors, and explained in his 1865 catalogue: 'To insure the peculiar look of *light all round*, which objects have on a dull day at sea, it was painted for the most part in the open air on dull days, and when the flesh was being painted, on cold days.'[18] The reason for painting flesh in the cold is explained by Brown's diary entry for 2 Sept. 1855, when he was giving the finishing touches to the painting:

To-day fortune seemed to favour me. It has been intensely cold – no sun, no rain, a high wind. But this seemed the sweetest weather possible, for it was the weather for my picture, and made my hand look blue with the cold, as I require it in the work. So I painted all day out in the yard, and made the man's hand more what I want than it has looked yet.[19]

Most of the painting of flesh was done under similar conditions in the early months of 1853. 'Emma coming to sit to me in the most inhuman weather from Highgate. This work representing an out-door scene without sunlight, I painted at it chiefly out of doors when the snow was lying on the ground.'[20] No more need be said on this score, but Brown's concluding sentences from his explanation of 1865 are also of interest:

Absolutely without regard to the art of any period or country, I have tried to render this scene as it would appear. The minuteness of detail which would be visible under such conditions of broad daylight, I have thought necessary to imitate, as bringing the pathos of the subject home to the beholder.[21]

Thus, Brown's goal was an absolute realism in which minute detail is appropriate both because it is what we would see, and also for psychological reasons. The psychological explanation was not uniquely Brown's; Ruskin had given a comparable explanation of the accessory details in Holman Hunt's *Awakening Conscience* in 1854.[22] John Gere has also pointed out that similar instances of heightened awareness in moments of stress are described in Tennyson's *Maud* and Rossetti's poem *The Woodspurge*.[23]

The earliest and largest of Brown's landscapes of the 1850s is *An English Autumn Afternoon* (Pl. 9), which he also began in 1852. He painted on it for approximately a month during October 1852, again from 15 Sept. to around 20 Oct. in 1853, and for two months more between October 1853 and the following summer when he sold it at auction. In January 1855 Brown borrowed the painting back and worked on it again before sending it to the British Institution, where it was exhibited as *English autumn afternoon, Hampstead – scenery in 1853*. When he sold the painting in 1854, Brown estimated that he had given it six months of work.[24] He received nine guineas, the frame having cost him four, and even then it was bought by a friend.

The picture is a view from the artist's back window in Hampstead over the Heath; Kenwood House and Highgate Church are visible in the distance. This suburban view

[16]*Ibid.*, p. 31.
[17]See above, p. 17
[18]Brown, 1865, p. 9.
[19]Rossetti, 1900, p. 192.
[20]*Ibid.*, p. 112.

[21]Brown, 1865, p. 9.
[22]Ruskin, 1903–12, XII, 334.
[23]Ironside and Gere, 1948, p. 24n.
[24]Rossetti, 1900, pp. 111–14.

35

provoked Ruskin's one recorded comment about Brown's art. Coming upon the painter in Rossetti's studio in the summer of 1855, Ruskin asked Brown why he had chosen 'such a very ugly subject'. Brown, feeling that Ruskin had intended a deliberate insult, answered curtly, 'Because it lay out of a back window', and left it at that.[25] But Ruskin's question is understandable, even if Brown suspected his motives. Why should so much labour have been spent in recording scenery which by Ruskin's standards was of so little interest, which lacked any elements of natural grandeur or natural beauty? It is a question which comes up again and again in Ruskin's criticism; we have seen it before in his comments on the background of Millais's *Ophelia*. Brown's reply was not meant to satisfy Ruskin, but it was to the point. The picture is the landscape of his own personal experience. It does not have the scenic interest which Ruskin wanted – and which we can see in Brown's earlier *Winandermere* – but shows an intimate, domestic view, full of signs of human activity and human presence. This is what the artist saw from his window, and this personal association sanctions the subject.

The human presence is most evident in the foreground, where a boy and girl are relaxing and enjoying the view. They give the painting a slightly sentimental air, but Brown did not want too much sentiment read into them, and in his remarks about the picture in 1865 he declared that they were not lovers, but mere 'boy and girl, neighbours and friends'.[26]

Foreground figures looking into a picture are a device for leading the viewer's eye into the landscape by associative means. There are numerous antecedents dating back to Jan Van Eyck. An English example, similar in feeling, is Constable's inclusion of the Bishop of Salisbury and his wife in the foreground of his *Salisbury Cathedral from the Bishop's Grounds* (Victoria and Albert Museum). Other examples are in the work of Francis Danby, for whom Brown had high respect.[27] Danby's *Painter's Holiday* (collection of Mr. and Mrs. Paul Mellon), which Brown would have seen when it was exhibited at the Royal Academy in 1844, shows a painter reclining on a high foreground, like Brown's, and watching the sun set over an extensive landscape.

Brown also uses an age-old device, the so-called plateau landscape, which again dates back to Jan Van Eyck, in placing the figures on a high foreground, above and separate from the rest of the landscape. As in fifteenth-century paintings, it provides a means of transition from large foreground figures to a distant expanse of landscape. While there are numerous earlier English examples of the plateau landscape, including Danby's *Painter's Holiday*, it also appears in Brown's earlier historical compositions, *The Body of Harold Brought before William the Conqueror* and *Chaucer at the Court of Edward III*. In his first use of it in the cartoon of *Harold*, Brown was probably following the example of Delacroix's *Crusaders Entering Constantinople*. In the Delacroix and in Brown's two earlier pictures the plateau landscape is the device of a figural painter. We could consider *An English Autumn Afternoon* also as a figural picture with a separate landscape background, but it is one in which the relative importance of foreground and background has been reversed. Following Brown's lead, variations of the plateau landscape appear frequently in later landscapes of the Pre-Raphaelite circle, most frequently in those of Thomas Seddon (whose brother owned *An English Autumn Afternoon*), John Brett, and Holman Hunt. For all of them it allowed a combination of close foreground detail with panoramic views, for which they, like Brown, were willing to sacrifice spatial continuity.

[25]Rossetti, 1899, pp. 38–9.
[26]Brown, 1865, p. 8.
[27]Ford Madox Brown, 'The Progress of English Art

as not Shown at the Manchester Exhibition', *Magazine of Art*, XI, 1888, p. 122.

A result of the high vantage-point of the plateau landscape is a high horizon. While in *Winandermere* the sky fills over two thirds of the composition, it accounts for less than one third of *An English Autumn Afternoon*. We have seen that the high horizons of the pictures exhibited by Hunt and Millais in 1851 were denounced in *The Times* as part of the servile imitation of the false perspective of remote antiquity. It is almost an axiom of art history that the high horizon belongs to the earliest stages of landscape painting,[28] and in Brown's art this change and most of the other changes from *Winandermere* do seem to indicate a reversion to a more primitive style. *An English Autumn Afternoon* has more apparent affinities stylistically with Jan Van Eyck than with Claude Lorraine or Constable. In 1846, before he had any contact with the future members of the Pre-Raphaelite Brotherhood, Brown had painted a 'Holbein of the 19th Century' in which he wished 'to substitute simple imitation for scenic effectiveness, and purity of natural colour for scholastic depth of tone.'[29] *An English Autumn Afternoon* is a later product of the same process of seeking a more simple, direct truth, but the primitive qualities are no longer the result of consciously emulating early art as the way of achieving it. Brown had learned his lessons. In October 1852 he had commenced two pictures: *The Last of England* and *An English Autumn Afternoon*. His assertion in 1865 of the freedom of one from any dependence upon the past – 'Absolutely without regard to the art of any period or country, I have tried to render this scene as it would appear' – is equally appropriate for the other. But, in *An English Autumn Afternoon* he rendered the scene not as it would appear, but as it did appear. He described the picture as 'a literal transcript of the scenery round London, as looked at from Hampstead'.

The scenery is viewed at a certain time and under the conditions of that time. Here is Brown's description:

The smoke of London is seen rising half way above the fantastic shaped, small distant cumuli, which accompany particularly fine weather. The upper portion of the sky would be blue as seen reflected in the youth's hat; the grey mist of autumn only rising a certain height. The time is 3 P.M., when late in October the shadows already lie long, and the sun's rays (coming from behind in this work) are preternaturally glowing, as in rivalry of the foliage.[30]

That Brown should want to paint a literal transcript of the view is what we might expect. That he should provide a detailed explanation of the atmospheric and meteorological conditions is slightly surprising. The sky forms a small and relatively neutral part of the painting; the terrain, not the sky, is the primary interest. We see none of the dramatic clouds that dominate Constable's views on Hampstead Heath, or Brown's earlier *Winandermere*. Yet, Brown, like Constable, associates particular cloud formations with other conditions of the weather, and he points out four different aspects of the sky visible in his picture: rising smoke, grey mist of autumn, small distant cumuli, and a blue upper sky. The distant clouds are pink in the light of the late afternoon sun. The entire foreground is in shadow, and consequently in details such as the boy's hat we see the reflected blue of the upper sky. But the hat is so completely blue, while other foreground details such as the white bench are relatively unaffected, that it appears to be a blue hat. Despite Brown's working directly from nature, the effect seems eccentric, as if it were painted on the basis of theory rather than observation, and it brings to mind Henry Richter's bluish draperies of some forty years earlier.

As well as the reduced importance of the sky, *An English Autumn Afternoon* shows several

---

[28]'A high horizon is everywhere a sign of the Primitives', Max Friedländer, *Landscape, Portrait, Still-Life: Their Origin and Development*, trans. R. F. C. Hull (New York, 1963) p. 26.
[29]See above, p. 6
[30]Brown, 1865, pp. 7–8.

other compositional changes from *Winandermere*. Although the foreground is in shadow, it is not as dark as the foreground of the earlier picture. Tonal contrast between foreground and distance has been radically reduced, and in its place comes over-all strength of colour. Similarly the *repoussoir* clumps of trees and series of framing *coulisses* of the earlier composition have disappeared. Immediately beyond the foreground plateau a dense area of foliage runs across the picture like a wall. The eye is not led through open spaces into the distance but must jump across this compositional barrier. The foliage is treated neither as clearly delineated individual leaves, as by Hunt and Millais, nor in large masses, but in myriad small touches of color. Where various planes of foliage are seen through, or juxtaposed to, one another, the separate touches tend to merge into one plane of colour. The result is a confusion of conventional, illusionistic, spatial depth. As in the Pre-Raphaelite pictures of 1851, composition in two-dimensional relationships is replacing three-dimensional space.

Brown gives no indication in his diary or in the 1865 catalogue that this flattening process was a result of conscious effort. Rather it seems to have been a result of his willingness to sacrifice any conventional means of organizing or clarifying space in order to record exactly what he saw. Even the shape of the picture appears to be a product of his attempt to give as pure an approximation of the visual experience as possible. Following the lead of the German Nazarenes and numerous English artists, Brown started using shapes other than the normal rectangle for some of his pictures in the 1840s. In the earlier examples he adopted medieval or renaissance forms: *Chaucer at the Court of Edward III* was originally planned as a Gothic triptych.[31] *The Last of England* is still a Renaissance tondo, but there is no such obvious source for the horizontal ovals which Brown gave to *An English Autumn Afternoon* and *Windermere*. There are seventeenth- and eighteenth-century precedents, which would have had little appeal for Brown, in the decorative shapes of overdoors and the like. In his case the most likely reason for employing the shape is that it corresponds with what we accept as the normal field of binocular vision.

Brown painted two small landscapes, *The Brent at Hendon* (Pl. 12b) and *Carrying Corn* (Pl. 14), in 1854, and a third, *The Hayfield* (Pl. 15), in 1855. During these years he kept a diary, which was published in 1900 by William Michael Rossetti. Brown painted landscapes largely as a diversion, inspired by his enjoyment of the natural world. In 1854 and 1855, he made a number of excursions in the country with his wife, and his diary entries describing them record his love of landscape for its own sake, regardless of his requirements as a painter. For example, on 22 August 1854, he felt disgusted with everything and was unable to work, so they took a trip to St. Albans on the top of a bus: 'We should have thought more of the fields, no doubt, were we not so much used to them of late. However, one field of turnips against the afternoon sky did surprise us into exclamation, with its wonderful emerald tints.'[32] On 13 October they went for a walk: 'Exquisite day: hedges all gold, rubies and emeralds, defying all "white grounds" to yield the like.'[33] Both these passages show Brown seeing with the eyes of a painter, but not looking for potential pictures. He is a stroller, enjoying his surroundings. At other times he did try to channel his enjoyment into pictures; a diary entry dated 21 July 1855, demonstrates his difficulties:

Looked out for landscapes this evening; but although all around one is lovely, how little of it will work up into a picture! that is, without great additions and alterations, which is a work of too much time to suit my purposes just now. I want little subjects that will paint off at once. How despairing it is to view the loveliness of nature towards sunset, and know the impossibility of imitating it! –

[31]See the oil sketch in the Ashmolean Museum, reproduced in Hunt, 1905, I, 123. [32]Rossetti, 1900, p. 117. [33]*Ibid.*, p. 143.

at least in a satisfactory manner, as one could do, would it only remain so long enough. Then one feels the want of a life's study, such as Turner devoted to landscape; and even then what a botch is any attempt to render it! What wonderful effects I have seen this evening in the hayfields! the warmth of the uncut grass, the greeny greyness of the unmade hay in furrows or tufts with lovely violet shadows, and long shades of the trees thrown athwart all, and melting away one tint into another imperceptibly; and one moment more a cloud passes and all the magic is gone. Begin tomorrow morning, all is changed; the hay and the reapers are gone most likely, the sun too, or if not it is in quite the opposite quarter, and all that *was* loveliest is all that is tamest now, alas! It is better to be a poet! still better a mere lover of nature, one who never dreams of possession.[34]

This passage reveals two elements not entirely in harmony with one another: Brown's awareness of his limited capabilities, and, once again, his response to the beauty of the landscape. Essential to these paintings is the 'loveliness' of some natural effect. Brown looked for 'little subjects that will paint off at once', but he chose subjects which he admired and then found impossibly difficult to paint.

His purpose was to paint potboilers. At the time, Brown and his family were miserably poor, and his painting excursions were interspersed with visits to the pawn-broker. While many of his major paintings were dragging on for years (*Work* from 1852 to 1865, *The Last of England* from 1852 to 1855), these landscapes were painted to produce an immediate income. All considered, the undertaking was impractical. Brown could not command high prices for his landscapes, and, from temperament and lack of experience, he could not paint them off at once. He invariably bogged down in difficulties and put in large amounts of time. As he decided on 21 Sept. 1854:

Altogether these little landscapes take up too much time to be profitable . . . I cannot help it, but somehow whatever I am about I must go through with to the extremity. This, if the work happens to be of importance, is a most happy quality; but on the other hand it is a most unprofitable mania when the occasion that calls it forth is trivial.[35]

Brown's doubts about his capabilities are a theme running through his diary. To be a successful landscape painter requires 'a life's study'. Lacking this, Brown could not work with assurance; it 'requires all my energy and attention to master the difficulties attending a style of work I have not been bred to'.[36] Individual details become insurmountable problems causing doubts and delays:

It would seem that very small trees in the distance are very difficult objects to paint, or else I am not suited to this sort of work; for I can make nothing of this small screen of trees, though I have pottered over [them] sufficient time to have painted a large landscape, the men of English schools would say.[37]

These are not the comments of a master sure of himself and of his art. Brown's approach to landscape is tentative and searching, and this is reflected in the finished pictures. There is no consistent production; each picture is unique, an isolated object, the result of a fresh attack upon fresh problems.

Although his first purpose was the literal depiction of natural scenery, Brown realized that he could never achieve exact imitation. For one thing, he was aware that he could not cope with nature's changeability, and that the effects he wished to paint would not wait to be painted. Furthermore, no degree of copying in itself was adequate for the complexities of even the more permanent aspects of nature: 'Nature, that at first sight appears so lovely, is on consideration almost always incomplete; moreover there is no painting intertangled foliage without losing half its beauties. If imitated exactly, it can only be done as seen from one eye, and quite flat and confused therefore.'[38]

[34]*Ibid.*, pp. 188–9.
[35]*Ibid.*, pp. 130–31.
[36]*Ibid.*, p. 130.

[37]*Ibid.*, p. 134.
[38]*Ibid.*, p. 124.

Brown wrote this on 1 Sept. 1854, while looking for a place to paint *The Brent at Hendon*, the first of the small landscapes (Pl. 12b). The problems of painting intertangled foliage were evidently real ones; the picture *is* quite flat and confused. In the crowded oval space, the effect of the foliage is further complicated by reflections in the stream. There is a conflict within the picture between Brown's technique of painstaking literalness and a subject that is essentially romantic. The subject is not the forest primeval, but it is the city-dweller's equivalent. In 1865 Brown descibed the Brent as 'a most romantic little river.' It was part of the surroundings of London which were disappearing before urban expansion, but when the picture was painted, 'once embowered in the wooded hollows of its banks the visitor might imagine himself a hundred miles away.'[39] The appeal is to nostalgia, even escapism, and the mood is emphasized by the little figure of a woman reading a letter, which Brown added to make the picture more sentimental.[40]

Brown began *The Brent at Hendon* on 2 Sept. 1854. A few days later, he started a second landscape, *Carrying Corn* (Pl. 14), which he painted simultaneously. He worked on the *Brent* in the mornings until 26 Sept. and on *Carrying Corn* in the evenings until 13 Oct. He sold both the following June for ten and twelve pounds respectively, and a month later, on 28 July 1855, he began the third landscape, *The Hayfield* (Pl. 15). This painting occupied him until 24 Oct 1855, with additional work on the foreground and some repainting in December. Brown sold it in the following August to William Morris for forty pounds.

Carrying Corn and *The Hayfield* both show harvest scenes, the former seen just before sunset, the latter just after, and in both a full moon is low in the sky. Like *The Brent* they depict a rural England still untouched by the modern city and the industrial revolution, and they share some of its nostalgic romanticism. In both, farmworkers are carting off hay or wheat; in the foreground of *Carrying Corn* a woman is picking turnips, and in *The Hayfield* an artist watches the activity. Brown's diary records his choosing the site of *Carrying Corn*: 'About three out to a field, to begin the outline of a small landscape. Found it of surpassing loveliness. Cornshocks in long perspective form, hayricks, and steeple seen between them – foreground of turnips – blue sky and afternoon sun.'[41] The following year the site he chose for *The Hayfield* was 'a very lovely bit of scenery'. He did not describe the scene further in his diary, but he did in the 1865 catalogue: 'The stacking of the second crop of hay had been much delayed by rain, which heightened the green of the remaining grass, together with the brown of the hay.'[42]

In these paintings we can see Brown attempting to record exactly what he saw. The amount of detail that they contain reflects his labours at one site for a period of a month and a half and at the other for almost three months. Yet the results do not seem very natural. They show the same tendency towards two-dimensionality that we have seen in *An English Autumn Afternoon*, but in these smaller pictures, because of their relative simplicity, it is even more evident. Everything becomes woven into a surface pattern. Details which we might expect to stand out, such as the woman picking turnips in the foreground of *Carrying Corn* or the children in the cart in *The Hayfield*, appear to be deliberately unemphasized, even left unfinished, so as not to contradict the pattern. As in *An English Autumn Afternoon*, the emphasis on the surface at the expense of illusionistic space is the outgrowth of neglect or avoidance of space-creating compositional formulae. This is partly a result of Brown's limited competence; he had never learned the tricks of landscape painting. But his lack of experience allowed him to look at landscape with a remarkably

[39]Brown, 1865, p. 10.   [41] *Ibid.*, p. 125.
[40]Rossetti, 1900, p. 130.   [42]Brown, 1865, p. 10.

fresh eye. He seems to have been oblivious of anything to be learned from previous painting which could help him slide over his problems, approaching his landscapes almost as if they were the first ever painted. The results have a freshness, an individuality, and a slight feeling of naïveté more akin to Pol de Limbourg and Jan Van Eyck than to what we usually consider the mainstream of nineteenth-century naturalism, running from Constable to Monet.

Compared to the landscapes of Constable, Brown's pictures appear stylized. We do not accept them as realistic pictures of the surroundings of Hampstead in the way that we readily accept Constable's views of the same vicinity. Brown's pictures show too much too clearly; they are like wide-eyed visions of a world of pastoral harmony and tranquillity. The twilight hour, the scenes of harvesting (rather than ploughing and planting), the relative importance and the placing of the figures, and the transformation of landsape space into surface pattern have little in common with Constable, but they do recall Samuel Palmer of the Shoreham period. In the 1850s Palmer was still alive and active, but it is unlikely that Brown was aware of his early works done in Shoreham in the 1820s and early 1830s. The young Palmer, the disciple of Blake, scorned naturalism, and in the Shoreham paintings he deliberately tried to be visionary and spiritual; Brown was ostensibly only trying to paint potboilers showing straightforward views of rural scenery. Both artists, however, lacked any interest in traditional landscape virtues; Palmer's admiration for the 'very ancient Italian and German masters' and his disapproval of what the moderns 'call their effects' anticipate Brown's later rejection of 'scenic effectiveness'. Palmer's descriptions of the strength and clarity of distant hills – 'we are not troubled with aerial perspective in the valley of vision' – could be applied to Brown's *Hayfield*.[43] In Palmer, visionary clarity verges on the hallucinatory, and in Brown there is a slight tendency to similar imbalance. In *Carrying Corn*, for example, there is something disturbing about the prominence of the foreground turnips. Brown painted these landscapes after his move to Hampstead, where he was 'most of the time intensely miserable, very hard up, and a little mad . . . broken in spirit and but a melancholy copy of what I once was.'[44] He wrote these words describing the previous two years in his diary in August 1854, just before beginning the first of the landscapes. His diary during the period of these paintings alternates widely between depression and exaltation. The pleasure he was able to draw from nature provided a release from his problems, and his small, idyllic landscapes seem to have become vehicles into which he unknowingly projected an emotional load far transcending his original money-making goals.

After *The Hayfield*, Brown's next landscape was a small watercolour, *Hampstead from My Window*, which he painted from his studio almost two years later, in the spring of 1857 (Pl. 13a). He included it in an exhibition of British pictures sent to America later in the same year, and it was sold in Philadelphia. It differs considerably from the group of paintings that preceded it. It is smaller and in a different medium. In subject it has few of the romantic overtones of the group of landscapes of 1854–5; rather it shows Brown's domestic environment, and in this respect, as in several others, it is comparable to *An English Autumn Afternoon*. The view in the watercolour is of Hampstead seen from Kentish Town rather than from Hampstead toward Highgate, but in both works we look over foliate foregrounds and across the Heath. As in *An English Autumn Afternoon* the foliage is treated as small touches of colour in an almost *pointilliste* fashion, with comparable ambi-

[43]A. H. Palmer, *The Life and Letters of Samuel Palmer* (London, 1892), pp. 14, 17. [44]Rossetti, 1900, p. 113.

guities of planes. There is no foreground; we are above ground level and look out of the window through a screen of trees whose bottoms are cut off by the picture frame. As a result, the dots of foliage have no horizontal ground plane to situate them in depth. They are on the immediate surface of the watercolour, making it more strongly two-dimensional than any of Brown's earlier landscapes. We see through the foliage to diminutive figures on a street below, and over it to open space beyond, but the distant view forms only a small part of the picture.

The last of this series of landscapes is *Walton-on-the-Naze* (Pl. 13b and Col. Pl. 3). Brown stopped keeping his diary in 1858, so instead of our being able to follow his day-by-day progress, we do not even know surely in what year *Walton-on-the-Naze* was painted. It is signed and dated 1860, and in the catalogue of Brown's exhibition it is dated 1860, but it may have been begun in the autumn of 1859 as recorded by Hueffer.[45] The painting shows a scene on the east coast of Essex, near Harwich; the time is late summer or early autumn. Brown's entry in his catalogue mainly describes the scenery; it also contains a brief mention of the figures: 'The lady and little girl, by their let-down hair, have been bathing – the gentleman descants learnedly on the beauty of the scene.'[46] These figures, absorbed by the scenery before them, probably represent Brown, his wife, and his daughter, and the picture appears to be a souvenir of a seaside vacation.

The figures make the picture more than pure landscape. From Brown's diary entries, we have seen his strong feeling for natural scenery. His involvement seems to have destroyed detachment. For Constable, the landscape is nature, something with a life of its own outside himself; for Brown, his own reaction to the landscape is inextricably present. The beauty of a place is important, but the artist makes us as aware of his response as of the landscape. In two of Brown's landscapes, *An English Autumn Afternoon* and *Hampstead from My Window*, the subject is his own landscape, the view he sees every day from his window. In two others, *The Hayfield* and *Walton-on-the-Naze*, he includes figures who probably represent himself. These figures seen from the rear are, like the young couple in *An English Autumn Afternoon*, a compositional crutch, a device to lead the viewer into the picture; they belong, likewise, to a long tradition of figures looking into the distance. But whereas in much Romantic painting of the earlier nineteenth century, that of Caspar David Friedrich for the prime example, we feel that the figures convey a rather melancholy mood, a desire for escape into the space they contemplate, or beyond, in Brown's landscapes there is only contentment. The landscape is limited, the figures belong to it, and they embody the artist's own happy relation with the scene. The artist makes clear his delight in the world by showing himself there enjoying it.

The figures in *An English Autumn Afternoon* and *Walton-on-the-Naze* are of a different social class from those of most Romantic landscape paintings. Instead of picturesque peasants and fishermen, we see subjects of the middle-class world of artist and patron enjoying their middle-class pleasures. Brown's subject of a seaside holiday in *Walton-on-the-Naze* was, however, far from the first of its kind. Frith's *Life at the Seaside* (*Ramsgate Sands*, Royal Collection) was exhibited in 1854, and its popular success virtually established a new *genre* of painting. For Frith the contemporary holiday scene is an excuse for a picture packed with amusing or sentimental anecdote. Brown's paintings are free (or almost free) of this narrative element, and he began painting subjects of middle-class leisure independently of Frith; *An English Autumn Afternoon*, boy and girl lolling in the foreground, was begun in 1852, two years before Frith exhibited *Life at the Seaside*. Brown painted these subjects

[45] Hueffer, 1896, p. 439.　　　　[46]Brown, 1865, p. 11.

42

primarily from 'love of the mere look of things', and in this respect, while they differ considerably from Frith's works, they seem akin to the early paintings of Boudin or Monet.

However, the look of things for Brown was quite different from the look for the Impressionists. *Walton-on-the-Naze* gives an extraordinary amount of information about the place. Brown's look was not a rapid glance, but a steady gaze taking in the myriad features of the landscape. We are aware of those features in much the same way as the woman in the picture, whose companion points them out to her one by one. The figures examining the landscape give it a narrative unity. The corn shocks in perspective rows lead the eye into the picture, and the rainbow arching over the landscape provides an enclosing frame. But there is no single focus for the painting as a whole; there is a separate, precise focus for each object. Things lack the feeling of inevitable relationship that objects in a more traditionally composed and organized painting would normally have. In looking at the picture we notice various details – the square-rigged ship on the horizon, a field mouse in the foreground, tiny figures at work in the middle distance – separately and unexpectedly. The picture shares the hyper-real clarity of vision of *The Hayfield* and *Carrying Corn*, but compared to them *Walton-on-the-Naze* is less compact, less tautly composed. It is more spacious and leisurely, more like a dream than a vision. The antiquated ship on the horizon is like a ghost ship, and the rainbow and the moon, just faintly visible, enhance the feeling of dream-like unreality.

The white building at the centre of the picture recalls one of the best-known English watercolours, Thomas Girtin's *White House, Chelsea Reach* (Tate Gallery). It is possible that Brown was aware of the Girtin, which had been engraved, when he made such a marked accent of the small building. There are also other points of similarity between the watercolour and Brown's painting: the windmills to the buildings' left, the meandering interplay of land and water, the clouds low over the horizons, and the twilight or near twilight hours. In both there is a flat monotony about the scenery which is relatively rare in English landscape (and also rare in Girtin's work). There are also glaring differences; Brown's smallness of touch, his much greater profusion of detail, and the inclusion of foreground figures all contrast with Girtin's breadth and simplicity. Girtin's colours are cool greys and blues; Brown's are vibrant greens and purples. These differences demonstrate some of the transformation of English painting in the sixty years between the two works. But Brown's painting does have something of the almost magical stillness and serenity of mood of the earlier watercolour. The divorce between Pre-Raphaelitism and the English landscape tradition was not absolute.

Walton-on-the-Naze is still in the same style as Brown's pictures of the 1850s, but it is his last work in which rigorous naturalism is of much importance. In 1861 he was a founding member of Morris, Marshall, Faulkner and Company, and in the early 1860s he spent much of his time designing furniture and stained glass for the firm. Designing for stained glass seems to have had a substantial effect upon his later painting, almost all of which falls into curvilinear, two-dimensional patterns and is radically different from his art of the 1850s. Landscape elements appear throughout his paintings from after 1860, but they are relatively unambitious, and they reveal little of the scrupulous fidelity of his earlier works.

In one later painting, *The Coat of Many Colours* of 1866 (Pl. 16a), Brown copied the background from an Eastern landscape by Thomas Seddon (Pl. 52a).[47] This shows a concern

47 *Ibid.*, p. 21.

for historical and geographical exactitude; however, at the same time, it shows an abandonment of that direct confrontation with nature which lay behind all of his art of the previous decade. Furthermore, although the derivation is obvious, Brown altered Seddon's view to emphasize the linear pattern of the paths on the distant hillsides. All Brown's landscape backgrounds of the 1860s and later are relatively linear and schematic; they are more like those in his painting of the 1840s than those of the 1850s. The background of *Byron's Dream* of 1874 (Pl. 16b), for example, recalls the pattern of fields in the background of *Chaucer at the Court of Edward III*. The same curvilinear schematization is visible in the landscape passages in Brown's frescoes in the Manchester Town Hall, which were the main occupation of the last fifteen years of his life.

Brown lived in Manchester for the sake of his frescoes from 1881 until 1887, and he painted one landscape there, *Platt Lane* (Pl. 17a), which is dated October 1884. According to Hueffer, Brown intended it as a study for his fresco *Chetham's Life Dream* in the Town Hall.[48] However, the background of the fresco shows a different site, and there is no evident connection. Brown painted *Platt Lane* directly on the spot, using a cab to protect himself from the weather. Despite this, it shows the same curvilinear stylization as Brown's later figural works. The composition, dominated by the linear patterns of bare branches and of the curving lane, may have been inspired by Atkinson Grimshaw (Pl. 17b).[49] The picture has an air of naive quaintness, which is appealing, but it has little in common with Brown's landscapes of the 1850s, and compared to them it seems relatively unambitious.

[48]Hueffer, 1896, p. 367. [49]See below, p. 161

44

IV
John Everett Millais

NEITHER Holman Hunt nor John Everett Millais developed a feeling for landscape comparable to that of Ford Madox Brown. As painters of landscape neither stands on the same level. Nonetheless, landscape elements appear throughout their art – both in figural compositions and in occasional pure landscapes.

The earliest extant landscape of any consequence by either artist is a watercolour by Millais in Birmingham, *The Gipsy* (Pl. 18a). It is signed and dated 1846, that is, when Millais was seventeen years old, and two years before the foundation of the Pre-Raphaelite Brotherhood. The watercolour shows no hint of Millais's future Pre-Raphaelite style; it does, however, demonstrate the young artist's fluency in the vocabulary of the 1830s and 1840s. The composition contains framing trees, a road leading into the picture, alternating lights and shades, and a subdued tonality with one touch of bright colour on the foreground figure. It recalls works by William Collins, W. F. Witherington, and a host of contemporary watercolourists, and it is itself an example of the conventionally composed picture, with little or no fresh observation of nature, against which the Pre-Raphaelites were to rebel.

Another work which the available evidence also indicates is early is the small *Landscape, Hampstead* in Liverpool (Pl. 18b). It is not dated, and it is not close stylistically to any known works. In a letter of 1878 Millais accepted it as his work and described it as 'a sketch from Nature done many years ago . . . I think I painted it from Hampstead or thereabouts.'[1] Millais had friends who moved to Hampstead in 1848, and during visits to them he painted landscapes in the vicinity. A *Hampstead Heath* (location unknown) is dated 1848 and described as 'an extremely elaborate and patient sketch' by M. H. Spielmann.[2] So this seems the most likely date for the picture in Liverpool. It is a study of a group of farm buildings whose main interest lies in their picturesque dilapidation. It shows a warm palette of reds and browns, care and competence in the depiction of the buildings, and fairly broad handling in the foreground. As yet there is no hint of the minute details or brilliant colours of Pre-Raphaelitism. If the picture dates from the summer of 1848, it is mainly of interest in demonstrating that just before the formation of the Pre-Raphaelite Brotherhood the new winds blowing had had no apparent effect on Millais's treatment of the natural world. For Millais, as for everyone else, Pre-Raphaelitism was initially a figural art whose central impulse was archaizing. However, by the next year this was beginning to change.

The Kingfisher's Haunt, a small oil sketch destroyed in the Second World War but of which a photograph exists (Pl. 19a), is probably the product of an early attempt by Millais to make a Pre-Raphaelite study from nature. There is conflicting evidence about both its subject and its date. J. G. Millais dates it 1856.[3] Ford Madox Brown described it in his diary in August 1854 and called it recent.[4] There is a small painting by Holman Hunt,

[1] Bennett, 1967, p.23.
[2] Spielmann, 1898, p. 71. In addition, Mary Bennett (1967, p. 23) notes that the painting is on a panel made by T. Brown, 163 High Holborn, and that directories list T. Brown at that address only until 1853–4.
[3] Millais, 1899, II, 469.
[4] Rossetti, 1900, p. 123.

The Haunted Manor (Pl. 19b), which shows the identical foreground. As even the plant life is the same in the two works they must have been painted at the same time, and the Hunt is dated 1849. In *Pre-Raphaelitism and the Pre-Raphaelite Brotherhood* Hunt describes a stream and pool at Ewell in Surrey of which he began a picture at an earlier date yet, probably in 1847.[5] He gives no indication that Millais also painted the same subject. When Millais's *Kingfisher's Haunt* was in the John Miller sale in 1858 it appeared in the catalogue with the subtitle *A Study in Wimbledon Park*.[6]

The answer is probably that Hunt's picture begun in 1847 was not *The Haunted Manor*. He wrote that he began a painting of a pool, which is not exactly the subject of *The Haunted Manor*. As Hunt usually signed his pictures with the date when he painted from nature, and not with the date of completion,[7] it seems most likely that the two artists began studies from nature together in 1849, possibly in Wimbledon Park. As the backgrounds are not the same, it appears that they finished them separately at later dates. The picture Brown saw in August 1854 and described as 'quite recent – a waterfall with a little lady and gent, and a child in the background' was surely *The Kingfisher's Haunt*. So this may be the date when Millais completed it; J. G. Millais's 1856 is apparently an error.

The Kingfisher's Haunt is primarily a study of foreground detail. The little waterfall and surrounding plants are the subject of the picture. The point of view is from above looking down on the immediate foreground, which fills the composition. The horizon is at the very top. Thus, the painting is not strictly comparable to the *Landscape, Hampstead*, which is a study of larger objects well within the depth of the picture. But the change from a relatively conventional landscape view to a closely focused study of detail in the imme-diate foreground parallels the change in Millais's larger figural pictures at the same time. The plants around the waterfall are painted with the same microscopic accuracy as those in *Ferdinand Lured by Ariel*, *The Woodman's Daughter*, and *Ophelia*. As in these pictures, rationally ordered space is sacrificed to concentration upon natural detail; this marks a reversal from the Hampstead picture, in which there is no detail at all. For the picture's colour we must rely upon Ford Madox Brown's diary: 'The foliage and foreground icy cold and raw in colour; the greens unripe enough to cause indigestion.' These words indicate a substantial change from the innocuous browns of the earlier landscape in the direction of the shrill greens of *The Woodman's Daughter*.

As evidence that the background was added at a later date we have not only Ford Madox Brown's 'quite recent' but also the stylistic evidence of the figures, which recall the couples that appear in several of Millais's drawings of 1853 and 1854, for example the figures in *Rejected*, dated 1853 (private collection).[8] The view under the trees to the horizon is like that in the background of *The Woodman's Daughter*, but the handling seems looser and appears from the photograph to be comparable to that in Millais's small painting of *Waiting* (Pl. 22), which is dated 1854. There is, however, a marked contrast between the generalized treatment of the foreground in *Waiting* and the leaf-by-leaf attention to detail in *The Kingfisher's Haunt* which substantiates the theory that the latter was begun at an earlier date.

We have seen that Millais in *Ferdinand Lured by Ariel* treated the natural setting as botanic detail, with almost no concern for spatial depth. In *The Woodman's Daughter* he expanded the background to show a distant view through the woods, but the space seems artificially

[5]Hunt, 1905, I, 70–72.

[6]Christie's, London, 20–22 May, 1858, no. 153. I am indebted to Mary Bennett for this reference.

[7]See below, p. 59

[8]Ironside and Gere, 1948, pl. 61.

contrived, suggesting Paolo Uccello more than nature. In the summer of 1851, in *Ophelia*, he returned to a constricted space, filling the entire picture with closely studied foliage. In his second picture of 1851, *A Huguenot, on St. Bartholomew's Day, Refusing to Shield Himself from Danger by Wearing the Roman Catholic Badge* (Pl. 40a), which he began painting in September or October, he restricted the space still more closely by painting the figures before an ivy-covered wall running to the top of the picture. The *Huguenot* shows botanic detail comparable to that in Millais's other paintings, but because much of the background consists of a brick wall, plant life plays a less dominant role than in *Ophelia*. On the other hand, the wall running across the picture forbids any penetration at all through the depths of foliage, as is still possible in *Ophelia*. Like Hunt's figures in *The Hireling Shepherd*, Millais's are on the surface of the picture. But unlike *The Hireling Shepherd*, in the *Huguenot* there is no space behind the figures. The result is a two-dimensional composition in which the figures appear inlaid into the flat background rather than standing before it.

When the *Huguenot* was exhibited at the Royal Academy in 1852 it was well received; in fact, it was Millais's first great popular success. However the *Art Journal* and some other periodicals criticized its flatness, blaming it on a lack of aerial perspective.[9] This criticism drew a scornful rebuttal from Ruskin in the unlikely vehicle of the third volume of *The Stones of Venice*.[10] Ruskin argued that the aerial perspective of most modern artists was a gross exaggeration; if we can see objects in clear weather at distances of miles, distances of a few feet or yards should have no visible effect. In the *Huguenot*, if the figures were standing about three feet from the wall, the aerial perspective calculated by scientific principle would be 'less than the 15,000th part of the depth of any given colour'. Ruskin concluded that Millais's perspective was accurate and that perspective as usually shown was 'entirely conventional and ridiculous; a mere struggle on the part of the pretendedly well-informed, but really ignorant, artist, to express distances by mist which he cannot by drawing.' The argument is convincing on its own terms, but Ruskin did not assert that Millais's accurate perspective gave any suggestion of the three feet between the figures and the wall. His argument that the effect of aerial perspective on tone and colour is so slight as to be hardly noticeable except over vast distances is, nonetheless, of considerable interest because of its claim of scientific truth for the over-all evenness of tonality which had been appearing in Pre-Raphaelite pictures to the detriment of traditional three-dimensional illusionistic space.

In March 1852 Millais wrote to his friend Thomas Combe that his next picture would not require much out-of-door work and that he hoped to enjoy the summer 'without a millstone of a picture hanging about my neck'. The picture he proposed painting would have 'nothing but a sheet of water and a few trees – a bit of flooded country, such as I have seen near you at Whitham.'[11] This was to have been the background of *The Eve of the Deluge*, a picture Millais had been contemplating since 1850, but which he never painted. Instead, he painted in time for the Royal Academy exhibition of 1853 two pictures of couples, repeating the sentimental formula which had made the *Huguenot* his first popular success. One, *The Order of Release, 1746* (Tate Gallery), which Millais began in December 1852, is perhaps of greatest interest because Effie Ruskin was one of the models. The figures appear before a black background, and the consequent simplicity led the *Athenaeum* to declare that Millais had escaped so successfully from 'the trammels of the school which he founded' that it wondered why he consented to be fettered by them in his other work.[12]

The other work, *The Proscribed Royalist, 1651* (private collection), shows a Puritan girl

[9]*Art Journal*, 1852, p. 173.
[10]Ruskin, 1903–12, XI, 59–60.

[11]Millais, 1899, I, 162.
[12]Bennett, 1967, p. 35.

visiting a Cavalier hidden in a hollow tree.[13] Millais painted the background out of doors at Hayes, near Bromley in Kent. Despite his hope of avoiding work out of doors, he was in the country from June until November. The background consists almost entirely of plant life: leaves, ferns, and the roots and trunk of the tree in which the Royalist hides. This botanic detail makes *The Proscribed Royalist* seem closely comparable to *Ophelia*, but in one respect it shows an advance. Millais painted the picture in sunlight, and he took the Puritan's dress to Hayes to paint it out of doors on a lay figure. He painted the actual models in the studio, but Arthur Hughes, who posed for the Cavalier, reported that Millais moved from his regular studio to a small back room where direct sunlight could fall on the figures.[14]

In October 1852 Millais wrote again to Thomas Combe expressing his intention of painting *The Deluge* in 1853.[15] It now would not require any outdoor painting, so Millais would be able to take a holiday abroad with the Combes. When the summer of 1853 came, he kept to part of this plan; he did not paint *The Deluge*, and he did not go abroad with the Combes, but neither did he begin another picture requiring a landscape background, and in June he set off for a holiday in Scotland. His companions were his brother William Millais and John and Effie Ruskin. The trip was the Ruskins' idea; Effie mentioned it in a letter to her mother as early as 31 March. Holman Hunt was also invited to accompany the group, but did not go because of a last-minute tooth-ache.[16]

The party arrived at Brig o'Turk in the Trossachs north of Glasgow on the first of July 1853. They remained until the end of October. Ruskin left on 26 Oct. to go to Edinburgh to lecture, and Millais followed a day or two later. During the stay an attachment developed between Millais and Effie Ruskin which led to her leaving Ruskin in the following year and marrying Millais in 1855. The emotional complications of the situation explain the low spirits and ill health displayed by Millais almost from the moment of their arrival. Ruskin wrote to his mother in October, 'Sometimes he is all excitement, sometimes depressed, sick and faint as a woman, always restless and unhappy. I think I never saw such a miserable person on the whole.'[17]

The trip was intended as a vacation. As Ruskin wrote to a friend in August: 'Both Millais and I came down here to rest; he having painted, and I corrected press, quite as much as was good for either of us; but', Ruskin added, 'he is painting a little among the rocks, and I am making some drawings which may be useful to me.'[18] Although everyone proclaimed Millais's need of a rest, almost as soon as they arrived at Brig o'Turk Millais and Ruskin began to plan a picture which was to become more of a burden to Millais than anything he had yet done. This was his portrait of Ruskin standing by the stream running through Glen Finglas (or Glenfinlas, as they generally referred to it) a short distance from their lodgings (Pl. 20). At the suggestion apparently of Ruskin's father, Millais planned a picture of Effie Ruskin at a window in Doune Castle, which he never painted, and a companion picture of her husband. They settled on a site for Ruskin's portrait by 4 July but then had to wait until the end of the month for a canvas to come from London before Millais could begin to paint. During the interval Millais painted 'for practice' a small picture on millboard of Mrs Ruskin sitting on the rocks by the stream (Pl. 21a).[19] There is contradictory evidence about the exact date when Millais began the larger portrait of

[13]Reproduced in Millais, 1899, I, 173.
[14]*Ibid.*, p. 175.
[15]*Ibid.*, p. 172.
[16]Lutyens, 1967, pp. 40, 49–51. Holman Hunt, un-dated letter to Edward Lear, John Rylands Library,

Manchester, Rylands Eng. MS. 1214, f. 11.
[17]Lutyens, 1967, p. 97, and 59–104 *passim*.
[18]Ruskin, 1903–12, XII, p. xxii.
[19]Lutyens, 1967, pp. 64–9.

Ruskin but it seems most likely to have been on 28 July, when Ruskin wrote to his father, 'you will be delighted to hear that my portrait is verily *begun* today and a most exquisite piece of leafage done already, close to the head . . .' Henry Acland, Ruskin's friend who was later to own the picture, was visiting the party at Brig o'Turk when the picture was begun, and Ruskin reported that 'he says it is in every way perfect both for me and Millais.'[20]

As work began, Ruskin kept in his diary a record of each week's progress:

Millais's picture of Glenfinlas was begun on Wednesday; outlined at once, Henry Acland holding the canvas, and a piece laid in that afternoon. More done on Thursday – about an hour's work on Friday – Saturday blank – Monday blank – Tuesday out at 6 in the morning painting till 9, and from 12 till 5 – Wednesday 11 to 6 – Thursday 11 to 6 – Friday 11 to 5 – Saturday 11 to 5 . . .[21]

Ruskin kept this record for ten weeks; the painting took longer. Millais was still working on it on 16 Oct., and according to Ruskin, 'It is not nearly done yet.'[22] After the Ruskins left for Edinburgh on 26 Oct., Millais planned to stay on at Brig o'Turk, but inclement weather almost immediately put a halt to his labours. On 29 Oct. he wrote to Hunt from Edinburgh, 'I have sent home the picture of Ruskin for the weather was terrible and would have killed me outright, so I intend coming for a week or so in March when it is dry, although colder than now.'[23]

When the spring came, Millais tried to avoid his return visit. On 8 April 1854, he called on George Price Boyce, who recorded in his diary, 'He wanted to finish the picture of Ruskin (looking on falling water) from some spot nearer than the Highlands. I recommended him the neighbourhood of Capel Curig.'[24] Millais planned to follow this advice and during April announced to his friends his intention of going to Wales; however, in May he decided to return to Scotland. Before leaving he wrote to F. J. Furnivall, a friend of Ruskin's, that he was going in order to finish the background properly: 'For a time I intended to finish the waterfall from Wales but Ruskin did not seem satisfied with this notion as the rocks are of quite a different Strata there.'[25] Millais was back at the New Trossachs Hotel at Glen Finglas by 24 May, and he worked on the painting for another month. During both visits to Scotland he was plagued by rainy weather and various mishaps, so he spent by no means all his time on the picture. On the other hand, as with his other works, he left the figure painting to be done in the studio. Ruskin posed between January and April 1854, and his hands were not completed until the following autumn.

Ruskin's wife left him in April 1854; in July their marriage was annulled. These events did not lessen Ruskin's enthusiasm for the picture, although completing it became an odious duty for Millais. He wanted to drop it as early as December 1853, but continued with it at Ruskin's insistence. When Ruskin finally had the painting in his possession he wrote to Millais expressing his delight with it and asking for Millais's proper address 'as I may often want to write to you, now'. To this, Millais replied insisting upon 'the necessity of abstaining from further intercourse' because of 'the barrier which cannot but be between us personally'.[26]

Since 1851 Ruskin had taken a possessive interest in Millais. The portrait allowed him an opportunity of participating in Millais's work which he obviously relished – to the degree that the picture seems to have meant more to him than his wife. His description of the site to his father reveals his enthusiasm:

[20]*Ibid.*, p. 75.
[21]J. Howard Whitehouse, *Vindication of Ruskin* (London, 1950) p. 123.
[22]Ruskin, 1903–12, XII, p. xxiv.
[23]Lutyens, 1967, p. 103.
[24]Boyce, 1941, p. 20.
[25]Lutyens, 1967, p. 215.
[26]*Ibid.*, pp. 247–48.

Millais has fixed on his place – a lovely piece of worn rock, with foaming water and weeds and moss, and a noble overhanging bank of dark crag – and I am to be standing looking quietly down the stream – just the sort of thing I used to do for hours together – he is very happy at the idea of doing it and I think you will be proud of the picture – and we shall have the two most wonderful torrents in the world, Turner's *St. Gothard* – and Millais's *Glenfinlas*. He is going to take the utmost possible pains with it – and says he can paint rocks and water better than anything else – I am sure the foam of the torrent will be something quite new in art.[27]

Ruskin maintained his excitement throughout the summer. On 16 Oct., he wrote to Furnivall that Millais was painting 'a picture of a torrent among rocks, which will make a revolution in landscape painting.'[28]

Remarkable in both these letters is Ruskin's description of the picture primarily as a landscape painting. Its new or revolutionary qualities were to be not in portraiture but in the treatment of nature. This one-sided emphasis was partly due to the fact that Millais concentrated during his time in Scotland on the landscape detail, leaving the figure for his London studio. Hence, the details of rocks and water were the aspects of the picture receiving the most attention during the summer. However, Ruskin's letter to his father was written before the daily routine of painting had begun, and when he had the picture in his possession he wrote to Millais that he had to get reconciled to 'the figure's standing in the way.'[29] His attitude toward the picture reflects his basic interests and not just his preoccupation of the day. Since beginning *Modern Painters* Ruskin had consistently devoted more attention to landscape painting than to any other aspect of contemporary art. His early defence of the Pre-Raphaelites was based entirely on their treatment of natural detail, and in the pamphlet *Pre-Raphaelitism* he had drawn a hypothetical comparison between Millais and Turner. The two both set out to paint the same mountain valley. Turner has 'a memory which nothing escapes, an invention which never rests, and is comparatively near sighted.' Millais, in contrast,

sees everything, small and large, with almost the same clearness; mountains and grasshoppers alike; the leaves on the branches, the veins on the pebbles, the bubbles in the stream; but he can remember nothing, and invent nothing. Patiently he sets himself to his mighty task; abandoning at once all thoughts of seizing transient effects, or giving general impressions of that which his eyes present to him in microscopical dissection, he chooses some small portion out of the infinite scene, and calculates with courage the number of weeks which must elapse before he can do justice to the intensity of his perceptions, or the fulness of matter in his subject.[30]

This is a presentiment of Millais's spending some fifteen weeks painting the veins on the pebbles and the bubbles in the stream of a small portion of a mountain valley in Scotland. In 1851, at approximately the time when he was writing the pamphlet, Ruskin tried to get Millais to accompany him to Switzerland.[31] In 1852 he complained about Millais's painting a 'rascally garden-rolled-nursery-maid's paradise' for background instead of real nature.[32] Now, in 1853, he had Millais painting exactly what he approved of, and he worked to see that Millais painted it as he wanted it. In Ruskin's letters there are references to 'managing' Millais, and he explained to Furnivall in October,

I have stopped all this time to keep Millais company – to keep him up to the Pre-Raphaelite degree of finish – which I have done with a vengeance, as he has taken three months to do half a background two feet over, and perhaps won't finish it now. But I have got maps of all the lichens on the rocks, and the *bubbles* painted in the foam.[33]

He kept a time-table of Millais's progress, he held an umbrella over him while he worked,

---

[27]Ruskin, 1903–12, XII, p. xxiv.
[28]*Ibid.*
[29]Lutyens, 1967, p. 247.
[30]Ruskin, 1903–12, XII, 359.

[31]Millais, 1899, I, 116.
[32]See above, p. 30
[33]Ruskin, 1903–12, XII, p. xxiv.

and he made at least one large and careful drawing of the rocks in the background of the painting (Pl. 21b).

Ruskin's role in the painting of his portrait is the first example of the sort of personal direction that he would later give to the landscape painters Inchbold and Brett, and it is more extensively documented than these later efforts. However, despite Ruskin's efforts, Millais's style in the portrait is not radically different from that of preceding years. Ruskin's comments of 1851 about Millais's inability to seize transient effects or to give general impressions are equally true of *The Woodman's Daughter* of that year, of *Ophelia* of the following, and of the *Portrait of Ruskin*. There is no space, no sky, no atmosphere; there is not even a hint of shadow linking the figure to his environment. Ruskin seems pasted on the surface of the picture. This is partly the result of Millais's painting the figure separately with Ruskin posed on a flight of steps. It also reflects Ruskin's argument in *Modern Painters* that specific and historic facts (such as the lichens and striations of the rocks) are more important than general and transitory ones (such as light and atmosphere) and that expression of the latter should not obscure the former. From the beginning, Millais planned that there would be no sun in the picture, which delighted Ruskin: 'Everett paints so brightly that he cannot possibly have too quiet a subject.'[34] Previously, Millais's *Ophelia* had had a quiet subject, and he excluded from the portrait the same things that he had excluded from the earlier picture. As Ruskin's remark to Furnivall about keeping Millais 'up to the Pre-Raphaelite degree of finish' indicates, his influence on Millais stylistically was to encourage him to stick to the paths he was already following. He did force Millais to struggle with new features of the landscape – gneiss rock, lichens, falling water – and these caused difficulties. 'Everett never having painted rock foreground before did not know how troublesome it was',[35] Ruskin wrote rather lightly in August. By October Millais was writing to Hunt: 'You know how dreadfully these out of doors affairs hang fire. This is a wretched [sic.] picture not larger than your sheep of last year [Hunt's *Strayed Sheep*, Pl. 28a]. There is some falling water in it which is very perplexing.'[36]

During the stay at Brig o'Turk the whole group busied itself with painting and sketching, and there is a substantial body of additional works dating from the trip. Millais's small *Waterfall* (Pl. 21a), showing Effie seated on the rocks, has already been mentioned. This picture has usually been identified as a study for the background of the *Portrait of Ruskin*. Strictly speaking, this is incorrect. *The Waterfall* was begun earlier, but it does not show the same site. Millais painted the background of the portrait directly from nature, making no more elaborate studies for it than a slight pencil sketch in the Ashmolean Museum. Compared to the portrait, *The Waterfall* is a much slighter production. It is considerably smaller ($10\frac{1}{2}$ by $12\frac{1}{2}$ inches), and the foreground rocks and water are less crisply detailed and have little of the verisimilitude of those in the larger painting. The differences demonstrate that the vastly longer time which Millais spent on the portrait was employed to effect. The background of *The Waterfall* shows some distance and a bit of sky, but it is treated summarily and may have been added to complete and make saleable the original foreground sketch.

Millais also made a number of humorous drawings, some of which show the hardships of working out of doors in the Scottish climate. His hat and umbrella are blown into the stream in one, rain prevents the group from sketching in a second, and they are attacked by midges in a third.[37] In another drawing, inscribed *Two Masters and their Pupils*, Millais

[34]Lutyens, 1967, p. 77.
[35]*Ibid.*, p. 85.
[36]*Ibid.*, p. 94.

[37]Mary Lutyens, 'Millais's Portrait of Ruskin', *Apollo*, LXXXV, 1967, pp. 246–53, pls. 5, 9, and 12.

shows himself seated on the rocks working at the portrait on a rustic easel while Effie Ruskin sits behind him reading.[38] The inscription refers to the instruction Millais was giving Mrs Ruskin in drawing and painting. A small and amateurish painting of a waterfall in the collection of Mary Lutyens may be by Effie.[39] Another painting of a waterfall by Millais's brother William is in the collection of Lord Sherfield (Pl. 83b). Finally, there is Ruskin's drawing of *Gneiss Rock in Glenfinlas* (Pl. 21b). It appears to show part of the rocks on the left side of the background of Millais's portrait, but from a viewpoint that is lower and looking more downstream. The linear patterns in the rock are clearly shown, and we can easily visualize Ruskin's using the drawing to demonstrate to Millais the laws of rock formation. Because Ruskin's drawing is a close study of a limited area, it is in some respects a more successful work than the painting, which extends similar study over a wider area and combines it with a portrait to dissipate the effect. Ruskin's remark about 'the figure's standing in the way' was not just self-effacing nonsense.

Millais's break with Ruskin was accompanied by his withdrawal from Pre-Raphaelite circles. In the autumn of 1853 he was elected an associate member of the Royal Academy. While Rossetti, Ford Madox Brown, and their friends were becoming increasingly hostile to the Academy, Millais was becoming a staunch member of the establishment camp. The break was not absolute: Millais remained throughout his life a close friend of Holman Hunt, and he did exhibit at the Pre-Raphaelite-sponsored exhibition in Russell Place in 1857. On the other hand, he did not become a member of the Hogarth Club, the Pre-Raphaelite exhibiting society founded in 1858. Ruskin was a member of the Hogarth Club, and it is probable that Millais did not join in order to avoid contact with him,[40] but this is symptomatic. After 1854 Ruskin became an ever more active figure in Pre-Raphaelite circles while Millais gradually dropped out. After Millais's marriage to Effie in July 1855 they lived in Scotland until 1862.

As we have seen, Millais insisted that his contacts with Ruskin be broken off, but the ill will he held toward Ruskin was not reciprocated. In 1855 Ruskin started writing an annual review of the Royal Academy and other annual exhibitions in London, which is now usually known as *Academy Notes*. Ruskin claimed 'entire impartiality' for his *Notes*,[41] but, in fact, he used them to proselytize for his beliefs and for his Pre-Raphaelite friends. And in *Academy Notes*, at least in the first two years, Millais was the brightest star: the artist who in 1855 had painted 'the only *great* picture exhibited this year; but this is *very* great;' and whose pictures exhibited in 1856 would 'rank in future among the world's best masterpieces.'[42]

Ruskin eulogized Millais not only in the face of personal conflict but also in the face of radical changes in Millais's art. After 1853 Millais never painted with the same Pre-Raphaelite detail that we see in the *Portrait of Ruskin* and in his earlier work. Ruskin noted the departure, and initially he approved of it. About *The Rescue* (National Gallery of Victoria, Melbourne), the *great* picture of 1855, in which Millais showed a fireman saving three children from a blazing home, Ruskin wrote:

The execution of the picture is remarkably bold – in some respects imperfect. I have heard it was hastily finished; but, except in the face of the child kissing the mother, it could not be much bettered. For there is a true sympathy between the impetuousness of execution and the haste of the action.[43]

[38]Mary Lutyens, 'Portraits of Effie', *Apollo*, LXXXVII, 1968, p. 194, pl. 14.
[39]Lutyens, *Apollo*, LXXXV, 1967, p. 248, pl. 3. This picture was sold at Christie's, London, 19 Nov. 1965, no. 8, by Sir William Dyke Acland as by William Millais.
[40]Scott, 1892, II, 47.
[41]Ruskin, 1903–12, XIV, 5.
[42]*Ibid.*, pp. 22, 56–7.
[43]*Ibid.*, p. 23.

In outdoor painting, we can see the slackening in Millais's small *Waiting*, signed and dated 1854 (Pl. 22). In composition, this picture of a girl sitting at a stile does not show significant change from earlier works such as *The Woodman's Daughter* or *The Proscribed Royalist*. The background consists of trees running to the top of the picture. The greens are as bright as in Millais's earlier pictures. However, if we look at the foreground there are no longer separate blades of grass, but a general green area in which brush strokes suggest an occasional blade. The wall over which the stile is built is of a uniform texture and colour, with the individual stones summarily outlined in black. Their lack of detail makes one feel that, after painting the rocks and lichens of the Ruskin portrait, Millais decided that he had had enough. Millais did not exhibit the picture (he exhibited nothing at the Royal Academy in 1854), but a writer in the *Art Journal* saw it in a private collection in 1857 and noted, 'in the secondary material there is greater breadth of manipulation than is generally found in Millais's works.'[44]

In abandoning exact botanical and geological detail, Millais abandoned the most distinctive quality of his work of the previous few years, but he also gained from the change. There is, for once, an effective feeling of the fall of light in *Waiting*; it is evident both in the dappled effect of sunlight falling through the woods in the background and in the contrast of highlights and shadows upon the foreground grass. In addition, mood is not swamped by detail. The girl in *Waiting*, although much smaller relatively than Ophelia, dominates the picture as Millais's earlier heroine does not. The artist is no longer the conscientious slave of what he sees, rejecting nothing, selecting nothing. He now uses the natural world for the sake of other ends.

The masterpieces of Millais's changed style are *The Blind Girl* (Pl. 23) and *Autumn Leaves* (Pl. 24a), two of the five pictures that he exhibited at the Royal Academy in 1856. A third, *Peace Concluded, 1856* (Minneapolis Institute of Art), elicited Ruskin's talk about 'the world's best masterpieces', but it is of an interior subject. Both *The Blind Girl* and *Autumn Leaves* show figures posed out of doors before landscape backgrounds.

Millais began the background of *The Blind Girl* at Winchelsea in the autumn of 1854, but he did not paint the figures, middle distance, and foreground until 1856, when he was living in Scotland. There is no conspicuous break between the earlier and later portions of the painting. However, by the standards of his earlier work, the foreground and middle distance are broadly painted. There are still individual flowers and blades of grass, but these are selected details which provide an illusion of high finish, more like the dandelions in Hunt's *Rienzi* than the painstaking thoroughness of Hunt's and Millais's subsequent works. When Ford Madox Brown saw *The Blind Girl* he praised it in his diary as 'a religious picture and a glorious one', but he also commented: 'It is a pity he has so scamped the execution.'[45] If we consider the change from *Ophelia* we can understand why Brown tempered his praise.

There is nothing in Millais's earlier work to which we can compare the further background. It is a view of open, rising ground with the buildings of Winchelsea clearly recognizable on top of the rise. For the first time in Millais's art, space and distance are important. The background is still, however, not a conventional landscape setting. The hill behind the figures goes up more than it goes back. The horizon is almost at the top of the painting, and there is little tonal modification between foreground and distance. Spatial recession is established only by the smaller sizes of animals, trees, and buildings, and these provide uncertain measurement. It is difficult, for example, to estimate the pitch

[44] *Art Journal*, 1857, p. 310.　　　　[45] Hueffer, 1896, pp. 120–21.

of the slope or the distance from the animals in the middle distance to the buildings on the horizon.

Above the horizon, the sky forms a significant part of the painting, likewise for the first time in Millais's art. Although the sky accounts for less than one fifth of the picture, the double rainbows set against lowering grey clouds give it a dramatic prominence. *The Blind Girl* is one of the first Pre-Raphaelite attempts to make weather other than open sunniness a significant part of the picture. To do this Millais had to abandon dependence upon direct observation. The double rainbows are a studio concoction whose colours Millais originally got wrong and later had to repaint. Millais had earlier copied the natural world objectively, for its own sake; here he manipulates nature as a pictorial element. Because of the high horizon, the dramatic sky, and the brilliant green of the fields, the landscape is full, active, and close to the surface of the painting. It is not a subordinate backdrop for the figures, but an essential part of the subject. The spectacle of rainbows and landscape, which the blind girl cannot see, provides the meaning of the picture. Nonetheless, if Millais manipulates nature, it is only within naturalistic limits; we must recognize the beauty which the girl cannot see. The brilliant contrast of the green hill against the grey sky is convincing as a momentary effect seen just after a storm. And the distant background is a scrupulous view of the 'Ancient Town' of Winchelsea seen from the east. The strip of buildings and trees, at once objectively detailed and, because of the distance, seen in terms of masses and as a whole, is one of the loveliest passages in Pre-Raphaelite painting. The buildings march in ordered rhythm across the horizon and are shown with a clarity and chastity which make us accept the honesty of the artist's vision and feel the joys inherent in the possibility of sight.

Millais painted *Autumn Leaves* in the autumn of 1855 at Annat Lodge, where he was living, near Perth. According to his wife's diary, he wanted it to be a picture 'full of beauty and without subject.'[46] In the eyes of Ford Madox Brown he came close to succeeding, but in Brown's opinion this was not an unmixed blessing: 'I saw Millais' picture of the year, *Autumn Leaves* – the finest in painting and colour he has yet done, but the subject somewhat without purpose, and looking like portraits.'[47] The figures, four girls gathering leaves, pose in the foreground. Two of them gaze out of the picture in a manner that connects them more with the viewer than with each other or their two companions, who are staring pensively into the pile of burning leaves before them. Behind them, we see autumnal woods and a sunset over purple hills. The subject is mellow – sunset, autumn, burning leaves – the day, the season, nature is at its languid end, not thriving and blossoming, as in *Ophelia*. A story is not told, but mood is evoked by the associative appeal of the imagery. The treatment of nature is like the subject: suggestive rather than precisely defined. The colours – red and gold in the foreground leaves, blue and purple in the distance, the sky gold over the horizon – are in themselves emotive and over-ripe. The pile of leaves at the centre of the picture seems elaborated, but it shows none of the fineness of observation of Millais's earlier works. Past the foreground figures there is no detail. On the left a man raking leaves is only a faintly suggested ghostly presence. The trees are a loosely brushed-in area of reddish browns. The town of Perth in the valley beyond is lost in the evening mist, and the distant hills are silhouettes against the sky.

In front of *Autumn Leaves* talk about the Pre-Raphaelites' 'childlike reversion from existing schools to Nature herself' no longer seems appropriate. Millais's goal was a picture 'full of beauty'. Although Millais certainly would have seen no conflict between truth and

[46]Bennett, 1967, p. 41.   [47]Hueffer, 1896, p. 120.

1b. Arthur Hughes, *The Long Engagement* (Plate 41c)

1a. John Everett Millais, *Ferdinand Lured by Ariel* (Plate 2a)

a.

b.

c.

d.

2a. William Holman Hunt, detail from *The Hireling Shepherd* (Plate 5)

2b. Ford Madox Brown, detail from *The Pretty Baa-Lambs* (Plate 8)

2c. John William Inchbold, detail from *At Bolton* (Plate 60a)

2d. John Brett, detail from *The Stonebreaker* (Plate 69b)

beauty, five years earlier truth had been the goal, and beauty happened as a consequence. Now, the order has been reversed. The kind of botanic truth shown by Millais in an earlier picture such as *Ophelia* depended on close personal observation and resulted in a view of nature of startling individuality and originality. *Autumn Leaves* still depended upon observation; Millais painted it from the view from his own garden. But autumnal colours and sunset skies were hardly a discovery of Millais's. An older artist like Danby had made a speciality of sunset effects. To say that Millais turned to a tried-and-true formula is too strong, because the effects were unprecedented in his own work, but he had left the spring-time of independent discovery.

Ruskin did not mention *The Blind Girl* in his *Academy Notes* of 1856, although much later he did write one of his most rapturous descriptive passages about it in *The Three Colours of Pre-Raphaelitism*.[48] He lauded *Autumn Leaves* in *Academy Notes*, calling it 'by much the most poetical work the painter has yet conceived.' He described the background as, 'as far as I know, the first instance of a perfectly painted twilight. It is as easy, as it is common, to give obscurity to twilight, but to give the glow within its darkness is another matter; and though Giorgione might have come near the glow, he never gave the valley mist.'[49] Ruskin had complained in the first volume of *Modern Painters* that he had never seen a clear twilight properly painted, 'that effect in which all details are lost, while intense clearness and light are still felt.' Even Turner had failed by making the effect appear too misty, 'but it remains to be shown that any closer approximation to the effect is possible.'[50] Millais had at last done it, surpassing not Turner but Giorgione. In Ruskin's review of Millais's *Peace Concluded* he was even more extravagant with Venetian comparisons, declaring that 'Titian himself could hardly head him now,' and he placed Millais on a pedestal which he shared only with Turner among the artists of all time.[51]

If Ruskin's enthusiasm now seems somewhat excessive, perhaps in 1856, when he could see *Autumn Leaves* without looking at it over the decline of Millais's later art, it might have been possible to see the painting only as an omen of promising developments. However, other viewers noting the changes in Millais's art were more restrained. Ford Madox Brown was not the only person to have mixed feelings. The critic of *The Times*, for example, saw new weaknesses as well as new strengths:

Millais contributes several works of very various merit. The best is *Autumn Leaves* – girls burning these leaves – and here may at once be seen the advance made in his style. Compare the leaves with the straw in the ark of several years ago [*The Return of the Dove to the Ark* (Ashmolean Museum, Oxford)]. There every straw was painted with a minuteness which it was painful to follow. Here the leaves are given with great truth and force, but the treatment is much more general and the work more vapid. Throughout all his works the same increasing insipidity of touch may be seen; but in all of them will not be seen colour as good as in this work or expression so true.[52]

Today, we can see that after 1856 Millais never again came near the heights that he reached in that and preceding years, and that, in fact, *Autumn Leaves* contained many of the seeds of the deterioration of his later art.

The decline can be seen in *A Dream of the Past: Sir Isumbras at the Ford* (Pl. 24b), the chief picture that he exhibited at the Royal Academy in 1857. It depicts a medieval knight ferrying two children across a river on his charger. The children are wide-eyed cousins of those in *Autumn Leaves*, but while the children in the earlier picture have at least a moody

[48]Ruskin, 1903–12, XXXIV, 148–51.
[49]*Ibid.*, XIV, 66–7.
[50]*Ibid.*, III, 340n.
[51]*Ibid.*, XIV, 56–57.
[52]Quoted in Hunt, 1905, II, 113.

remoteness, those in *Sir Isumbras* are all sugar. Behind them is a twilight taken straight from *Autumn Leaves*. There is still some illusion of detail, for example in the foreground plants, but the treatment is coarse. Millais spent less than a fortnight painting the picture's background, although *Sir Isumbras* was larger than any of his previous Pre-Raphaelite works. If we remember the amount of time he spent on the backgrounds of *Ophelia* or the *Portrait of Ruskin*, much of the difference between Millais's earlier and later art is explained. Millais talked of the new breadth of his execution in contrast to Pre-Raphaelite detail,[53] but, despite the loosening of technique, a picture like *Sir Isumbras* is made out of hard edges and sharp contrasts; it has no more breadth of vision or feeling than Millais's earlier work. The reason for the change was Millais's desire to achieve a speedier execution and consequently a larger production, in order to provide an income to support his wife and rapidly growing family.

Ruskin was as aghast at *Sir Isumbras* as he had been enthusiastic about *Autumn Leaves*. He began his discussion of the picture by explaining his praise of the previous year's works. They had promised to place Millais among the 'great Imaginative masters', although there had been 'a slovenliness and imperfection in many portions' which Ruskin had passed over as accidental. Now, however, the change from *Ophelia* 'is not merely Fall – it is Catastrophe', and Ruskin saw no hope but 'in a return to quiet perfectness of work.'[54]

Millais did not return to quiet perfectness of work. He exhibited nothing at the Royal Academy in 1858, but in 1859 he exhibited two large pictures of outdoor subjects. Both have moody, ambiguous subjects which again depend on *Autumn Leaves*. One, *The Vale of Rest* (Tate Gallery), which shows nuns digging a grave, has yet another sunset. The other, *Spring* or *Apple Blossoms* (Pl. 25a), is of a group of girls taking tea in an orchard. It has a background of flowering trees which at first glance appears comparable to Millais's earlier foliate backgrounds, but the handling is closer to that in *Sir Isumbras*. Ruskin wrote a long and thoughful review of these pictures, in which he still found greatness, but greatness undermined by crudity.[55] Here are his comments about the background of *Apple Blossoms*:

When we look at this fierce and rigid orchard – this angry blooming (petals, as it were, of japanned brass); and remember the lovely wild roses and flowers scattered on the stream in *Ophelia*; there is, I regret to say, no ground for any diminution of the doubt which I expressed two years since respecting the future career of a painter who can fall thus strangely beneath himself.

Ruskin concluded with the assertion that Millais still had greater powers than any other artist, but he was misusing them, or not using them. 'Here, we have a careless or insolent indication of things that might be; not the splendid promise of a grand impatience, but the scrabbled remnant of a scornfully abandoned aim.'

Perhaps Ruskin's criticisms in 1857 and 1859 and a generally unsympathetic public response made Millais feel that he was fighting on the wrong ground. After 1859 significant landscape passages disappeared from his painting; almost all of his pictures from the early 1860s are of interior subjects. Much of Millais's activity in the 1860s was concerned with book illustration, in particular illustrations of Trollope's novels. These illustrations occasionally have landscape settings, and one, the frontispiece to *Orley Farm*, published in 1862, is a full landscape composition. It shows a woman milking a cow in the foreground and a house, Orley Farm, on top of a slope behind her. The rising hillside and high horizon are faintly reminiscent of *The Blind Girl*, but in every respect the illustration is a

[53]Millais, 1899, I, 342.
[54]Ruskin, 1903–12, XIV, 106–11

[55]*Ibid.*, pp. 212–16.

slight work. It is not based on observation but on Trollope's description in the opening pages of the novel.

Beginning in 1870 and continuing to the end of his life, Millais did regularly paint landscapes (Pl. 25b). These have nothing to do with Pre-Raphaelitism, but belong to the sphere of late Victorian popular and sentimental painting. In style and content they are not far from the landscapes of Benjamin Williams Leader and other late Victorian landscapists. The painter William Blake Richmond, a friend of Millais's, wrote that people interested the artist more than things, 'Even in his landscapes I think I can always detect a kind of human sentiment pervading them, a mood of Nature akin to a human mood which prompted them,'[56] The paintings show anthropomorphized landscapes. The subjects are Millais's feelings, and the feelings are commonplace. The titles in themselves are indicative of the pictures' banality: *Chill October, Flowing to the Sea, The Fringe of the Moor, The Moon is Up and Yet It Is Not Night, Lingering Autumn, Over the Hills and Far Away*. Millais's explanation of *Chill October*, the first of these later landscapes, is indicative of the attitude in which all of them were painted: 'I chose the subject for the sentiment it always conveyed to my mind, and I am happy to think that the transcript touched the public in a like manner.'[57] The inspiration was not the landscape, but the sentiment it *always* conveyed. From the original Pre-Raphaelite child-like reversion to nature, we have come full circle to landscapes which are hardly about nature at all.

[56]Millais, 1899, II, 442.   [57]*Ibid.*, p. 29; *Chill October* is reproduced facing p. 26.

V

William Holman Hunt

IN HIS MEMOIRS, Holman Hunt describes an effort that he made to paint a picture of a pool at Ewell in the summer of 1847: 'The difference between the scene as it was presented to my untutored sight, and any single landscape by the great painters that I knew, suggested the doubt, when I had begun the subject on my drawing-board, whether it was not one which a practical painter should avoid.' After a few days, he gave it up, 'blaming only my want of masterliness'.[1] This small incident is indicative of Hunt's entire career. If we recall Millais's watercolour of 1846, *The Gipsy*, or his small *Landscape, Hampstead* of 1848 (Pl. 18), some of the differences between the two men are demonstrated. In the 1840s Millais accepted the prevailing styles and worked comfortably within them. Hunt, on the other hand, had to abandon his picture because of the conflict between his own perception of nature and his inherited values. This integrity runs all through Hunt's career, making him the most forceful proponent of Pre-Raphaelitism and giving to his late art an interest not shared by that of most of his colleagues. In contrast, Millais, except in his few Pre-Raphaelite years, followed the path of least resistance, and even as a Pre-Raphaelite his art had an ease and sureness denied to Hunt. As Hunt's book demonstrates, he conceived his role as a holy mission, and his life was a series of struggles where nothing came easily.

In the summer of 1848, when Dante Gabriel Rossetti was working in Hunt's studio, the two artists made a sketching excursion to Greenwich and Blackheath. An apparent product of this outing is a small oil painting by Hunt (Pl. 26a), which bears on its back an inscription probably by the artist's widow: 'Love at First Sight: Study made in Blackheath Park for a picture he intended to paint / W. Holman Hunt / Sept. 1848.' In *Pre-Raphaelitism and the Pre-Raphaelite Brotherhood* Hunt places the excursion just before he moved into a new painting room in August 1848 and before beginning work on the figures in *Rienzi*.[2] The picture includes two figures and three deer. These were apparently added to enhance what was intended as a simple study for a background. They are small and rather slight, and Hunt seems to have had difficulty with them. The reproduction in *Pre-Raphaelitism and the Pre-Raphaelite Brotherhood* shows the man on the right in a different costume and position from that in the painting as it now exists.[3] In the picture, the man is smaller than the woman and appears proportionately too small for his place in the spatial depth of the picture. The legs of two of the deer in the foreground are cut by the picture frame, prefiguring Hunt's frequent later practice of slicing his figures by the edge of the picture.

Although the label on the back implies that the picture is a study for a work that was never painted, Hunt did make use of it in his *Druids* (Pl. 26b), begun a year later. The cluster of dead trees in the upper centre of the *Druids*, seen through the Druidic avenue, is based on that in *Love at First Sight*, and we can also recognize the pair of trunks on the left and the trees rising over the mass of foliage above and to the right. Hunt may also have

[1]Hunt, 1905, I, 71–2.
[2]*Ibid.*, p. 114.
[3]*Ibid.*, p. 117.

used these same trees as the model for the tops of the trees seen above the heads of his figures and through a row of poplar trunks in *Rienzi*. The further trees in *Rienzi* have a similar outline, and Hunt was working on *Rienzi* at the time of and after his outing to Blackheath. However, as this is part of *Rienzi* that Hunt repainted in 1886, the evidence of its similarity or dissimilarity is not conclusive. What is of greater significance is the fact that while Hunt went to the Lea Marshes to paint 'the background and foreground' of the *Druids*, he did not paint all the background directly from nature but based it partly on an earlier sketch, made before he had conceived the subject of the picture. As we have seen, the distant background of the *Druids* does not share the precise detail of the foreground.[4] The trees in *Love at First Sight* are more carefully treated than the corresponding portion of the *Druids*, in which they have been reduced by about a third, but they are not painted with leaf-by-leaf precision. The foreground shows no detail at all. The colour, except in the figures, is rather heavy and dull, with little suggestion of the brilliant pitch that was soon to appear as a hallmark of Hunt's art.

In 1849 Hunt painted at least two landscape studies. In July William Michael Rossetti recorded in his *P.R.B. Journal* that Hunt had made a study in colour of a cornfield at Ewell.[5] This may have been the 'lovely hasty rub in of a cornfield against a deep blue sky' by Hunt which George Price Boyce saw at Rossetti's on 3 March, 1854.[6] It may possibly be either the *Cornfield at Ewell* which was owned by Hunt's daughter in 1951 but has since disappeared, or a *Landscape* given by the artist's widow to Sir Kenneth R. Swan and lent by him to the Holman Hunt exhibition of 1969.[7] This latter *Landscape* has an unusual narrow vertical shape and is possibly a fragment. It has a broadly brushed foreground which is clearly a later addition to a view of fields and trees along the horizon similar to the background of the *Druids*.

The other study is *The Haunted Manor* (Pl. 19b), which is signed and dated 1849. This picture has been identified as the painting of the pool at Ewell which Hunt began in 1847.[8] As we have seen, he wrote that he gave up on the study, so, if this identification is correct, the date 1849 would indicate when he returned to the study and completed it. The picture does appear to have been painted at two separate times, the inch or two of further view along the top being much more brightly coloured than the rather heavy foreground.

There is however substantial reason for doubting if this is the picture begun in 1847. First, it is not a picture of a pool, but of a waterfall. Second, Hunt does not indicate in his memoirs that he ever completed the study begun in 1847. Third, as we have seen, the subject is the same as Millais's *Kingfisher's Haunt*, which in 1858 bore the subtitle *Study in Wimbledon Park* (Pl. 19a).[9] If there is any validity in this identification, Hunt's picture must also have been painted at Wimbledon Park, not at Ewell. Hunt frequently gave his pictures the date when he worked on them from nature, not when he completed them (*The Hireling Shepherd* is dated '1851. Ewell' although finished in London in 1852; *The Scapegoat* [Pl. 29a], completed in Jerusalem in 1855, is inscribed 'Oosdom, Dead Sea 1854'). Hunt first exhibited *The Haunted Manor* in 1856 at the Liverpool Academy, and it seems unlikely that he would have waited so long to exhibit it unless he had also waited to finish it. The background, full of golden light and blue shadows, has no similarity to the background of the *Druids*, which was begun in 1849. It is impossibly precocious for the Hunt of 1849, but accords with his art of the middle and later 1850s. Furthermore, none of Hunt's works painted before 1849 show an interest in elaborate foreground detail. The

[4]See above, p. 11.
[5]Rossetti, 1900, p. 216.
[6]Boyce, 1941, p. 70.

[7]Bennett, 1969, p. 46, no. 37.
[8]*Ibid.*, p. 20.
[9]See above, pp. 45–6.

detail in *Rienzi* consists of a few separate dandelions, and there is none in the foreground of *Love at First Sight*. In 1849 Hunt's *Druids* and Millais's *Ferdinand Lured by Ariel* begin to show the elaboration of botanic detail which would characterize much of both artists' work in subsequent years. What we see in *The Haunted Manor* and *The Kingfisher's Haunt* are two close studies of natural detail, which the artists apparently made working side by side in 1849 in anticipation of their larger paintings begun in the same year. In both cases they finished their studies by adding backgrounds at a later date.

Although the backgrounds differ considerably, the centre sections of the pictures show the identical stones and plants. Yet, the differences between the two are striking. They reveal Hunt and Millais, within a year of the formation of the Pre-Raphaelite Brotherhood, as considerably farther apart than Monet and Renoir mutually painting *La Grenouillère* in 1869. The differences are in part due to the artists' different points of view: Hunt's low, close, and frontal; Millais's looking at the waterfall obliquely from above and from a greater distance. But the viewpoints themselves are the results of choices which reflect the personalities of the men: Hunt, blunt and direct; Millais, more facile and elegant. We can see the same contrast in the four-square composition of Hunt's *Rienzi* and the more elegant but spatially less coherent composition of Millais's *Isabella*. Millais's version, because it shows the waterfall from a greater distance, has a smaller scale and more comprehensive view. In Hunt's, on the other hand, there is a sense of physical solidity, bulk, and weight which is lacking in Millais's. Details such as the water-plants above the fall have a simple integrity as separate things, while in the Millais they merge together in a complicated tangle.

The waterfall and surrounding plants fill most of Hunt's composition. They are studied as physical objects, carefully delineated and solidly modelled, but without concern for conditions of outdoor light and atmosphere. Sunlight falls only in the bit of added landscape along the top of the picture. Unlike the background of Millais's picture, which recedes to a distant horizon, Hunt's is packed with detail: a fence and hayrick to the left, and the house which gives the picture its name to the right. All are bathed in a vibrant golden light which gives them a prominence disproportionate to the amount of space they occupy. The contrast to the sombre, earthy massiveness of the foreground makes them appear almost as magical, or haunted, visions, and Hunt's title indicates he was fully aware of this supernatural effect.

We have already discussed Hunt's major exhibited pictures from *Rienzi* of 1849 to *The Hireling Shepherd*, which he began in the summer of 1851 and exhibited the following year. While in the country in 1851, Hunt also began *The Light of the World* (Pl. 27a), which he did not finish and exhibit until 1854. This painting was Hunt's first to achieve any popular success, and it is still his best-known work. Because it is a part of nineteenth-century religion as well as art, *The Light of the World* is a difficult picture to look at. But in addition to being a religious tract, it is also an outdoor night scene painted with Hunt's usual rigour.

Although Hunt may have intended *The Hireling Shepherd* to embody a symbolic message, we have seen that when it was first exhibited it was received and criticized primarily as a work of extreme realism or naturalism. The opposite is true of *The Light of the World*. When it was exhibited at the Royal Academy in 1854 along with *The Awakening Conscience*, which Hunt intended as its material counterpart, the two immediately raised questions about what they meant. Ruskin responded to these questions on behalf of Hunt, who was then in the East, by writing a pair of letters to *The Times*. These letters are mainly about the pictures' symbolic meanings, but in the letter about *The Light of the World*

Ruskin also insisted upon its truth, and he drew a distinction between true Pre-Raphaelite work and its imitations:

The true work represents all objects exactly as they would appear in nature in the position and at the distance which the arrangement of the picture supposes. The false work represents them with all their details, as if seen through a microscope. Examine closely the ivy on the door in Mr. Hunt's picture, and there will not be found in it a single clear outline. All is the most exquisite mystery of colour; becoming reality at its due distance. . . . The spurious imitations of Pre-Raphaelite work represent the most minute leaves and other objects with sharp outlines, but with no variety of colour, and with none of the concealment, none of the infinity of nature.[10]

Ruskin did not cite specific examples of the spurious imitations, but he declared they covered half the walls of the Academy. That Ruskin felt it necessary to draw this distinction is indicative of how common minutely drawn detail was in English painting in the 1850s. The differences he points out are a result of the extraordinary labours of Hunt and Millais in working directly out of doors. They not only painted elaborate detail, they painted it directly from nature, and their originality lay as much in the observation behind their works as in the treatment. Ruskin commented that Hunt's ivy did not show sharp outlines. Despite the minuteness of detail, Pre-Raphaelitism was not a linear style. Hunt and Millais painted from nature; they did not draw. They saw and recorded in terms of the touch of colour rather than the drawn outline. Neither artist made careful black-and-white outline drawings of natural detail such as those by the German Nazarenes or by an English painter like Leighton.[11]

Hunt painted *The Light of the World* as a night scene to convey his message of Christ as the bearer of light to the sinner. Ruskin in his letter about the painting interpreted the reddish light from Christ's lantern as the light of conscience, and he contrasted it to the light of Christ's nimbus, which he described as the light of the hope of salvation. Thus, the light has a symbolic function, like the ivy and weeds on the door, which, according to Ruskin, indicate that the door to the human soul has long been unopened.[12] Hunt began painting the background out of doors by moonlight on 7 Nov. 1851, while he and Millais were in the country. He had a straw hut built to protect him from the cold, and he continued to work out of doors at night until they returned to London on 6 Dec. His subsequent work on the painting in his London studio on Cheyne Walk was also done at night during periods of full moon. For Christ's lantern he had a lantern made to his designs, and he painted the foreground detail by the light it cast.

The Light of the World is the first of several outdoor night scenes by Hunt. It shows considerably less natural detail than the contemporary sunlit *Hireling Shepherd*, and the colours are also, of course, much more subdued. Those in the foreground have a reddish glow from the light cast by the lantern; those in the moonlit background are cool greens. A by-product of Hunt's work on *The Light of the World* in the winter of 1853 is a small nocturnal view over the Thames from Hunt's studio (Pl. 27b). It shows the deep green water of the river illuminated by golden moonlight on the left and by lights from buildings on the opposite shore on the right. This is only a small oil sketch ($5\frac{3}{4}$ by $7\frac{3}{4}$ inches), which Hunt made from his window and gave to Millais, but it is nonetheless remarkable for its breadth and simplicity. Hunt could do without the insistent detail and strident colours of his sunlit paintings, and this small, almost Whistlerian, sketch demonstrates to what degree he could adapt himself to what he saw before him.

Although Hunt commenced *The Light of the World* in the same year as *The Hireling*

[10]Ruskin, 1903–12, XII, 331–2.
[11]See below, p. 177.

[12]Ruskin, 1903–12, XII, 329–30.

Shepherd, he completed it only in time to send to the Royal Academy in 1854. In the meantime he had painted another outdoor picture. When he exhibited *The Hireling Shepherd* at the Royal Academy in 1852, an admirer, Charles Maude, commissioned him to paint a replica of the group of sheep in the painting's background. Hunt agreed to the commission, but he later sought and received permission to paint an original picture of sheep instead. He spent the summer and autumn of 1852 at Fairlight, near Hastings, painting the picture, *Strayed Sheep* (Pl. 28a), and an additional small landscape, *Fairlight Downs – Sunlight on the Sea* (location unknown). Robert Martineau, who in the previous year had started taking instruction from Hunt, had a place near Fairlight, and it was probably because of his proximity that Hunt decided to work there. Through Martineau, Hunt acquired another disciple, Edward Lear, who shared lodgings with him during his stay. Lear had been painting landscapes professionally since the 1830s. He had not been very successful, but his choosing to be instructed by Hunt, who was fifteen years his junior, and who had never yet exhibited a pure landscape, is testimony to the impact of the landscape passages in *The Hireling Shepherd*.[13]

Strayed Sheep was commissioned as a picture of sheep, and so it is more than a landscape. It has also frequently been interpreted as more than a picture of sheep. F. G. Stephens wrote in 1860 that it was 'of men, not of sheep'.[14] Ruskin in his Oxford lectures of 1883 claimed that *Strayed Sheep* was in its deeper meaning the first of Hunt's sacred paintings, and he applied to it the lines from *Isaiah* liii.6 beginning 'All we like sheep have gone astray'.[15] There also seems to be another kind of symbolism in the picture. Hunt first exhibited it at the Royal Academy in 1853 under the title *Our English Coasts, 1852*, which, Stephens wrote, 'might be taken as a satire on the reported defenseless state of the country against foreign invasion'. This interpretation is not as frivolous as it at first might seem. Hunt's picture composed of a flock of sheep on a cliff, with the sea below to the left, echoes Landseer's *Peace*, which appeared at the Royal Academy in 1846 and in 1852 was in the National Gallery in the Vernon Collection (Pl. 28b). In *Pre-Raphaelitism and the Pre-Raphaelite Brotherhood* Hunt cited *Peace* as a work 'of real point and poetry', which should never be forgotten despite his lower opinion of Landseer's ordinary productions.[16] The point of *Peace* was as a pendant to a companion picture of *War* (destroyed: formerly Tate Gallery). It shows not only sheep, one of which grazes in the mouth of an abandoned cannon, but also goats, a shepherd dog, gulls, and a picknicking family. There are biblical overtones in the imagery: in the figures, who suggest a Holy Family, as well as in the sheep, but they enhance the pacific mood of the scene rather than transform it into a vehicle of religious symbolism. We have seen that in 1850 Landseer also exhibited a *Lost Sheep*, appending to it a biblical quotation.[17] However, this picture of a shepherd carrying a sheep had no visual similarity to *Strayed Sheep*, and as Hunt originally titled his picture *Our English Coasts* their later similarity of titles is accidental. Landseer's *Peace* shows the Channel coast near Dover with its defences fallen into disrepair, and Hunt's *Strayed Sheep* also shows the unguarded Channel coast, whatever else it may mean as well.

Strayed Sheep is a picture of sea, cliffs, sheep, and plants, all lit by brilliant sunlight. It is in a lighter and brighter palette than *The Hireling Shepherd*, or, indeed, almost any preceding oil painting except some of Turner's later works, and, whereas Turner was generally looked upon as extravagantly visionary, Hunt's picture is a sunlit view of a recognizable

[13]See below, p. 152.
[14]Stephens, 1860, p. 23.
[15]Ruskin, 1903–12, XXXIII, 274.

[16]Hunt, 1905, I, 48.
[17]See above, p. 20.

spot on the South Coast of England. His sunlight does not dissolve objects but emphasizes their particular qualities. It glows through the thin membranes of the sheeps' ears, and it illuminates each leaf, blossom, and butterfly separately. Hunt's concern is with what light does to the colour of the specific object or surface, not with the general visual effect. Each thing is obtrusively itself, tightly painted and brightly coloured. The wool of the foreground sheep, if examined closely, reveals an incredible welter of small touches of different colours – red, blue, pink, yellow – as if the artist had examined each strand separately. The earth in the foreground is reddish in sunlight, but violet in shadow. The grey rocks in the centre of the painting become blue in shadow, and the shadows under the legs of the sheep lying down on the upper right are clear blue. We have seen coloured shadows before, in *The Hireling Shepherd* and in Ford Madox Brown's *Pretty Baa-Lambs* and *An English Autumn Afternoon*, but in *Strayed Sheep* Hunt pursued his study of reflected colour with greater consistency throughout the picture. We see it not only in the minutely observed foreground details, but also in the distance. The bit of sky above the cliff is little more than a luminous void, but the sea on the left is broken up into prismatic blues, greens, and violets. The horizon is indistinct and, at the point where the promontory of the cliff meets the sea, lost in haze. F. G. Stephens explained this as a result of the sun shining upon the further side of the cliff:

the sunlight lying upon the place was reflected into a whitish hazy glare, originated by the exhalations that arise from the cliff, which showed above and around it, softening the line of the horizon on the sea, though the cause was invisible, – a very subtle piece of observation, which we never remember to have seen painted before.[18]

Hunt remained at Fairlight working on *Strayed Sheep* until December 1852. Because he spent more time on it than he had intended, he decided that he must ask more than the seventy pounds he had originally agreed upon with Maude. Through the winter of 1852–3 he delayed delivering the picture, and he considered painting yet another sheep picture to fulfil the commission. His correspondence at this time is full of unhappy references to the painting, which ceased when Maude agreed to pay an additional fifty pounds.[19] In 1853 Hunt sent the picture to the Royal Academy, where it was well received. Even the *Art Journal*, which had been consistently hostile, praised it. In the following year it won the fifty pound prize at the Birmingham Academy, and in 1855 it was selected to be among the English pictures sent to the *Exposition Universelle* in Paris.

Of the Pre-Raphaelite pictures shown in the Paris exhibition, which, among others, also included *The Light of the World* and Millais's *Ophelia*, *Strayed Sheep* seems to have made the strongest impression. Thomas Armstrong, who was a student in Paris in 1855, wrote in his memoir that he expected the French to disapprove of a kind of work so utterly new and unknown, and he was surprised on the opening day of the exhibition to see a group of French artists standing before *Strayed Sheep* and admiring it.[20] Armstrong also wrote that he tried to give Delacroix some idea of the Pre-Raphaelite movement before the exhibition began. He apparently had some success; on 30 June 1855, Delacroix recorded in his journal that he had spent the morning looking at the English pictures, which he had admired very much: 'I am really astounded by Hunt's sheep.'[21] The French critics generally recognized the picture's originality but had mixed opinions about its success. In general, they agreed that it may have been truthful, but that it did not appear very natural.

[18]Stephens, 1860, pp 23–4.
[19]John Rylands Library, Manchester, Rylands Eng. MS. 1214, ff. 4–9; Troxell, 1937, p. 37; Hunt, 1905, I, 336–8.

[20]L. M. Lamont, ed., *Thomas Armstrong, C.B.: A Memoir* (London, 1912), p. 6.
[21]Eugène Delacroix, *The Journal*, trans. Walter Pach (New York, 1937) p. 476.

The *Art Journal*, in a survey of French criticism of English pictures at the exhibition, quoted the *Athenaeum Français*: 'The grass gives the individuality of each blade, each with its own light, its reflection and its shadow – each part astonishes by the truthfulness of its reproduction, and nevertheless the whole wants truth, and wholly fails to recall nature.'[22] Another critic quoted by the *Art Journal*, Maxime du Camp, saw Hunt as a disciple of Landseer who by his 'false and fantastic tints' succeeded in painting a picture which seemed to be seen through a prism.[23] Du Camp was perhaps more perceptive than the *Art Journal*, which found the Landseer connection ludicrous. Théophile Gautier devoted a chapter of his *Beaux-Arts en Europe* to Millais and Hunt. He compared *Strayed Sheep* to a work by Charles de la Berge, a French painter with a reputation for a fanatical love of finish, and, declared Gautier, the Hunt made the de la Berge look like a 'vague pochade'. Hunt's details took on an exaggerated importance, as if seen through a microscope; a blade of grass was as important as a tree. No painting in the exhibition was as disconcerting; although it appeared most false, it was 'précisément le plus vrai'.[24]

Gautier thought that Millais and Hunt would create a school in England, but he doubted that they would be imitated in France, for the practical reason that their methods were too demanding. On both counts Gautier was correct, although we could adduce additional reasons why French artists did not imitate Pre-Raphaelite detail. Nonetheless, Hunt's equation of light and colour, which produced a prismatic palette, did anticipate central interests in subsequent French painting. At the end of the century, Robert de la Sizeranne, in *La Peinture Anglaise contemporaine*, a work of unquestioning Anglophilic enthusiasm, did claim that Pre-Raphaelitism had contained the germ of all contemporary painting, and he made *Strayed Sheep* his chief example:

The blood-red sheep in indigo bushes, on rocks chiselled like sugar-candy, under an audacious sky, recall the worst excesses of our 'luminists'; and, remembering that this picture dates forty-one years back, it is a question whether it is not one of the earliest manifestations of the open-air school, and whether the violet horses of M. Besnard are not the descendants, by a strange pedigree, of the red sheep of Mr. Hunt. With all his extravagances Hunt made a colour speak which before him had slumbered heavily. Sometimes it is only a flash, but by this flash it may be seen how right the P.R.B. were to desert the studio for the fields, and a misunderstood tradition for nature . . .[25]

Although de la Sizeranne was right in recognizing the revolutionary and prophetic qualities in Hunt's picture, there is no evidence that it had any actual influence on the younger French artists. In England, with more historic justification, similar claims were made for the picture. In 1859, Ruskin cited *Strayed Sheep* in *Academy Notes*, along with Hunt's *Valentine Rescuing Sylvia from Proteus* and Turner's *Sun of Venice* and *Slave Ship*, as an example of a magnificent effect of sunshine colour 'of a kind necessarily unintelligible to the ordinary observer', which he contrasted to the popularly effective sacrifice of colour in Cuyp, Claude, Wilson and all other supposed masters of sunshine.[26] In his Oxford lectures of 1883, published as *The Art of England* in 1884, Ruskin reconsidered the picture, which he had seen exhibited at the Fine Art Society in London the previous year. In the first lecture of the series, which was devoted to Hunt and Rossetti, Ruskin claimed that a new 'attentive' landscape had arisen in England. The first example had been the apparently unimportant picture, *Strayed Sheep*, which

[22]*Art Journal*, 1855, p. 252
[23]*Ibid.*, 1856, p. 79.
[24]Théophile Gautier, *Les Beaux-Arts en Europe – 1855*, première série (Paris, 1857) pp. 42–3.

[25]Robert de La Sizeranne, *English Contemporary Art*, trans. H. M. Poynter (London, 1898), pp. 76–7.
[26]Ruskin, 1903–12, XIV, 225–6.

at once achieved all that can ever be done in that kind ... It showed to us, for the first time in the history of art, the absolutely faithful balance of colour and shade by which actual sunshine might be transposed into a key in which the harmonies possible with material pigments should yet produce the same impressions upon the mind which were caused by the light itself.

All earlier work had either subdued nature into narrower truths or had been conventional:

Turner's, so bold in conventionalism that it is credible to few of you, and offensive to many. But the pure natural green and tufted gold of the herbage in the hollow of that little sea-cliff must be recognized for true merely by a minute's pause of attention. Standing long before the picture, you were soothed by it, and raised into such peace as you are intended to find in the glory and stillness of summer, possessing all things.[27]

In 1859, Ruskin pronounced it impossible to paint sunshine colour with the pitch of light which has true relation to the shadow. But he declared that sunshine was necessary to landscape, and that the public would come to understand its expression. Now, twenty-four years later, the public was apparently ready for Hunt, if not for Turner. Hunt's colours were still not literally true, but he had found the equivalents to give the optical impression of sunlight.

Hunt began his second picture, *Fairlight Downs – Sunlight on the Sea*, in August 1852, while still working on *Strayed Sheep*. It has disappeared, but according to descriptions by F. G. Stephens and William Michael Rossetti it was a view of the sea from the Sussex Downs on a grey, hazy day. In the foreground there were green downs, ploughed fields, haystacks, trees, some sheep, and a spaniel, but all this was of subordinate importance to the prismatic effect of shifting light and colour over the sea.

The sky, mysteriously broken with pale tints of green and drifts of violet-ashen cloud, shifts over the expanse of brilliant sea, emerald-green to the left, passing into dancing ripple and the broad blinding space of central light, with streaks of opaque blue and orange rifts up to the horizon.

Thus William Michael Rossetti.[28] Stephens described the colour of the sea as that of turquoises and pearls.[29]

In 1858 Hunt paid a return visit to Fairlight, where he painted a small portrait of a girl, *The Schoolgirl's Hymn* (Ashmolean Museum, Oxford), which he exhibited in 1859. The background of this picture shows a view over fields to a sea of pale blues, greens, and violets. He may have finished *Sunlight on the Sea* during this visit, as he first exhibited it only at the end of 1858. The critic Philip Gilbert Hamerton saw *Fairlight Downs – Sunlight on the Sea* when it was exhibited and discussed it in an article, 'The Relation between Photography and Painting', comparing it to a marine photograph by Gustave le Gray. Hamerton concluded that Hunt's painting was truer than the photograph in light and dark, in perspective, and in containing more factual information.[30] On the other hand, the critic for the *Art Journal* saw only exaggeration: 'So subservient here is nature to execution, that we feel only the insolence of manner.'[31]

At the beginning of 1854, after completing *The Light of the World* and *The Awakening Conscience*, Hunt set off on a trip to the Holy Land in fulfilment of a long-standing ambition. His main reason for going was religious: he wished to paint biblical subjects in their actual settings and he apparently first intended to paint a picture of *Jacob in the Wilderness*, set in the desert of Sinai. Hunt arrived in Cairo in January 1854. There he was joined by the landscape painter Thomas Seddon, who had preceded him to the East. The two made plans for their excursion to Sinai, practising for the trip by camping in a tent near the

[27]*Ibid.*, XXXIII, 272–3.
[28]Rossetti, 1867, p. 244.
[29]Stephens, 1860, pp. 54–5.

[30]Hamerton, 1874, pp. 58–9.
[31]*Art Journal*, 1858, p. 355.

Pyramids and seeking the advice of Edward Lear, who was also in Egypt at the time and was an experienced traveller. However, the project had to be abandoned; on 27 March Seddon wrote to his fiancée:

You will be, perhaps, surprised to hear that our plans are changed; but the fact is, that Hunt discovered, two or three weeks ago, that when Jacob left his father's house he was a middle-aged man of forty, which has stopped him from painting a picture of him in the wilderness, as he had intended to have done at Sinai; so that, not being a landscape painter, he thought he could not spend a whole summer there.[32]

Instead, Hunt and Seddon travelled to Jerusalem. As soon as they arrived there, in June 1854, Hunt set to work upon an ambitious figural painting of *The Finding of Christ in the Temple* (City Art Gallery, Birmingham). He originally hoped to have this picture ready for the next year's Royal Academy exhibition, but, because of various difficulties, chiefly the lack of willing models, he was not able to complete the picture in the East. He brought the partly completed canvas back with him to London in 1856 and continued to work on it there, finally finishing it in 1860. The picture is set inside the Temple. In the background there is a view of the Mount of Olives, which Hunt based on a 'Map-like sketch' made from the roof of the Mosque As Sakrah, but this forms only a small part of the painting.

In the autumn of 1854, when Hunt realized that he would not be able to exhibit *The Finding of Christ in the Temple* in 1855, he decided to put it aside and take up another subject, one in which there would be no problems with human models: *The Scapegoat* (Pl. 29a). He still had trouble with his models, one of which died, and he did not have *The Scapegoat* ready for the 1855 exhibition either, as he completed it only in June of that year, but he did exhibit it in 1856. The subject, which Hunt explained in a note in the catalogue, is the Old-Testament Scapegoat who is driven from the Temple on the Day of Atonement, bearing the sins of the community.[33] He wears around his horns a scarlet fillet, which will become white if the sins are forgiven. In the book of Leviticus, the goat is said to bear the iniquities into a land not inhabited, which in Hunt's visualization has become the barren shore at the southern end of the Dead Sea.

The picture is thus of a religious subject, based on the Bible and also upon the *Talmud*. It is symbolic; the goat is a prototype of the Saviour. But the goat is also a goat, and in the context of Hunt's art he is related to the sheep of *The Hireling Shepherd* and *Strayed Sheep*. Like those pictures, *The Scapegoat* has a connection with Landseer. When Hunt thought of the subject, while studying the Jewish ritual, it struck him as one suited for Landseer: 'I had in fact resolved to take the opportunity to talk to him of it; but now I reflected that in Syria I had a possibility of painting it worthily which he could never have . . .'[34] Hunt's thinking of Landseer may have led to his visualization of the barren shore where the goat has wandered to expire. The subject parallels pictures of animal drama by Landseer such as *The Sanctuary* of 1842 (Royal Collection), which shows an exhausted stag, who has fled his pursuers to the deserted shore of a highland loch.[35] In the background of *The Sanctuary*, on the other side of the water, the sun sets over a range of mountains. Derek Hill has suggested that a sequel to *The Sanctuary*, the painting Landseer exhibited in 1844 as *Coming Events Cast Their Shadows Before* (*The Challenge*; Pl. 29b), may have inspired Hunt's picture.[36] Its subject of two stags about to fight is not as close as that of *The Sanctuary*, and it is seen by

[32]Seddon, 1858, pp. 61–2.
[33]Reprinted in Bennett, 1969, p. 42.
[34]Hunt, 1905, I, 447.
[35]Reproduced in *Engravings from Landseer* (Boston, 1876) pl. III.

[36]Derek Hill, 'Landseer as Craftsman', in *Paintings and Drawings by Sir Edwin Landseer*, exhibition catalogue, (Royal Academy of Arts, London, 1961), p. xiii.

moonlight rather than the setting sun of *The Sanctuary* and *The Scapegoat*; but in the foreground Landseer's bellowing stag stands on a barren shore across which dead trees lie, and in the distance, again on the far side of a body of water, there is a range of mountains. Their bottoms are in shadow, but the upper parts are lit by the moon, giving the setting of impending struggle a feeling of visionary unreality. Hunt's goat stands on the salt marshes at the edge of the Dead Sea, his feet breaking through the crust. Around him are the skeletons of animals which previously died there, and in the background, across the sea, are the mountains of Edom, whose upper reaches are a flaming violet in the setting sun. The setting is, if anything, even more unworldly and inhospitable than that of Landseer's painting.

Hunt decided to paint *The Scapegoat* in the early autumn of 1854. With some friends, he made a trip to the Dead Sea in October to look for a site, finally selecting a salt-encrusted shore at Oosdom, which he believed to be the biblical Sodom,[37] at the southern end of the Sea. He deferred beginning the painting until the correct season, well after the Day of Atonement. On 13 Nov. 1854, he left Jerusalem to encamp at Oosdom and begin the picture's background. It is unclear how long Hunt stayed there; apparently it was not over a fortnight. He took a white goat with him from Jersusalem, but, as in *The Hireling Shepherd*, he did no more than the landscape on the spot, leaving the goat to be painted back in Jerusalem. Hunt was well aware of what an extraordinary venture he had undertaken, and he kept a diary of the trip. From this we learn that he began by copying in the distant mountains, and that he worked at all parts of the picture except the goat. Because of the impatience of his Arab guides, he had to cut his stay shorter than he intended. When he left, no part of the picture was entirely finished.

I left reluctantly altho' what is done already inclines me to continue it at home in hopes of making a picture of some interest in its components – it would not all be painted so scrupulously from nature as I should like but at least I have made every exertion to obtain the proper opportunity and some truth in its features must be the result I hope.[38]

In Jerusalem, after his return, he painted the goat, a camel's skeleton from one found locally, and the rest of the foreground details. He painted the sky from the roof of a friend's house which allowed him a view of the mountains beyond the Dead Sea.

The lengths to which Hunt went to paint his background emphasize the fact that *The Scapegoat* is not only a picture of a goat, or of a religious symbol; it also contains an extensive landscape, which purports to be an accurate representation of a specific place. There is no scriptural source for showing the goat on the shores of the Dead Sea; the choice of location was apparently Hunt's idea. His belief that a picture of the place would be of interest for its own sake was why he did not forego the subject in favour of Landseer but painted it himself. In March 1855 he wrote to Rossetti, 'I don't know I should have thought the subject demanding immediate illustration had I not had the opportunity of painting this extraordinary spot as background from nature.'[39] While at work on the painting he was informed of the existence of an etching of the subject of *The Scapegoat*. He had believed that no one had painted the subject before, but the new information did not disturb him: 'I don't care for anything that could be designed in England as the interest of the illustration depends upon the locality so much'.[40] In his diary of the trip to the Dead Sea Hunt described a view to the south of the Sea which he had seen en route:

[37]Letter to Thomas Combe dated 7 Sept. 1855, John Rylands Library, Manchester, Rylands Eng. MS. 1213, f. 12.

[38]John Rylands Library, Manchester, Rylands Eng. MS. 1210, f. 7.

[39]Troxell, 1937, pp. 40–41.

[40]Letter to Thomas Combe dated 31 March 1855, John Rylands Library, Manchester, Rylands Eng. MS. 1213, f. 5.

Never was so extraordinary a scene of beautifully arranged horrible wilderness . . . I can understand the use of art in thinking how interesting a picture of such a scene would be, and in thinking that I was doing right morally in undertaking a work of similar value in conveying important knowledge I commended myself to God's merciful protection.[41]

When Hunt exhibited the picture at the Royal Academy he began the explanatory note in the catalogue with an identification of the site before going on to explain the biblical meaning of the subject.

The location, in addition to its own topographical interest, was also appropriate to Hunt's subject. Hunt's description of the site in his diary shows that he saw a deep significance in its desolate beauty:

The mountains lie afar beautiful as precious stones but near they are dry and scorched, the rose colour is the burnt ashes of the grate, the golden plain is the salt and naked sand. The Sea is heaven's own blue like a diamond more lovely in a king's diadem than in the mines of the Indies but as it gushes up through the broken ice-like salt on the beach, it is black, full of asphalt ocum – and in the hand slimy, and smarting as a sting. No one can stand and say it is not accursed of God. If in all there are sensible figures of men's secret deeds and thoughts, then is this the horrible figure of Sin – a varnished deceit – earth joys at hand but Hell gaping behind, a stealthy, terrible enemy for ever.[42]

Hunt seems to have done everything in his power to emphasize the unworldly, hellish aspects of the scene. The goat stands in as hopeless a situation as could be imagined; his doom is foreshadowed by the skeletons surrounding him. The setting sun has turned the sky orange and the distant mountains into lurid purples and violets. In a small version of the picture (City Art Gallery, Manchester), in which Hunt experimented with a black rather than white goat, he also introduced a rainbow, 'the celestial image of heaven's mercy,'[43] but in the finished picture three is no such sign of hope.

The background of *The Scapegoat* is the most extensive and most ambitious landscape that Hunt had yet painted. The picture is a bit larger than *The Hireling Shepherd* and considerably larger than *Strayed Sheep*, and the landscape is relatively more important in the composition than in either of these works. It also contains a distant view which is more important than the study of foreground detail. *The Scapegoat* is comparable in Hunt's art to *The Blind Girl* and *Autumn Leaves* in Millais's, and all three pictures were exhibited in 1856. Like Millais's pictures, *The Scapegoat* also shows some loosening of the minute Pre-Raphaelite handling of previous years. The foreground detail and the wool of the goat do not have the same crispness nor elaboration as comparable parts of *Strayed Sheep*. The background also seems less crisp than anything in Hunt's previous works, but there is nothing in any of them which is at all comparable. Like the background of *Autumn Leaves*, it shows distant hills at sunset, and there is a new range of emotive colours. But whereas Millais was slipping toward a more conventional vision, so that Ruskin could compare him to Giorgione, Hunt was becoming more extraordinarily personal. Throughout the painting we can see the concern with reflected light and colour of Hunt's earlier pictures pushed to new extremes. In previous pictures, however garish or forced their colours might seem, Hunt had at least applied his vision to the depiction of the familiar English landscape. In *The Scapegoat* his lack of pictorial inhibition was combined with a landscape which was both unfamiliar and, by English standards, fantastic. Hunt may have painted what he saw, but by choice he saw strange things, and he saw them at their most vivid pitch. He chose to paint at sunset, and he waited for months in Jerusalem before finishing the picture so he

[41]John Rylands Library, Manchester, Rylands Eng.   [42]*Ibid.*, f. 5.
MS. 1210, f. 4v.   [43]Hunt, 1905, I, 456.

could paint pink clouds into the normally empty sky. The colours are seen with an intensity and expressive power which go beyond naturalistic observation. Behind the goat, the landscape screams out in oppressive, strident chords which underscore the message of impersonal and implacable doom.

The public reaction to *The Scapegoat* was mixed. Most critics did not see a deep meaning in the subject, and many were dubious about the picture's value as a record of the place. The *Art Journal* decided that the picture was 'useless for any good purpose'. The only interesting thing to its critic's eye was the deposit of salt in the foreground; he declared flatly that the mountains of Edom were not as red and blue as Hunt had painted them.[44] Even Ford Madox Brown, who admired the painting – 'by the might of genius, out of an old goat, and some saline incrustations, can be made one of the most tragic and impressive works in the annals of art' – was disturbed by the background which was 'hard in colour, and eats up the foreground'.[45] Ruskin devoted a long review to *The Scapegoat* in *Academy Notes*, but he also had mixed feelings. He praised Hunt for undertaking it, and he asserted its value as a record of the place:

Of all the scenes in the Holy Land, there are none whose present aspect tends so distinctly to confirm the statements of Scripture, as this condemned shore. It is therefore exactly the scene of which it might seem most desirable to give a perfect idea to those who cannot see it for themselves; it is that also fewest travellers are able to see; and which, I suppose, no one but Mr. Hunt himself would ever have dreamed of making the subject of a close pictorial study.

He praised the temper and the toil which produced the picture, but, 'regarded merely as a landscape, or as a composition', the picture was a total failure. It lacked nearly all the 'effective manipulation' of Hunt's earlier works. It had no good hair-painting, nor hoof-painting, and the animal in the exact centre made it look like a sign. The mountains were also a failure, but Ruskin forgave this, because 'the forms of large distant landscape are a quite new study to the Pre-Raphaelites, and they cannot be expected to conquer them at first'. Ruskin also forgave Hunt's making the reflection in the water brighter than the sky above it, though when Millais did the same thing the following year he called it 'singularly disgraceful'. In Hunt's case, Ruskin surmised, correctly, that the water and the sky were painted separately at different seasons. Thus, although both were painted from nature, they were discordant, and the reflected colours could not be toned down because of their complexity.[46]

Before 1854 Hunt painted only an occasional pure landscape, as opposed to landscape backgrounds to other kinds of pictures. The earlier landscapes that we now know can be classified as studies or ancillary works rather than as independent pictures. It is worth noting that Hunt did not exhibit any of his earlier landscapes until after his trip to the East, and in the cases of *The Haunted Manor* and *Fairlight Downs – Sunlight on the Sea* he may not have completed them until then. In the East, he did paint a considerable number of landscapes in watercolour, three of which he exhibited along with *The Scapegoat* at the

[44]*Art Journal*, 1856, p. 170.
[45]Hueffer, 1896, p. 125.
[46]Ruskin, 1903–12, XIV, 61–6 and 108. Hunt protested against the criticism of the reflections in a letter to Ruskin dated 4 May 1858: 'There can be no doubt that in fact the light reflected in water is more or less lower in tone than the sky above – it is brought down thus however into violent opposition with the darkest parts of the subject which to the eye gives it a luminosity such as no opposition of mere pigment will produce unless the literal truth of proportion is departed from. To the eye in some cases the reflection is *quite as bright* as the sky itself – Millais who always works by an impression and not on theory – painted his water thus in the *Dream of the Past* [Pl. 24b]. Your matter of fact criticism however confused him so that on its return in repainting parts in his studio he dimmed the water and I hesitate not to say spoiled the picture. Candidly I believed your strictures on *The Scapegoat* have not depressed its value.' (Formerly collection of Mrs. Elizabeth Burt, partly quoted in Sotheby, 1970, no. 908.)

Royal Academy in 1856, as soon as he returned. The topographic interest of their subjects was clearly the motivation for these works, as it was for the background of *The Scapegoat*, and Hunt exhibited them with titles indicating exactly what they showed. Previously his landscape studies and landscape backgrounds had had no topographic interest. In *Strayed Sheep*, which does show a specific place, the distinctive character of the place is not very important, and when Hunt exhibited the picture he did not indicate the location; the interest is not in the place but in nature. In the East, Hunt reversed his priorities, and his Eastern landscapes have some of the quality of a tourist's mementoes of famous and faraway places.

Hunt did not go to the East to paint landscapes, but in Egypt, where he first arrived, he discovered that he could not easily paint figural subjects. He disliked the Egyptian scenery:

The country offers nothing with more than antiquarian interest as landscape; the Pyramids themselves are extremely ugly blocks, as one always knew, and arranged with most unpicturesque taste . . . There are palm trees about, which attract my passing admiration, but for all else one might as well sketch in Hackney Marsh.[47]

He professed no interest in modern Cairo, but he did feel a duty to record traditional manners and customs that were passing away,[48] and he began two genre subjects: *A Street Scene in Cairo: The Lantern Maker's Courtship* (City Art Gallery, Birmingham) and *The Afterglow in Egypt* (Southampton Art Gallery). He had difficulties in both works in getting models to sit, and he finished neither picture until long after his return to England. He had no such troubles with landscape, so, despite protestations of not wishing to be a *paysagiste*, he began to paint views in watercolour. By limiting his landscapes to this medium, he apparently felt he was making less of a commitment to the lower category of subject.

Soon after Hunt's arrival in Egypt, he encamped with Thomas Seddon at Giza, near the Sphinx. Both artists painted watercolours of the Sphinx. Hunt's, which he exhibited at the Royal Academy in 1856, shows the head of the Sphinx seen from the rear, with a view over the desert beyond to the pyramids of Saqqara on the horizon (Pl. 50a). At the time Hunt and Seddon were at Giza the French Egyptologist Mariette was excavating the Sphinx, and Hunt's curious view may have been intended to show the recently uncovered rock. It is almost a geological study of pittings and striations. In the foreground lies a dead snake, probably the one whose killing Hunt described in a letter to Thomas Combe.[49] He may have included it in the watercolour for the amusement of Seddon, who had a passion for snakes and snake-charmers. At Giza Hunt also began two watercolours of gazelles in the desert: a small one signed and dated 1854 (Walker Art Gallery, Liverpool), and a larger one, which he did not complete until 1866.[50] In the former a single gazelle is the main subject; in the latter four gazelles are seen in the midst of a panoramic desert landscape. These beasts, along with the snake in *The Sphinx* and a flock of ducks in the foreground of a slighter watercolour of *The Great Pyramid* (private collection),[51] suggest that Hunt in the period following the success of *Strayed Sheep* was as ready to become an *animaliste* as a *paysagiste*. Indeed, *The Scapegoat*, begun later in 1854, was a considerably more ambitious undertaking than any of Hunt's pure landscapes.

Seddon remained at Giza, with a few interruptions, until he and Hunt left Egypt for

[47]Letter to Millais dated 16 March 1854, Hunt, 1905, I, 380n.
[48]*Ibid.*, 377, 380n. See also Holman-Hunt, 1969, p. 122.
[49]Letter to Thomas Combe dated 26 April 1854, formerly collection of Mrs. Elizabeth Burt, quoted in Sotheby, 1970, no. 887. See also Hunt, 1905, I, 380n.

[50]Sold Christie's, London, 9 Nov. 1971, no. 152, and reproduced in the catalogue; also reproduced in Hunt, 1905, I, 390. The Liverpool watercolour is reproduced in Bennett, 1969, pl. 45.
[51]Bennett, 1969, pl. 44.

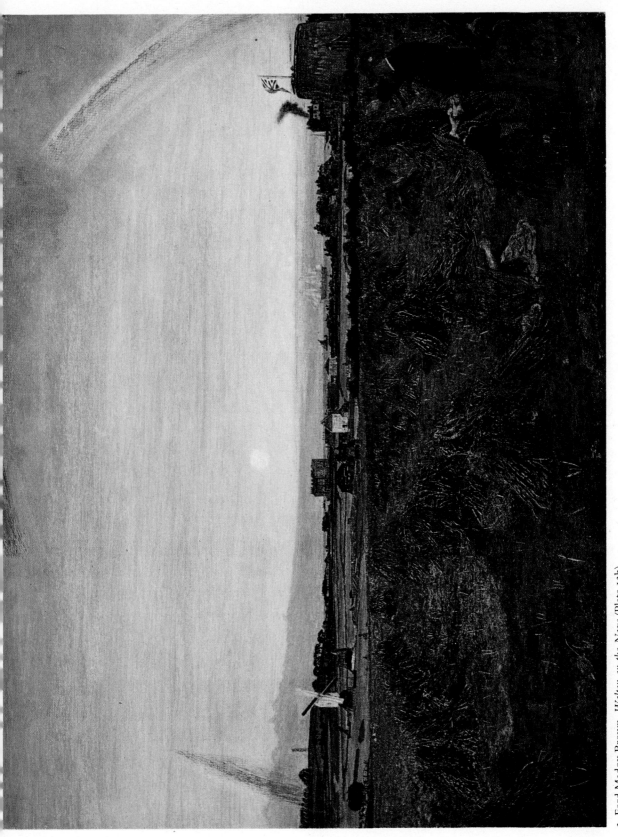

3. Ford Madox Brown, *Walton-on-the-Naze* (Plate 13b)

4. William Holman Hunt, *The Plain of Rephaim from Mount Zion* (Plate 32a)

Jerusalem, but Hunt moved back to Cairo, returning in April to Giza to finish his view of the Sphinx.[52] In Cairo he painted a watercolour which he exhibited in 1857 as *Sketch from a House in New Ca., Looking Towards Gebel Mokattum*, but which has since usually been known as *Cairo: Sunset on the Gebel Mokattum* (Pl. 30a). The Gebel Mokattum, or el Muqattam, is the range of barren hills bordering the city to the East. The real subject of this watercolour, and to a degree of that of the Sphinx, is the colour of the desert, which Hunt did find beautiful despite his dislike of Egyptian scenery.[53] In *The Sphinx* the desert is golden; in *Sunset on the Gebel Mokattum* it is a brilliant pink, and the buildings of Cairo in the middle distance are orange in the late afternoon sun. In both the colours are at an even higher pitch than in *Strayed Sheep*, Hunt's most recent attempt at painting sunlight. Cast shadows on the hills and in the foreground of *The Sphinx* are bright blue, and in *Sunset on the Gebel Mokattum* the foreground, which is in shadow, is blue and violet.

Hunt and Seddon left Egypt in mid-May 1854. They arrived in Jerusalem on 3 June. Hunt remained there until October 1855, then travelled overland north to Beirut, and sailed for home in November 1855. He was more enthusiastic about Palestine than about Egypt. To his pious eyes most of the landmarks had an intrinsic interest and appeal, but he also found the landscape beautiful for its own sake. Long passages in his memoirs describe his rapturous response to the scenery. He repudiated the prevailing opinion that the scenery in itself was devoid of attraction. Agriculturally, much of it was unproductive,

But there is a beauty independent of fruitfulness, which perhaps it is too much to expect all to see, just as it is unreasonable to require the ordinary observer to appreciate the proportions and lines of a human skeleton . . . Syria is intrinsically beautiful. The formation of the country, the spread of the plains, the rise of the hills, the lute-like lines of the mounts, all are exquisite; and with these fundmental merits there is often enough of vegetation to add the charm of life to the whole.[54]

Now Hunt did wish to make a pictorial record of the scenery, and he wrote to Rossetti complaining that he was unable to do so:

I should be dreadfully sad in leaving the place with so little of its countless beauties on canvas or in any way portrayed, for in fact, I can promise literally nothing. The figure picture I am doing has no landscape, and the other is of a distant place. One can do nothing in so short a time as a twelvemonth.[55]

Nonetheless, although Hunt promised literally nothing, he did make several watercolours in and around Jerusalem and on his trip north at the end of his stay.

At the Royal Academy in 1856 he exhibited two which he had made in Jerusalem. These were *View from the Mount of Offence, Looking Towards the Dead Sea and the Mountains of Moab: Morning*, which is usually known as *The Dead Sea from Siloam* (Pl. 30b), and *Jerusalem by Moonlight: Looking over the Site of the Temple to the Mount of Olives*, which is reproduced in Hunt's memoirs as *Mohamedan Festival at Jersusalem* and has also been called *Jerusalem during Ramazan* (Pl. 31a).[56] These two pictures are approximately the same size as *The Sphinx* and *Sunset on the Gebel Mokattum*, fourteen inches being the horizontal and larger dimension of each. Hunt also made one larger watercolour in Jerusalem, *The Plain of Rephaim from Mount Zion* (Pl. 32a and Col. Pl. 4), which is fourteen by twenty inches, and a second the same size of *Nazareth* (Pl. 32b), but he did not exhibit these two works until 1861. In his memoirs Hunt mentioned working on the former landscape just before his departure from Jerusalem; the latter he began during a stay of several days at Nazareth on his journey to Beirut. In a diary he kept during the trip he recorded working on the water-

[52]Seddon, 1858, p. 71.
[53]Hunt, 1905, I, 380n.
[54]*Ibid.*, II, 42.

[55]21 March 1855, Troxell, 1937, p. 41.
[56]Hunt, 1905, I, 411.

colour of *Nazareth* from 24 through 27 October, labouring each day from before sunrise until sunset. On 25 Oct. he wrote, 'If I can only advance it enough it will be a great pleasure to me all my days in England', but he left off two days later with sorrow that he could not bring the drawing to a higher state of completion.[57]

Hunt's remark in his diary implies that he intended to keep *Nazareth* in his own possession. However, in 1861 it was bought by Thomas Plint along with *The Plain of Rephaim, Jerusalem during Ramazan, The Dead Sea from Siloam,* and *Cairo: Sunset on the Gebel Mokattum.* Plint died shortly after, and in the sale of his collection at Christie's in 1862 the Hunt watercolours were accompanied by the following note in the catalogue: 'The five well-known works, begun from nature in 1855, and completed in 1861, lately exhibited'.[58] As the three smaller watercolours had all been exhibited in 1856 and 1857 (and again in 1861), the 'completed in 1861' could only refer to the two larger ones, which first appeared publicly only in 1861.[59]

Jerusalem during Ramazan was apparently the first watercolour begun in the Holy Land. In *Pre-Raphaelitism and the Pre-Raphaelite Brotherhood* there is a description of its commencement:

One evening at home, when the moon was shining splendidly, I raised myself to look over the high wall on my roof, and stood gazing on the impressive view of the Mosque As Sakrah [on the site of the Temple], the swaying dark cypresses; the arcades and eastern wall stood backgrounded by the Mount of Olives. It was a poetic and absorbing scene, and watching it from hour to hour for the most suitable light and shade, the moonlight effect enchanted me, and I proceeded to make a drawing.[60]

There is no mention of the torchlit procession which can be seen in the centre of the picture. Hunt's inspiration was the poetic effect of the moonlight. Thus, the scene shows a continuation of the interest in nocturnal effects which he had displayed in *The Light of the World* and in his slight sketch of the *Thames by Night.* As in those works, there is a combination of artificial light and natural moonlight, and the colours are predominantly pale blues and greens. Despite the difference in colour, the composition is similar to that of *Cairo: Sunset on the Gebel Mokattum.* Both watercolours show views across cities to hills beyond, and both have running across the foregrounds the parapets of the roofs which provide the vantage-points. In the lower left corner of *Jerusalem during Ramazan* a woman leans across the wall to watch the procession; *Cairo: Sunset on the Gebel Mokattum* shows a child looking over the wall and a woman sifting grain.

Hunt's other Eastern landscapes also have high vantage-points. This is not so conspicuous in *The Sphinx,* but we are high enough to see to Saqqara some ten or eleven miles to the South. In *The Plain of Rephaim from Zion* and *Nazareth* there are figures on high foreground promontories which are squeezed into the corners of the compositions. In *The Dead Sea from Siloam* the land drops away from the vantage-point so abruptly that there is no actual foreground, but we see the tops of the trees growing on the slope before us and a small figure climbing in them.

The foreground figures and their situation above the landscapes recall Ford Madox Brown's use of foreground figures and plateau landscape in *An English Autumn Afternoon* (Pl. 9). Like Brown, Hunt was not primarily a landscape painter, and his repeated use of similar arrangements is an obvious device to give his views some compositional structure.

[57]John Rylands Library, Manchester, Rylands Eng. MS. 1211, ff. 69–70.

[58]Christie's, London, 7 March 1862, nos. 192–6.

[59]See Bennett, 1969, p. 77, no. 160, and p. 79, no. 170,

where, however, the date of exhibition is given as 1862. The three smaller watercolours had previously hung in Hunt's dining room; see Boyce, 1941, p. 31.

[60]Hunt, 1905, I, 408–09.

In his placing of the figures on a foreground plateau we can discern Brown's influence, transmitted by Hunt's travelling companion, Thomas Seddon. Seddon used the plateau landscape both in the East in his *Jerusalem and the Valley of Jehoshaphat* (Pl. 51b), and earlier in *Léhon, from Mont Parnasse* of 1853 (Pl. 51a). Before Seddon travelled to the East, Brown had been his mentor, and the composition of *Léhon, from Mont Parnasse* depends obviously and heavily upon *An English Autumn Afternoon*.

In *Cairo: Sunset on the Gebel Mokattum* and *Jerusalem during Ramazan* the figures are innocuous and seem to exist only to serve a compositional function. But the activity in the foregrounds of Hunt's other Eastern watercolours deserves attention. The snake in *The Sphinx* and the figure in the trees in *The Dead Sea from Siloam* have been mentioned. In *Nazareth* there are two youths, one of whom is reaching for a stone with his left hand in order, apparently, to kill another snake. In *The Plain of Rephaim* a bearded man in Eastern garb carries a small child up the rocky hillside. They are accompanied by another, larger child. The man has lost his hat, which falls through the air below him, and below it are two boys, the lower parts of whose bodies are cut by the picture frame. One boy has his arm upraised, but whether it is to hail the man, attack him, or catch his hat, it is impossible to tell. The impression given is that the man is rescuing the child he carries from the boys. However, Hunt mentions in his memoir that he worked on the watercolour in a high wind, so the incident may have only to do with that.[61]

In all the watercolours the figures are placed at the very edge of the composition, and they are usually cut by the frame at the bottom of the picture. In *The Plain of Rephaim* the left side of the picture also slices off the arm of the boy accompanying the bearded man. We have seen that in *Love at First Sight* Hunt cut through the lower extremities of the deer in the foreground with the bottom of his picture. In *Strayed Sheep* the animal nearest us and those along the right hand edge of the picture are again only partly visible within the rectangle of the picture space. Hunt repeated this practice in later works such as the watercolour *Festa at Fiesole* of 1868 (Pl. 34b) and the oil painting *The Plain of Esdraelon from the Heights above Nazareth* of 1870-7 (Pl. 33b). In all these examples except *Strayed Sheep* the figures or animals are only appendages to the landscapes. The works give the feeling that Hunt felt he had to include figures to enliven the compositions, but then he ruthlessly shoved them aside so they would be in the way as little as possible. But he seems also to have wanted to suggest by the way he cut off the compositions or activities that the space of the picture is only an arbitrary slice of a larger whole. The snake in *The Sphinx*, for example, makes the image less self-contained, because it implies an action and an actor who is not shown. In *Fairlight Downs - Sunlight on the Sea*, according to William Michael Rossetti's description, a black spaniel chased a walking-stick which had been thrown by its unseen master from outside of the picture space: 'Slight as it is, this small familiar incident brings the whole thing home to you with doubled force of undiluted fact.'[62] What Rossetti, writing in 1858, implies is that Hunt was attempting to enhance the sense of the picture's reality by a snapshot-like exclusion of part of the incident, like Degas but a decade earlier.

Hunt painted *The Dead Sea from Siloam* in the light of early morning.[63] It shows the view looking East from Jerusalem toward the Dead Sea, and, as we can see from the shadows of the trees on the lower right, looking into the morning sun. He painted *The Plain of Rephaim* in the evenings, an hour or two before sunset. The view is to the South,

---

[61]*Ibid.*, II, 34.
[62]Rossetti, 1867, p. 244.

[63]Letter to Thomas Combe dated 7 Sept. 1855, John Rylands Library, Manchester, Rylands Eng. MS. 1213, f. 12.

and the light falls from the right. The foreground and distant hills are brightly lit, but most of the middle distance is in shadow. In *Nazareth*, upon which because of his limited time Hunt worked throughout the day, the effect is of general open sunniness with little shadow. The view is from the hills north of the town, which is nestled in the middle distance. Beyond stretches a vast, barren landscape, similar to those in *The Plain of Rephaim* and *The Dead Sea from Siloam*. The colours of all three are comparable to those of *Cairo: Sunset on the Gebel Mokattum* although not at quite such a vivid pitch. The mountains in the far distance of *The Dead Sea from Siloam* are seen faintly through the morning mist over the Sea, and the mountains in the distance of *Nazareth* also appear somewhat de-materialized in the brilliant light.

In all three watercolours, however, most of the expanse of landscape is depicted with Pre-Raphaelite precision. As we have seen, what Hunt admired in Syria was the beauty of the larger lines of the landscape. What his views show with insistent clarity is the rigid rocky structure of the terrain, traversed by the long lines of roads, walls, and aqueducts. The horizons are high; the skies are empty, or nearly empty. Vegetation is of minimal importance, and the foregrounds serve mainly as foils for the distant views. If we recall the overweening importance given by Hunt to details of plant life in *The Hireling Shepherd* and *Strayed Sheep*, we can see the very different focus in these later landscapes. Their large lines give visual embodiment to his comparison of the formation of the country to the human skeleton. Hunt never returned to the microscopic botanic study of the years before 1854, but, unlike Millais, he never abandoned the integrity of vision that lay behind that study. His Eastern landscapes are just as scrupulous as his earlier works, and in their way they are perhaps even more original.

In addition to the six finished Eastern watercolours which we have been discussing, Hunt painted or drew a large number of lesser views during his first trip to the Holy Land. Many of these are chiefly of documentary interest as records of the trip, and they are reproduced as such in *Pre-Raphaelitism and the Pre-Raphaelite Brotherhood*. Occasionally in the medium of pencil, or pencil and body colour, Hunt shows himself capable of an economy and simplicity otherwise rare in his art, but he was never a sensitive draughtsman, and it is impossible to claim high quality for these works. Hunt also made a small etching of the Sphinx by moonlight, with what is apparently the artists' tent in the foreground,[64] and he began at least two drawings which he never completed, of the same size as *The Plain of Rephaim* and *Nazareth*. One of these is of *The Sea of Galilee* (Pl. 33a). At sunrise on 30 October 1855, the day after Hunt left Nazareth, he began the view from the southern end of the sea, with the town of Tiberias in the foreground. He waited to colour the drawing until he had seen the effect of evening. His discovery that there was cholera in the town prevented this, forcing his precipitate departure, but he did finish the drawing in out-line. A watercolour by Arthur Hughes showing the scene by night, which was based on this sketch and upon Hunt's description of the moon rising over the water, is reproduced in *Pre-Raphaelitism and the Pre-Raphaelite Brotherhood*.[65] The other unfinished view was apparently begun in September 1854 on an excursion to Hebron. Hunt worked on it again on his first trip to the Dead Sea to look for a site for *The Scapegoat*.[66] Unlike Hunt's outline drawing of *The Sea of Galilee*, this is an unfinished watercolour (Pl. 31b), and it reveals only slight traces of pencil with no careful outline underlying the colour. The most distant portions of the view are the most highly finished, and the nearer foreground is still bare; there is no hint of the figures and incidents which enliven the foregrounds of Hunt's

[64]Reproduced in Hunt, 1905, I, 378. [66]*Ibid.*, I, 452.
[65]*Ibid.*, II, 47.

finished watercolours. Probably because it is unfinished, it shows an uncluttered largeness of vision which makes it in some ways the most immediately impressive of all Hunt's Eastern works.

On his way home to England, Hunt visited Constantinople and the Crimea. In January 1856 he began a large watercolour, *The Sleeping City* (Ashmolean Museum, Oxford), showing the cemetery at Pera, near Constantinople.[67] Hunt brought it home with the lower part blank and did not finally complete it until 1888. It is mainly a study of foreground objects: trees and foliage fill the background. The result seems like a return to an earlier, more claustrophobic kind of Pre-Raphaelitism, but without the precise detail of Hunt's and Millais's works from the early 1850s.

On later trips to the East in 1869–72, 1875–8, and 1892–3, Hunt painted a few additional landscapes. The most ambitious is a view in oil, *The Plain of Esdraelon from the Heights above Nazareth*, which Hunt began in 1870 as a study for the background of his large *Shadow of Death* (City Art Gallery, Manchester). It exists in a version without figures (private collection),[68] a larger version in the Ashmolean Museum in which there are shepherds and sheep in the foreground (Pl. 33b), and another version also with figures (private collection). The smaller version without figures still has some of the strength of vision of the watercolours of 1854 and 1855. In the Ashmolean version everything is softened to the same slightly fuzzy texture which appears in much of Hunt's later art. The palette is as bright as ever, but the effect seems rather heavy-handed. Hunt exhibited this picture along with *The Afterglow in Egypt* at the opening exhibition of the Grosvenor Gallery in 1877, where next to works by Whistler and Burne-Jones they must have looked garish and old-fashioned. There also exist watercolours of Jerusalem dated 1869 (collection of Mrs. E. M. S. C. Tompkin) and 1892 (William Morris Gallery, Walthamstow), but they are only weaker echoes of Hunt's earlier work. The watercolour of 1892 seems, in fact, to have been based on a painting made during their first trip by Thomas Seddon.[69]

After 1856 Hunt continued to paint landscapes in watercolour on trips he made away from London. There are groups of landscapes from an excursion to Devon and Cornwall in the autumn of 1860 and from two stays in Italy between 1866 and 1869. There are also individual landscapes from trips to Switzerland in 1875 and 1883–4, and from Greece and Corfu, which he visited on his last trip to the East in 1892.

Hunt's trip to Devon and Cornwall in 1860 was a walking tour made in the company of Tennyson, Francis Turner Palgrave, Thomas Woolner, and the painter Val Prinsep. The watercolours Hunt made on the trip come closest of all his works to conventional English landscape views. *Helston, Cornwall* (Pl. 34a) shows rolling, open fields with a stream bordered by trees. It has none of the exotic colour of Hunt's Eastern landscapes, and even in terms of Hunt's English pictures, the sunburnt orange-yellow of the fields seems more subdued than the brilliant greens of *The Hireling Shepherd* and *Strayed Sheep*. Nonetheless, it is still strongly coloured. Greens and violets play through the prevailing colours of the fields, and the shadows in the trees and the distant hedge-rows on the farther hills are blue. Another smaller watercolour, *Autumn Tints – Ivy Bridge, Cornwall* (collection of Lord Sherfield), shows a wooded scene with a rich play of reflected light and colour recalling the background of *The Haunted Manor*. In addition, Hunt made a number of watercolours of waves breaking on the coast. These represent a unique and not very successful venture

[67]Reproduced, *ibid.*, II, 84.
[68]Reproduced in Bennett, 1969, pl. 81.

[69]See below, p. 102.

75

into imagery of movement and natural dynamism, and they have little in common with any of his other works.[70]

Hunt was in Italy from August 1866 until September 1867, and again from early in 1868 until the summer of 1869. He lived mainly at Florence, but in 1868 he visited Naples and made several watercolours nearby. In 1869 he was elected an honorary associate member of the Old Water-Colour Society and sent two watercolours of Italian subjects to its summer exhibition. These have disappeared, but from contemporary descriptions they sound most interesting. According to F. G. Stephens's review in the *Athenaeum*, one, *Interior of the Cathedral at Salerno*, was a view from the altar over the brightly coloured floor of the nave. Its effect was one of brilliant daylight: 'The whole is suffused with light at its fullest power without glare, and superb as the multifarious details are, aerial perspective is perfectly preserved in the greatest variety of tints and wealth of tones.'[71] In the judgement of the critic for the *Art Journal*, 'This, as other drawings by Mr. Holman Hunt, may possibly be admired more by artists than the general public; the result strikes us as more clever than agreeable.'[72]

Hunt's second watercolour exhibited in 1869 was *Moonlight at Salerno*, which was a view across the harbour from a high vantage-point; in the foreground a man read a newspaper by moonlight. Its main interest apparently lay in the colour of the water and the reflected light of the moon. According to the *Art Journal*, it possessed 'doubtless rare qualities of light and colour, iridescent and opalescent on the sea as it sparkles under the golden moonlight', but 'to ordinary eyes' it seemed too blue. Although this watercolour is lost, a small *Fishing Boats by Moonlight* (Cecil Higgins Art Gallery, Bedford) shows a similar subject of a harbour at night. Another nocturnal watercolour painted by Hunt in Italy is *The Ponte Vecchio, Florence* (Pl. 36a). In this work as well, interest lies in the reflections in the water, which provide a mirrored repetition of the bridge and the buildings along the Arno, but illumination now comes from the lights of the city rather than the moon. As in Hunt's earlier oil sketch of *The Thames* of 1853 (Pl. 27b) the colours are in restricted range, and the work has a sobriety quite unlike the dazzle of his sunlit views of approximately the same time.

Hunt's wife died in Florence in December 1866. His return in 1868 was for the sake of erecting a memorial to her. During this second stay in Italy, he lived outside the city at Fiesole, for reasons of health, and there he 'executed a few watercolour drawings from the hills, and so kept myself in the pure air'.[73] He exhibited one of these, *Festa at Fiesole* (Pl. 34b), at the Old Water-Colour Society in 1870. Another showing the same view is *Sunset in the Val d'Arno* (Pl. 35b). In 1870 Hunt also exhibited *Sunset at Chimalditi* (or *Camaldoli*; Pl. 35a). It is similar to the two Florentine watercolours, but is a view over the Bay of Naples.[74]

These panoramic vistas recall Hunt's Eastern watercolours of 1855. *Festa at Fiesole* is a plateau landscape, and its foreground, showing the Royal band on the road to Fiesole, is prominent enough to give the picture its title and the subtitle of *True Merit Overlooked*. However, except for the one onlooking and overlooked small boy, all the figures are squeezed into a corner and cut across by the frame. They are rather clumsily drawn, in contrast to the carefully delineated landscape beyond them, and when it was exhibited they were criticized as 'bilious-looking' and 'little short of ridiculous'.[75] The foreground in

[70]Davies, 1936, pls. VI and VIII.
[71]*Ibid.*, p. 16.
[72]*Ibid.*, p.14.

[73]Hunt, 1905, II, 256.
[74]See Bennett, 1969, p. 87, no. 213.
[75]Davies, 1936, pp. 18–21.

Sunset at Chimalditi is limited to the tops of plants whose lower portions are cut off by the bottom of the picture. No actual ground is visible, but the plants establish that we are on a promontory. A tall sunflower rising almost to the top of the picture on the right provides a *repoussoir* foil to the distant emptiness of the landscape below. Turner in his pictures of the vicinity of the Bay of Naples, *The Bay of Baiae* of 1823 and *The Golden Bough* of 1834 (both in the Tate Gallery), had progressively whittled away the foreground masses of traditional Claudian compositions. Hunt's reduction of the foreground trees to a solitary thin stalk seems like a further step in this development. In the third panoramic landscape, *Sunset in the Val d'Arno*, he eliminated all but a suggestion of immediate foreground. There remain only a wisp of smoke in the lower left corner and a small clump of foliage in the lower right; beyond, the picture consists entirely of the landscape far below our vantage-point. The composition does not seem the less successful for the loss of the foreground; however, this is the only one of Hunt's finished panoramic landscapes in which he dispensed so completely with foreground elaboration. In the others, he seems to have felt that something was necessary, no matter how extraneous it might be to the rest of the composition.

The topographical interest in these watercolours is more limited than in Hunt's Eastern views, and none stresses notable local features. In fact, Ruskin, who owned *Sunset at Chimalditi*, referred to it as *Sunset on the Egean* or as a Greek sunset.[76] The primary interest of of all three is the sun. In *Festa at Fiesole* it is behind dark cypress trees, creating an incandescent burst of orange and red light and making the sky a patchwork of yellow and blue. In *Sunset in the Val d'Arno*, the sun is behind clouds and its beams fall on the valley. In *Sunset at Chimalditi* it is not behind anything, but is just above the horizon, surrounded by a dazzling halo of light.

When Hunt exhibited *Festa at Fiesole* and *Sunset at Chimalditi* in 1870, F. G. Stephens tried to explain the works:

The aim, as we understand it, of the painter has been to render by means of painting two of those effects of light on the retina which, because of their extreme delicacy and marvellous difficulty, have not been attempted before; unless by Turner, with circumstances less favourable than those under which Mr. Hunt has worked, the appearance of intense radiance on the eye in looking at a landscape has not yet hitherto been successfully attempted.[77]

Stephens declared that Hunt had succeeded perfectly. The critic for the *Art Journal* was less enthusiastic, but perhaps more searching:

The works he has here exhibited may be accounted as extraordinary phenomena both in Nature and Art, and yet as an earnest endeavour to paint what is unpaintable, this strange and startling attempt is not unworthy of respect. As a kind of kaleidoscopic arrangement of colour, this study of sky, earth, and water taken from a mountain top [*Sunset at Chimalditi*] is curiously interesting. But we do not regard the effect depicted as true to outward nature, it is rather the result of a frenzied vision; the eye when dazzled by effects of light sees colours which do not exist outwardly and physically, but only inwardly and within the mind's consciousness. It is an interesting question, not easy of solution, how far a painter is justified in throwing into his picture a poetic cast of thought, a frenzy of colour, which corresponds not to nature but to his individual idiosyncracies. Turner's practice must be taken as an argument that cuts both ways, and we cannot but consider that Holman Hunt falls into an extravagance which even in Turner is not excused. The *Sunset* before us wants the moderation of Art and the modesty of Nature.[78]

Despite approval on the one hand, and disapproval on the other, Stephens's 'effects of light on the retina' and the *Art Journal*'s 'eye when dazzled by effects of light' are not far apart.

[76]Ruskin, 1903–12, XXXIV, 169, and XXXVII, 20.   [78]*Ibid.*
[77]Davies, 1936, pp. 19–20.

The latter's criticism of the extravagance of Hunt's colour recalls French criticism of *Strayed Sheep* in 1855.[79] In the period between *Strayed Sheep* and the Italian landscapes, Hunt's art became less ostensibly naturalistic. Whereas *Strayed Sheep* seems to have looked forward to Impressionism, *Sunset at Chimalditi* looks back to Turner. Both Stephens and the *Art Journal* mentioned Turner in discussing the watercolours, and it is significant that Ruskin bought *Sunset at Chimalditi*, the only work by Hunt he ever owned. He placed it in the drawing school at Oxford, along with many of his Turners, and described it in a letter to Charles Eliot Norton as 'so true that everybody disbelieves its being true at all.'[80]

After 1869 Hunt never again painted landscapes with the same concentrated energy. The most ambitious of his later landscapes are a pair of watercolours of Alpine scenes, which he painted in 1875 and 1883. The first of these he exhibited at the Old Water-Colour Society in 1879 under the title *Study of Moonlight Effect from Berne Overlooking the River Nydeck to the Oberland Alps* (Rijksmuseum, Amsterdam). It has a plateau composition; two figures on a terrace in the foreground look out at the river valley and the moonlit fleecy clouds above. The other, *The Apple Harvest – Valley of the Rhine, Ragaz* (City Art Gallery, Birmingham), which Hunt exhibited in 1885, shows a mountain valley with peasants working in the foreground. The hour is mid-day, and the colours are bright in the sun, but the figures are clumsy and the work seems heavy-handed. Still later watercolours are a large *Stratford-on-Avon*, signed and dated 1888 (Coventry), a night scene, *The Square, Athens*, painted in 1892 and exhibited in 1893 (collection of Mrs. E. M. S. C. Tompkin), and a smaller twilight *Corfu*, which is signed and dated 1893 (with Leger Galleries, London, 1969).[81]

In addition to Hunt's watercolour landscapes, many of his later paintings have extensive outdoor passages. The Holy Family in *The Triumph of the Innocents* (Walker Art Gallery, Liverpool) moves through a nocturnal landscape, and the ritual of *May Morning on Magdalen Tower* (Lady Lever Art Gallery, Port Sunlight) takes place before the streaming pink clouds of dawn.[82] In 1863, the marriage of the Prince of Wales inspired Hunt to paint *London Bridge at Night* (Pl. 37a), showing the rejoicing crowd streaming across the torch-lit and banner-bedecked bridge. It is a curious response to the event, as there is no sign of the royal couple. Hunt was interested in the 'Hogarthian humour' of the scene and in recording a scene of contemporary history, in this instance the appearance of a London crowd.[83] He exhibited the picture privately the following year. A pamphlet published at the time describing the picture and pointing out its numerous incidents[84] – the apprehension of a thief, a soldier angry at a chimney sweep, etc. – indicates that Hunt was interested in the kind of anecdotal detail that had brought Frith's paintings such popular success. The picture is also Hunt's most ambitious night piece. The main light of the painting comes from flares and illuminations along the bridge, but these are contrasted with the softer light of the moon in the upper left corner of the picture, a contrast reminiscent of works by Joseph Wright of Derby. There are also reflections of the lights in the river, as well as wind and a London fog, all elements usually associated with mood and mystery, but here treated with factual literalness.

In the same years Hunt, instructing his sister in painting, began a picture of pigeons for her to finish. His sister apparently soon lost interest, and Hunt went on to finish the

[79]See above, pp. 63–4.
[80]Ruskin, 1903–12, XXXVII, 20.
[81]For reproductions see Hunt, 1905, II, op. p. 352, and p. 382; and Bennett, 1969, pls. 88 and 89.
[82]Reproduced in Bennett, 1969, pls. 83 and 95.

[83]Hunt, 1905, II, 243.
[84]Reprinted in W. Holman-Hunt, *Pre-Raphaelitism and the Pre-Raphaelite Brotherhood*, 2nd edn. rev. (London, 1913) II, 406–08

painting. It is signed and dated *66–75*, but according to *Pre-Raphaelitism and the Pre-Raphaelite Brotherhood*, Hunt completed it in 1866.[85] He exhibited it at the Royal Academy in 1867 with the title *The Festival of St. Swithin* (Pl. 36b). It is primarily a picture of pigeons in and about their dovecote, but there is a landscape below and beyond, and, as the name implies, it is also a picture of rain. Rain falls in sheets across the picture; it hits the roof of the dovecote and spatters in the air, and along the edges it collects and falls in drops. For once in Hunt's painting there is palpable moisture in the atmosphere, and the scale of colour is subdued to a prevailing grey.

In Jerusalem in 1875 Hunt painted *The Ship* (Pl. 37b), based on sketches he had made on the P. and O. ship coming to the Holy Land in the same year. The picture illustrates Tennyson's quatrain from *In Memoriam*:

> I hear the noise about thy keel,
> I hear the bell struck in the night,
> I see the cabin window bright,
> I see the sailor at the wheel!

Consequently, it is a night scene, with the bright lights of cabin and deck and the red flame from the smoke stack contrasted with the moonlit sky. Hunt painted *The Ship* as an experiment with materials available in Jerusalem, those he had sent from England having failed to arrive, and it has deteriorated more than any other of his pictures. Nonetheless, it is a strange and striking painting, and it demonstrates once again that Hunt's literal vision was also a highly personal one.

[85]Hunt, 1905, II, 253–4.

VI

Outdoor Painting by other Members of the Pre-Raphaelite Circle

OF THE ORIGINAL members of the Pre-Raphaelite Brotherhood, only Hunt and Millais displayed a strong interest in out-of-door painting. Thomas Woolner was a sculptor. William Michael Rossetti was not an artist at all, and Frederick George Stephens was one only briefly. Both Rossetti and Stephens became critics who were to remain loyal advocates and, eventually, historians of the movement. James Collinson, on the other hand, soon resigned from the Brotherhood and abandoned painting when he was converted to Roman Catholicism and entered a Jesuit monastery. After leaving the monastery in 1854 or 1855 he took up painting again, but he was no longer part of the Pre-Raphaelite group. One painting by Collinson of a mother and child in a landscape is in the Mellon collection (Pl. 38a). A label on the back gives Collinson's address as Queen's Road, Chelsea,[1] which was his address listed in the Royal Academy catalogue of 1855, the first year Collinson exhibited following his monastic interlude. He could not have been there much before the spring of 1855, as a letter dated 4 June 1855, from William Michael Rossetti to Holman Hunt, who was then in the East, contained the announcement that Collinson had 're-appeared in the light of the sun', and that he was living with Richard Burchett, a master in the government school of art at South Kensington.[2] Burchett was also a Catholic convert, and his address in 1855 was 11 Queen's Road. He painted one memorable landscape of *A Scene in the Isle of Wight* (Victoria and Albert Museum), which shows a view across Sandown Bay to Culver Cliff in the distance.[3] Collinson's painting has the same view in the background. The treatment of detail by both artists is daintily precise, but neither picture has Pre-Raphaelite brilliance or vibrancy. As Holman Hunt said about Collinson's earlier work, 'with form so lacking in nervousness as his, finish of detail is wasted labour.'[4]

Collinson was at best a minor artist, so whether a picture like this should be considered technically Pre-Raphaelite is an academic question. Other than Hunt and Millais, the only member of the original Brotherhood who made a significant contribution as an artist was Dante Gabriel Rossetti, and Rossetti's indifference to what Hunt considered the ruling principle of the movement was notorious. Rossetti painted his first picture as a Pre-Raphaelite, *The Girlhood of Mary Virgin* (Tate Gallery), under Holman Hunt's direction, and in a naive way it does show some of the concern with natural detail that characterizes the early works of Hunt and Millais. But while in Hunt's and Millais's painting the tentative naturalism of 1848 and 1849 led to much more ambitious treatment of nature in their pictures of the early 1850s, Rossetti moved in the opposite direction. *The Girlhood of Mary*

---

[1]*Painting in England 1700–1850 from the Collection of Mr. and Mrs. Paul Mellon*, exhibition catalogue (Royal Academy of Arts, London, 1964–5) p. 37, no. 127.
[2]John Rylands Library, Manchester, Rylands Eng. MS. 1216, f. 65.

[3]Reproduced in Graham Reynolds, *Victorian Painting* (London, 1966) pl. 103. Burchett's address was listed in the British Institution catalogue; he did not exhibit at the Royal Academy in 1855. Collinson remained at 11 Queen's Road through 1858.
[4]Hunt, 1905, I, 84.

Virgin includes a row of carefully painted leaves along the top and a bit of landscape out the window, but in his painting of the following year, *Ecce Ancilla Domini!* (Tate Gallery), almost all traces of the outside world have disappeared, and there remain two figures in a bare room. Rossetti did make a few sporadic later attempts at painting outdoor scenes. In the autumn of 1850, when Hunt went to Knole Park to paint the background of *Valentine Rescuing Sylvia from Proteus*, Rossetti accompanied him so that he might also paint out of doors. Hunt describes how he fared:

I ran up occasionally to see him, and found him nearly always engaged in a mortal quarrel with some particular leaf which would perversely shake about and get torn off its branch when he was half way in its representation. Having been served thus repeatedly, he would put up with no more such treatment, and left canvas, box, and easel for the man to collect when at dusk the barrow came for my picture, he stalking back to the lodgings to write and to try designs.[5]

Rossetti's struggles with nature were for the background of a large picture, whose subject he originally planned to be *Il Saluto di Beatrice*. It is worth noting that Rossetti, who had no previous experience at all in painting landscape, began to work directly out of doors on a large canvas; he did not begin by making smaller and more controllable studies from nature. He soon left off, but he took up the canvas again in 1872 as *The Bower Meadow* (Pl. 38b), which has two women playing a lute and a zither in the foreground and a group of dancing figures behind them. The background, the product of his outing of 1850, shows a screen of trees across the horizon and open meadow between the trees and the figures. It is similar to the further background of Hunt's *Druids*, begun in 1849 (Pl. 26b), and to Hunt's small, related *Love at First Sight* (Pl. 26a), which he began on an earlier excursion with Rossetti. But the background trees form only a minor part of *The Bower Meadow*, and in the foreground there is none of the leaf-by-leaf detail of the foreground of the *Druids*.

In his painting of a modern moral subject, *Found* (Wilmington Society of the Fine Arts, Wilmington, Delaware), Rossetti attempted an extensive city-scape. However, although his ambitions were high, they never reached fruition, and he left the picture unfinished. For a time he worked on it while staying with Ford Madox Brown. An entry in Brown's diary, dated 12 Nov. 1854, describes Rossetti painting a calf: 'He paints in all like Albert Dürer, hair by hair, and seems incapable of any breadth; but this he will get from going over it from feeling at home. From want of habit, I see Nature bothers him, but it is sweetly drawn and felt.'[6] Nature never ceased to bother Rossetti, and when he abandoned *Found*, he abandoned all attempts at naturalism. His real forte was inventive design, and his finest achievements as a painter are his quaintly decorative watercolours from the later 1850s. In these the settings are often highly elaborated, but they have little to do with natural appearances. One of the earliest and most beautiful of Rossetti's watercolours, *Dante Drawing an Angel on the Anniversary of Beatrice's Death* (Ashmolean Museum, Oxford), does have a landscape background. It is a fanciful view of Florence seen through a window, and it seems mainly the product of Rossetti's imagination. This watercolour was seen by Ruskin in April 1854, just when Effie was about to leave him and his friendship with Millais was floundering. On 10 April he wrote to Rossetti and praised it in unlikely, but for Ruskin characteristic, terms:

I think it a thoroughly glorious work – the most perfect piece of Italy, in the accessory parts, I have ever seen in my life – nor of Italy only – but of marvellous landscape painting. I might perhaps, if we were talking about it, venture to point out one or two things that appear to me questionable.[7]

[5]*Ibid.*, p. 237. Rossetti himself described the experience in a letter to John Lucas Tupper; see Rossetti, 1900, p.23.

[6]Rossetti, 1899, p. 21.

[7]Troxell, 1937, pp. 25–6.

This was the beginning of a friendship between Ruskin and Rossetti which flourished more or less into the 1860s. At first, Ruskin nurtured a hope that his new friend would take some interest in landscape. There is an amusing series of letters written by Ruskin to Rossetti in October 1855. First, Ruskin wrote, 'If I were to find funds could you be ready on Wednesday morning to take a run into Wales, and make me a sketch of some rocks in the bed of a stream, with trees above, mountain ashes, and so on, scarlet in autumn tints?' In the second, he pacified the artist, who had apparently taken offence at the suggestion: 'I should never think of your sitting out to paint from Nature. Merely look at the place; make memoranda fast, work at home at the inn, and walk among the hills.' Finally, the series closes with Ruskin chastising Rossetti, who had been ready to take the money to go to Paris, but not to paint landscapes in Wales.[8] Ruskin also proposed that they visit Switzerland together in 1856, but the trip did not come to pass.[9]

Many of Rossetti's works of the 1850s and later do include landscape backgrounds, but he was able to paint them without a direct study of nature. In 1856, to complete his water-colour *Writing on the Sand* (British Museum), he borrowed two sketches by George Price Boyce of the Devonshire coast.[10] In 1863 he was collecting stereoscopic photographs of cities to use for the background of his *Helen of Troy* (Kunsthalle, Hamburg), and later his erstwhile assistant, Charles Fairfax Murray, provided him with both sketches and photographs from Italy to base backgrounds on.[11]

Millais and Hunt, rather than Rossetti, established the pattern of Pre-Raphaelitism in the 1850s, and the most obvious characteristic of the new style was the elaboration of natural detail. That by 1853 the movement was generally thought of in terms of close natural detail is demonstrated by a pair of small pictures of *Puck and the Moth*, which a painter named Edward Hopley exhibited at the British Institution in that year (Pl. 39). These pictures, which, according to the *Art Journal*, were intended to contrast 'the spirit of pre-Raffaelism with that of post-Raffaelism',[12] are almost identical in subject and in treatment of the figure. But, while in one the surroundings are murky and subordinated to the figure, in the other they are filled with microscopic plant life and there is a charming landscape background across which chugs a diminutive train. In the same year Hopley wrote *A Letter on Pre- and Post-Raffaelism*, in which he argued that the moral of a picture must suffer when struggling against 'irresistible littleness and indubitable cobwebs and caterpillars'.[13]

The quintessential Pre-Raphaelite composition consists of a single figure or a simple group of figures before an ivy-covered wall or a foliate background. Millais established it in *Ferdinand Lured by Ariel* (Pl. 2a and Col. Pl. 1a), and he repeated it in his most popular paintings of the following years, the *Huguenot* (Pl. 40a) and *The Proscribed Royalist*. *Ophelia* is essentially the same picture turned on its side (Pl. 4). The appeal of the arrangement lay in its simplicity and lack of the artificiality to which the Pre-Raphaelites objected in more ambitious compositions. The simplicity of the figural arrangement allowed the artist to devote that much more attention to the careful copying of the natural world. In the early 1850s for the Pre-Raphaelite followers, as for Millais, nature generally consisted of detail seen at close range. In the middle of the 1850s Millais's backgrounds opened out into more

[8]Rossetti, 1899, pp. 103–04.
[9]Ruskin, 1903–12, V, p. xlix.
[10]Boyce, 1941, p. 38.
[11]Doughty and Wahl, 1965–7, II, 479; and William Michael Rossetti, *Dante Gabriel Rossetti as Designer and*

Writer (London, 1889) p. 110.
[12]*Art Journal*, 1853, p. 88.
[13]Quoted in the *Athenaeum*, 6 Aug. 1853, p. 943. See also Fredeman, 1965, pp. 226–7, no. 66.3.

extensive views in *Autumn Leaves* and *The Blind Girl*, and a comparable opening out followed in the painting of other artists of the group.

The first close associate of the Pre-Raphaelite Brotherhood was Charles Allston Collins, who shared the critical vicissitudes of Hunt and Millais as early as 1850. His art is clearly dependent on that of Millais, and his best-known picture, *Convent Thoughts* (Pl. 3a), reflects the composition of Millais's *Ferdinand Lured by Ariel*, which had been exhibited a year earlier. Collins's technical abilities were limited, and all his figures have a stiffness which gives his paintings a look of amateurish awkwardness. However, he was responsible for one of the first Pre-Raphaelite landscape paintings to be exhibited: *May in Regent's Park*, shown at the Royal Academy in 1852. The picture has disappeared, but it was described by contemporary critics. It showed a view of the park from the window of a neighbouring house (Collins lived in Hanover Terrace, overlooking the Park), and one reviewer suggested that it was seen through an eyeglass.[14] The *Art Journal* characterized the picture as, 'certainly among the most eccentric of the curiosities of landscape painting', but went on to say that it was exquisitely painted.[15] The *Athenaeum* accused Collins of exaggerating Millais's mannerisms:

The botanical predominates altogether over the artistical, – and to a vicious and mistaken extreme. In nature there is air as well as earth, – she masses and generalizes where these facsimile makers split hairs and particularize. They take a branch, a flower, a blade of grass, place it close before them and as closely copy it, – forgetting that these objects, at the distance imagined in the picture, could by no means be seen with such *hortus siccus* minuteness.[16]

This picture appears to have been Collins's most venturesome attempt at an outdoor subject. As a pure landscape, it stands apart from *The Hireling Shepherd* and *Ophelia*, which were exhibited in the same year. Collins was with Hunt and Millais when they were at Ewell painting the backgrounds of these pictures in the preceding summer and autumn. He began there a picture of *The Nativity* with an elaborate background of 'chestnut foliage and arboreal richness'. This *Nativity* evolved into a scene of more modern charity, showing a French woman bringing a cloak to a poor family in a shed. It was exhibited at the Royal Academy in 1854 as *A Thought of Bethlehem*, but Collins may have subsequently reworked or partly effaced it, and it may eventually have been destroyed. In 1873, Holman Hunt found the canvas off the stretcher on Collins's deathbed. Hunt implies that the canvas contained just the background painted at Ewell.[17] Collins's last picture to appear at the Royal Academy was *The Good Harvest of 1854*, which he exhibited in 1855 (Pl. 40b). It shows a continuing dependence upon Millais; the background of ivy on a brick wall comes straight from the *Huguenot*. In 1857 Collins exhibited works at Liverpool and in the Pre-Raphaelite exhibition in Russell Place, but he soon after gave up painting for writing.

Another associate of the Pre-Raphaelites, whose painting career was even shorter, was Walter Howell Deverell. His early death in 1854 cut off what was certainly a much more promising talent than that of Collins. Deverell's *Scene from 'The Twelfth Night'*, of 1850 (private collection), is a complex figural composition reminiscent of Millais's *Isabella*. His *Scene from 'As you Like It'*, exhibited at the Royal Academy in 1853 (City Art Gallery, Birmingham), is compositionally simpler, showing three figures before a wooded back-

[14]*British Quarterly Review*, XVI, 1852, p. 213.
[15]*Art Journal*, 1852, p. 166.
[16]*Athenaeum*, 22 May 1852, p. 582.
[17]Hunt, 1905, I, 272–73, and II, 313. See also Millais, 1899, I, 133, where it is stated that the picture was never finished. The fullest discussion is in Anne Julie d'Harnoncourt, 'The Awakening Conscience: A Study of Moral Subject Matter in Pre-Raphaelite Painting, with a Catalogue of Pictures in the Tate Gallery', unpublished master's thesis, Courtauld Institute of Art, University of London, 1967, pp. 31 and 77n.

ground. Deverell painted the picture while sharing a studio with Rossetti in Red Lion Square, and he painted the Forest of Arden 'from the dusty foliage of that dingy precinct'.[18] More interesting as outdoor paintings are *The Irish Vagrants* (Art Gallery of Johannesburg) and *The Pet* (Tate Gallery). The former, which Deverell left unfinished, has an extensive background, whose rolling fields and rows of cornshocks recall the background of Hunt's *Hireling Shepherd* rather than the usual foliate backgrounds based on Millais. *The Pet* of 1852–3 shows a woman with a birdcage in the doorway of a conservatory, and a garden beyond. Its compositional simplicity is accompanied by a breadth of handling that differs considerably from the carefully copied detail in most Pre-Raphaelite pictures of this early date. John Gere has pointed out that Deverell's breadth is combined with a lack of didactic or narrative purpose, and he has suggested that Deverell, had he lived, might have succeeded, where Millais failed, in achieving a breadth of form without a diminution of the quality of his painting.[19]

Deverell and Collins were both close to the early history of the Pre-Raphaelite Brotherhood, and both were considered for membership in the Brotherhood. In actual output, however, neither compares in importance with Arthur Hughes, whose best works rank alongside those of Millais, Hunt, and Brown. The appeal of his art stems largely from its delicate sentiment. He could not be considered a bold explorer of the natural world, as in their various ways were Millais, Hunt, and Brown, but landscape settings do play a major role in most of his painting.

Hughes was converted to Pre-Raphaelitism by reading *The Germ* in 1850.[20] His first work of note was a picture of *Ophelia*, which he exhibited at the Royal Academy in 1852 (Pl. 41b). That was the year that Millais exhibited his *Ophelia*, but apparently Hughes, although he had previously met Hunt and Rossetti, did not meet Millais until varnishing day of the 1852 exhibition and knew nothing of Millais's picture. His version differs from Millais's both in composition and in general style. Ophelia sits at the edge of the water, shredding flowers into the brook. In the immediate foreground the plants in and along the edge of the water are precisely delineated, but the rest of the painting dissolves into unPre-Raphaelite vagueness which suggests a deep space quite unlike Millais's spacelessness. Colour is not tied to descriptive detail as in the Millais, but is itself evocative of mood. The sky is deep green above, and the haze over the horizon is a murky purple. The foreground colours are darker than the brilliant ones achieved by Millais using a wet white ground, and the water is almost black. Against it, the lighter greens of the grass-covered shore, the orange and green of the scum, and the orange rock with purple lichens to the right of the girl create a patterned effect.

Hughes was twenty years old in 1852. The modelling of the figure of Ophelia is still reminiscent of the life class and shows evident *pentimenti*. Nonetheless, the picture is impressive from the haunting quality of the landscape; its atmospheric effect suggests the possibility of Hughes's art developing along other lines than those of Millais's exclusively botanical scrutiny. Indeed, Hughes's *Ophelia* anticipates Millais's later effort to gain breadth and mood in his *Autumn Leaves* of 1856. However, when Hughes met Millais in 1852 he fell heavily under his sway. A series of pictures from the 1850s – *April Love* (Tate Gallery), *The Long Engagement* (Pl. 41c and Col. Pl. 1b), *The Tryst* (Tate Gallery), and *Fair Rosamund* (National Gallery of Victoria, Melbourne) – follow the pattern set by Millais in *Ferdinand Lured by Ariel* and the *Huguenot*. *April Love*, which Hughes exhibited at the Royal Academy in 1856, is generally the most admired. According to Robert Ross, it was painted

[18]Scott, 1892, I, 285.   [20]*Ibid.*, p. 41.
[19]Ironside and Gere, 1948, p. 28.

in the open air in the garden of a Mr. Cutbush at Maidstone.[21] The setting is most important in *The Long Engagement*, which Hughes began in 1853 as *Orlando in the Forest of Arden*, painting the background from nature with the usual Pre-Raphaelite care. In August 1854 he wrote to William Allingham describing the difficulties:

Painting wild roses into *Orlando* has been a kind of match against time with me, they passing away so soon, like all lovely things *under* the sun (eh?) and as sensitive as beautiful. The least hint of rain, just a dark cloud passing over, closes them up for the rest of the day perhaps. One day a great bee exasperated me to the pitch of madness by persisting in attacking me, the perspiration pouring down my face in three streams the while – and another I had to remain for three hours under a great beech tree with roots all unearthed, and years upon years of dead leaves under his shade, listening to the rain plashings.[22]

In 1855 Hughes submitted the picture to the Royal Academy, where it was rejected. He then repainted it, replacing the figure of Orlando with a pair of ageing Victorian lovers, and exhibited it at the Royal Academy in 1859 with a quotation from Chaucer:

> For how myght sweetness ever hav be known
> To hym that never tastyd bitternesse.

The painting represents a complete change in Hughes's style from that of his own *Ophelia* to that of Millais's. The drawing and colouring of every leaf and blossom are clear, separate, and precise. There is no spatial depth; the background is entirely filled with foliage pressing upon the figures, and the bright colours bring each detail forward to the surface.[23] The figures do not stand out from their setting; everything is of equal value, and the couple only emerges as part of an over-all surface pattern. When compared to Millais, Hughes seems even more rigid in avoiding any suggestion of depth and more consistent in the treatment of the picture's surface. We feel the forms taken in pictures such as Millais's *Ophelia* were the result of the artist's peculiar approach to recording natural phenomena, but in Hughes's picture the stylization is a product of consciously controlled denial of traditional pictorial space. Nevertheless, the foliate and floral surroundings give the picture its meaning. The subject *is* the long engagement, and our awareness of nature growing, blossoming, and reproducing itself heightens the poignancy of the enforced sterility of the two protagonists.

Millais in his pictures exhibited in 1856 introduced a new breadth of space and of effect. Hughes followed him in his *Home from Sea*, which he began in the summer of 1856 (Pl. 42a). This painting also has a complicated history. It is signed and dated 1863, and Hughes exhibited it at the Royal Academy in that year; however, in main lines it dates from 1856 and 1857.[24] The background was painted from nature during the summer of 1856 in the churchyard at Chingford, Essex. The figure of the boy crying on the grave was painted in the spring of 1857. Hughes exhibited the picture in the summer of 1857 as *A Mother's Grave* at the Pre-Raphaelite exhibition in Russell Place, and later in the same year in America as *Home from Sea – The Mother's Grave*. The figure of the boy's sister was added later, probably in 1863, the date on the picture. The painting is still highly detailed, still, by landscape standards, a close study of a circumscribed area. But, in contrast to *The Long Engagement*, *Home from Sea* does reveal an attempt to establish space within the picture. There is a ground plane which recedes to the church at a recognizable distance in the

[21]Robert Ross, 'April Love: A Note', *Burlington Magazine*, XXVIII, 1916, p. 171.
[22]H. Allingham and E. B. Williams, eds., *Letters to William Allingham*, London, 1911, p. 51.
[23]'This is a professedly "Pre-Raffaelite" work, with everything in it rushing out of the frame, and introducing as much of the crudity of the manner as can be shown on a limited field.' *Art Journal*, 1859, p. 170.
[24]Ironside and Gere, 1948, p. 43.

background. The foreground details such as the flowers on the trunk of the tree to the right and the branches above the figures are highly finished, but they do not fill the picture, and, consequently do not seem as obtrusive as the foliate detail in *The Long Engagement*. In some respects – shape, placement of figures, intensity of greens, sheep in the background – *Home from Sea* is closer to Holman Hunt's *Hireling Shepherd* than to any picture by Millais. However, if we recall the dependence of Hughes's earlier paintings upon those of Millais, it is probably correct to see the opening-out of his art as part of the same pattern, in this instance depending more upon *The Blind Girl* than upon *Autumn Leaves*.

A drawing of the composition of *Home from Sea*, as it originally existed, without the sister, is in the Ashmolean Museum. Robin Gibson has pointed out that the attitude of the boy lying on the ground in grief can be traced back to the frontispiece of the first issue of *The Germ*: an etched illustration by Holman Hunt to Thomas Woolner's poem 'Of My Lady in Death'. But Robin Gibson has also noted that Hughes himself had painted a picture of a figure lying in a landscape possibly as early as 1849.[25] In this work, *The Young Poet* (Pl. 41a), the composition stems from traditional imagery of the melancholy poet, as it appears, for example, in Joseph Wright of Derby's *Sir Brooke Boothby* (Tate Gallery). After 1856 Hughes painted several additional pictures of figures lying out of doors on the ground. They include *The Woodman's Child* of 1860 (Tate Gallery), *The Rift within the Lute*, which Hughes exhibited at the Royal Academy in 1862 and which shows an obvious dependence on traditional images of melancholy (City Art Gallery, Carlisle), and *The Compleat Angler* of probably after 1870, which shows a girl lying by a stream, reading a book (collection of Lord Henley).

Comparison of *Home from Sea* with *The Young Poet* shows not only the much greater detail in Hughes's work after he came into the Pre-Raphaelite sphere of influence, but also changed spatial relationships. The ground upon which Hughes's earlier poet lies appears to recede continuously from the bottom edge of the picture to the horizon, which is just above the figure's head but at an indeterminate distance in space. In *Home from Sea* the immediate foreground, upon which the boy lies, slopes upward; above him, at about the middle of the picture, the angle of vision changes, and we look across a horizontally receding plane to the old church and surrounding trees, which reach almost to the top of the painting. The figures and their surroundings are pushed forward to the surface of the painting instead of being in its space, as is the poet, and there is little feeling of depth in the background behind them. The abrupt horizontal recession across the churchyard creates a mannerist space that we can recognize intellectually, but, in effect, the background, like that of Millais's *Blind Girl*, goes up more than it goes back, and the whole composition crowds toward the surface. Originally, the composition must have broken into two distinct halves across the middle of the picture. Hughes may have added the upright figure of the girl to please a client, but she also links the upper and lower halves of the painting. In a second, smaller version of *The Rift within the Lute*, which was bought by the same client, Hughes also added an upright figure, to similar effect.[26]

The Woodman's Child shows a small girl sleeping in the foreground while her parents are tiny figures at work in another sharply receding background. The picture has no evident connection with Millais's earlier *Woodman's Daughter*, or with Patmore's poem on which the Millais was based. *The Rift within the Lute* was exhibited with lines from Tennyson's *Idylls of the King*, but it does not appear to be a specific illustration; in its background are a small hunter and a hound. The second version, with a male figure

[25]Gibson, 1970, p. 456.   [26]*Ibid.*, pp. 455–6.

added, is more obviously Arthurian, and the figures are identified on the frame as Enid and Geraint. Both *The Woodman's Child* and *The Rift within the Lute* have forest settings, and the natural details, including in the former a squirrel and a bird watching the sleeping child, are more prominent than in *Home from Sea*.

Another group of works by Hughes from around 1860 have sunsets in their backgrounds. The most ambitious of them is *The Knight of the Sun* of 1860 (Pl. 42b), which shows a dying knight being carried through a forest while the sun sets in the distance. The effect of the sunset, which is reflected in a river, was clearly inspired by Henry Wallis's *Stonebreaker* exhibited in 1858 (Pl. 43a), but behind both pictures lay Millais's *Autumn Leaves* and *Sir Isumbras*, exhibited in 1856 and 1857.[27] The forest setting, like the settings of *The Woodman's Child* and *The Rift within the Lute*, is painted with painstaking attention to detail. Although Hughes was obviously influenced by Millais in other ways, he did not quite so readily abandon Pre-Raphaelite detail. Hughes's details in *The Knight of the Sun*, however, no longer have the brilliant pitch of colour of those in his earlier *Long Engagement*. They are subdued because it is twilight, and so that the sunset can glow more effectively, without undue competition. By subordinating his foreground colours, Hughes did exactly what early critics of the Pre-Raphaelites claimed they were incapable of: he made the whole more important than the parts. But in doing so, Hughes also sacrificed the vibrancy of a picture like *The Long Engagement*, in which every leaf and petal is alive with a life of its own. Robert Ross wrote that Hughes's earlier works were 'like some brilliant Easter morning in a radiant spring'.[28] Alas, Hughes's spring lasted for only a few years. He may have tried to retain it, but the twilight of *The Knight of the Sun* marks a drawing back to a more conventional vision. Hughes continued to paint pictures with outdoor settings – and occasional pure landscapes – through the rest of his long life. Many still follow Pre-Raphaelite prototypes from the 1850s. For example, a *Portrait of Arthur P. Davison* of 1868 (private collection) shows a little boy before yet another brick wall descended from Millais's *Huguenot*. Other late works are less obviously Pre-Raphaelite. *The Potter's Courtship*, exhibited at the Royal Academy in 1886 (Laing Art Gallery, Newcastle upon Tyne), has a blue Mediterranean background which is closer to Alma-Tadema than to Pre-Raphaelite pictures. Whatever the stylistic connections, Hughes's later art is not very interesting. As John Gere has written, it does not even have 'the positive quality of vulgarity', which distinguishes the later works of Millais.[29]

By the middle of the 1850s, Pre-Raphaelitism was no longer simply a matter of Hunt, Millais, Rossetti, and a few close friends, but had achieved a widely-felt influence in English painting. In the introduction to his *Academy Notes* of 1856, Ruskin announced that the Pre-Raphaelites had 'completely and confessedly' won the battle: 'animosity has changed into emulation, astonishment into sympathy, and . . . a true and consistent school of art is at last established in the Royal Academy of England.'[30] Ironically, by 1856 Millais's style was beginning to show change, and in the following year Ruskin was to lament his disastrous decline. Millais's art was the model for most Pre-Raphaelite imitators, and most of them followed him into mediocrity. The Pre-Raphaelite Renaissance, which Ruskin so jubilantly hailed in 1856, was by 1860 largely a thing of the past. And by that year, Ruskin had ceased publishing his *Academy Notes*. Nonetheless, in the years 1855–9 a surprising number of remarkably good pictures were exhibited by artists who had lately come to the Pre-Raphaelite fold, and who for the most part would soon desert it. The most notable of

[27] *Ibid.*, p. 452.
[28] *Burlington Magazine*, XXVIII, 1916, p. 207.
[29] Ironside and Gere, 1948, p. 41.
[30] Ruskin, 1903–12, XIV, 47.

these later adherents were William Lindsay Windus, John Brett (both of whom are discussed in later chapters), and Henry Wallis.

Wallis's education included not only the usual study at the Royal Academy schools, but also a period spent in Paris at the Ecole des Beaux-Arts and the studio of Gleyre. However, whatever French influence there may have been in his art is less apparent than that of Pre-Raphaelitism. He first exhibited at the Royal Academy in 1854, and he created a sensation in 1856 with *The Death of Chatterton* (Tate Gallery), which Ruskin called, 'faultless and wonderful: a most noble example of the great school'. Two years later Wallis exhibited a picture of a dead stonebreaker with a quotation from *Sartor Resartus* for a title (Pl. 43a and Col. Pl. 5), which Ruskin declared the picture of the year, 'and but narrowly missing being a first rate of any year'.[31]

The Death of Chatterton is an interior scene, with only a view over the London skyline through a garret window, but the other picture is an outdoor painting and a remarkable one. The stonebreaker lies dead upon his litter of rocks at sunset. Behind him are a fern-covered bank, a river in a valley below, and hills beyond. In a sense, the picture follows the Pre-Raphaelite pattern of the single figure in an elaborate and brightly coloured environment, but the extensive background and sunset effect reflect the later development of Pre-Raphaelitism in Millais's *Autumn Leaves*. Some details such as the leaves above the horizon are minutely and separately painted, but in the larger mass of the bank behind the dead man, the minutely drawn foliate detail of Hunt, Millais, or Hughes is absent. Throughout the foreground Wallis's colours have an extremely high key. They are thinly painted over a white ground, and the effect is dazzling. As there is relatively little detail – simply areas of green and red, suggesting patches of grass and earth – the foreground comes to the surface primarily as abstract colour. Individual details such as the rodent at the dead worker's foot, and even the stonebreaker himself, do not stand out, but are absorbed as part of the pattern. The figure is painted in earthier colours than his setting. Nature glows vibrantly, but the dead man recedes into the landscape and becomes the quieter in death.

In *Academy Notes* Ruskin wrote that Wallis's foreground seemed somewhat hastily painted, but he forgave it as the colours were beautiful and it would have been in false taste to elaborate the subject further. He was more critical of the distance, which suffered from 'a too heavy laying of the body of paint'. The blue of the hills was 'too uniform and dead', and the sky above them had 'no joy nor clearness when it is looked into'. Although joy is possibly the last quality we would expect to find in a painting of such a gloomy subject, it is possible to see what Ruskin means. In treatment of both foreground and background, Wallis seems to have adopted Pre-Raphaelite effects of colour without basing them on the scrupulously detailed observation of Pre-Raphaelitism. But, although Ruskin partially disapproved, Wallis was remarkably successful in retaining the vibrancy of early Pre-Raphaelite colour and handling while incorporating them into a broader effect.

Unfortunately, much of Wallis's œuvre has disappeared, and of his other known works only *The Death of Chatterton* is of comparable quality or interest. A small oil sketch dated 1859, *Coast Study, Sunset* (Walker Art Gallery, Liverpool), also shows a twilight subject, but the handling is heavier and broader than that in *The Stonebreaker*.

Personally, Wallis seems to have been on the periphery of the Pre-Raphaelite group. In 1854 Rossetti wrote in reply to a query by the collector Francis McCracken that he had only seen one picture by Wallis and that he considered it inferior to a picture of high merit such as Deverell's *Irish Vagrants*.[32] In 1857 Wallis did not participate in the Pre-Raphaelite

[31]*Ibid.*, pp. 60 and 170.   [32]Doughty and Wahl, 1965–7, I, 198.

exhibition held at Russell Place, but he did later belong to the Hogarth Club, whose membership consisted of the Pre-Raphaelite group and some associates. In 1858 he ran off with George Meredith's wife. He travelled extensively in later years and became an expert on ceramics. He also worked in watercolour and was elected an associate member of the Old Water-Colour Society in 1878 and a full member two years later.

Another member of the Hogarth Club, who seems otherwise to have had only slight personal contact with the Pre-Raphaelite group, was William Shakespeare Burton. In 1856 he exhibited *The Cavalier and the Puritan* at the Royal Academy (Pl. 43b). The picture was not included in the first edition of the exhibition catalogue, but it was well hung. Ruskin found the subject not very intelligible, but the painting masterly, and the painter 'capable of the greatest things'.[33] The picture has a subject in seventeenth-century costume, like that of Millais's *Proscribed Royalist*, and the elaborately and minutely detailed setting seems to depend upon Millais's example. This is Burton's only early work now known. According to F. G. Stephens, 'After this supreme effort of his art had failed to secure that honour it merited the painter lived an almost embittered man.'[34] The artist disappeared so completely from sight that Stephens, writing in 1886, thought that he had long been dead, though in fact he lived until 1916 and in later years painted pictures of religious subjects.

Even more obscure is William J. Webbe, who seems to have had no recorded personal contact with the members of the Pre-Raphaelite Brotherhood. In Percy Bate's *Pre-Raphaelite Painters*, which contains much information about minor followers of the movement, he is mentioned in only one sentence. However, two roundels dated 1854 and 1855 show Pre-Raphaelite elaboration of microscopic foreground foliage pushed to an almost insane extreme. *A Hedge Bank in May*, dated 1854 and exhibited at the British Institution in 1855 (Stone Gallery, Newcastle upon Tyne),[35] depends upon Holman Hunt's *Strayed Sheep*, exhibited in 1853. The heads of two sheep appear over the hedge-bank. Cut off by the frame at the top of the picture are the four feet of another sheep or lamb, and at the bottom of the picture a snake slithers through the grass. The slightly larger *After Sunset*, dated 1855 and exhibited at the Society of British Artists in 1856 (Pl. 44a), shows a rabbit in the midst of a similar jumble of leaves and flowers. In both pictures the technique is drier and more linear than Hunt's. In 1856 Ruskin described Webbe's *White Owl* at the Royal Academy as a careful study, but he criticized it for lacking the softness of feathers.[36]

From 1855 through 1860 Webbe lived on the Isle of Wight, and in addition to pictures of animals he also exhibited a few landscapes. In 1862 he travelled to the Holy Land, and all his subsequent exhibited works in the 1860s were of Eastern subjects. *The Lost Sheep* of 1864 (Pl. 44b) shows another subject dependent on Hunt's pastoral imagery, and the landscape seems equally to show his influence. A shepherd carries a sheep before mountains of pink and blue and a sky of green. The spiky weeds in the foreground, pink and violet, could have grown from the seeds of those in *The Light of the World*. Despite Webbe's obvious and loyal emulation of Hunt, he is not mentioned in *Pre-Raphaelitism and the Pre-Raphaelite Brotherhood*, but in the first volume is reproduced a drawing of *The Church of the Sepulchre* which is apparently by Webbe, so he and Hunt may have had some personal contact.[37]

[33]Ruskin, 1903–12, XIV, 66.
[34]*Athenaeum*, 11 Sept. 1886, p. 342.
[35]Reproduced in Jeremy Maas, *Victorian Painters* (London, 1969) p. 227.
[36]Ruskin, 1903–12, XIV, 51.
[37]Hunt, 1905, I, 420.

In Scotland, the impact of Pre-Raphaelitism can be seen most evidently in the work of Jospeh Noel Paton. Born in 1821, the same year as Ford Madox Brown, Paton was older than the members of the Pre-Raphaelite Brotherhood, and he was a successful artist before they had formed their group. He competed in the competitions for the Houses of Parliament and won prizes in 1845 and 1847. His successful picture of the latter year, *The Reconciliation of Oberon and Titania* (National Gallery of Scotland, Edinburgh), was bought by the Royal Scottish Academy in 1848. The subject is an imaginary fairyland, which is teeming with tiny figures drawn in minute and highly finished detail. On the basis of its success and that of a sequel of 1849, *The Quarrel of Oberon and Titania* (National Gallery of Scotland), Paton was elected an associate member of the Royal Scottish Academy in 1847 and a full member in 1850.

In the 1850s Paton incorporated Pre-Raphaelite close observation of nature into his already laborious style. The best example is *The Bluidie Tryste* of 1855 (Pl. 45), which shows the obvious influence of Millais, specifically of *The Proscribed Royalist*. The waterfall in the foreground is reminiscent of Millais's waterfall in the *Portrait of Ruskin*. Paton and Millais had been friends since 1843, when they were students in the Royal Academy schools together. Paton could have seen the *Portrait of Ruskin* in Millais's studio, and they may have had some contact when Millais was in Scotland working on the picture, as well as from 1855 onwards when Millais lived in Scotland. In August 1853, Ruskin wrote to his father from the Trossachs mentioning Paton as one of the Scottish artists looking forward to his forthcoming Edinburgh lectures.[38]

Paton exhibited *The Bluidie Tryste* at the Royal Academy in 1858. Ruskin gave it a mixed review; he disliked the gloomy subject and the lack of subtlety in the colour, but he praised the draughtsmanship and Paton's intense care: 'There is more natural history in it than in most others in the rooms; the little pinguicula alpina on the left, the oxalis leaves in the middle, the red ferns, and small red viper on the right, are all exquisitely articulated as far as form goes.'[39]

Ruskin declared that Paton's minute execution proved him capable of all perfection, despite the weakness of colour. However, *The Bluidie Tryste* seems to have been Paton's supreme attempt at this kind of Pre-Raphaelite botanic scrutiny. *Hesperus, the Evening Star, Sacred to Lovers* of 1857 (Museum and Art Gallery, Glasgow), which Paton exhibited at the Royal Academy in 1860, has much less detail and a sunset effect once again recalling *Autumn Leaves*.

Noel Paton's younger brother, Waller Hugh Paton, painted brightly coloured and highly detailed landscapes which have been called Pre-Raphaelite. He seems to have had no direct connection with the artists in London, but in 1858 Ruskin wrote a letter to the *Witness* in Edinburgh defending one of his pictures, *Wild Water, Inveruglas*, against criticism made in the *Scotsman*.[40] This picture, like most of Waller Paton's output, has disappeared.

Another older artist of Scottish origin was William Bell Scott. He was born in 1811, and hence was a mature artist by the time Pre-Raphaelitism came into being. He was also a poet, and his connection with the Pre-Raphaelites stemmed from Rossetti's admiration for his poetry. From 1843 until 1864 Scott was Master of the Government School of Design in Newcastle, so, although he became a close friend of Rossetti and other members of the group, sheer physical distance kept him apart.

Scott's best-known works are a series of scenes from the history of Northumberland,

[38]Ruskin, 1903–12, XII, p. xxvii. For Paton's friendship with Millais, see Millais, 1899, II, 403–9.

[39]Ruskin, 1903–12, XIV, 155–6.

[40]*Ibid.*, p. 329.

which he painted for the court at Wallington Hall, near Newcastle. These occupied him from 1856 until 1861. The subjects range in time from the Roman occupation of Britain to the nineteenth century. Several of them have extensive landscape backgrounds which show the places where the events were supposed to have taken place. When Rossetti saw a photograph of the first of the paintings, *St. Cuthbert*, he wrote to Scott in February 1857 to praise it:

I suppose it is the only picture existing as yet of so definitely 'historical' a class, in which the surroundings are real studies from nature; a great thing to have done . . . The whole scene too, and the quiet way in which the incident is occurring, at once strike the spectator with the immense advantage of simple truth in historical art over the 'monumental' style.[41]

Rossetti was praising Scott for doing what Holman Hunt had also set out to do in religious pictures on his trips to the East. The picture admired by Rossetti shows Cuthbert consenting to become bishop in 675. The setting is Cuthbert's retreat in the Farne Islands off the coast of Northumberland. In the National Gallery of Scotland there is a watercolour study for the background, inscribed 'Landing Place, St. Cuthbert's Island', and another study for the wall behind the figures, made from a different site. There are also various other studies for the Wallington murals including an extensive landscape for *The Building of the Roman Wall*. The watercolour studies show little Pre-Raphaelite character, and the same may be said of the backgrounds of the finished pictures Scott based upon them.

The most interesting picture of the series is *Newcastle Quayside in 1861*, which brings history up to the present (Pl. 46a). The composition depends upon Ford Madox Brown's *Work*, but whereas Brown's picture shows an age-old form of labour set in Georgian Hampstead, Scott's shows the full impact of the industrial revolution. The labourers hammering in the foreground are men from Robert Stephenson's locomotive works. They work in a picturesque jumble of motifs from modern Tyneside, including in the lower right corner a plan of a locomotive and a newspaper dated 11 March 1861, which contains advertisements for a panorama of Garibaldi in Italy, for a photographer, and for Scott's School of Design. The composition is a kind of plateau landscape, as in more conventional ways are several of the other Wallington paintings. In this case, the foreground activity appears to be taking place on the upper floor of a building, the side of which has been cut away to form an open loggia overlooking the commercial activity on the quay below. In the distance is Robert Stephenson's recently built High Level Bridge, across which steams a train.

Scott had previously used a similar composition in *Albrecht Dürer of Nuremburg* of 1854 (Pl. 46b). In this picture the German artist stands on the balcony of his house looking down at the busy medieval square before the Tiergärtner Tor. The painting's meticulous topographical accuracy reflects a spirit akin to that of Pre-Raphaelitism. However, prior to 1854 most of Hunt's and Millais's energies had been devoted to close examination of botanic detail, not ambitious topographical views. In 1852, Charles Collins had exhibited *May in Regent's Park* which was a view from a window, and by 1854 Ford Madox Brown had painted *An English Autumn Afternoon*, which does show an extensive view from a high vantage-point. The angle at which we see the woman feeding chickens in the lower left of Brown's painting is close to that of our view of the nearest figures in the square in Scott's painting. But Scott's topographical clarity, his articulation of foreground and distance by light and shadow and modification of tone, and his more linear treatment of detail, accompanied by less tightly stippled use of paint, make his work quite distinct from Brown's.

[41]Scott, 1892, II, 35–6.

His view of a bustling medieval town has as much in common with Samuel Prout as with Brown and the Pre-Raphaelites, and if Scott is more precise and accurate than Prout, an important reason is Scott's lifelong devotion to Dürer, the subject of his picture.

In later works Scott was more obviously affected by Pre-Raphaelitism. A group of paintings from 1863 show careful foliate detail and tighter, drier use of paint than *Albrecht Dürer of Nuremburg*. Later works meticulously Pre-Raphaelite in spirit are the paintings of the graves of Keats and Shelley in Rome, which date from 1873 (Ashmolean Museum, Oxford). The pictures of 1863 all include sunsets, and one of them, *The Gloaming: Manse Garden in Berwickshire* (Pl. 47a), has a Gothic tower silhouetted in the dusk. Pictures like this, and others showing empty seashores at twilight (William Morris Gallery, Walthamstow, and collection of M. D. E. Clayton-Stamm),[42] bring to mind German Romantic landscapes by Caspar David Friedrich, Carl Gustav Carus, and Carl Wagner, and they may indeed owe a debt to German art. Scott travelled in Germany in the 1850s because of his curiosity about contemporary German painting. He retained sufficient interest in German art and culture to form a collection of Dürer's prints and to publish a monograph on Dürer in 1869. In 1873 he published a book on modern German art.

Although Scott was influenced to some degree by Pre-Raphaelitism, he did not adopt the Pre-Raphaelite method of painting directly from nature. He believed that the best education for an artist was daily sketching in a pocket sketch-book. Because Holman Hunt did not have the habit of constantly making rapid records of what he saw about him, Scott felt he was a limited artist, 'a slave to the circumstances under which he worked'.[43] As we have seen, Scott based his Wallington murals on watercolour studies. Large numbers of additional sketches by him also exist. These sketches (Pl. 47b) often show a rapid calligraphic drawing and a liveliness of colour which gives them a verve and freedom otherwise rare in Pre-Raphaelite works. But they are manifestations of the continuation of a duality which Hunt and Millais eliminated by painting directly out of doors. The sketches, like so many sketches by earlier artists, are very appealing, but the finished works based upon them lack that sense of freshness of vision, which Hunt's and Millais's works from the 1850s do have, despite their leaf-by-leaf detail.

Frederick Sandys appeared on the Pre-Raphaelite horizon in 1857 with a caricature of Millais's *Sir Isumbras* in which the knight's horse has become a donkey labelled 'J. R. Oxon', the knight is Millais, and his two passengers are Holman Hunt and Rossetti. On the basis of this unlikely beginning Sandys and Rossetti became close friends. Sandys's art has much more to do with Rossetti's than with the naturalistic side of Pre-Raphaelitism; in fact, it has so much to do with Rossetti that their friendship ended in 1869 when Rossetti began to think that Sandys was plagiarizing his ideas.[44] Like Rossetti, Sandys did not work chiefly in oil, although he did paint a number of oil paintings. He was primarily a draughtsman of incredible virtuosity, and his chief contribution to the history of English art lies in the black-and-white illustrations which he made during the 1860s. Many of these illustrations have landscape settings drawn in complex and minute detail, and for them he made equally minute preparatory studies. George Du Maurier, freshly arrived in London and trying to establish himself as an illustrator, could only marvel at Sandys's execution and the ten to twelve hours of work a day behind it. Du Maurier noted the effort which Sandys put into his studies: 'If he has a patch of grass to do in a cut, an inch square, he

[42]For the latter, which is in watercolour, see M. D. E. Clayton-Stamm, 'William Bell Scott: Observer of the Industrial Revolution', *Apollo*, LXXXIX, 1969, p. 387, fig. 4.

[43]Scott, 1892, II, 44.

[44]Rossetti, 1903, pp. 393–4, and 441–4.

makes a large and highly finished study from nature for it.'[45] Many of these preparatory studies are known. They are generally larger than the finished woodcuts, and they are minutely and beautifully drawn. An example is a pencil drawing of *Wild Arum and Grass* (Pl. 48a). The drawing measures $7\frac{5}{16}$ by $6\frac{1}{8}$ inches; Sandys used it for a tiny detail of the foreground plants in his woodcut *The Old Chartist*, which measures only $4\frac{3}{16}$ by 5 inches overall (Pl. 48c). In addition, there are three other studies of natural detail for *The Old Chartist* in Birmingham. Sandys employed two of these for other works as well: he used a pen-and-ink drawing of a thistle also in a woodcut of 1863, *Life's Journey*, and he used a watercolour study of ivy growing on a post (Pl. 48b) in an oil *Portrait of the Reverend James Bulwer* (Pl. 49a).[46]

Sandys's finished woodcuts, such as *The Old Chartist* and *Life's Journey*, have an emphasis on botanic detail in their foregrounds, crowded compositions, and high horizons, all of which indicate an affinity with earlier Pre-Raphaelite work. Among the illustrators of the 1860s, all of whose activity followed the lead of the Pre-Raphaelites' illustrations to the Moxon Tennyson of 1857, Sandys has the closest relation with the Pre-Raphaelite naturalism of the previous decade. This relation can also be seen in his oil paintings. His *Autumn* (location unknown; a small version is in Birmingham) has a subject of youth and age and a landscape setting of a river and bridge at twilight, which depend quite obviously on Millais's *Sir Isumbras*. The *Portrait of the Reverend James Bulwer* has a background wall with ivy growing on it which is yet another descendant of Millais's *Huguenot*.

Yet, despite his personal as well as stylistic connections, Sandys's method of working was quite distinct from the Pre-Raphaelites' and stemmed from another tradition. He was a native of Norwich, and he continued to list a Norwich address in the Royal Academy catalogues until 1865, although during the early 1860s he resided for periods of months with Rossetti at Cheyne Walk. Sandys had plenty of exposure to the artists of his native city. One of his chief patrons, the Reverend Bulwer, had earlier patronized John Sell Cotman and owned a large collection of drawings by Cotman and other Norwich artists. A number of Sandys's early drawings are copies after Cotman, and he started making his own careful drawings from nature in Norfolk before he had any contact with the Pre-Raphaelites. These early drawings show more carefully naturalistic detail than do those of Cotman, but their detail is paralleled in the work of a younger Norwich artist, John Middleton. When Sandys came into contact with the Pre-Raphaelites, he continued to draw from nature; he did not paint directly. The number of drawings which exist by him and the reappearance of motifs in more than one finished work suggest that his practice was to make sketches independently and then compose his pictures or illustrations from separate studies he had previously made. But he also made studies as he needed them. A diary which he kept while working on the portrait of the Reverend Bulwer shows that he made drawings for the ivy in the background (City Art Gallery, Birmingham) after he had begun the painting. When he copied in the background from the drawings, he eliminated numerous details, making the ivy less complex than in the original sketches.

Sandys was not the only artist to be drawn into the Pre-Raphaelite orbit at the end of the 1850s by the magnetism of Rossetti. Two others were William Morris and Edward Burne-Jones. As students together at Oxford in the mid-1850s they became aware of Ruskin and of Pre-Raphaelitism. Several letters written by Burne-Jones while at Oxford indicate that the message of *Modern Painters*, which had possessed such potent appeal for Holman Hunt a decade earlier, still had not lost its force:

[45]Du Maurier, 1951, p. 99.

[46]See William S. A. Dale, 'A Portrait by Fred Sandys,' *Burlington Magazine*, CVII, 1965, pp. 250–53.

He [Ruskin] is the most profound investigator of the objective that I know of: the whole work is evidence of a painfully careful study of nature, universally and particularly; in aesthetics he is authority. Above all things I recommend you to read him, he will do you more good in twenty chapters than all the mathematics ever written.[47]

In 1856 William Morris, who was wealthy, gave tangible proof of his admiration for the early Pre-Raphaelite paintings by purchasing Arthur Hughes's *April Love* and Ford Madox Brown's *Hayfield* (Pl. 15). But the appeal for both Morris and Burne-Jones of the kind of careful study of the natural world which these pictures represent and which *Modern Painters* calls for was soon to give way to that of the more poetic and more decorative art of Rossetti. Both began to paint under Rossetti's direction, but Rossetti started them working with conventional Pre-Raphaelite care. He wrote to William Bell Scott about Morris's first picture, *Sir Tristram after His Illness in the Garden of King Mark's Palace, Recognized by the Dog He Had Given to Iseult*, 'It is being done all from nature of course.' Earlier, in February 1857, he had written to Scott about Burne-Jones's drawings, which were 'marvels of finish and imaginative detail, unequalled by anything unless perhaps Albert Dürer's finest works.'[48] Morris's first picture has disappeared; his one known easel picture, *La Belle Iseult*, of 1858 (Tate Gallery), has an interior setting and is little more than a pastiche of Rossetti's Arthurian watercolours of 1857, such as *The Wedding of St. George* or *The Tune of Seven Towers* (both Tate Gallery), which Morris owned. Burne-Jones's early drawings show an equally strong dependence upon Rossetti; his *Going to the Battle*, drawn in 1858 or 1859 (Fitzwilliam Museum, Cambridge), for example, reflects both Rossetti's *Before the Battle* of 1858 (Museum of Fine Arts, Boston) and his earlier illustration of *St. Cecilia* for the Moxon Tennyson. Like Rossetti's *St. Cecilia*, Burne-Jones's drawing has an outdoor setting, but one in which the creation of a medieval world is more important than the study of nature. The drawing is larger than Rossetti's, and the detail is more elaborate and more minute, but as Rossetti's letter to Scott hints, Burne-Jones drew so minutely at least partly in emulation of Dürer.[49]

Many of Burne-Jones's later paintings have extensive landscape backgrounds, and in a few cases they show specific places. The background of *Aurora* (Queensland Art Gallery, Brisbane, Australia) is based on a sketch of a canal at Oxford made in 1867.[50] Three watercolour landscapes by Burne-Jones at Birmingham were made apparently as studies for the background of *Green Summer* of 1864. The landscapes are not very interesting in themselves; all three are studies for background masses of trees, and their foregrounds are empty. In the finished *Green Summer*, the landscape setting was reduced to a subordinate role in the composition.[51] Often, when Burne-Jones's backgrounds are more important, they depend more upon earlier art than upon the artist's own response to nature. In some examples, as in *The Mill* (Victoria and Albert Museum), the earlier art is Venetian; in many others it is Pre-Raphaelite. Behind the foliate elaboration of the *Briar-Rose* series of 1870–90 (Buscot Park, Berkshire lies Millais's *Ophelia*. In *The Briar Wood*, the first painting of the series (Pl. 49b), there is no spatial depth, and the entire background is filled with botanic detail. However, Millais's picture is a record of the painstakingly observed variety of natural detail, while in the Burne-Jones there is just one kind of plant, which is repeated over the entire picture surface, drawing it into a consistent two-dimensional pattern. Natural details are used, but naturalism is no longer important. Burne-Jones

[47]Burne-Jones, 1904, I, 79.
[48]Scott, 1892, II, 37, 39.
[49]See Ironside and Gere, 1948, p.57.

[50]Burne-Jones, 1904, I, 304–05. Reproduced in Ironside and Gere, 1948, pl. 83.
[51]Reproduced in Ironside and Gere, 1948, pl. 91.

frankly stated that the 'Direct transcript from Nature', which the Pre-Raphaelites in the 1850s had tried to achieve, was of no interest to him:

I suppose by the time the 'photographic artist' can give us all the colours as correctly as the shapes, people will begin to find out that the realism they talk about isn't art at all but science; interesting, no doubt, as a scientific achievement but nothing more. Some one will have succeeded in making a reflection in a looking glass permanent under certain conditions. What has that to do with art?[52]

Although Burne-Jones was only four years younger than Millais, he started to paint over a decade later, and as an artist he belongs to another generation. The term 'second-generation Pre-Raphaelites' has been used for Burne-Jones and Morris. Their generation was the same as Whistler's; their main contribution was to the Aestheticism which came to dominate progressive English art in the 1870s. The conflict between this new taste and the naturalistic orientation of the 1850s came into the open in 1877 with Ruskin's attack upon Whistler and the ensuing legal action. Burne-Jones appeared as a witness in the trial on Ruskin's behalf because of old loyalties, but he could almost as easily have been on the other side. Burne-Jones had been taken up by Ruskin during the 1860s, but their friendship foundered around 1870 because of differences in their beliefs. Burne-Jones was offended by Ruskin's dislike of Michelangelo. Ruskin disapproved of Burne-Jones's working methods, and he could not understand the painter's lack of interest in the natural world: 'Nothing puzzles me more than the delight that painters have in drawing mere folds of drapery and their carelessness about the folds of water and clouds, or hills, or branches. Why should the tuckings in and out of muslin be eternally interesting?'[53] Around 1870, not only Burne-Jones, but also Leighton, Poynter, Albert Moore, and Whistler were more interested in folds of drapery than in hills or branches. All of these artists owed debts to Pre-Raphaelitism, but for none of them was the close study of nature any longer important in the way that it had been for Hunt, Millais, and Brown, and almost all their contemporaries during the 1850s.

[52]Burne-Jones, 1904, II, 261.　　　　　[53]*Ibid.*, p. 18.

VII
Thomas Seddon

WE HAVE seen that in the years following 1851, Hunt, Millais, and Ford Madox Brown studied the natural world more and more closely, and that Ruskin discussed and defended the works of the first two in terms of landscape painting. Hence, it should come as no surprise that as the Pre-Raphaelite impulse became widespread around the middle of the 1850s a number of artists tried to paint pure landscapes based on Pre-Raphaelite principles. These artists, for the most part, came to Pre-Raphaelitism slightly later than such painters as Hughes and Deverell, discussed in the preceding chapter; however, they did rapidly gain considerable prominence in the second half of the 1850s. This prominence was short-lived, and most of them are entirely forgotten today. But the importance that at least one biased observer ascribed to Pre-Raphaelite landscape painting is manifested by the amount of attention devoted to these painters in Ruskin's *Academy Notes*, whose years of publication, 1855–9, correspond to the period of their greatest activity. Slightly later, William Michael Rossetti, discussing the International Exhibition of 1862, wrote, 'Landscape of late years has come almost wholly into the domain of Praeraphaelitism', and the artists he deemed worthy of mention were the same group that Ruskin had praised and encouraged in *Academy Notes*.[1] One centre of Pre-Raphaelite landscape painting was Liverpool. The Liverpool artists were in close touch with developments in London, but they form a separate group because of their geographical isolation, and they are discussed in a separate chapter. The impact of the movement on a number of artists who were not intimate members of the Pre-Raphaelite group is discussed in the last three chapters. Four artists – Thomas Seddon, George Price Boyce, John William Inchbold, and John Brett – were close personal associates of the Pre-Raphaelite group, and in all of them, in one way or another, Ruskin took an active interest. The works of these four men, along with the landscapes of Ford Madox Brown and Holman Hunt, provide the central material for any consideration of Pre-Raphaelite landscape painting.

The oldest of these artists and the first to come into the Pre-Raphaelite milieu was Thomas Seddon. Born in 1821, Seddon was the son of a well-known furniture-maker. In 1841, to prepare himself to enter the family business, he went to Paris for a year to study ornamental art. Following his return he worked as a furniture-designer through the 1840s, but, although he was reasonably successful, winning a prize for a sideboard from the Society of Arts in 1848, he had ambitions for 'higher art'. It is possible that in Paris he had come into contact with the group of expatriate English artists which included Ford Madox Brown, as in London these artists, now returned home, were his teachers. Seddon first studied drawing at night with Charles Lucy in Camden Town. Lucy had been a student of Delaroche in Paris and was a friend of Ford Madox Brown; the two shared a studio in 1844 and 1845. Seddon also drew from the model at the Clipstone Street Artists Society, and by 1850 he was working in Madox Brown's studio.[2] He began a copy of Brown's

---

[1]Rossetti, 1867, p. 160.

[2]Hueffer, 1896, p. 75. For further details of Seddon's early life see Seddon, 1858, pp. 1–25.

Chaucer (presumably the version now in the Tate Gallery), and in 1851 Brown gave him the study for the picture's background, the *View from Shorn Ridgeway* (Pl. 7a). Brown and Seddon remained close friends until Seddon's death in 1856. Throughout Brown's diaries and letters are references to advising and helping Seddon, and, according to both Rossetti and Holman Hunt, Brown was largely responsible for Seddon's first picture exhibited at the Royal Academy, a painting of *Penelope*, shown in 1852.[3] In 1850 Seddon was instrumental in establishing in Camden Town the North London School of Design for the instruction of workingmen in drawing. Brown served as an instructor in the school, and was for a period beginning in 1852 its headmaster. Brown was also friendly with the rest of the Seddon family: in 1849 he painted portraits of Seddon's parents in exchange for a sofa, and Charles Seddon, one of Thomas Seddon's brothers, was the purchaser of *An English Autumn Afternoon*.

Seddon began painting landscapes while still working in the furniture business. In the summer of 1849 he spent several weeks painting at Bettws-y-Coed in North Wales, and in the summer of the following year he painted at Barbizon. His work from this period has disappeared, and his later work shows no hint either of the influence of David Cox, who was the dominant figure at Bettws-y-Coed, or of the Barbizon masters. According to the *Memoir* of Seddon written by his brother John Pollard Seddon, he was already more concerned at this time with careful detail than with painterly breadth:

He would stoutly maintain that it was far better to secure but two or three good studies during the usual stay which each artist was able to make, than to confine their practice, as was usual, to mere sketching. Instead of the single day which they usually devoted to an important scene and a large canvas, in his opinion weeks would hardly suffice.[4]

In December 1850 Seddon had an attack of rheumatic fever which was almost fatal, and only after this did he give up his role in the furniture trade to become an artist in earnest. To recuperate he went to Wales, remaining there from August 1851 until early in 1852. In a letter written in September 1851 he mentioned making a study of Tintern and two other studies. One of these may have been the *Scene on the River Wye* which he sent to an exhibition of sketches in the winter of 1852.[5] At the Royal Academy in 1852 he exhibited his *Penelope*, and in the summers of 1852 and 1853 he went to Dinan in Brittany. He became engaged to a girl from Dinan, whom he married in 1855, and in the last few years of his life Dinan was his second home. In 1852, he painted a small landscape, *A Valley in Brittany*, which he exhibited at the Royal Academy in 1853. In a letter to Ford Madox Brown written from Dinan on 1 Sept. 1852, he described it as a complicated undertaking, with 'specimens of every tree in the universe'.[6] In 1853 he painted a larger landscape showing the ruined priory of Léhon just outside Dinan. He exhibited this picture at the Royal Academy, in 1854 as *Léhon, from Mont Parnasse, Brittany* (Pl. 51a).

Léhon, from Mont Parnasse is the earliest landscape by Seddon that we can now identify, and it reveals the strong influence of Ford Madox Brown. In fact, it closely reflects *An English Autumn Afternoon*, which Brown had begun the previous year. Like that painting, Seddon's picture shows a group of casual figures on a high foreground promontory, overlooking but distinctly separate from a valley below. In the valley, the tiny figures of a religious procession leaving the ruined monastery correspond to the agricultural

[3]Doughty and Wahl, 1965–7, I, 335, and Hunt, 1905, II, 128.
[4]Seddon, 1858, p. 7.
[5]*Ibid.*, pp. 17–18, and *Spectator*, 18 Dec. 1852, p. 1212.
[6]Seddon, 1858, p.21.

labourers in Brown's picture. The horizon is high, and most of the picture is filled with the carefully delineated foliage of the trees in the middle distance, but a further range of hills is visible in the far distance. All this again reflects *An English Autumn Afternoon*, but in comparison Seddon's picture seems less purely visual than Brown's; Seddon appears more concerned with describing than seeing. While Brown's subject is a suburban view of no particular significance in itself, which was chosen because it lay outside a back window, Seddon's picture shows the picturesque ruins of a medieval monument. Throughout Brown's picture there are ambiguities, the result of his apparent unwillingness to impose an order upon the confusion of nature as he saw it. In Seddon's picture everything is clear and precise; Brown's spatial confusion has been resolved, and things fit together in an orderly fashion. Also, reflecting Seddon's relative inexperience as a painter, his picture is stiffer and drier in execution. Nonetheless, *Léhon, from Mont Parnasse* is far from an inconsiderable accomplishment. It reveals the painstaking attention to detail that was to characterize Seddon's later Eastern landscapes, as well as an ability to combine detail with a panoramic sense of the landscape as a whole. The religious procession fills only a small part of the picture area, but the entire landscape focuses upon it, and both procession and landscape gain dignity by the juxtaposition.

All Seddon's other pictures now known are associated with the trip that he made to the East with Holman Hunt in 1853 and 1854. Seddon's reasons for making this trip were mixed. Partly they were religious. According to his brother, he had contracted in Paris 'a taste for pleasure and dissipation', for which, following his illness, he tried to atone. Through his letters written from the East runs a heavy stream of penitent religiosity. But Seddon was also aware of his inexperience as an artist. He hoped to give his works a saleability by giving them the unusual and extra-artistic interest of the biblical landscape. Furthermore, he hoped to profit from the example and advice of his travelling companion, Holman Hunt.[7] Although he preceded Hunt to the East by several weeks, he waited for his arrival to begin an important work, in order to have his advice on 'the best points of view'.[8]

Seddon arrived in Cairo on 8 Dec. 1853. There, while waiting for Hunt, he had the brief companionship of another Hunt disciple, Edward Lear, who was setting off on a trip up the Nile. Although Seddon delayed commencing any big work, he did sketch various subjects, including Richard Burton fresh back from his trip to Mecca.[9] Seddon completed three of his Egyptian sketches after his return to England and exhibited them at the Royal Academy in 1856. Their titles – *An Arab Sheikh and Tents in the Egyptian Desert – Painted on the Spot*; *Dromedary and Camels at the City of the Dead, Cairo, with the Tomb of Sultan El Barkooh in the Background*; and *Interior of a Deewan, Formerly Belonging to the Copt Patriarch, near the Esbekeeyah, Cairo* – suggest that Seddon's initial interest was in the exotic and picturesque qualities of the East, rather like those displayed in the works of John Frederick Lewis. It is possible that Seddon's decision to paint in the East was in part inspired by the sensational success of Lewis's Eastern subjects exhibited at the Old Water-Colour Society in 1850 and 1852. After Seddon's return, when he sold a picture of a camel to Lord Grosvenor, he proudly reported to Ford Madox Brown that it would hang with two works

[7]Hunt, 1905, I, 362.
[8]Seddon, 1858, p. 36.
[9]*Ibid.*, pp. 32–3. Seddon's drawing was reproduced in Burton's account of his trip, *Personal Narrative of a Pilgrimage to El Medinah and Meccah*, 2nd edn. (London, 1857) I, facing p. 28, as *An Arab Shaykh in his Travelling Dress*. What is apparently a copy of Seddon's sketch by Edward Lear, dated 23 Dec. 1853, is in the Harvard College Library; see *Edward Lear: Painter, Poet and Draughtsman*, exhibition catalogue (Worcester Art Museum, Worcester, Mass., 1968) no. 28 and pl. 79.

by Lewis, 'which is honorable company' (Holman Hunt, on the other hand, dismissed Lewis as a painter of 'Egyptian Social Scenes').[10]

Seddon's practice of sketching in Cairo was in accord both with the methods of older artists such as Lewis and with the advice of Ford Madox Brown, who had apparently felt that Seddon should paint his pictures back in England.[11] But although sketching was encouraged by Brown, it did not find a place in the stricter Pre-Raphaelite dogma of Holman Hunt, and when Hunt arrived in Cairo at the end of January 1854, Seddon stopped sketching. In February the two artists encamped at the Pyramids of Giza. Hunt soon returned to Cairo, but Seddon remained at Giza for most of his time in Egypt working on a picture of the Pyramids. Like Hunt, Seddon was disappointed by the Egyptian scenery, and he professed little admiration for the Pyramids:

I must say that both Pyramids and Sphinxes, in ordinary daylight, are merely ugly, and do not look half as large as they ought to look, knowing their real size; but in particular effects of light and shade, with a fine sunset behind them, for example, or when the sky lights up again, a quarter or half an hour afterwards – when long beams of rose-coloured light shoot up like a glory from behind the middle one into a sky of the most lovely violet – they then look imposing, with their huge black masses against the flood of brilliant light behind them.[12]

His view of the Pyramids was much as described above: after sunset, 'with a village on the left, and a sedgy pool of water, in which they are reflected'.[13]

At Giza, Seddon also made a carefully finished watercolour showing excavations taking place before the Sphinx (Pl. 50b).[14] In his published correspondence there is no reference to this drawing, but a letter dated 27 March 1854 gives a description of the activities shown:

It is very amusing just now to watch the operation which Mr. Marriette is carrying on for the French Government round the Sphinx, where he is searching for an entrance. There are about one hundred children removing the sand. Some eight or ten men and bigger boys fill small round baskets with sand, and there are two groups, one of boys and the other of girls. Some older ones lift the baskets on to the heads of the children, who carry them up the slope in two long processions, the head boy and girl singing, and the others all joining in chorus, and laughing and joking and shouting, while two or three majestic old Arabs stand by as overseers, with store of vociferation and blows, not serious, which, coming on their loose drapery, only just keeps them at work, and rather increases the laughter than otherwise.[15]

'Mr. Marriette' was, of course, the great French Egyptologist who founded the Egyptian Department of Antiquities. His activities were also recorded by Holman Hunt in a drawing of Fellah children carrying sand.[16] Hunt's watercolour of the back of the Sphinx (Pl. 50a) shows the geological structure of the rock, which Mariette's excavations had partly revealed. Seddon's view is more anecdotal and more conventional than Hunt's. His watercolour is also more linear and less strongly coloured than Hunt's, but the two works are approximately the same size, and their compositions balance in a way that suggests that they may have been conceived as pendants.

[10]Seddon, 1858, p. 141, and Hunt, 1905, I, 270.
[11]Hueffer, 1896, p. 99.
[12]Seddon, 1858, pp. 52–3.
[13]Reproduced in *British Art Fifty Years Ago*, exhibition catalogue (Whitechapel Art Gallery, London, 1905) pp. 54–5. A sketch of the composition is reproduced in Seddon, 1858, p. 52.
[14]Inscribed on the back: 'The Great Sphinx at the Pyramids of Ghizel painted on the spot in the spring of 1853 during the excavations carried on by Mons. Marrith for the French Government./ Thomas B. Seddon / 137 New Bond St. London / bought Feby 26, 1856 of the painter, his friend, by G. P. Boyce for 30 gs.' The 1853 is obviously an error; the watercolour is signed and dated 1854 on the front.
[15]Seddon, 1858, pp. 64–5.
[16]Reproduced in Hunt, 1905, I, 383.

Seddon and Hunt left Egypt in May and arrived in Jerusalem on 3 June. Seddon immediately encamped on a hill south of the city, and there he remained for the rest of his stay. His main project was an elaborate picture, *Jerusalem and the Valley of Jehoshaphat from the Hill of Evil Counsel* (Pl. 51b), which he painted from a hundred yards higher up the hill than his tent. He also began a smaller view of *Mount Zion* and two watercolours. Like Hunt, he was more enthusiastic about Palestine than about Egypt, and, as in the case of Hunt, this was partly due to religious reasons:

Besides the beauty of this land, one cannot help feeling that one is treading upon holy ground; and it is impossible to tread the same soil which Our Lord trod, and wander over His favourite walks with the apostles, and follow the very road that He went from Gethsemane to the cross, without seriously feeling that it is a solemn reality, and no dream.[17]

But there was more to the Holy Land: 'Independently of the undying interest that must ever belong to Jerusalem, the country is exceedingly beautiful, and by no means the barren place I expected'. Seddon was delighted to see hills again after spending six months on 'a plain of flat mud like Egypt'. He filled his letters with rapturous descriptions of the country, and he set to work with enthusiasm. His routine was single-minded and simple: 'I get up before sunrise, breakfast, and paint till eleven; then read, *darn*, dine, or sleep till two; then paint till six; then I have to return, put up my things, and go out for a walk'.[18]

He could live outside the city in isolation and stick to this routine because he planned to stay in the Holy Land for a strictly limited time. On 3 August he wrote that he had done about half his large picture, and that he hoped to leave within five weeks.[19] Because of illness, he was forced to postpone his departure, but he did leave on 19 October, and he was back in Dinan by 4 November (Hunt remained a year longer, leaving Jerusalem in October 1855). Seddon had still not completed all his pictures by the date of his departure but planned to finish them in Dinan, using sketches and photographs. A friend in Jerusalem, James Graham, was a photographer, and Seddon admired his views:

I hope to bring some of them to England for him, so that I shall be able to show them to you [Seddon's fiancée] and supply my own want of sketches. They are extremely valuable, because perfectly true as far as they go; however, they will never supplant the pencil, for there is much in photographs that is false; the greens and yellows become nearly as black as the shadows, so that you often cannot distinguish which is shadow and which grass.[20]

This is Seddon's only recorded reference to Graham's photography; there is no evidence to what extent, if at all, he used photographs in finishing his pictures.[21]

Seddon stayed two months in Dinan; then he returned to London, and in the spring of 1855 he held a private exhibition of his works. This seems to have been quite successful, but his *Pyramids* was rejected at the Royal Academy. In the autumn of 1855, he exhibited the watercolour *The Great Sphinx at the Pyramids of Giza* at the Liverpool Academy. In 1856 he exhibited three Egyptian sketches at the Royal Academy, and in the fall of that year he exhibited *Jerusalem and the Valley of Jehoshaphat* and *Mount Zion* at Liverpool.

[17]Seddon, 1858, p. 85.

[18]*Ibid.*, p. 97.

[19]*Ibid.*, p. 106.

[20]*Ibid.*, p. 111.

[21]A watercolour replica of *Jerusalem and the Valley of Jehoshaphat* (Ashmolean Museum, Oxford) is painted over a photograph, but according to the donor, Miss H. M. Virtue Tebbs, the photograph was of the original picture, not the actual landscape (note on the back of the watercolour). This is apparently the work by Seddon referred to in a letter from Rossetti to James Anderson Rose dated 26 June 1865: 'As to the drawing, I must tell you one thing about it, it is painted in [? water-] colour over a photograph from the picture. I do not mistrust it [however] on that account, as I possess a similar thing by Seddon, now ten years old, which is as good as the first day.' (Doughty and Wahl, 1965–7, II, 557). For a qualified assertion that the picture was based on the photograph see Aaron Scharf, *Art and Photography*, (London, 1968) pp. 77 and 264.

Apparently Hunt and Seddon were not as close as their joint travel would suggest. Seddon's pranks on their trip from Cairo to Jerusalem seem to have irritated Hunt,[22] and in Jerusalem, living apart, they had little contact with one another. Upon Seddon's return to London in January 1855, Madox Brown recorded in his diary: 'Hunt, he tells me, gave him no advice at all; he has been prepossessed against him, I fear . . .'[23] In Seddon's letters from Jerusalem there is almost no mention of Hunt, and the only attention to Seddon's pictures recorded in Hunt's memoirs was at the very end of Seddon's stay in Jerusalem:

Seddon had asked me to pronounce upon his picture of Jerusalem and Siloam from Aceldama. It was painted throughout elaborately and delicately, but it was scarcely in the pictorial sense a landscape. Sitting before the spot I pointed out to him how completely the tones and tints failed in their due relation, and how essential it was that he should supply the deficiency, explaining that in conventional art the demand for variety of tones was satisfied by exaggeration and tricks, and that these had increased the due expectation for effect to such an extent that when a work was done strictly from Nature, unless all the variety that Nature gave was rendered by the painter, the spectator had good cause for declaring the work crude and false; in short, that the more truth there was in one direction, the greater there must be in others. I calculated that to do the scene any justice he must work upon his canvas fully another three weeks.[24]

Seddon did not follow Hunt's advice, but returned home without completing the picture: 'I told him that I would toss all my pictures into the fire rather than stay a moment over the time I had fixed'.[25] Although he worked on his pictures for two additional months in Dinan, when he showed them to Ford Madox Brown, Brown also was dismayed: 'His pictures are cruelly PRB'd . . . The high finish is too obtrusive. However, they present qualities of drawing and truthfulness seldom surpassed; but no beauty, nothing to make the bosom tingle. Could I but have seen them in progress: I will do all I can to make him improve them yet, but it is late'.[26] Brown did do what he could, and he repainted the sky of Seddon's *Pyramids* himself.[27] There is no mention in Brown's diary of *Jerusalem and the Valley of Jehoshaphat*, but, with or without Brown's advice, Seddon did work on it in London early in 1855. On 5 March he described it as quite finished, and 'much improved by a rather deeper blue sky'.[28] The *craquelure* which is now apparent in the sky may be the result of this repainting. Otherwise, as Brown feared, by the time Seddon was in London it was too late to make much change in such an elaborately wrought painting. Seddon defended the accuracy of his vision – 'I really believe that there was no more atmosphere at the time' – but he resolved to avoid such 'peculiarities' in the future.[29]

Jerusalem and the Valley of Jehoshaphat is a plateau landscape, showing a foreground hillside with a sleeping shepherd and a flock of sheep and goats, a valley over which the eye must jump, and a panoramic landscape beyond. It is comparable in composition to *Léhon, from Mont Parnasse*, but the view is less intimate. Most of the landscape is seen at a considerable distance, and, therefore, the scale is small. The hills are bare, rather than covered with trees, so that geological detail is of prime importance, and, because of the nature of the terrain, the effect is rather arid. The painting does reveal a concern with reflected light and colour corresponding to that of Brown and Hunt. The shadows of the trees on the hill to the right are bright blue, and throughout the picture shadows are seen in terms of colour. However, there is relatively little shadow in the picture, most of which shows bare earth under burning sunlight, and the contrasts between light and shadow are harsh and unsubtle. We do not feel that Seddon saw in terms of light and colour, as did Brown. The

[22]Hunt, 1905, I, 391–5.
[23]Rossetti, 1899, p. 158.
[24]Hunt, 1905, I, 447.
[25]Seddon, 1858, p. 131.

[26]Rossetti, 1899, p. 158.
[27]Hueffer, 1896, p. 122.
[28]Seddon, 1858, p. 134.
[29]*Ibid.*, pp. 144–5.

painting seems more like a drawing to which colour has been added; indeed, the carefully drawn patterns of terraces and erosion on the distant hills take on rhythms of their own, giving to the picture a remarkable quality of calligraphic fantasy. *Jerusalem and the Valley of Jehoshaphat* is probably the supreme example of Pre-Raphaelite attention to physical fact exclusive of all other interests, but this stemmed from the artist's limitations, or inexperience, and, as we have seen, the artist and his closest associates agreed that the result was not entirely satisfactory.

Seddon also continued to work on his *Mount Zion* after his return to England, completing it by adding to the foreground an eagle which he painted from one shot and sent to him by a friend in Jerusalem.[30] This picture has disappeared, but the detail of the eagle suggests that it may be reflected in Holman Hunt's watercolour view of the same site dated 1892, which also has an eagle in the foreground (William Morris Gallery, Walthamstow).

The two watercolours which Seddon began in Jerusalem are described in a letter which the artist wrote from his tent on 25 June 1854:

Today I have been going on with a watercolour drawing of the mountains of Moab, beyond the Dead Sea, looking down the Valley of Hinnom. I have taken them half an hour before sunset, when they are bathed in a mist of rosy light, while the valley in front is in shadow. It never does to be too confident, but, if it is finished as it is begun, it will be the best watercolour landscape that I have done. I began that, and another of Joab's well, and the great threshing-floor in front, with the oxen treading the corn, as watercolour is not so laborious as oil.[31]

The latter watercolour is *The Well of Enrogel* (Pl. 52a), which shows the activities in the valley immediately below Seddon's tent. The small scale and careful detail recall *Jerusalem and the Valley of Jehoshaphat*. As in the painting the view is from above, and in the immediate foreground there is a small figure whose body is cut by the frame in a manner reminiscent of Holman Hunt. This watercolour provided the model for the background of Ford Madox Brown's *Coat of Many Colours* (Pl. 16a).[32]

The other watercolour is quite different (Pl. 52b). It is a view of the mountains beyond the Dead Sea some forty or fifty miles away. The Sea itself is not visible. The view is seen in terms of the light and colour of the hour just before sunset. The sky is green, as Seddon described it in one of his letters.[33] The mountains in the late afternoon sunlight are deep violet, and the foreground is in strongly differentiated shadow. Stylistically, the watercolour is closer to Holman Hunt's Eastern landscapes than to Seddon's other works, and, although Seddon described it in coloristic terms early in his stay in Jerusalem and promised that it would be the best he had done, Hunt's hand may, in fact, be present. Hunt claimed to have completed one of his travelling companion's watercolours when Seddon returned home.[34] If, as indicated in Seddon's letters, he began only two watercolours while at Jerusalem, Hunt's participation seems more probable in *The Mountains of Moab* than in the drier *Well of Enrogel*. It is impossible to say how much of the finished picture is due to Hunt, but wherever the responsibility, it does have a breadth and richness of colour unequalled in Seddon's few other known works.

In London Seddon not only continued to work on the pictures which he brought back from the East, but also began to paint new Eastern subjects. The most important of these was a large *Arabs at Prayer in the Desert*, which he left unfinished at his death (Pl. 53a). In Cairo Seddon had made several sketches of camels and arabs, and this picture seems to have been based upon them. In painting a major work in the studio and basing it on

[30]*Ibid.*, pp. 133, 135.
[31]*Ibid.*, p. 94.
[32]See above, p. 43.

[33]Seddon, 1858, p. 92.
[34]Hunt, 1905, II, 128.

sketches rather than direct observation, Seddon was departing from strict Pre-Raphaelite practice, and the result looks more like an Eastern subject by John Frederick Lewis than one by Holman Hunt. Indeed, Seddon may have been inspired by Lewis's *Well in the Desert*, which had been exhibited at the Old Water-Colour Society in the spring of 1855, shortly before Seddon began his picture.[35]

A slighter picture which Seddon apparently painted entirely after his return is a *View on the Nile*, dated 1855 (Pl. 53b). In his letters from Egypt Seddon described two trips on the Nile, the first to Saqqara in December 1853, the second a longer trip through the Delta with Hunt on their way to Jerusalem the following May. The picture combines elements from both trips: the sunset effect recalls Seddon's description of 'the picturesque palm trees, and long sloping yards of the boats, looking black as night against the red golden sky' on the trip to Saqqara, while the water buffalo in the foreground are from the latter voyage.[36] The chief interest of the picture is in the colour of the Egyptian sunset, and there is relatively little topographic detail. This emphasis on effect can probably be explained as Seddon's response to the criticism which his Eastern views had drawn: of being overliteral, dry, and without atmosphere. As he wrote in May 1855, 'I know in my style of painting it is the side likely to err on, and I shall try and shew in my work this summer here that I do not do so'.[37] Unfortunately, without the 'peculiarities' of Seddon's earlier pictures, the *View on the Nile* is a rather characterless work. Its composition is reminiscent of Dutch river landscapes, and it displays none of the individuality which, whatever their short-comings, Seddon's other Eastern landscapes do have.

Having achieved some reputation as a painter of the Holy Land, Seddon returned to the East in the autumn of 1856. He intended to paint views of the Dead Sea and of the cedars of Lebanon,[38] but he contracted dysentery *en route* and died in Cairo on 23 Nov. 1856, just a month after his arrival. Following his death, meetings were held, an exhibition arranged, and a subscription was put under way to purchase *Jerusalem and the Valley of Jehoshaphat* for the National Gallery. The most interesting aspect of this activity – aside from the fact that *Jerusalem and the Valley of Jehoshaphat* did enter the National Gallery – was the participation of Ruskin.

Ruskin had visited Seddon's exhibition in 1855, and, according to the artist, he had been enthusiastic:

Mr. Ruskin also came and stayed a long time. He was very much pleased with everything, and especially *Jerusalem*, which he praised wonderfully; and in good truth it is something for a man who has studied pictures so much to say, 'Well, Mr. S., before I saw these, I never thought it possible to attain such an effect of sun and light without sacrificing truth of colour'.[39]

This opinion differs from that of Seddon's friends, and it is difficult to consider truth of light and colour among the strengths of Seddon's works known today. Ruskin, if not mis-quoted, may have been flattering Seddon; in any case, when he later praised Seddon's work, it was for other, more limited reasons. Ruskin spoke at a meeting held at Holman Hunt's house shortly after Seddon's death. There, he credited Seddon's art with a utili-tarian value:

[35]Lewis's exhibited watercolour was probably similar to, and possibly identical with, the watercolour in the Victoria and Albert Museum catalogued as *A Halt in the Desert*, which shows a well and is signed and dated 1855 (reproduced in *The Old Water-Colour Society's Club: 1925–1926: Third Annual Volume* [London, 1926] pl. IX).

[36]Seddon, 1858, pp. 33–4, 80.
[37]*Ibid.*, p. 144.
[38]Holman Hunt, letter to Edward Lear dated 31 Dec. 1856, John Rylands Library, Manchester, Rylands Eng, MS. 1214, f. 19.
[39]Seddon, 1858, p. 137.

Mr. Seddon's works are the first which represent a truly historic landscape art; that is to say, they are the first landscapes uniting perfect artistical skill with topographic accuracy being directed with stern self-restraint to no other purpose than that of giving to persons who cannot travel trustworthy knowledge of the scenes which ought to be most interesting to them. Whatever degrees of truth may have been attained or attempted by previous artists have been more or less subordinate to pictorial and dramatic effect. In Mr. Seddon's works the primal object is to place the spectator, as far as art can do, in the scene represented, and to give him the perfect sensation of its reality, wholly unmodified by the artist's execution.[40]

Ruskin spoke again at a *conversazione* held on 6 May 1857 at the Society of Arts in connection with the exhibition of Seddon's work.[41] In this talk he suggested that Seddon was an artist of no unique talent; his work was important not because it was remarkable, but because it was of a class that could and should be imitated by other artists. Ruskin then went on to place Seddon within the context of Pre-Raphaelitism. He defined the movement as 'the pursuit of truth in art, with a useful purpose', but he added that there were two distinct types of Pre-Raphaelites:

There were the poetical Pre-Raphaelites and the prosaic Pre-Raphaelites, and the prosaic were the more important of the two. The spirit of the present age was strictly scientific, and all that they could do more than was done in the earlier ages must be on the side of truth, and could not be on the side of imagination . . . Science had brought forward the disposition to test facts more accurately, which was adverse, more or less, to imagination, but which should direct to the grasping of facts around them; and it was this special direction of painting, which, he believed, ought to be cultivated.

If an artist had imaginative powers they would come out anyway, but it was a great waste to try to make all minds imaginative.

In all ages, there were two great classes of artists, men of inventive minds, and men of more or less prosaic minds; and the great danger of following the theory of beauty only, was to make the matter-of-fact minds comparatively useless, and yet they were the most common amongst them. There were more men capable of pursuing a simple problem, or representing a simple fact, than there were men capable of following at any distance in the path of the great inventive painters.

Seddon had painted at least one imaginative picture, his early *Penelope*, which Ruskin called 'noble', but the artist had measured his strength and turned 'from the paths of imagination to those of historical and matter-of-fact representation.' Ruskin thought that the change had come at a propitious moment. Because of the destruction of monuments and places of beauty which was taking place at an accelerated pace all over Europe, 'he was anxious that pictures in modern days should be addressed to the representation simply of facts, to the representation either of architecture or scenery, of which the associations were likely to be swept away by what was called modern progress or improvement'.

This was a curiously limited role to be urged by the champion of Turner, who was still in the process of writing *Modern Painters*; however, the proposal repeats a theme which had appeared in Ruskin's pamphlet *Pre-Raphaelitism*, published in 1851. Questioning whether the artist had any useful function, Ruskin had there concluded that the artists's 'true duty' was, 'the faithful representation of all objects of historical interest, or of natural beauty existent at the period; representation such as might at once aid the advance of the sciences and keep faithful record of every monument of past ages which was likely to be swept away in the approaching era of revolutionary change.'[42] The main addition in the speeches on Seddon was the term 'historic landscape'. In the first volume of *Modern Painters* Ruskin had used the word 'historical' in a different sense, defining as 'historical' those truths 'which

[40]Ruskin, 1903–12, XIV, 465n.   [42]*Ibid.*, XII, 349.
[41]*Ibid.*, pp. 464–70.

tell us most about the past and future states of the object to which they belong'.[43] He applied this concept to landscape, but he did not use the expression 'historic landscape'. In 1851 Ruskin emphasized the value of pictures as historical records; now he also assigned to them the role of substituting for travel. This idea did appear elsewhere in his criticism; for example he praised *The Scapegoat* for giving a perfect idea of a scene to people who could not see it for themselves.[44]

Holman Hunt had ideas about the value of a work of art similar to those of Ruskin, and he felt that much of *The Scapegoat*'s value lay in conveying knowledge about the place. He also took a dutiful interest in recording traditional Eastern manners and customs that were about to disappear.[45] And, of course, he was much more responsible than Ruskin for Seddon's following the path of 'matter-of-fact representation'. Apparently Ruskin had not known Seddon before his Eastern trip, and had not, therefore, directly encouraged him. He never mentioned Seddon's painting on any other occasion; so it seems that the two talks on Seddon were inspired by the special circumstances rather than by any particular admiration for his work. Nonetheless, in discussing Seddon's art, Ruskin expressed theories which were central in his assessment of Pre-Raphaelite landscape painting. The role which he ascribed to Seddon was that which he was to urge upon younger artists like John Brett, and he later measured Brett's *Val d'Aosta* by the same standards of historic landscape which he had used for Seddon.[46]

Jerusalem and the Valley of Jehoshaphat was the first – and for a long time, the only – Pre-Raphaelite picture in a public collection. It therefore attracted a degree of attention that otherwise it would hardly have deserved, and in books such as Richard and Samuel Redgraves' *Century of Painters of the English School*, published in 1866, or Philip Gilbert Hamerton's *Life of Turner*, published in 1878, it stood for the movement. Neither of these books had anything new or illuminating to say about Seddon's picture, but Hamerton's book elicited a response from John Pollard Seddon, the artist's brother, who wrote to the *Athenaeum* in 1879. He accepted Hamerton's discussion of the picture as fair, but then pointed out that *Jerusalem and the Valley of Jehoshaphat* was exceptional in his brother's *oeuvre*, and he went on to question the application of the term 'Pre-Raphaelite' to Seddon:

I remember well his correcting me with earnestness when I applied to him the term 'Pre-Raphaelite', which Mr. Hamerton has in this passage used with regard to him. 'Do not call me so'; said he, 'I greatly admire much in the works of my friends who have assumed the name, but I do not wholly agree with them, and I have my own ideas as to painting, which I shall endeavour to work out independently'.[47]

Although this letter was written twenty-three years after Seddon's death, there is no reason to doubt that it reflects the artist's view of himself. *Jerusalem and the Valley of Jehoshaphat* is an exceptional work, and it may have seemed so to the artist. We have seen that due to the initially unfavourable reaction to this picture and to Seddon's other Eastern pictures, the artist did resolve to change his style, and the direction of this change was away from Pre-

[43]See above, p. 9.

[44]See above, p. 69.

[45]See above, pp. 67 and 70. Hunt wrote to William Michael Rossetti on 12 Aug. 1855 from Jerusalem: 'I am not satisfied with the thousand books of travel that come out every year, but even these in all their triviality and superficiality are a keen reproof to painters. I have a notion that painters should go out two by two, like merchants of nature, and bring back precious merchandise in faithful pictures of scenes interesting from historical considerations or from the strangeness of the subject itself. . . . I think this must be the next stage of P.R.B. indoctrination and it has been this conviction which brought me out here, . . . I remember that Ruskin details a scheme corresponding in some degree but with some reservations as to the men to be thus employed.' (Letter formerly in the collection of Mrs. Elizabeth Burt, quoted in part in Sotheby, 1970, no. 889).

[46]See below, pp. 130-1.

[47]*Athenaeum*, 22 March 1879, p. 386.

Raphaelitism toward a more conventional vision. Yet, because of Seddon's early death, he can not be said to have succeeded in working out his ideas independently. All of Seddon's landscapes were painted between 1852 and 1856. Consequently, his known *oeuvre* has a unity and consistency which we can not find in the larger outputs, dating from much longer working careers, of artists such as Inchbold and Brett. In their careers, Pre-Raphaelitism was an interlude, as it might well have been in Seddon's had he lived longer. But in his few working years he was not able to emerge from the shadows of Brown and Hunt. Despite disclaimers, and despite the limited and derivative nature of the works themselves, Seddon was the purest Pre-Raphaelite landscape painter.

VIII

George Price Boyce

G EORGE PRICE BOYCE was born in 1826. He was trained as an architect, and in 1846 he went to work for the firm of Wyatt and Brandon. After three years he gave up architecture to become a painter. However, buildings appear in many of his paintings, and they are always drawn with a sureness and precision that reflects his training. As a painter he worked primarily in watercolour; his first master was David Cox, whom he met in Wales in 1849.[1] Boyce's diary for 1851, the first year in which he kept it, records lessons from Cox on a subsequent trip to Wales.[2] Cox's influence is evident in most of Boyce's early watercolours, and as late as the autumn of 1855 Boyce was painting broad atmospheric watercolours of Welsh scenery following Cox's example.[3]

At some time before 1851 Boyce met Thomas Seddon. The two painted together at Dinan in 1853, and Boyce later bought Seddon's watercolour of *The Great Sphinx* (Pl. 50b). Through Seddon, Boyce met Dante Gabriel Rossetti, who became his closest friend among the Pre-Raphaelite group. In 1858 Rossetti based the background of his watercolour *Writing on the Sand* (British Museum) on two sketches by Boyce of Babbacombe Bay in Devonshire. Through Rossetti in 1853 Boyce met Hunt and Millais, and in 1854 he met Ruskin. Shortly after Ruskin had first called upon Rossetti in the spring of 1854 he was taken round to Boyce's to see two drawings by Rossetti in Boyce's collection. Ruskin also looked at some of Boyce's own drawings and started to give advice, which Boyce recorded in his diary:

On my expressing my liking for after sunset and twilight effects, he said I must not be led away by them, as on account of the little light requisite for them, they were easier of realization than sunlight effects. He was very friendly and pleasant and encouraging in manner, and showed no conceit, grandeur, or patronizing mien . . . He said he would be glad to call again and see my drawings.[4]

In the summer of 1854 Boyce went to Venice on a trip apparently inspired by Ruskin. There are two letters in the Yale University Library from Ruskin to Boyce dated 14 June and 28 June 1854. These were obviously written in reply to requests for advice. In the first, Ruskin apologized for having encouraged Boyce to travel: 'I am vexed at thinking that I have perhaps been partly instrumental in leading you into the expense and trouble of a long journey, when there was quite enough material to employ you delightfully nearer home.' He recommended that Boyce work in Verona and that in Venice he should draw the exterior of St. Mark's: 'It answers precisely to your wishes, as expressed in your note, *near* subject – good architecture – colour – light and shade.'

Boyce apparently did commence a study of the exterior of St. Mark's, and in the second letter Ruskin applauded the undertaking: 'I am sure you will find it delicious.' However,

---

[1]For this and other details of Boyce's life, see Arthur E. Street, 'George Price Boyce, R.W.S.', *The Old Water-Colour Society's Club: Nineteenth Annual Volume*, London, 1941, pp. 1–8. This accompanies "Extracts from Boyce's Diaries: 1851–75', *ibid.*, pp. 9–71.

[2]Boyce, 1941, pp. 10–11.

[3]An example is *Llyn Hilsi, Wales* (collection of John Gere), which is signed and dated 29 Oct. 1855.

[4]Boyce, 1941, p. 21.

Boyce seems also to have expressed an interest in the interior, which Ruskin tried to discourage: 'The outside is the finer study – the inside is too Rembrandtesque – too much dependent on flashing of gold out of gloom – which is always effective – but comparatively vulgar – and for the rest – exhausted in idea by many painters before now.'

This echoes the advice which Ruskin gave Boyce when they first met. In both cases, he inveighed against dark effects, and, although he did so because they were easy or vulgar, the advice also reflects the constant theme in Ruskin's criticism that clear delineation is more important than pictorial effectiveness. It is related to Ruskin's idea of the usefulness of recording monuments and places of interest, which he expressed in his pamphlet *Pre-Raphaelitism*, and which he here urged upon Boyce. He suggested that Boyce stop in Rouen on his way home, because northern architecture was being destroyed far faster than Italian. Three years later, Ruskin repeated this point more emphatically in his speech on Thomas Seddon.

Ruskin, when in Venice in 1852 preparing *The Stones of Venice*, had collected photographs of Venetian architecture, which he compared to his own drawings. Apparently Boyce did likewise, and his comments drew a reply from Ruskin in a note appended to his second letter: 'What you say of Calotypes is quite true – you know they not only misrepresent colour but violently exaggerate shadow and thereby lose all truth – except of drawing.' Extreme clarity, combined with an exaggerated perspective, gives many of Boyce's later watercolours what might be considered a photographic look. In 1865, he bought five photographs from Julia Margaret Cameron ('for which, being an artist, I paid half-price').[5] However, there is no evidence that Boyce ever used photographs for his own work, and in 1854 he and Ruskin seem to have been in complete agreement about the failings of the medium.

Boyce remained in Venice and Verona until November 1854. In December, in London, he attended a lecture by Ruskin at the Architectural Museum. After the lecture the two men spoke. Ruskin immediately invited himself to come look at Boyce's recent drawings and expressed the hope that Boyce was by now 'a confirmed Pre-Raphaelite'.[6] As we have seen, in 1855 Boyce was still painting Welsh scenery in a style which was almost the antithesis of Pre-Raphaelitism, and his Venetian watercolours also reveal him as far from being a 'confirmed Pre-Raphaelite'. A number of the Venetian views are remarkably broad and atmospheric (Pl. 54a). On coarse paper, like that often used by Cox, and in a murky, almost monochromatic palette, they show that Boyce still retained his liking for twilight despite Ruskin's advice. Boyce also made more careful architectural studies in Venice and Verona, and these come closer to being the kind of careful record urged by Ruskin (Pl. 54b). However, Boyce had drawn architectural subjects before 1854, notably in Westminster Abbey,[7] and it is difficult to see any distinctly Pre-Raphaelite quality in the drawings from his trip.

In the summer of 1856 Boyce was in Switzerland, at Giornico in the Ticino Valley between Bellinzona and the St. Gothard Pass. This was Ruskin country (he had studied the topography of the Ticino in preparation for his discussion of Turner's *Pass of Faido* in the fourth volume of *Modern Painters*, published in 1856), so it is probable that this trip was inspired by Ruskin as well. At Giornico, Boyce injured his hip while 'giving chase to a trio of country lasses'.[8] This injury was serious enough to force him to stop work for a long

[5] *Ibid.*, p. 50.
[6] *Ibid.*, p. 22.
[7] For example, *Edward the Confessor's Chapel, Westminster Abbey*, begun in 1852 (Victoria and Albert Museum), reproduced in Léon Soldes, *Masterpieces of British Art* (London, 1940) pl. 8.
[8] Boyce, 1941, p. 22.

period. There are very few recorded works by Boyce from 1857; to the Pre-Raphaelite exhibition in Russell Place and the American Exhibition of British Art in 1857 he sent works dating from before 1856. But in the last years of the 1850s and in the early 1860s, following this break in his career, he was active, and in the works of these years we can see a distinct Pre-Raphaelite character.

A good example is *The Mill on the Thames at Mapledurham* (Pl. 55a and Col. Pl. 8a), which is signed and dated July 1860. Like most of Boyce's works from this period it shows scenery on the Thames between Reading and Oxford. The subject is a picturesque rustic building, which is delineated in minute detail. The colours, especially the greens of the foliage, are bright and quite unlike those of Boyce's watercolours of the early 1850s. The effect is one of rural domesticity, rather than natural grandeur. The space is strictly limited by the buildings and trees running across the picture, and it is populated by minutely-drawn genre figures, ducks, and domestic animals.

The sense of intimacy is even greater in *At Binsey, near Oxford* (Pl. 55b), which is dated September 1862. A mother and child are seated in the foreground; two guinea-hens scavenge in the grass before them; and a rustic fence and farm buildings close off the view. The foliage of a pair of trees fills the upper half of the composition, forming a screen of delicately drawn leaves across the surface of the picture. There are, of course, birds in the branches. Screens of trees through which farm buildings may be seen appear in a number of other watercolours. An earlier example is *Streatley Mill* of 1859, which also has a pair of figures reclining in the foreground reminiscent of those in Ford Madox Brown's *English Autumn Afternoon*. A later example is *Windmill Hills, Gateshead-on-Tyne* of 1864-5, in which the murky city of Newcastle is faintly visible in the background (Laing Art Gallery, Newcastle upon Tyne).[9]

Many of Boyce's other watercolours from the 1860s also show restricted spaces and emphasized foregrounds. The most appealing are a pair from 1863, which are almost identical, of a *Red Barn at Whitchurch* (Pl. 56a).[10] These show enclosed barnyards whose foregrounds contain heaps of straw in which small pigs seem to swim, their black silhouettes rising gracefully out of the straw like porpoises out of the sea. A watercolour in the Tate Gallery, *Landscape: Wootton, Autumn*, dated 1864-5 (Pl. 56b), has a field with crows in the foreground and a fence running in sharp perspective to a red brick building in the distance. The spatial relations in this work and in others by Boyce recall those in pictures by Ford Madox Brown. The emphasized foreground and relatively small building are like those in *Carrying Corn* (Pl. 14) and *The Pretty Baa-Lambs* (Pl. 8). The screen of trees in *At Binsey* is comparable to the screen of trees through which the landscape is seen in Brown's watercolour of *Hampstead from My Window* (Pl. 13a); a later and broader watercolour by Boyce, *From a Window at Ludlow* of 1871 (Pl. 57b), shows an even closer compositional similarity.

Boyce's first foreign travel after his accident at Giornico was to Egypt in the winter of 1861-2. There he shared a house in Giza with two artists, Egron Lundgren and Frank Dillon, neither of whom had any Pre-Raphaelite connections.[11] Possibly because of the influence of his companions, Boyce's Egyptian watercolours do not show Pre-Raphaelite qualities comparable to those of his domestic English subjects from just before and after his trip. At their most ambitious, they seem like broader and simpler versions of John Frederick Lewis's Eastern subjects, without any of Lewis's virtuosity. Boyce left Egypt

[9]*Ibid.*, pls. II and VII.   [11]Roget, 1891, II, 405.
[10]And *Ibid.*, pl. VI.

before his two companions, and back in London in April 1862, he showed Rossetti the results of his trip. Rossetti 'did not like what I had done in the East. Said that all things that artists brought from the East were always all alike and equally uninteresting.'[12]

In the middle of the 1860s Boyce's art began to lose the bright colouring and minute detail of his work of a few years earlier. Although throughout his life most of his work retained a distinctive precision and clarity, many of his works from the 1870s and 1880s such as *From a Window at Ludlow* (Pl. 57b) show a loosening of touch. In 1862 Boyce took Rossetti's old rooms in Chatham Place, Blackfriars, overlooking the Thames. Like Rossetti, he was a friend of Whistler; and in February 1863 Whistler began an etching of the Thames from Boyce's window. Boyce himself soon began to make studies of the river and its urban surroundings. In June he recorded in his diary that he had made 'a study of moonlight effect on river from my balcony'.[13] An example of this kind of study, *The Thames by Night from the Adelphi*, is in the Tate Gallery (Pl. 57a). 1863 was well before Whistler started painting his Nocturnes, the first of which date from his trip to Valparaiso in 1866, and it is tempting to think that Whistler's interest in nocturnal views of the river might owe something to Boyce. Nine years before, in 1854, Ruskin had tried to discourage Boyce's liking for 'after sunset and twilight effects'. His renewed interest in these effects is symptomatic of the breakdown in the 1860s of the Pre-Raphaelite impulse toward strict objectivity.

Boyce was elected an associate member of the Old Water-Colour Society in 1864 and a full member in 1878. He died in 1897 after a long career of producing competent and attractive, if slightly dull watercolours. He had independent means and was perhaps as avid a collector as an artist (he owned works by Corot, Daubigny, and Delacroix, as well as by Rossetti, Seddon, and Inchbold). His diary shows that he was always modest about his own work, and it was apparently because of his unassuming nature that he took so long to advance from associate to full membership in the Old Water-Colour Society. In later years, however, he had one vocal admirer, the Pre-Raphaelite-turned-critic, F. G. Stephens. In Stephens's descriptions of English private collections, which appeared periodically in the *Athenaeum*, Boyce's works invariably received glowing praise. Thus, the larger version of the *Red Barn at Whitchurch*, which Stephens saw in the collection of Lowthian Bell near Durham, was singled out because of the breadth and dignity with which the artist had treated 'homely, if not ignoble materials'. As the Bell collection contained a sizable group of works by Boyce, Stephens began his article about the collection with a general discussion of Boyce's art: 'He comes nearer to Mr. Holman Hunt among living artists in his execution, which is faithful, strong, elaborate, powerful in colour and tone, and marked by learned and careful drawing . . . Their nearest point of resemblance is, that they are, probably, the two most uncompromising realists in Europe.'[14] This is a strong statement, claiming much more than Boyce would have claimed for himself. If, in perspective, it seems remarkably insular, it does suggest that there is at least a distinct individuality to Boyce's art, visible beyond the artist's modesty and the limitations of scale and medium. Although Boyce's name rarely appears in the modern literature on Pre-Raphaelitism, and then only because of his diary, he was more than just a friend of Rossetti.

[12]Boyce, 1941, p. 41.
[13]*Ibid.*, pp. 44–5.

[14]*Athenaeum*, 18 Oct. 1873, pp. 500–01.

IX

John William Inchbold

JOHN WILLIAM INCHBOLD was an artist of considerably greater stature than either Seddon or Boyce, but until recently he was even more nearly forgotten, and he remains more elusive. He was a bachelor 'of a sensitive and retiring disposition', who left relatively few traces of his life other than his art. The most complete account of his life appeared in the catalogue of a small memorial exhibition held in the year of his death, and already for the anonymous author of that brief notice many of the details of Inchbold's life seem to have been cloaked in obscurity.[1]

Inchbold was born in Leeds in 1830, the son of the proprietor of the *Leeds Intelligencer* (which later became the *Yorkshire Post*). He had some instruction in drawing in Leeds, and then went to London at the age of sixteen or seventeen to learn lithography in the firm of Day and Haghe, with which his father had connections through publishing. He also studied at the Royal Academy schools, and in 1849 and 1850 he exhibited watercolours at the Society of British Artists.

There are groups of watercolours by Inchbold from 1849 showing subjects on the Yorkshire coast near his native Leeds (Pl. 58a; his first exhibited watercolour in 1849 was *Scarborough and Whitby Point, from Filey Rocks*), and from 1849 and 1850 of views on the Thames (Pl. 58b). All these early works are remarkably broad. They show none of the prevailing early Victorian tendency toward careful detail, much less any evident awareness of Pre-Raphaelitism. The Thames sketches show the atmospheric effects of certain times of day, chiefly dawn, and the transparent washes, which make even St. Paul's appear to be dissolved in light and atmosphere, bring to mind on a less accomplished level some of Turner's watercolours made on his first trip to Venice in 1819, such as *San Giorgio Maggiore, Sunrise* (Turner Bequest, British Museum).[2] However, it is unlikely that Inchbold could have been aware of these works, as they had always remained in Turner's possession.

In 1851 Inchbold exhibited two watercolours at the Royal Academy, and in the following year he exhibited a single work, apparently in oil. None of these works can now be identified. The titles of the two watercolours, *Study from Nature – Evening* and *Sketch in November*, suggest that these works may have continued the artist's interest in atmospheric effects of the two previous years. By 1852, however, there was a change. Inchbold's exhibited picture was only titled *A Study*, but William Michael Rossetti, in his review of the Royal Academy exhibition in the *Spectator*, classed it with Charles Collins's *May in Regent's Park* and a picture by William Millais as an example of the progress of Pre-Raphaelitism in landscape painting; its subject, according to William Michael, was a tree-stump and scattered leaves.[3]

This is the first mention of Inchbold in connection with Pre-Raphaelitism. We do not know how or when he came into contact with the movement, but as a student at the

---

[1] *Loan Exhibition of Works by G. J. Pinwell, Sam Bough, J. W. Inchbold* (Royal Water-Colour Society Art Club, London, 1888), pp. 7–10.

[2] Reproduced in Martin Butlin, *Turner: Watercolours* (London, 1962) pl. 9.

[3] *Spectator*, 19 June 1852, p. 593.

Academy schools at the end of the 1840s he would have had abundant opportunity to fall under its sway. In the following years Inchbold became a rather uneasy personal associate of the Rossettis. There are several references to him in Dante Gabriel Rossetti's letters, but their tone is usually less than affectionate: 'I hate Inchbold or should be happy to call on him with you'; 'Inchbold is less a bore than a curse'.[4] To this latter stricture, William Michael Rossetti, who edited the letters, added the protest that he knew Inchbold well and liked him, but he had to admit, 'there was in him something between uneasy modesty and angular self-opinion, not promoting smoothness of intercourse.'[5] Inchbold was also a friend of Swinburne, who in the autumn of 1864 spent three months with him in Cornwall, working on *Atalanta in Calydon*. Following Inchbold's death in 1888, Swinburne wrote an ode in his memory, and in a letter written at the same time gave another hint of Inchbold's quirkiness of character: 'He had not many friends, being very shy and rather brusque in manner, so that people were apt to think him odd.'[6] For Swinburne, however, Inchbold was 'a very old and dear friend', whose apparent oddness was far outweighed by his 'inexhaustible kindness and goodness, and his beautiful sincerity and simplicity of character'. In 1869, when Inchbold was on hard times, even Dante Gabriel Rossetti, his previous opinions notwithstanding, took a central role in organizing a lottery on his behalf.[7]

Inchbold's Pre-Raphaelitism is very evident in what was apparently his second oil painting to be shown at the Royal Academy, *The Chapel, Bolton*, exhibited in 1853 (Pl. 59a).[8] The subject is drawn from Inchbold's native Yorkshire; the ruins of Bolton Abbey are less than twenty miles from Leeds. In the Royal Academy catalogue Inchbold accompanied the picture with two lines from the first canto of Wordsworth's *White Doe of Rylstone*, which is set at Bolton:

> Nature softening, and unsealing,
> And busy with a hand of healing.

Although the picture is more than an illustration of these lines, the subject is in close accord. It is not a straightforward, topographically informative view of the ruins, but a picture of crumbling stone, covered by lichens and ivy, and surrounded and partly hidden by foliage and flowers.

The composition of *The Chapel, Bolton* echoes in reverse that of Inchbold's *Thames, Early Morning*, being based on architectural mass receding diagonally into the picture. This similarity is not coincidental; Inchbold relied on a few compositional formulae, which he repeated over and over throughout his career. A similar spatial structure can also be seen in some of the watercolours of the Yorkshire coast (Pl. 58a). But, although *The Chapel, Bolton* and *The Thames, Early Morning* have similar compositions, they are completely different in effect, and the difference is due to Pre-Raphaelitism. The painting has the

[4]Doughty and Wahl, 1965–7, I, 285, and II, 497.
[5]Rossetti, 1903, p. 64. See also Rossetti, 1906, I, 228–9.
[6]Lang, 1959–62, V, 258.
[7]Rossetti, 1903, p. 380; Doughty and Wahl, 1965–7, II, 684–5. See also two letters from Inchbold to F. G. Stephens describing Rossetti's help to him, quoted in Grylls, 1957, I, 216.
[8]As in the case of many of Inchbold's works, the identification of this picture is not absolutely certain. On the basis of an old photograph of a painting formerly in the Leathart collection, which is identical in all details, the picture now in Northampton (Pl. 59a) appears to be the same work. In the catalogue of the exhibition of the Leathart Collection at the Goupil Gallery in 1896 the measurements were given as 19½ by 27 inches, while those of the present picture are 25½ by 33 inches. However, in the 1896 catalogue there were errors in the measurements of other works, and it seems less likely that Inchbold would have made such an exact replica of such a highly detailed work than that the compiler of the catalogue made a mistake. The date on the Northampton picture is now almost illegible and can be read as either 1853 or 1855; in the Leathart ctalogue of 1896 the picture was listed as dated 1853.

hallmarks which we have seen in pictures such as Millais's *Ophelia* and *Huguenot* of a year earlier: microscopic detail, bright colours, and shallow space. There is none of the feeling of atmosphere which forms such a predominant part of the earlier watercolour, and the mass of the building, instead of forming a *repoussoir* leading the eye to a distant vista, creates a barrier which is continued by the trees on the left. As in Millais's works, botanic detail fills a large part of the picture, and the beauty of the conscientiously delineated leaves and blossoms gives the picture most of its charm. When we compare it to the earlier watercolour we can see the price Inchbold paid for this charm. So could the critic for the *Art Journal*, who, when it was exhibited in 1853, dismissed it with one sentence: 'This picture very much requires the relief of light and warmth'.[9]

At the Royal Academy in 1855 Inchbold exhibited a second picture painted at Bolton Abbey, this one entitled *At Bolton* (Pl. 60a). Again he included lines from *The White Doe of Rylstone* in the catalogue:

> And through yon gateway, where is found,
> Beneath the arch with ivy bound,
> Free entrance to the churchyard ground,
> Comes gliding in with lovely gleam,
> Comes gliding in serene and slow,
> Soft and silent as a dream
> A solitary Doe!

Wordsworth's poem begins with a description of a crowd gathering for a service in the chapel which still exists within the ruins of Bolton Priory. As soon as the people have gone inside, the doe appears, as described in the lines quoted. In subsequent lines the people leaving the chapel see the doe and discuss her as part of the legend of Rylstone, the telling of which forms the substance of the poem.

Here, the picture illustrates the poem: the white doe does appear before the gateway to the churchyard. But beyond that there is no narrative element. No people are present, and there is little feeling of their proximity. The mood of solitude is enhanced by a rabbit, not mentioned in the poem, sitting on the ground to the left of the doe. The interest in the picture, as perhaps inevitable in a landscape painting, is not in Wordsworth's story but in its setting: in the ancient stones of the ruined walls and the view over the valley of the Wharfe beyond.

The background view, which is lovely in its own right, is more extensive than that in the earlier Bolton picture, but it is still severely restricted to what can be seen through the arched opening of the walls. It forms a tiny part of the composition, less than one twelfth of the total picture surface. For the rest, the painting is a picture of foreground grass and stone walls, and as such it is another variant of a standard Pre-Raphaelite type stemming from Millais's *Huguenot*. As Inchbold's deer is thematically and proportionately less important than Millais's lovers, the background is more important and more elaborate. An arch in one wall reveals a second wall, which is embellished by a blind arcade as well as by the arched opening to the landscape beyond. But essentially the effect of the picture is one of two-dimensional surfaces enriched by the two-dimensional details of ivy, lichens, and the colour and texture of the stone.

As in Inchbold's earlier picture of Bolton, and indeed all his other oil paintings from the 1850s, the paint is thinly applied over a white ground, in some places so thinly that the white shows through unaffected by the local colour (Col. Pl. 2c). The result is quite distinctive and cooler, less harsh, than that of the colours in the early pictures by Millais and Hunt.

[9]*Art Journal*, 1853, p. 149.

Inchbold clearly had trouble in painting the doe, and the *pentimenti* around the legs are a reflection of the difficulty of retouching when painting in transparent colours over a white ground.

At the Royal Academy in 1855 Inchbold exhibited two additional pictures. One was entitled *A Study in March* and accompanied by another quotation from Wordsworth: 'When the primrose flower peeped forth to give an earnest of the spring'. This may be the undated picture in the Ashmolean Museum, usually called *In Early Spring* (Pl. 60b), which belongs stylistically to this period, and which does have primroses in the foreground. Also, the picture is small and of a restricted subject, so it could properly have been called a study. The distant background is of little importance, and most of the picture consists of a foreground slope, upon which the primroses grow, and bare trees, whose leafless branches form an elaborate filigree against the sky. Beneath the largest tree are a ewe and two lambs, which, like the primroses, are part of the new life of spring.

In light of the fact that the three pictures by Inchbold which we have so far considered were all accompanied in the Royal Academy catalogues by quotations from Wordsworth, it is worth recalling that Ruskin in the first volume of *Modern Painters* had held up a passage form Wordsworth as an example of careful finish:

The thoroughly great men are those who have done everything thoroughly, and who, in a word, have never despised anything, however small, of God's making, and this is the chief fault of our English landscapists, that they have not the intense all-observing penetration of well-rounded mind; they have not, except in one or two instances, anything of that feeling which Wordsworth shows us in the following lines:

> So fair, so sweet, withal so sensitive; —
> Would that the little flowers were born to live
> Conscious of half the pleasure which they give.
> That to this mountain daisy's self were known
> The beauty of its star-shaped shadow, thrown
> On the smooth surface of this naked stone.

That is a little bit of good, downright, foreground painting – no mistake about it; daisy, and shadow, and stone texture and all. Our painters must come to this before they have done their duty.[10]

In 1856, in the third volume of *Modern Painters*, Ruskin cited this passage when defending himself against charges of inconsistency for praising both Turner and the Pre-Raphaelites: 'Our painters did come to this, did do their duty, and did paint the daisy with its shadow'.[11]

Ruskin and the Victorians have been criticized for admiring Wordsworth for the wrong reasons, for his minute fidelity of natural description, when, in fact, this was not one of the poet's real interests. Humphry House has suggested that the quotations from Wordsworth in the first volume of *Modern Painters* would only strike the eye of a man concerned about such things.[12] There is some truth to this; most critics cite Girtin or Constable in relation to Wordsworth, not Inchbold. Nonetheless, the descriptions that Ruskin quoted are in the poetry, and a painter like Inchbold obviously felt an affinity. Inchbold himself wrote verse, publishing in 1876 a volume of sonnets entitled *Annus Amoris*, and many of his poems, bearing such titles as 'Early Spring' or 'Love's Autumn Buds', show a heavy debt to Wordsworth. Yet, although the foreground of Inchbold's *Study in March* is painted with a care which Ruskin (who called it 'exceedingly beautiful')[13] might have found worthy of Wordsworth, the passage accompanying the picture in the Royal Academy catalogue does not describe the primrose, but cites it as the embodiment of a season. In the picture,

[10]Ruskin, 1903–12, III, 177–8.
[11]*Ibid.*, V, 175.

[12]Humphry House, 'Man and Nature: Some Artists' Views', *The Listener*, XXXIX, 1948, p. 615.
[13]Ruskin, 1903–12, XIV, 22.

the individually studied flowers are not ends in themselves, as they sometimes seem to be in Ruskin's discussions, but parts of a larger nature. The details are factual, but there is a poetry of fact, as we can see in Wordsworth, and in much of Ruskin. The subject of the picture is not botanical illustration, but the poetry of the season, and this is a subject fully in harmony with the poetry of Wordsworth.

Inchbold painted a few other works which, from their titles and contemporary descriptions, appear to have contained comparably close – or closer – studies of natural detail. He exhibited one, *A Study*, 'The *Common Grass*', at the British Institution in 1854, and another, *Mid-Spring*, at the Royal Academy in 1856. He accompanied the latter work with a quotation from Tennyson, 'You scarce can see the grass for flowers', and apparently the picture was as full of minutely painted flowers as the quotation implies. As the *Art Journal* wrote, 'The flowers certainly faded, the grass withered, and the leaves fell before this picture could have been painted'.[14] Even Ruskin felt that Inchbold had taken an impracticable project, and in *Academy Notes* he urged the artist to choose subjects with more mass of shade.[15]

Paintings such as this, and the other pictures we have considered so far, are Inchbold's most characteristically Pre-Raphaelite works. But the almost exclusive concentration upon foreground detail, which distinguishes all of them, was not his only concern. During the same period, 1853–6, he painted another group of pictures which show extensive landscape views. The first of them is *Anstey's Cove, Devon* (Pl. 61). Although signed and dated 1854, this painting must have been substantially painted in 1853, as it was completed by April 1854, in time to be submitted to the Royal Academy. It was rejected, but before that happened Millais saw it among the pictures sent in to the Academy and described it in a letter to Holman Hunt as 'a lovely landscape with the sea and cliffs (not in the least like yours) quite original and exquisitely truthful and refined'.[16] 'Yours' refers to Hunt's *Strayed Sheep*, exhibited at the Royal Academy the year before. Although *Strayed Sheep* was the one conceivable Pre-Raphaelite prototype for Inchbold's picture (except possibly for Hunt's lost small *Fairlight Downs: Sunlight on the Sea*), the pictures, as Millais noted, are not very similar. Inchbold's view of rocky cliffs and sea is more like his own water-colours of the Yorkshire coast made in 1849 (Pl. 58a). *Anstey's Cove* is clearly Pre-Raphaelite; the colours are bright throughout, and the foliate detail in the foreground is as beautifully and delicately drawn as that in Inchbold's more intimate studies. The sea-mews in flight recall and may have been inspired by the swallows in Hunt's *Hireling Shepherd*. But Pre-Raphaelitism is here welded on to older types of landscape composition. The curving shore line, seen from above, recalls not only Inchbold's pre-Pre-Raphaelite watercolours, but also much earlier views of the Lakes of Albano and Nemi by Claude Lorraine, Richard Wilson, and John Robert Cozens. There is no evidence of how aware Inchbold may have been of such earlier works, and if we compare his picture with any of them the differences are as evident as and more important than the similarities. The sky is of minor importance in the Inchbold, and there is none of the vaporous suggestiveness of a Cozens: the cliffs on the far side of the cove are clear and hard, precisely faceted and brightly coloured. It can be argued that the composition was dictated by the configuration of the place depicted, but the artist chose his subject and his vantage-point, and in his later works views from high vantage-points looking over curving shores appear repeatedly. These compositions are a type of the plateau landscape, which we have seen used by other

[14]*Art Journal*, 1856, p. 168.
[15]Ruskin, 1903–12, XIV, 59–60.

[16]Holman-Hunt, 1969, p. 128.

Pre-Raphaelite artists, but Inchbold's use of the high foreground is not markedly similar to that in Brown's *English Autumn Afternoon* or Seddon's *Léhon, from Mont Parnasse*, which are roughly contemporary. No human figures are visible in *Anstey's Cove*, and it has none of the cosy harmony of Brown's and Seddon's landscapes. The subject is not Inchbold's own environment, but a place of impersonal scenic grandeur. Comparable scenery can be seen in another Devonshire landscape, which is also signed and dated 1854 (Pl. 59b). This picture, which was left to the Tate Gallery by Inchbold's chief patron, Sir John Russell Reynolds, has been variously called *The Dewar-Stone, Dartmoor* and *The Moorland*. It seems related to, but not identical with, the picture which Inchbold exhibited at the Royal Academy in 1855 as 'The Moorland' – Tennyson. The Tate picture is small (13¾ by 20½ inches) and is less tightly painted than Inchbold's other pictures of this time. By the standards of Pre-Raphaelite finish it appears almost sketchy and too insubstantial to have been the object of the praise which Ruskin lavished upon the exhibited picture.[17] Nonetheless, there probably was some connection. Ruskin praised Inchbold's painting of lichens, and the Tate painting does have a large lichen-covered boulder in the foreground. Also, Ruskin's editors associated the reference to Tennyson in the Royal Academy catalogue with a line from 'Locksley Hall' – 'O the dreary, dreary moorland! O the barren, barren shore!' – which is not inappropriate to this bleak and murky prospect inhabited by a solitary crow.

Even more inhospitable is the terrain shown in *The Cuillin Ridge, Skye* (Pl. 62). This picture is not dated, but it probably can be identified as *The Burn, November – The Cucullen Hills*, which Inchbold exhibited at the Royal Academy in 1856. *Cucullen* is one of the many variants of *Cuillin*, the name of the bare and precipitous range of mountains on the Isle of Skye. In the foreground there is carefully painted foliage, like that in the foreground of *Anstey's Cove*, but it is squeezed into a corner, and behind it the burn forms a barrier blocking rather than encouraging our entrance into the further landscape. There are a few hardy sheep on the hills in the middle distance, but no humans are present, and there are no roads, cottages, or other marks to indicate that people have ever penetrated this forbidding land. None of Inchbold's other known early pictures show any figures either, but subjects such as Bolton Abbey at least imply that someone was there once.

In many of Inchbold's titles indications of time are more important than indications of place. For example, his two watercolours at the Royal Academy in 1851 were *Study from Nature – Evening* and *Sketch in November*. In 1855 came *A Study in March* and in 1856, *Mid-Spring*. In the title *The Burn, November – The Cucullen Hills* both time and place are specified, and in the picture both are important. The mountains are painted with a hard clarity, which demands our belief in their topographic accuracy,[18] but they are also seen under the long shadows of evening. Before them hangs a thin strip of cloud, which is both a specific temporal effect, and a reflection of the extraordinary atmospheric effects for which Skye is famous. Over the distant horizon, to the right of the mountains, is an orange and purple sunset. This forms a relatively small part of the picture as a whole, but it is significant as a change from the clear sunlit detail in all the pictures now known which Inchbold sent to the Royal Academy from 1853 to 1855. In 1856 Millais's *Autumn Leaves* and Holman Hunt's *Scapegoat* also appeared at the Royal Academy, so Inchbold's sunset appears to be part of a larger Pre-Raphaelite redirection. In his case this was not an entirely new departure. In the Tate Gallery *Moorland* of 1854 the distance is lost in purple haze, and enough of

[17]Ruskin, 1903–12, XIV, 21–2.
[18]The subject of the picture, which until 1965 had been labelled *Ben Eay, Ross-shire*, was, in fact, identi- fied by Mr. Donald Reid on this basis. The view is from near Sligachan. I am grateful to Mr. Ian Lowe for this information.

Inchbold's watercolours of 1849 and 1850 show atmospheric effects of dawn and evening to make the sunset in *The Cuillin Ridge* seem like a continuation or revival of a pre-Pre-Raphaelite preoccupation.

Despite the departure from strict Pre-Raphaelitism that Inchbold's interest in atmospheric effects might imply, the works which he exhibited in the years 1852 through 1856 established him as the most prominent Pre-Raphaelite landscape painter. In 1857, in a letter describing the artists participating in the American Exhibition of British Art, William Michael Rossetti wrote that Inchbold ranked 'perhaps highest of the strictly Pre-Raphaelite landscape painters', and he added as an inevitable corollary, 'Much praised by Ruskin'.[19] Ruskin had known Inchbold since at least 1854, when he wrote his letter to *The Times* explaining Holman Hunt's *Awakening Conscience*. The first version of the letter had also included remarks about Inchbold and Charles Robert Leslie. When the letter was not printed, Ruskin, thinking it too long, eliminated the comments about Leslie and Inchbold and resubmitted it.[20] We do not know what he said about either artist, but as Inchbold's picture of that year, *Anstey's Cove*, was rejected by the Academy, Ruskin probably voiced a protest. Also, as Ruskin could not have seen the picture on the Academy's walls, we can assume that he probably saw it in the artist's studio. In March of the following year he borrowed one of Inchbold's pictures to show to Charles Kingsley to convert the writer to Pre-Raphaelitism. In May he put off visiting Rossetti so that he could see Inchbold before Inchbold left town,[21] and in the same month, in the first *Academy Notes*, he proclaimed Inchbold's *Moorland* 'the only thoroughly good landscape' in the Royal Academy exhibition. In May of 1856 Ruskin criticized Inchbold's choice of subject in *Mid-Spring*, but he praised the 'exquisite painting of withered heather and rock' in *The Burn, November – The Cucullen Hills*, and by 24 June they were together at Lauterbrunnen in Switzerland. In 1857 Ruskin did not go to the Alps, but he commissioned four drawings of cottages from Inchbold, who was at Chamonix. In 1858 they were together for two weeks at Fluelen and Bellinzona in Switzerland.[22]

Although the documentation of their relationship is slight, not going beyond the few dates and references just cited, it seems clear that Ruskin's interest in Inchbold was the result of the artist's application of Pre-Raphaelitism to landscape subjects. And it seems equally clear that Inchbold went to Switzerland directly or indirectly because of Ruskin. The Alps were one of Ruskin's passions. His own most ambitious drawings are of Alpine subjects. Long descriptions of the mountains fill his writings, and in *Modern Painters* he urged that more pictures be painted of the Alps.[23] As soon as Ruskin met Millais he invited him to Switzerland, and in one of his first published defences of the Pre-Raphaelite movement he fantasized about Millais's painting a mountain landscape.[24] Ruskin only succeeded in getting Millais as far as the Trossachs, but it was perhaps inevitable that, when a younger artist emerged who was a Pre-Raphaelite landscape painter, he would soon be in Switzerland, with Ruskin at his side. Ruskin not only commissioned Alpine subjects from Inchbold, he also worked to see that they were properly painted. A letter from Ruskin to his father, dated 9 August 1858, gives a picture of the treatment:

The two little drawings of which you speak in my bedroom are Inchbold's; the cottage, one I

[19]MS., Yale University Library. See Fredeman, 1965, p. 54, for the attribution of this letter.
[20]Ruskin, 1903–12, XIV, 38.
[21]Rossetti, 1899, pp. 96 and 79; reprinted in Ruskin, 1903–12, XXXVI, 190 and 201.
[22]Ruskin, 1903–12, XIV, pp. xxiii, 21, 59–60, and VII, p. xxxiii. Joan Evans and John Howard Whitehouse, eds., *The Diaries of John Ruskin* (Oxford, 1956–9) II, 516.
[23]Ruskin, 1903–12, III, 429.
[24]See above, p. 50. He also tried to get Rossetti to Switzerland; see Ruskin, 1903–12, V, p. xlix.

chose and made him draw at Lauterbrunnen; the Thun, bought when he couldn't sell anything, to help him a little. It isn't good for much, but is like a sweet Swiss evening. I wanted and ordered of him (paying him when he was at Chamouni last year) four more cottages; but he got entirely off the rails at Chamouni, and the cottages are failures. I stayed with him, or rather, made him stay with me, at Bellinzona, in order to make him understand where he was wrong. He was vexed with his work and, yet, thought it was right, and didn't know why he didn't like it, nor why nobody liked it. It was a delicate and difficult matter to make him gradually find out his own faults (it's no use *telling* a man of them), and took me a fortnight of innuendoes. At last I think I succeeded in making him entirely uncomfortable and ashamed of himself, and then I left him.[25]

In 1857, the year following his first visit to Switzerland, Inchbold exhibited one Alpine subject at the Royal Academy, *The Jungfrau, from the Wengern Alp*, and one at the Pre-Raphaelite exhibition in Russell Place, *Mid-day on the Lake of Thun*. He exhibited nothing at all in London either in 1858 or 1859. In 1860 he sent the same or another *Lake of Thun* to the Royal Academy and a picture entitled *Above Lucerne* to the Liverpool Academy. This picture may be *The Lake of Lucerne, Mont Pilatus in the Distance*, dated 1857, which is Inchbold's sole Alpine picture from these years now known (Pl. 63 and Col. Pl. 6a). Another, *A By-Path to Chamouni*, apparently from Inchbold's stay at Chamonix in 1857, was engraved in the *Art Journal* in 1871.[26] According to the short text which accompanied the plate, Inchbold painted the picture on the spot during a residence of several months near Sallanches, which is a few miles to the west of Chamonix.

Both *A By-Path to Chamouni* and *The Lake of Lucerne* show vast views, combining leaf-by-leaf foreground foliage with prospects of distant mountains. In *The Lake of Lucerne* the vantage-point is high above the lake, and the composition is built around the curve of the shore, like that of *Anstey's Cove*, but the foreground in *The Lake of Lucerne* is considerably less important than in *Anstey's Cove*. The top of a plant reaches into the picture, and there are vines along a wall, but no ground plane is visible. This abbreviation of the foreground is comparable to that in the watercolours which Holman Hunt brought back from the East in 1856.

An even more noteworthy change from *Anstey's Cove* can be seen in the palette of *The Lake of Lucerne*. Whereas in the former picture the colours are bright, in the latter they are light. They are blues and greens, as in the earlier picture, but now so uniformly pale that the picture looks like a watercolour. Inchbold's method of allowing the white ground to show through almost unaffected by the local colour is particularly evident in the foregound leaves, but nowhere in the picture is there much depth of colour. Nor is there any feeling of the richness of oil paint, which, despite the detail, we can still feel in a picture such as *Anstey's Cove*. The painting appears to have been painted as thinly as possible with a uniform stipple and a minimum of oil medium. The result is a uniformly flat, matt surface.

Despite or because of these 'peculiarities' (the term used by the *Art Journal* to describe the difficulties which the engraver of *A By-Path to Chamouni* had to overcome), *The Lake of Lucerne* is a jewel-like small painting, which makes the disappearance of Inchbold's other Alpine works from the 1850s seem a major loss. The feeling of almost visionary calm over the placid lake surrounded by mountains is akin to the mood that wafts over many of the Alpine watercolours of John Robert Cozens. It also seems to look forward to the more self-consciously subjective views of Alpine lakes by the Swiss painter Ferdinand Hodler. *The Lake of Lucerne* represents the end of Inchbold's truly Pre-Raphaelite pictures, but it is the most beautiful of them all.

It is impossible to say to what extent *The Lake of Lucerne* was influenced by Ruskin. The

---

[25]Ruskin, 1903–12, XIV, p. xxiii.   [26]*Art Journal*, 1871, facing p. 264.

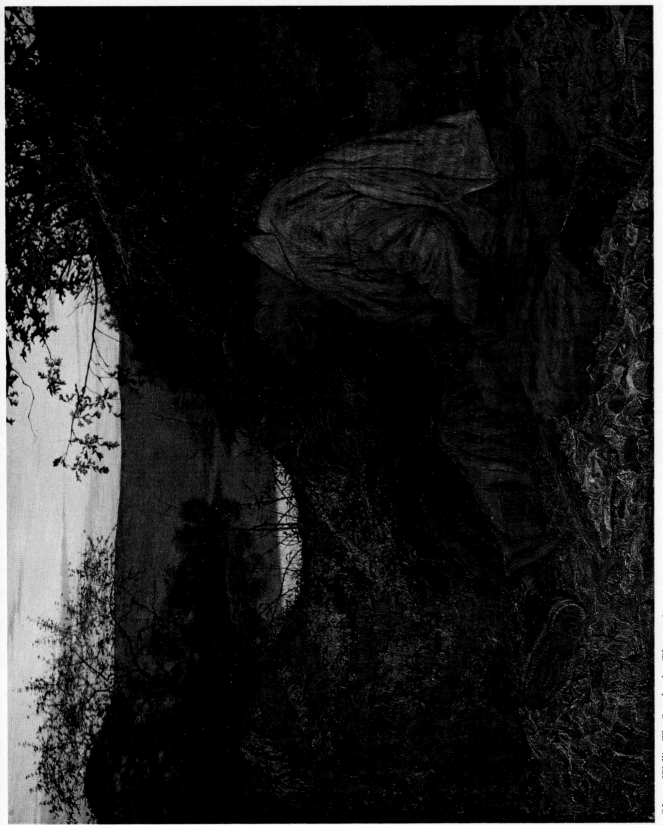

5. Henry Wallis, *The Stonebreaker* (Plate 43a)

6a. John William Inchbold, *The Lake of Lucerne, Mont Pilatus in the Distance* (Plate 63)

6b. John Brett, detail from *Val d'Aosta* (Plate 70)

location was one to which Ruskin repeatedly returned; indeed Fluelen, where he met Inchbold in 1858, is on the Lake of Lucerne. The effect of the distant mountains, with the outlines crisply drawn and the interiors lost in haze, is close to that in many of Ruskin's own drawings, and the similarity is heightened by the fact that Inchbold's picture looks so much like a watercolour. Yet all the evidence suggests that Ruskin did not think much of Inchbold's Swiss pictures. In his letter to his father, quoted above, Ruskin was scornful about Inchbold's drawings. In the *Academy Notes* for 1857 he ignored Inchbold's *Jungfrau, from the Wengern Alp* except for a passing mention in a discussion of a picture by Maclise.[27] As Ruskin was the one critic from whom Inchbold could have felt that he deserved some attention, there certainly was implied disapproval in his silence. Ruskin's disapproval may have been the reason why the artist did not exhibit at all in 1858 and 1859. Neglect publicly and 'a fortnight of innuendoes' privately must have been discouraging to a man as touchy and insecure as Inchbold.

Since Ruskin did not discuss Inchbold's Swiss works, we do not know why he failed to be enthusiastic about them. In 1856 he had criticized Inchbold for painting pictures without enough mass of shade, and he may have felt that the light palette of *The Lake of Lucerne* was a flagrant repetition of this fault. Also, he might well have felt that Inchbold relied too heavily on conventional compositional formulae. But this is speculation. In his letter to his father, Ruskin did not specify what went wrong when Inchbold 'got entirely off the rails at Chamouni', but he was complaining about Inchbold's drawings rather than his paintings.

A few watercolours by Inchbold dated 1857 and 1858 are known. None of them show Alpine subjects, but they may, nonetheless, reflect what Ruskin considered getting off the rails. These watercolours all show surprising breadth. If we take as an example a view of *Vesuvius and the Bay of Naples, from Posillipo*, which is dated 1857 (Pl. 64a), its looseness and freedom of handling seem very different from the stippled dryness of *The Lake of Lucerne*. There are elements in common between the two works: views over water to mountains, high vantage-points and consequently high horizons, and compositions built up from diagonals in the lower left corner, with the shore line curving beyond. But while in *The Lake of Lucerne* everything in the landscape is seen with pellucid clarity, in *Vesuvius and the Bay of Naples* there is no comparable detail, only a washy, atmospheric imprecision. The other watercolours of 1857–8 are essentially the same; in none of them does there appear even a vestige of Pre-Raphaelite detail. They are smaller, more informal works than a picture such as *The Lake of Lucerne*, and it may be that Inchbold was using different media in different ways. However, in the years 1853–6, the period of his most characteristically Pre-Raphaelite oil paintings, Inchbold appears to have done few, if any, watercolours. From the years following 1857 there is a comparable gap in his known oil paintings. He did exhibit a picture called *Furze Blossom* at Liverpool in 1860 and at the Royal Academy in 1861,[28] and he exhibited Cornish subjects in 1862 and 1863, but all these works have disappeared. The earliest oil paintings subsequent to *The Lake of Lucerne* which are now known date from visits which he made to Venice in 1862 and the following years. These Venetian pictures have much more in common with a watercolour such as *Vesuvius and the Bay of Naples* than with the oil paintings of the 1850s, and thus they suggest that the

[27]Ruskin, 1903–12, XIV, p. 96.
[28]This work must have been an oil painting because of the high price (£250) which Inchbold asked for it at Liverpool. For *The Burn – November – The Cucullen*

Hills and *The Jungfrau from the Wengern Alp* he had asked £150 and 150 gns. See Bennett, 1963, pp. 492, 495.

watercolours of 1857–8 represent not just the artist's different use of the medium, but the beginning of the end of Inchbold's adherence to strict, detailed Pre-Raphaelitism.

In all of Inchbold's Venetian pictures the Lagoon is more important than the city itself. They seem indebted to pictures of the Lagoon by Turner such as *The Campo Santo, Venice* (Toledo, Ohio) or *The Sun of Venice Going to Sea* (Tate Gallery); however, the views over water also continue a type of composition that had appeared repeatedly in Inchbold's art since his Thames and Yorkshire watercolours of 1849. In *Venice from the Public Gardens* (Pl. 65a), which is a sunset view of the city across the Lagoon, we see a variant of the familiar curving shore line, now moved from the left to the right-hand side of the picture. In a picture looking in the opposite direction from the Public Gardens (Pl. 64b) the only land in sight is a thin strip across the horizon. The immediate foreground is open water, in which the brightly coloured sails of a fishing boat are reflected. This emptiness and the picture's limited range of pale blue and pink colours seem the antithesis of the highly detailed and brightly coloured Pre-Raphaelitism of the 1850s. In this picture of early-morning calm we can see both the re-emergence of the interests which underlay Inchbold's Thames watercolours of 1849 and 1850 and a concern with compositional simplicity and tonal harmony which looks forward to Whistler.

Because it shows the city at twilight, the picture looking toward Venice from the Public Gardens seems even more Whistlerian. The sunset glow in the sky and its reflection in the Lagoon show a feeling for spectacular natural effects which looks back to the Tate *Moorland* and *The Cuillin Ridge*, but the city itself is only a dark silhouette along the horizon. Its towers, causing long reflections in the water, and the pinpoints of light within the darkness have an effect similar to those which appear in Whistler's nocturnal views along the Thames and in the few oil paintings from Whistler's Venetian trip of 1879–80.

We know that Inchbold was in Venice in the summer of 1862, when William Michael Rossetti met him there.[29] Drawings of Venetian subjects in the Oppé collection are dated 1862, 1863, and 1864. Neither of the paintings from the Public Gardens is dated, but Inchbold did exhibit a picture of the Public Gardens from the sea at the Royal Academy in 1865. Thus, Inchbold's Venetian pictures appear to be not only as much as seventeen years earlier than Whistler's Venetian works, but also to pre-date Whistler's first Nocturnes. There is no recorded proof that Whistler knew Inchbold, as there is in the case of Boyce, but since both moved in the circle of Swinburne and the Rossettis during the 1860s, it is more than likely that they came into contact.

In 1865 and 1866 Inchbold was in Spain. A landscape with orange trees in the foreground, showing the coast near Valencia, is dated 1865 (Pl. 65b). Another landscape, *Spring Time in Spain* (City Art Gallery, Birmingham) is the same size and apparently dates from the same trip although it bears the date 1869, when Inchbold completed it and sold it to James Leathart. In 1866 he also visited – or, at least, remembered – Yorkshire. In the Oppé collection are three small oil sketches, two of which are inscribed *Recollection – Barden Fells, 1866* and *Recollection – Strid, Barden Tower, 1866* (Pls. 66a and c). The Strid and Barden Tower are in Wharfedale, a few miles beyond Bolton Abbey. The sketches have little topographical detail, and, since they are titled *Recollections*, they were probably not painted on the spot. One bears Inchbold's London address, Lincoln's Inn Fields, along with his monogram and the date on the front of the picture. The three sketches are all broadly painted, and, although they show extensive landscapes, they are essentially two dimensional in effect. By 1866 we might well expect a kind of two-dimensional breadth

[29]Rossetti, 1903, p. 8.

reflecting Whistler and the by-now widespread acquaintance with Japanese prints, but Inchbold's sketches show less affinity with Whistler than did his Venetian pictures. On the contrary, these oil sketches seem to be extremely personal works, whose murky colours and strong brushwork create a mood of melodramatic turbulence. This is most evident in *Peat Burning*, the third sketch, in which the foreground is filled with red flames (Pl. 66c).

The sombre mood of the oil sketches can be seen on a more public scale in *Stonehenge from the East* (Pl. 66d), Inchbold's largest painting, which was rejected by the Royal Academy in 1869. This picture, which has now deteriorated badly, shows the monument under a cloudy sky, with the rays of the setting sun filtering through the stones. Following its rejection by the Royal Academy, Inchbold exhibited it in a 'Select Supplementary Exhibition' of refused pictures, and he wrote to both William Michael Rossetti and James Leathart trying to sell it. To the former, he explained his ambitions in the picture:

I have tried to secure architectural grandeur and natural sublimity, especially that religiousness by the introduction of the sun setting in the very centre of the altar-like portal; whilst the clouds are meant to suggest what is at once fiery and spiritual, the forms being (as often in nature) scarcely draped in cloudy matter. At the base is a barrow of the big past about which the everlasting flowers are opening seed-petals to the wind.[30]

1869 was a difficult year for Inchbold. In January he had to give up his studio in Lincoln's Inn Fields, and, according to William Michael Rossetti's diary, he lived successively with John Brett, Burne-Jones (without invitation), and Charles Augustus Howell. This evidently inspired Dante Gabriel Rossetti's limerick:

> There is a mad artist named Inchbold
> With whom you must be at a pinch bold:
> Or else you may score
> The brass plate on your door
> With the name of J. W. Inchbold.[31]

Inchbold never again had a proper London residence, and in subsequent years his address as listed in Royal Academy catalogues was either that of his patron Sir John Russell Reynolds or the Charing Cross Hotel, from where he was already writing to Leathart by October 1869. Throughout the year Inchbold seems to have had monetary problems. In January, Rossetti and Howell organized a lottery on his behalf, and through Inchbold's letters to Leathart, dating from October and November, runs an undisguised note of financial desperation.[32]

In April or early May of 1869 Inchbold went to the Isle of Wight, where he remained at least through August. In November, he wrote to Leathart from the Charing Cross Hotel that he had a picture recently done in the Isle of Wight, which was not yet framed. At the Royal Academy in the following year he exhibited a subject from the Isle of Wight, *The Under-cliffe, Spring Time* (Pl. 67a), and this picture, although dated 1870, must have been painted substantially in 1869 to have been ready in time for submission to the Royal Academy in April. This painting of a fresh and flowering coast has none of the portentous heaviness of the *Stonehenge*, and its blue sky and sunlit flowers in the foreground seem like a reversion to Inchbold's Pre-Raphaelite style of the 1850s. However, if we look again at *Anstey's Cove* (Pl. 61), the most obvious parallel to *The Under-cliffe*, we can see that the detail in the later picture is neither as elaborate nor as microscopically fine. In addition, the presence of figures in the Isle of Wight picture helps to create a more intimate mood than that of *Anstey's Cove* and Inchbold's other pictures from the 1850s. Although

[30]*Ibid.*, pp. 438–9.
[31]*Ibid.*, pp. 380, 495.

[32]There are eleven letters dated 1869 in the possession of Dr. Gilbert Leathart.

figures in landscapes were the rule rather than the exception in Pre-Raphaelite painting they were conspicuously absent from Inchbold's earlier pictures. Their appearance (beginning in *A By-Path to Chamouni* of 1857) humanizes the landscape and adds sentiment. The mood is light in *The Under-cliffe*, but nonetheless we feel it to be a deliberately sought mood, and this distinguishes the painting from the less subjective, more impersonal works of the 1850s.

Unfortunately, we do not know enough of Inchbold's work from the 1870s to say how typical *The Under-cliffe* might be. He exhibited another subject from the Isle of Wight at the Royal Academy in 1871. The subjects of watercolours dating from the first half of the 1870s range from lurid sunsets over the Yorkshire coast to delicately pretty views of Stratford-on-Avon. In 1874 an etching after a watercolour by Inchbold of *Charing Cross* appeared in the *Portfolio*, and the brief article accompanying it stated that in the last year or two Inchbold had been making a series of watercolour sketches along the Thames and elsewhere in London.[33] The etching is a nocturnal view of Charing Cross Station seen from across the river and shows an evident debt to Whistler. In 1876, the year of his volume of verse, *Annus Amoris*, a second etching after Inchbold, an interior of Westminster Abbey, was published in the *Portfolio*, and in 1879 another Westminster Abbey appeared, this time etched by the artist himself.[34] Inchbold probably revisited Venice in the 1870s, as he exhibited *The Green Horses of St. Mark's* at the Royal Academy in 1873, and he did visit North Africa, exhibiting an Algerian subject in 1878.

Some time in the later 1870s, possibly by 1877, the date on a watercolour of *Clarens* (private collection), Inchbold took up residence at Montreux on the Lake of Geneva, and he seems to have remained there except for occasional visits to England until his death (at his sister's home near Leeds) in January 1888. All of his recorded or dated works from 1880 onwards are views of the east end of the Lake of Geneva or the country immediately around it. He exhibited pictures of the Lake of Geneva at the Royal Academy in 1882 and 1885, and these along with a *From Pallano to the Dent du Midi*, also shown in 1885, were his only works to appear at the Academy during the 1880s. Swinburne, in a letter of 1883 describing Inchbold's studies of the Lake of Geneva, mentioned that there was one large picture.[35] This has disappeared, but a moderately sized ($20\frac{1}{4}$ by 31 inches) painting, inscribed 'Misty Morning Lake Leman' and dated 1883, is in the National Gallery of Ireland, and several watercolours are known. Some of the watercolours bear the dates 1880 or 1881, and many of them show variations of the same view, looking from a high vantage-point over the curving shore of the lake to the mountains in the South. In all of these views the Castle of Chillon is either distinctly or faintly visible, depending upon atmospheric conditions. A characteristic example is the *View Above Montreux*, dated 1880, in the Victoria and Albert Museum (Pl. 67b). Like all this group of watercolours it harks back in composition to the *Lake of Lucerne* of 1857 (Pl. 63). The delicate pattern of bare branches also recalls the minutely drawn branches in such earlier works as *In Early Spring* (Pl. 60b). But here the branches of the foreground trees are used as a foil to the hazy indistinctness of the rest of the landscape. The vaporous effect is subtle and lovely, but it is remote from the crystalline Pre-Raphaelite clarity of Inchbold's earlier works.

Through most of his life Inchbold seems to have been a rather pathetic figure. The American painter Elihu Vedder, who met Inchbold in Italy, wrote that there was 'some-

[33]*Portfolio*, 1874, pp. 180–81.
[34]*Ibid.*, 1876, op. p. 168, and 1879, facing p. 188. Inchbold later, in 1885, published a set of twenty-one

etchings entitled *Mountain and Vale*.
[35]Lang, 1959–62, V, 26–7.

thing forlorn' about him.[36] Inchbold himself in writing to William Michael Rossetti in 1869 about his *Stonehenge* found it necessary to apologize for the picture:

It is not, as you know, very easy to gain success perfect and complete in a picture like this, painted almost entirely from nature with another and entirely distinct vision before the imagination, and perhaps with a heart somewhat maimed and broken by that deadly and relentless opposition I seem to inspire most innocently in some quarters . . .[37]

William Michael Rossetti described Inchbold as an artist who, after starting as a Pre-Raphaelite landscape painter, was harassed by ill success into frittering away his powers.[38] For William Michael there was no question that Inchbold's later works represented a decline from his peaks of Pre-Raphaelite achievement. If we accept this judgement, it is tempting to see Ruskin as the villain. Inchbold's years in Switzerland seem to have been the time when he turned away from strict Pre-Raphaelitism, and the rough treatment which he received there from Ruskin may have caused not only the change but permanent damage as well. It is clear from Inchbold's letter to William Michael, quoted above, that he considered himself a damaged creature. Yet, to lay at Ruskin's feet chief responsibility for a career that lasted thirty years after their contact ended seems excessive, and when we look at Inchbold's career as a whole we should hesitate in ascribing to either Ruskin or the Pre-Raphaelite movement more importance than they deserve.

All of Inchbold's genuinely Pre-Raphaelite works which are now known date from within five years of one another, from 1853 to 1857. Although this was the period of his most memorable and, probably, most successful works, it was only an interlude. Both before it and after it, he painted in a very different fashion, and many of his later works have more in common with his juvenile works of 1849 and 1850 than with those from his Pre-Raphaelite years. Following Inchbold's death, Swinburne, who was a closer friend and had less of a Pre-Raphaelite candle to burn than William Michael Rossetti, described Inchbold's artistic output as comparable to Turner, without a mention of Pre-Raphaelitism.[39] When the etching after Inchbold's *Charing Cross* was published in *Portfolio* in 1874, the unsigned text accompanying it contained the following assessment of Inchbold's art:

Mr. Inchbold interprets his subjects with great taste and feeling, idealizing always to some extent, so that his drawings tend rather to a spiritual and not quite substantial conception of things, than to a material solidity; but in times of a vulgar yet powerful realism, this refinement is like poetry after prose.[40]

In Inchbold's *oeuvre* there is considerable variety, but this description of his art fits most of it, with the partial exception of those pictures dated from 1853 to 1857. 'Idealizing always to some extent' comes close to being the polar opposite of the quest for exact truth to nature which underlay Pre-Raphaelite naturalism. Vestiges of Pre-Raphaelitism remained a part of Inchbold's art; for example, as we can see from his letter to William Michael Rossetti quoted above, he continued to paint directly from nature even in works such as the *Stonehenge*, whose appearance is in no way Pre-Raphaelite. In all of Inchbold's later pictures Pre-Raphaelite directness was accompanied by 'a spiritual and not quite substantial conception of things'. The mists of subjectivity are usually more evident than the bright colours and careful detail of the Pre-Raphaelite quest for objectivity.

[36]Elihu Vedder, *Digressions* (Boston and New York, 1910) p. 161.
[37]Rossetti, 1903, p. 439.
[38]Rossetti, 1906, I, 229.

[39]Lang, 1959–62, V, 258.
[40]*Portfolio*, 1874, p. 180. This was probably written by Philip Gilbert Hamerton, the editor.

X

John Brett

JOHN BRETT was born in Surrey in 1831, the son of an army officer. He entered the Royal Academy schools in 1854 after having had some preliminary instruction in drawing in Dublin, where his father was stationed. Hence, although Brett was only a year younger than Inchbold, he began his painting career several years later, and he emerged on the Pre-Raphaelite scene much later. Inchbold first exhibited at the Royal Academy in 1851, and in the following year William Michael Rossetti categorized his art as 'Pre-Raphaelite'. Brett did not exhibit at the Royal Academy until 1856.

It appears that Brett originally intended to be a figural artist rather than a landscape painter. His first contribution to the Royal Academy consisted of three portraits, and in 1857 he exhibited a painting entitled *Faces in the Fire*, showing a boy seated by a hearth. A large number of portrait drawings by Brett are in the possession of the artist's descendants and are of high quality. Of his paintings the *Lady with a Dove* in the Tate Gallery best demonstrates his abilities as a figural artist. Dated 1864, this portrait of a Mme. Loeser is a work of such quiet sensitivity that even such an unlikely critic as C. H. Collins Baker, who was generally contemptuous of Victorian art, was able to praise it for not being Pre-Raphaelite at all.[1]

Numerous early landscape drawings, beginning with juvenile efforts from the 1830s, also belong to the artist's descendants, and an oil painting dated 1852, two years before Brett entered the Royal Academy schools, is in the Fitzwilliam Museum (Pl. 69a). None of these landscapes is very remarkable. The earlier ones are broadly handled but within the conventions of amateur sketching of the time. Those dating from 1853 to 1855 show increasing care and accuracy of draughtsmanship, reflecting the general mid-Victorian tendency toward tighter handling. They do not show any specifically Pre-Raphaelite influence, and they give no hint of the departure shown in Brett's first exhibited landscape, the *Glacier of Rosenlaui* (Pl. 68a), dated 23 August 1856, which he sent to the Royal Academy in 1857 along with *Faces in the Fire*.

Brett's trip to Switzerland in the summer of 1856, during which he painted the *Glacier of Rosenlaui*, was the turning point of his career. Rosenlaui and Wengern Alp, where Inchbold was working in 1856, are both in the Bernese Oberland, less than fifteen miles apart, so it was probably inevitable that the two landscape painters would come into contact, even though they apparently had not known each other before. In the following December, summing up the year's achievements in his diary, Brett wrote that he had first met Inchbold on the Wengern Alp and watched him work on *The Jungfrau from the Wengern Alp*, the picture Inchbold exhibited at the Royal Academy the following year.[2] This was the moment of revelation for Brett, who 'there and then saw that I had never

---

[1] C. H. Collins Baker and Montague R. James, *British Painting* (London, 1933), p. 205.

[2] Brett's diaries, letters, and, sketchbooks, upon which much of this chapter is based, are in the possession of the artist's descendants. I am grateful to Mrs. Joan Mitchell, Mrs. C. D. Wales, Mr. M. S. Hickox, and Mr. Patrick Brett for making this material available to me.

painted in my life, but only fooled and slopped, and thenceforward attempted in a reasonable way to paint all I could see.' Inchbold insisted that Brett remain in Switzerland to complete the *Glacier of Rosenlaui* as carefully as possible in every detail, and he even lent Brett money to enable him to do so.

Ruskin was also in the Bernese Oberland in the summer of 1856, and he visited Inchbold there. He did not see Brett, whom he had not yet met. Nonetheless, although Brett did not know Ruskin and had profited from watching Inchbold work, the *Glacier of Rosenlaui* is more Ruskinian than Pre-Raphaelite. The boulders in the foreground are drawn with such exactitude that the picture seems more like a geological illustration than a conventional landscape view. The actual Glacier of Rosenlaui is at the foot of two of the most spectacular peaks in the Alps, the Wellhorn and the Wetterhorn, but that is hardly evident from Brett's picture. His single-minded concentration on a few square yards of foreground detail is comparable to that shown in many of Ruskin's studies of Alpine rocks, and, like Ruskin's earlier studies, Brett's picture is based on careful draughtsmanship throughout. The colours are subdued, and, although the shadows in the crevices of the ice are blue, those under the foreground boulders are black. The sky is grey, and nowhere does the colour show Pre-Raphaelite luminosity or brilliance.

Brett's picture was not the only study of Alpine glaciers undertaken in the summer of 1856. While Brett was at Rosenlaui, T. H. Huxley and John Tyndall were also in the Bernese Oberland investigating glaciers. In 1857 they published a joint paper 'On the Structure and Motion of Glaciers'. Ruskin was soon plunged into the controversy which this paper aroused because of its attack on the theories of his friend and mentor James Forbes, but, despite the coincidence of time and subject, Brett's painting does not appear to have had any connection with Huxley's and Tyndall's investigations. Neither the structure nor the motion of the glacier seems to have been as important to the artist as the rocks lying before it. This careful study of rocks not only points to Ruskin as the picture's inspiration, but to a specific source in Ruskin's writings: the fourth volume of *Modern Painters*, which had been published on 14 April 1856.

Subtitled 'Of Mountain Beauty', the fourth volume of *Modern Painters* is more about geology than painting. Ruskin considered it the most valuable part of the entire work, and it had an impact in spheres other than the artistic one. According to Leslie Stephen, 'the fourth volume of *Modern Painters* infected me and other early members of the Alpine Club with an enthusiasm for which, I hope, we are still grateful'.[3] Stephen started to climb in the Alps in 1857, in part because of Ruskin, and the Alpine Club was founded in the same year. The core of Ruskin's volume is his discussion of the rock structure of the mountains. The rocks which make up the central mountain peaks he divided into two classes: compact crystallines (granites) and slaty crystallines (gneiss). All other rocks, such as slates and marbles, were by Ruskin's standards inferior and less beautiful. Ruskin concluded his discussion of mountain forms by pointedly lamenting the lack of any careful treatment of stones in modern painting: as stones are mountains in miniature, 'they seem to have been created especially to reward a patient observer'.[4] Yet, although Ruskin himself made countless careful studies of different rocks, to illustrate *Slaty Crystallines* in this chapter he used a daguerreotype instead of one of his own drawings, for the first and only time in *Modern Painters*. In the accompanying text he apologized for the illustration's inadequacy, which was due to the impossibility of showing the colour of the stone sur-

[3]Ruskin, 1903-12, XXVI, pp. xxiv and xvii-xli   [4]*Ibid.*, VI, 365-8.
passim; and *ibid.*, V, pp. lvii-lviii and lv-lxi *passim*.

face.[5] A few months after he had made this apology, he made what was probably his single most ambitious study of Alpine rock, showing a block of gneiss at Chamonix (Pl. 68b).

Brett's picture is a picture of what Ruskin wrote about, and because it is an oil painting it shows what Ruskin was unable to show in his black-and-white illustration. The distinctive characteristics of granite and gneiss as described by Ruskin are exactly those which distinguish the boulder without interior lines at the centre of the foreground of the *Glacier of Rosenlaui* from the larger, sinuously marked stone immediately behind it. The more fractured stone in the lower right corner appears to be an example of what Ruskin called slaty coherents. Although we can only speculate about Brett's response to Ruskin's geological discussions, everything we know about him makes it seem possible that he could have read and taken to heart the fourth volume of *Modern Painters* as soon as it was published. Once Ruskin and Brett met, Ruskin showed much greater respect for Brett's mind than he had for Inchbold's: in the fifth volume of *Modern Painters*, published four years after the fourth, Ruskin quoted Brett and described him as 'one of my keenest-minded friends'.[6] Like Ruskin, Brett had scientific leanings, and in later life he became an active astronomer. In 1870 he participated in a trip to Sicily sponsored by the Royal Astronomical Society to observe a solar eclipse. He subsequently became a fellow of the Society and published numerous observations of planetary detail in its *Notices*.

Although Brett first met Inchbold in the summer of 1856, he may have had earlier contact with other members of the Pre-Raphaelite circle. He was a friend of Coventry Patmore, who had been an intimate of the Pre-Raphaelite group since the formation of the Brotherhood. A drawing of the poet by Brett is dated 1855, and one of the three portraits Brett exhibited at the Royal Academy in 1856 was of Mrs. Patmore.[7] Also, in 1856 Brett rented a studio from Charles Lucy, the friend of Ford Madox Brown and first teacher of Thomas Seddon, and thus he had an additional means of contact with the group. By the autumn of 1856 he knew Dante Gabriel Rossetti. Rossetti saw the *Glacier of Rosenlaui* in Brett's studio and took it home to show Ruskin. According to the same diary entry in which Brett recorded his debt to Inchbold, Ruskin praised the picture unreservedly, but when the *Glacier of Rosenlaui* and *Faces in the Fire* appeared at the Royal Academy the following May, Ruskin mentioned neither of them in *Academy Notes*.

Following the Royal Academy exhibition of 1857, Brett sent the *Glacier of Rosenlaui* and a watercolour to the American Exhibition of British Art. He exhibited additional works at the Pre-Raphaelite exhibition in Russell Place in 1857 and at the Liverpool Academy, but from the evidence of the prices he asked and a few references in his letters it appears that all of them were drawings or watercolours.[8] One or two had titles such as *The Wetterhorn, Well Horn and Eiger, Switzerland*, suggesting that they were of vast Alpine panoramas, but the majority were of more modest subjects, and their titles – *Grass* or *Moss and Gentians from the Engels Hörner* – allow us to assume that they were close studies of natural detail. In 1858 Brett again sent watercolours to Liverpool, but for the last time. He exhibited only one work, *The Stonebreaker* (Pl. 69b and Col. Pl. 2d), at the Royal Academy in 1858, and in each of the following three years he exhibited only one picture per year.

The Stonebreaker is signed and dated 1857–8. Its subject is a young boy who must labour

[5] *Ibid.*, pl. 48 and p. 369.
[6] *Ibid.*, VII, 360–61.
[7] Derek Patmore, *The Life and Times of Coventry*

Patmore (London, 1949), frontispiece and facing p. 54.
[8] Bennett, 1963, p. 492.

while birds sing and his dog plays in the midst of a sun-filled landscape. At the same Royal Academy exhibition of 1858, Henry Wallis exhibited his picture of a stonebreaker who has succumbed to his back-breaking labour (Pl. 43a), accompanying it in the catalogue with a quotation from Carlyle. Brett's picture also has a message, but in contrast to the stark tragedy of Wallis's, it seems only sentimentally pathetic, in the more typically Victorian vein of Richard Redgrave's poor governesses. Indeed, the landscape in which the boy works is so lovely that it requires an act of intellect for us to think of the picture as an image of exploitation rather than of idyllic rural life.

Wallis's and Brett's pictures are so dissimilar that it seems irrelevant to ask whether either artist was aware of what the other was doing. Neither picture shows any evident connection with Courbet's *Stonebreakers* of a few years before, but Brett's painting could owe a slight debt to Landseer's *Stonebreaker's Daughter* of 1830 (Victoria and Albert Museum), which had been engraved. Both pictures have a somewhat ambiguous poignancy, and, more specifically, the Brett, like the Landseer, contains a white terrier. This is a small enough point, but in the 1850s any English artist painting a terrier could hardly have been oblivious to Landseer, especially if he had read his Ruskin.[9]

Brett's younger brother was the model for the child-labourer. The setting is Surrey. Box Hill near Dorking is in the background, and a milestone inscribed 'London 23' is in the foreground, pinpointing the site. The picture shows the same minute precision as the *Glacier of Rosenlaui* not only in the foreground but in the view of the slopes of Box Hill in the background as well. The colours of the foreground foliage are vibrantly bright in Pre-Raphaelite fashion, much brighter than any of the colours in the *Glacier of Rosenlaui*. However, in the background the colours are considerably modified so that the greens of Box Hill are markedly lighter and paler than those of the foreground plants. The effect of atmosphere is even more evident in the further distance on the right, which eventually becomes lost in a blue haze. Although by the standards of earlier English landscape painting this effect of atmosphere is hardly noteworthy, in terms of Pre-Raphaelite landscape it is. If we compare *The Stonebreaker* with Ford Madox Brown's *English Autumn Afternoon* (Pl. 9), the much greater tonal contrast between foreground and background in Brett's painting is evident. The result is more spacious and less two-dimensional in effect.

The Stonebreaker is usually said to have made Brett's reputation,[10] and certainly it is the painting upon which his modern reputation is based. It is a more attractive, as well as a more conventional picture than the *Glacier of Rosenlaui*. Yet, when exhibited, it was not well received, and it was ignored by most reviewers with the exception of Ruskin, who concluded his review of the Royal Academy exhibition by praising *The Stonebreaker* in glowing terms:

This, after John Lewis's, is simply the most perfect piece of painting with respect to touch in the Academy this year; in some points of precision it goes beyond anything the Pre-Raphaelites have done yet. I know no such thistle-down, no such chalk hills, and elm trees, no such natural pieces of faraway cloud, in any of their works.

The composition is palpably crude and wrong in many ways, especially in the awkward white cloud at the top; and the tone of the whole a little too much as if some of the chalk of the flints had been mixed with all the colours. For all that, it is a marvellous picture, and may be examined inch by inch with delight; though nearly the last stone I should ever have thought of anyone's sitting down to paint would have been a chalk flint. If he can make so much of that, what will Mr. Brett make of mica slate and gneiss! If he can paint so lovely a distance from the Surrey

---

[9]In his pamphlet *Pre-Raphaelitism* of 1851, Ruskin had ascribed Landseer's 'eminent success' to his 'healthy love of Scotch terriers'. Ruskin, 1903–12, XII, 365.
[10]For example, see Ironside and Gere, 1948, p. 46.

downs and railway-traversed vales, what would he not make of the chestnut groves of the Val d'Aosta! I heartily wish him good-speed and long exile.[11]

Ruskin's reference to Lewis is of interest because Brett himself, in later years, declared Lewis 'the greatest of all modern artists, except Turner'.[12] Ruskin had praised Lewis's *Frank Encampment in the Desert of Mount Sinai*, exhibited at the Old Water-Colour Society in 1856, as 'among the most *wonderful* pictures in the world', and he claimed that nothing comparable had been painted since Veronese. In the following years, however, he began to temper his admiration for Lewis; in 1858, while he was comparing Brett's execution to that of Lewis, he complained that Lewis's pictures were not dramatic enough, a complaint which would be echoed in Ruskin's criticism of Brett in the following year.[13]

There are traces of re-painting around the clouds at the top of the picture, so Ruskin's criticism may have prodded Brett to repaint them. The comment about mixing chalk with all the colours is a temperate echo of Ruskin's long-standing dislike of atmospheric effects, most vociferously expressed in his criticism of Claude. As a criticism of Brett, it was close to the mark, for Brett in a letter written to his sister in 1858, advising her on painting techniques, did recommend mixing white with the colours to make the paint more manageable. This is a different method from the usual Pre-Raphaelite one of painting in unmixed colours over a white ground, which Brett apparently used for the foreground plants in *The Stonebreaker*. In the same letter, the artist denied using any systematic method of tonal modification to give distance: 'If you paint the things the right colour, and put in only as much detail as you see, they will do, and won't want any forcing back.' To get the exact colour of nature, he advised his sister to look through a hole in a card, a method employed by Ruskin in his teaching at the Working Men's College.[14]

More interesting than Ruskin's praise or criticism of *The Stonebreaker* – and probably more puzzling to a contemporary reader – were his concluding remarks about the inferiority of chalk flint to mica slate and gneiss, and of the 'Surrey downs and railway-traversed vales' to the chestnut groves of the Val d'Aosta. These not only repeated his often-stated preference for Alpine scenery to English, but also referred to Brett's plans for his next undertaking (Pl. 70 and Col. Pl. 6b). Slightly over a month after Ruskin had wished him good-speed and long exile Brett set out for the Val d'Aosta. Ruskin's mouth-watering comments about a picture which was not yet begun encourage the suspicion that he was the instigator of the project. He did not commission Brett's *Val d'Aosta* – when Brett sent it to the Liverpool Academy in 1859 it was for sale[15] – but he was closely involved in its creation, and eventually he purchased it.

Why did Brett go to the Val d'Aosta rather than to the Valley of Chamonix on the other side of Mont Blanc, or to the Bernese Oberland, or to the Lake of Lucerne, all of which play a larger and more important role in Ruskin's writing? The most probable explanation is that Ruskin was planning to be in Turin during the summer and hence would be accessible if the artist needed his advice. Brett arrived at the town of Aosta at the end of June 1858 and immediately set to work at the Château St. Pierre, a few miles further up the valley. Ruskin arrived in Turin in the middle of July and remained there until the end of August. Just before leaving he wrote to his father:

Turin, August 26. I mentioned that Mr. Brett was with me at La Tour. He has been here a week today. I sent for him at Villeneuve, Val d'Aosta, because I didn't like what he said in his letter about his present work, and thought he wanted some lecturing like Inchbold: besides that, he

[11]Ruskin, 1903–12, XIV, 171–2.   [14]*Ibid.*, XV, 143.
[12]Brett, 1895, p. 639.   [15]Bennett, 1963, p. 492.
[13]Ruskin, 1903–12, XIV, 74–5, 159.

could give me some useful hints. He is much tougher and stronger than Inchbold, and takes more hammering; but I think he looks more miserable every day, and have good hope of making him completely wretched in a day or two more – and then I shall send him back to his castle. He is living *in* that castle which I sketched so long ago in Val d'Aosta – Château St. Pierre.[16]

La Tour is Torre Pellice, in the mountains to the southwest of Turin. The useful hints that Ruskin hoped to receive were for the final volume of *Modern Painters*, in which Brett is indeed quoted.[17]

One of Brett's sketchbooks contains a few drawings made during his visit to Turin. The most interesting are a pair showing rocky hillsides and bearing the initials J.M.W.T. One of these, dated 25 August, is a delicate pencil drawing with each rock and bush carefully delineated and modelled. This drawing is comparable to drawings throughout Brett's sketchbooks and is clearly by him, despite the posthumous initials of Turner. The other drawing is in pen and appears to be not by Brett, but by Ruskin. It is a more diagrammatic drawing in which the details of rocks and bushes are subordinated to the lines of the sloping hillside. Also bearing Turner's initials, this drawing contains an implied criticism of Brett's, demonstrating that Turner saw the grand lines of nature, not just niggling details. The only other hints that we have of Ruskin's hammering are a few descriptive notes of scenery, which Brett made in the same sketchbook on his return trip to the Val d'Aosta from Turin.[18] An example is his description of Verrès, between Ivrea and Chatillon: 'a little plain shut in by very fine mountain forms – a very good old fort or tower – also some very good bits of building – very few stones on plain – average trees – not much vine – about the best of the little towns in the valley.' These attempts to analyze the merits and faults of scenery, although not couched in Ruskinian language, were probably the results of Ruskin's urging Brett to give more consideration to choosing suitable subjects. A *leitmotiv* in Ruskin's discussions of Pre-Raphaelite works in *Academy Notes* was his criticism of their badly chosen subjects, and he may well have felt that Brett, after travelling half way across Europe to an Alpine valley, was still not painting a subject of appropriate grandeur. In 1851, on his most recent visit to the Val d'Aosta, Ruskin had compared the scenery in the upper part of the valley around Aosta, near where Brett was painting, unfavourably with that in the narrower lower part between Chatillon and Ivrea.[19] The notes in Brett's sketchbook all describe locations between Chatillon and Ivrea,[20] but Ruskin's advice, whatever it may have been, did not prevent Brett from returning to St. Pierre. He remained there working on the painting until the middle of November and exhibited the completed *Val d'Aosta* at the Royal Academy the following May.

Like *The Stonebreaker*, the *Val d'Aosta* is a plateau landscape, with a genre figure and a domestic animal in the foreground. But now the figure, a sleeping girl, is relatively anonymous and unimportant, and the foreground serves mainly as a *repoussoir* for the landscape beyond. This is a view up the valley of the Dora Baltea, looking to the west from the castle of St. Pierre at Villeneuve. The mountains in the distance are the Testa du Rutor, covered with snow, and Mte. Paramont, to its right. These are neither the highest nor the most dramatic mountains overlooking the Val d'Aosta. If Brett had travelled further up the valley to Courmayeur he could have painted the Italian flank of Mont Blanc, and from other points in the valley he could have seen the Matterhorn and Monte

[16]Ruskin, 1903–12, XIV, pp. xxiii–xxiv; Ruskin's sketch of the Château St. Pierre is reproduced *ibid.*, II, pl. 21.
[17]He is quoted as defining vulgarity as 'merely one of the forms of Death.' *Ibid.*, VII, 361.
[18]The book also contains sketches made on the journey

of Joseph Couttet, the Alpine guide, who had travelled with Ruskin during the summer and was now returning to his home in Chamonix.
[19]Ruskin, 1903–12, XIV, 236n.
[20]Other sites described are Pont-St. Martin and Montjovet.

Rosa. Even at St. Pierre, as T. S. R. Boase has pointed out, Brett turned his back on the most spectacular scenery.[21] La Grivola, due south of St. Pierre, and visible up the Val di Cogne, is higher than the mountains painted by Brett, and a more dramatic feature in the landscape. Brett also excluded picturesque features of another sort, showing neither his own Château St. Pierre nor the nearby Châtel Argent, two fortified medieval castles which form conspicuous landmarks in the valley. The *Val d'Aosta* is not a picture of romantic scenery or towering mountains, but of a valley with its peaceful agricultural life, which is enclosed by mountains. The distance from St. Pierre to Mte. Paramont is a little over twelve miles. The painting shows each tree, each vine, each cottage, even peasants working in the fields, through a substantial part of those twelve miles. The minute precision of handling equals that of *The Stonebreaker* and is more awe-inspiring because applied to such a vast panorama. The chief benefit of Brett's working in the Alps was not that he could see and paint high mountains – he avoided the highest and partly hid by cloud those he did show – but that he himself could have a high vantage-point from which he could see and paint ever more cottages and fields and trees.

Brett had English predecessors who had worked in the Val d'Aosta. Turner made at least one watercolour of the vicinity of St. Pierre (National Gallery of Scotland, Edinburgh).[22] But there is little in common between Turner's romantic imagery of natural forces and Brett's conscientiously detailed geographical statement. His documentation of not only the topography and geology, but also the cultivation and life of the valley, is close in spirit to the *Erdlebenbildkunst* of the Tyrolese artist Joseph Anton Koch, although if we look at an actual Alpine scene by Koch, for example *The Bernese Oberland* of 1815 (Osterreichische Galerie, Vienna),[23] the marked stylistic differences make any influence seem unlikely. However, a younger Austrian artist, Ferdinand Waldmüller, continued to paint comparable subjects, in a more meticulous style than Koch, past the middle of the century. In 1856 Waldmüller had an exhibition in London, at Buckingham Palace.[24] Brett could well have seen his works, but, again, it seems unlikely that Waldmüller would have had any real importance for Brett. What is most distinctive about the *Val d'Aosta*, the amount of information it provides, is not the result of imported ideas, but the culmination of the Pre-Raphaelite impulse to detailed naturalism.

When the *Val d'Aosta* appeared at the Royal Academy in 1859, one Pre-Raphaelite, or former Pre-Raphaelite, had little good to say of it. Millais wrote to his wife, 'There is a wretched little work like a photograph of some place in Switzerland, evidently painted under his [Ruskin's] guidance, for he seems to have lauded it up sky-high; and that is just where it is in the miniature room! He does not understand my work, which is now too broad for him to appreciate, and I think his eye is only fit to judge the portraits of insects.'[25] This comment mainly reflects Millais's dislike of Ruskin, but we also learn from it that the picture was badly hung. It was ignored by most of the press, but in *Academy Notes* Ruskin more than compensated:

Yes, here we have it at last – some close-coming to it at least – historical landscape properly so called – landscape painting with a meaning and a use. We have had hitherto plenty of industry, precision quite unlimited, but all useless, or nearly so, being wasted on scenes of no majesty or

[21]T. S. R. Boase, 'English Artists and the Val d'Aosta', *Journal of the Warburg and Courtauld Institutes*, XIX, 1956, p. 292n.

[22]Reproduced in *ibid.*, pl. 61e.

[23]Reproduced in Fritz Novotny, *Painting and Sculpture in Europe: 1780 to 1880* (Harmondsworth, 1960) pl. 25.

[24]*Ibid.*, pp. 112 and 245n. 3. For an example of Waldmüller's Alpine landscapes see *ibid.*, pl. 76A. See also Winslow Ames, *Prince Albert and Victorian Taste* (New York, 1968), p. 138.

[25]Millais, 1899, I, 342.

enduring interest. Here is, at last, a scene worth painting – painted with all our might (not quite with all our heart, perhaps, but with might of hand and eye). And here, accordingly, for the first time in history, we have by help of art, the power of visiting a place, reasoning about it, and knowing it, just as if we were there, except only that we cannot stir from our place, nor look behind us. For the rest, standing before this picture is just as good as standing on that spot in Val d'Aosta, so far as gaining of knowledge is concerned; and perhaps in some degree pleasanter, for it would be very hot on that rock today, and there would probably be a disagreeable smell of Juniper plants growing on the slopes above.[26]

Ruskin then proceeded to describe in detail what a 'simple-minded, quietly living person, indisposed towards railroad stations or crowded inns', might learn from the painting about 'what a Piedmontese valley is like in July'.

This concept of historic landscape is the same as that which Ruskin had applied three years earlier to Thomas Seddon. It will be remembered that Ruskin had called Seddon's art the first 'truly historic landscape art', whose purpose he defined as 'that of giving to persons who cannot travel trustworthy knowledge'.[27] That Brett's picture achieved this 'for the first time in history' is a reflection of Ruskin's indifference to Seddon's painting. His own involvement in the creation of the *Val d'Aosta* no doubt abetted his loss of memory.

Ruskin concluded his description of the painting by calling it, 'a notable picture truly; a possession of much within a few square feet'. But he then went on to criticize it in terms strong enough to negate most of his praise:

Yet not, in the strong, essential meaning of the word, a noble picture. It has a strange fault, considering the school to which it belongs – it seems to me wholly emotionless. I cannot find from it that the painter loved, or feared, anything in all that wonderful piece of the world. There seems to me no awe of the mountains there – no real love of the chestnuts or the vines. Keenness of eye and fineness of hand as much as you choose; but of emotion, or of intention nothing traceable. Not but that I believe the painter to be capable of the highest emotion: any one who can paint thus must have passion within him; but the passion here is assuredly not out of him. He has cared for nothing, except as it was more or less pretty in colour and form. I never saw the mirror so held up to Nature; but it is Mirror's work, not Man's.

Ruskin criticized particularly Brett's painting of the sky, and then in his final paragraph, he summed up the painting's strengths and weakness: 'Historical landscape it is, unquestionably; meteorological also; poetical – by no means: yet precious, in its patient way; and, as a wonder of toil and delicate handling, unimpeachable.'[28]

This criticism does not seem unjust, but from a partisan such as Ruskin it is surprising. The gist of much of his writing of the previous fifteen years had been to encourage exactly the kind of detached scientific observation that here reaches its apogee. In his speech on Thomas Seddon, when proselytizing for 'historic landscape', he had argued that artists should be as scientific as possible. 'If they imparted knowledge and industry enough, the imagination would come out.'[29] But Brett had imparted knowledge and industry enough, and the imagination had not come out. Ruskin had had high hopes for the painting and had even committed himself publicly to its success in the previous year's *Academy Notes*. That it failed to meet his expectations was more than a disappointment; it was a disillusion-

[26]Ruskin, 1903–12, XIV, 234.
[27]See above, p. 104.
[28]Ruskin, 1903–12, XIV, 236–7.
[29]*Ibid.*, p. 468 and see above, p. 104. See also the fourth volume of *Modern Painters*, where Ruskin urged that a topographical picture be 'as far as possible, the reflection of the place in a mirror; and the artist to

consider himself only as a sensitive and skilful reflector'. However, here, this goal was only for artists without much invention; those with inventive power were to treat the subject 'in a totally different way; giving not the actual facts of it, but the impression it made on his mind' (*ibid.*, VI, 31–2).

ment which coincided with, and perhaps helped to produce, a major redirection in Ruskin's career. After 1859, Ruskin ceased publishing *Academy Notes*, and he largely abandoned his active encouragement of contemporary artists. The failure of the *Val d'Aosta* was the failure of the movement which Ruskin had adopted and attempted to direct.

Ruskin's most specific criticism of Brett's picture had to do with the sky:

This absence of sentiment is peculiarly indicated by the feeble anger of the sky. Had it been wholly cloudless – burning down in one calm field of light behind the purple hills, all the rest of the landscape would have been gathered into unity by its repose; and for the sleeping girl we should have feared no other disturbance than the bleating of the favourite of her flock . . . But now she will be comfortlessly waked by hailstorm in another quarter of an hour; and yet there is no majesty in the clouds, nor any grand incumbency of them on the hills; they are but a dash of mist, gusty and disagreeable enough – in no otherwise to be dreaded.[30]

It was Brett's misfortune that he attempted to paint complex meteorological conditions at the same time that his critic was preparing the section of *Modern Painters* entitled 'Of Cloud Beauty'. In the summer of 1858, Ruskin made several studies of cloud effects over the mountains. He reproduced a number of them in the fifth volume of *Modern Painters*, and another, *A July Thunder Cloud in the Val d'Aosta, 1858*, served to illustrate a lecture, 'The Storm Cloud of the Nineteenth Century', which he gave in 1884.[31] In all these drawings the clouds are spectacular, dwarfing the mountains. Ruskin described his drawings as literal representations, but they have a romantic exuberance which makes Brett's clouds seem insipid in comparison.

What Brett's clouds do is conceal the outlines of the mountains. The painting is not only less spectacular meteorologically than it would have been if Brett had painted clouds like Ruskin's, but also less spectacular topographically than it would have been with an empty sky. Either kind of spectacle would have been a distraction, taking the viewer's mind and eye from the prosaic fields of the valley to more romantic heights. Brett's refusal to allow this to happen demonstrates the gulf between mid-century naturalism and earlier Romanticism, and, more specifically, the gulf between Brett and Turner. Nonetheless, the examples of Turner's keen observation which Ruskin cited in *Modern Painters* do often make Turner's pictures sound quite like the *Val d'Aosta*, and Ruskin had tried since 1851 to prove that Turner and the Pre-Raphaelites were fundamentally akin. He could mention Millais's portrait of himself in the same breath with Turner because the subjects of the two artists were so far apart that there was no real basis of comparison. However, Brett, by painting a vast Alpine landscape, did put himself in a position to be compared directly with Turner. Ruskin did not mention Turner in his review of Brett's picture, but Ruskin's feelings for the Alps and for Turner's paintings were so inextricably mixed, that he must have had him in mind. Seen in contrast to the paintings which provided a visual equivalent to Ruskin's own emotional responses to the mountains, Brett's scientific detachment must have seemed the more disappointing. Ruskin expressed his disappointment in the review of the painting; he did not suggest the possibility that the emotional level, which he demanded, and the load of factual information, which Brett presented, might have been in any way incompatible.

Despite his disappointment, Ruskin bought the picture. This may have been because Brett could find no other purchaser, and Ruskin felt responsible. He put it up for sale in 1869 and bought it in. He later mentioned it twice in his published writings. In 1875, in a revival of *Academy Notes*, he bemoaned the decline in Brett's art:

Since the days when I first endeavoured to direct the attention of a careless public to his conscien-

[30] *Ibid.*, XIV, 237.   [31] *Ibid.*, VII, pls. 68, 70, 71, and fig. 87; XXXIV, pl. II.

tious painting of the Stonebreaker and Woodcutter, he has gained nothing – rather, I fear, lost, in subtlety of execution, and necessitates the decline of his future power by persistently covering too large canvas. There is no occasion that a geological study should also be a geological map; and even his earlier picture, which I am honoured in possessing, of the Val d'Aosta, would have been the more precious to me if it had been only of half the Val d'Aosta.[32]

In 1880 Ruskin lent the picture to an exhibition in the Isle of Man and supplied a note for the catalogue. He described the circumstances under which the picture was painted, then continued:

I at that time hoped much from his zeal and fineness of minute execution in realizing, with Dürer-like precision, the detail of Swiss landscape. Had he sympathised enough with Swiss and Italian life, his work might have become of extreme value; but, instead, he took to mere photography of physical landscape, and gradually lost both precision and sentiment . . . There is no pretence of composition, or, as usually understood, of painter's skill in this picture. It is the careful delineation of what is supposed to be beautiful in itself; and it has lost, instead of benefited, by the unwise introduction of storm on the hills for the sake of variety. In good, permanent, and honourably finished oil-painting this picture cannot be surpassed; it is as safe as a piece of china, and as finished as the finest engraving.[33]

Both of these passages suggest that Ruskin considered Brett's decline to have begun almost during his work on the *Val d'Aosta*. It is generally believed that Brett's art began to deteriorate immediately afterwards, probably as a reaction to Ruskin's badgering. However, Brett's work from the following two years has disappeared, so we do not know how much it changed. His *Hedger*, exhibited at the Royal Academy in 1860, and *Warwick Castle*, exhibited in 1861, appear from their titles, from related drawings (Pl. 72b), and from contemporary descriptions to have been characteristic Pre-Raphaelite pictures in both subject and style.[34] Both entered collections of Pre-Raphaelite art. For *The Hedger*, Brett asked the same price as he had for the *Val d'Aosta*; for *Warwick Castle* he asked and received considerably more, but the latter was the largest picture he had yet painted.[35]

Brett spent the summer of 1861 again in the Alps, and he exhibited two Alpine subjects at the Royal Academy in 1862. In the winter of 1861–2 he was in Florence, where he made a watercolour of the Ponte Vecchio which he later sold to Ruskin's father. A letter from Ruskin to his father, dated 2 May 1863, refers to this drawing:

I have to-day your interesting letter about Brett. I am much obliged by what you have done for him: nor do I think it will be useless. I've written to him repeating what I told him three years ago – that painting large studies by way of pictures was simply ridiculous – that he must make small ones first, saleable, and learn to choose subjects. The little Florence will, I think, be very pleasant to me – it is sure to be 'preciously' like.[36]

This letter suggests that a strain had come into the friendship because of Ruskin's disapproval of Brett's way of working. His comment about choosing subjects repeats once again a complaint he had been making about the Pre-Raphaelites ever since 1852, but his criticism of Brett's 'painting large studies by way of pictures' is something we have not seen before. It sounds like a repudiation of the whole Pre-Raphaelite method of painting directly from nature. Ruskin does not state explicitly that only studies should be painted from nature, while finished pictures should be painted in the studio, but that is what the

[32]*Ibid.*, XIV, 293. 'Woodcutter' seems to be a reference to Brett's *Hedger*, exhibited at the Royal Academy in 1860, but Ruskin never mentioned this picture in print.
[33]*Ibid.*, p. 238n.
[34]See *Athenaeum*, 19 May 1860, p. 690, and *Art Journal*, 1860, p. 169, and 1861, p. 196.
[35]He asked £300 for both the *Val d'Aosta* and *The*

Hedger (Bennett, 1963, pp. 492, 495). *The Hedger* was bought by B. G. Windus. He sold *Warwick Castle* to Thomas Plint for £420 when it was still half-finished; he had originally asked £450 (diary, 30 Jan. 1861). It measured 37 by 49 inches.
[36]Ruskin, 1903–12, XXXVI, 441.

letter implies. Ruskin probably would have been happy if Brett never painted large pictures at all, and he continued to inveigh against the scale of Brett's paintings in the *Academy Notes* of 1875. In 1876 he wrote to a younger painter, Albert Goodwin, lamenting Goodwin's 'taking to oil and to large canvases', and his arguments to Goodwin can be applied to Brett. Although the letter was directed primarily against the use of oil, it also explains Ruskin's preference for small studies:

Large canvases mean the complete doing of what they contain, and the painting of not more than three or four in the year, while I think you have eyes to discern every summer three or four and forty, of which it is a treason to your genius to omit such record as would on small scale be easily possible to you.

And as a mere matter of personal comfort, twenty people can enjoy a small drawing for one who wants to cover half a furlong of wall.[37]

Ruskin's preamble to this advice was the assertion that 'all great efforts are failures . . . we only use our powers fully by doing what we know we can do well and enjoy doing, better and better every day.' Since Brett's *Val d'Aosta* was, if anything, a great effort, by Ruskin's later view of things it had been doomed to failure. Ruskin's disappointment with the results of the project which Brett had undertaken at his bidding was probably one of the causes for his later belief in the preferability of moderation in artistic ambitions, and his criticism of Brett in 1863 was one of the first manifestations of this belief. However, their friendship ended in the following year not because of Ruskin's disapproval of Brett's art, but because of a scientific disagreement. As Ruskin explained in a letter to Rossetti, written in 1865,

. . . I will associate with no man who does not more or less accept my own estimate of myself. For instance, Brett told me, a year ago, that a statement of mine respecting a scientific matter (which I knew *à fond* before he was born) was 'bosh'. I told him in return he was a fool; he left the house, and I will not see him again 'until he is wiser'.[38]

Brett returned to Florence in the winter of 1862–3 and spent the subsequent two winters in the vicinity of the Bay of Naples. To the Royal Academy of 1863 he sent a painting of *Florence from Bellosguardo* (Pl. 71a). Together with a second picture it was rejected, causing suspicions of foul play.[39] 1863 was the only year between 1856 and Brett's death that he was not represented at the Academy, but it did not do him any harm; as George du Maurier wrote to Thomas Armstrong, 'Brett whose picture was kicked out sold it immediately, which very likely wouldn't have happened had he met with justice.'[40] The view of Florence is from the south-west, looking across the city toward Fiesole and the Apennines. The time is late afternoon, as we can tell from the long shadows of the trees in the olive grove in the foreground, and the entire picture is suffused in a rosy glow. The Villa Brichieri at Bellosguardo, the home of Isa Blagden, was one of the focal points for the English community in Florence, and Brett's picture may well have been painted from its spacious terrace, which was renowned for its view. The atmosphere evoked in most reminiscences of Bellosguardo is of a world of rarefied, literate, and relaxed conversations, with the Val d'Arno below, 'vast and delicate, as if it were a painted picture'.[41] Into this cultivated milieu Brett could not have fitted very comfortably. His painting shows single-

[37]*Ibid.*, XXXVII, 212–13.
[38]*Ibid.*, XXXVI, 493–4.
[39]The suspicions were voiced by Coventry Patmore in a letter to Holman Hunt; see Sotheby, 1970, no. 905.
[40]Du Maurier, 1951, p. 204.

[41]Henry James, *William Wetmore Story and His Friends* (Boston, 1903), II, 95. See also Giuliana Artom Treves, *The Golden Ring: The Anglo-Florentines, 1847–1862*, trans. Sylvia Sprigge (London, 1956) pp. 177–193.

7. Daniel Alexander Williamson, *Spring: Arnside Knot and Coniston Range of Hills from Warton Crag* (Plate 81b)

8a. George Price Boyce, *The Mill on the Thames at Mapledurham* (Plate 55a)

8b. William Dyce, *Pegwell Bay, Kent – a Recollection of October 5th, 1858* (Plate 96a)

mindedness carried to the point of monomania. *Florence from Bellosguardo* does not surpass the *Val d'Aosta* in the amount of detail it contains, but, unlike the earlier picture, it is a view over a man-made environment where the shapes are essentially all the same. Instead of a continuously varying landscape, there is endless repetition of pitched roofs and rectangular windows. In painting a view of Florence Brett turned to what was perhaps the inevitable subject for a landscape painter belonging to a movement calling itself Pre-Raphaelite, and the result is one of the most extraordinary of all Pre-Raphaelite pictures. It is a Pre-Raphaelite *veduta*, a nineteenth-century equivalent of the elaborately detailed urban views of Canaletto and Bellotto. However, with eighteenth-century reasonableness, Canaletto and Bellotto did not choose points of view which would allow them to see every roof-top in the city. Brett himself may have decided that this type of all-inclusive panorama required too much sheer work. In subsequent years he frequently painted pictures from high vantage-points, but not of subjects demanding the detailed treatment of the *Val d'Aosta* or the *Florence*. In pictures which he sent to the Royal Academy in 1864 and 1865, *Massa, Bay of Naples* (Pl. 71b) and *Morants Court in May* (Pl. 72a), he continued to paint with minute Pre-Raphaelite care, but in neither work does the quantity of detail have such pronounced importance as in Brett's earlier paintings.

Massa, Bay of Naples is a coast scene, and water fills the foreground. The town of Massa is seen at some distance and occupies only a relatively small part of the picture as a whole. *Morants Court in May* shows a domestic subject, a farmhouse in Kent with a cow and calves in the foreground. The house and its surroundings are painted with delicate precision, but both foreground and distance play subordinate roles. If we compare *Morants Court* with *The Stonebreaker*, which is approximately the same size, we can see that, by eliminating intricate foreground foliage and an extensive background view, Brett reduced substantially his own labour (or – since we do not know how much work he devoted to either picture – our sense of his labour) and gained a more unified vision, less subdivided into separately observed details. However, separately observed details, laboriously recorded each and all, give *The Stonebreaker* a vibrant freshness which is no longer present in these works from the following decade. Brett's new sophistication, or prudence, was at the expense of the belief that a picture could be all-encompassing, which is one of the most distinctive ingredients of Pre-Raphaelite landscape painting.

Watercolours which Brett made near Goring-on-Thames in 1865 (Pl. 72c), on the Isle of Wight in 1866 (City Art Gallery, Birmingham), and at Yarmouth in 1868 (collection of Mr. and Mrs. C. D. Wales) are comparable to *Morants Court* in the amount of detail they show. His exhibited pictures from 1866 through 1870 have all disappeared, but the two paintings which he sent to the Royal Academy in 1871, *The British Channel Seen from the Dorsetshire Cliffs* (Pl. 73b) and *Etna from the Heights of Taormina* (Pl. 73a), are both now in museums. The latter picture is the result of Brett's trip to Sicily in the winter of 1870–1. When it was exhibited, the *Art Journal* called it 'a carefully mapped-out scene' in the 'now all but extinct style once known as Pre-Raphaelite'.[42] This is a fair enough description, although if we compare the picture with the *Val d'Aosta* we can see that it is more conventionally topographical and considerably less finely detailed. Brett was in Sicily for approximately two months; he had been in the Val d'Aosta for over five. The *Val d'Aosta* measures $34\frac{1}{2}$ by $26\frac{7}{8}$ inches; *Etna from Taormina* measures 33 by $48\frac{1}{2}$ inches. As Ruskin was to complain in 1875, Brett covered 'too large canvas. There is no occasion that a geological study should also be a geological map.'

[42] *Art Journal*, 1871, p. 177.

Like *Etna from the Heights of Taormina*, *The British Channel Seen from the Dorsetshire Cliffs* is a view from a height over a vast distance, but the view now is over water. The first pictorial evidence of Brett's interest in the sea stems from his visit to the Bay of Naples in the winter of 1863–4. Two watercolours dating from this trip (City Art Gallery, Birmingham, and collection of John Gere), as well as *Massa, Bay of Naples*, show scenes along the coast in which water is as important as land. At the Royal Academy exhibition of 1864 Brett also exhibited *A North-west Squall in the Mediterranean*. From 1865 until his marriage in 1870 he seems to have spent most of his time in various fishing or yachting ports around England and Wales. After his marriage he regularly spent his summers with his family aboard a yacht, cruising and sketching in the waters surrounding the British Isles. After 1871 he travelled no further abroad than Cherbourg and Etretat, and almost all of his later pictures are views either of or from the coast of Britain. While *Etna from Taormina* is a last echo of the 'all but extinct style once known as Pre-Raphaelite', *From the Dorsetshire Cliffs* can serve to represent all of Brett's paintings for the remaining two-thirds of his professional life.

Between 1870 and 1901 Brett sent an average of three pictures a year to the Royal Academy, measuring up to forty-two by eighty-four inches each, the size of *From the Dorsetshire Cliffs*. These were in addition to a mass of oil sketches produced during the summers. In the autumn of 1886 he exhibited a group of forty-six sketches and three small paintings in an exhibition entitled *Three Months on the Scottish Coast*. In the catalogue Brett stated that this exhibition represented an average summer's work, and he explained his working procedures. The sketches were painted from nature in single sittings of two or three hours, and each was supposed to be a single observation unadulterated. The small pictures were the products of days unfit for sketching out of doors. His large pictures, which he described as abstracts of several observations, were painted in the studio in the winter. Brett was proud of his efficiency and claimed that his practice of painting at once, without retouching, reduced his labour to about a third of that of most artists.[43] The sketches are generally all the same size, seven by fourteen inches, and the larger pictures, with only rare exceptions, retain the same proportions. Not surprisingly, in light of this standardized mass production, the seascapes all tend to look rather alike. The most memorable of them are the pictures of expanses of open sea such as *From the Dorsetshire Cliffs* or *Britannia's Realm* of 1880, both of which are in the Tate Gallery. Their clarity of vision combined with bright prismatic colours might be considered reminiscent of Pre-Raphaelitism, but the remote emptiness of these views is the antithesis of the loving closeness of Pre-Raphaelite detail. Despite Ruskin's criticism, Brett's later pictures do have precision, but it is only too easy to agree with Ruskin's lament about his loss of sentiment.

About that quality Brett had this to say: 'Sentiment in landscape is chiefly dependent on meteorology.'[44] Such a remark may well be true; it says essentially the same thing as Constable's 'It will be difficult to name a class of landscape in which sky is not the keynote, the standard of scale, and the chief organ of sentiment',[45] but it says it in a manner that has become mechanistically impersonal. Brett concluded his essay in *Three Months on the Scottish Coast* with the assertion, 'the out-of-doors world is entirely at the command of the landscape painter, and if he does not depict it accurately it is not because of the imperfection of his means and appliances, or the inherent weakness of his art, but merely because

[43]Brett, 1886, pp. 3, 7–8, *et passim*.
[44]*Ibid.*, p. 10.
[45]R. B. Beckett, *John Constable and the Fishers* (London, 1952) p. 82. About Constable, Brett had this to say:

'Constable took so superficial an interest in nature that he never took any pains to study her laws.' (Brett, 1895, p. 638).

he lacks intelligence and information.'[46] Brett had intelligence and information, and his later pictures do depict the out-of-doors world with a kind of cold accuracy. Some of the larger pictures are quite impressive, and many of the oil sketches are even sensitive. Sensitivity, however, did not hold a very important place in Brett's scientific scheme of things, and 'insensitive' is an adjective which has been applied frequently to his later works.[47] The pictures are, nonetheless, products of a lucidly systematic intelligence, and they brought the artist a considerable degree of success. *Britannia's Realm* was a Chantrey Bequest purchase in 1880, and in the following year Brett was elected an associate member of the Royal Academy. He remained an associate, never becoming a full member, but, except for Millais, no other painter from the Pre-Raphaelite group of the 1850s entered even that far into the fold.

[46]Brett, 1886, p. 18.
[47]Whistler's comment on *Britannia's Realm* was, 'Tin! if you threw a stone on to this it would make a rumbling noise.' Quoted by J. B. Manson, *The Tate Gallery* (London, 1930) p. 119.

XI

The Liverpool School

OUTSIDE London, the Pre-Raphaelites received their most friendly reception in Liverpool. The annual exhibition of the Liverpool Academy became a Pre-Raphaelite domain, and a group of local Liverpool artists fell heavily under Pre-Raphaelite influence.

In 1850, a young Liverpool painter, William Lindsay Windus, was persuaded by his patron, John Miller, to visit the exhibition of the Royal Academy in London to see what other painters were doing. There he saw Millais's *Christ in the House of His Parents*, and his excitement about this picture was apparently enough to form a basis for the general conversion of several of his associates. In 1851, Holman Hunt sent his *Valentine Rescuing Sylvia from Proteus* to the exhibition of the Liverpool Academy and it won the prize given annually to a work by a non-member. This success led to the Pre-Raphaelites' adoption of Liverpool as a regular place of exhibition – to an extent demonstrated by the large number of pictures recorded in Mary Bennett's 'Check-list of Pre-Raphaelite Pictures Exhibited at Liverpool'.[1] Between 1851 and 1859, Hunt, Millais, and Ford Madox Brown each won the annual prize twice. In the other three years it went to William Dyce, to Brown's friend Mark Anthony, and to Augustus Egg, who also had Pre-Raphaelite connections. When Millais's *Blind Girl* won the prize in 1857, it provoked violent opposition from a conservative faction of the Academy and in the press. The controversy drew a letter from Ruskin supporting the Academy's choice;[2] it also led to the formation of a rival group and to the eventual demise of the Liverpool Academy. The Liverpool artists themselves participated in some of the activities of the London Pre-Raphaelites. Several sent pictures to the 1857 exhibition in Russell Place and to the American exhibition of the same year, and the category of non-resident artistic members of the Hogarth Club was dominated by Liverpool painters.

Windus was the outstanding figure of the group, and he remains the best-known. His first work to show Pre-Raphaelite influence was *Burd Helen* (Walker Art Gallery, Liverpool), which he exhibited at the Royal Academy in 1856, and which drew Ruskin's glowing praise. Three years later, he exhibited *Too Late* (Tate Gallery). This picture also drew a long but less sympathetic review from Ruskin.[3] Both paintings reflect the influence of Millais in the figural style, and of Pre-Raphaelitism in general in their subjects. Both are outdoor pictures, but the landscape backgrounds are of relatively minor importance. *Burd Helen* is based on a Scottish Border ballad, and for the sake of verisimilitude Windus painted its background on the Isle of Arran. As in the early pictures of Hunt and Millais, the background seems to have been executed first and the figures added later in the studio. The background of *Too Late* is slightly more elaborate, but neither background is obtrusive or draws attention to itself to the extent that Millais's do. That of the latter picture is pale in colour and so thinly painted that it looks unfinished. As a result, it has an atmospheric breadth atypical of Pre-Raphaelitism.

[1]Bennett, 1963.
[2]Ruskin, 1903–12, XIV, 327–8.

[3]*Ibid.*, pp. 85–87, 233–4, 239.

A combination of calamities, including Ruskin's criticism of *Too Late*, almost brought Windus's painting career to an end after 1859. During the rest of his long life, he worked only infrequently, and he destroyed much of what he did. All his known later works are small, and most are sketches. There are, however, two small finished pictures, which are essentially landscapes. The earlier is *The Outlaw*, which Windus painted in 1861 and exhibited at the Liverpool Academy in 1862 (City Art Gallery, Manchester).[4] This is almost a problem picture, in which the problem is to find the subject. Two small figures are buried in the foliage in the extreme foreground, and a running hound is barely visible in the background. For the rest, the picture is a landscape seen entirely below the horizon. Except for the figures the colour is green without strong contrasts. The foreground foliage is painted in small detail, which increases its importance at the expense of the figures. The other painting is *The Stray Lamb* (Pl. 82b). According to James Smith, the artist's friend and patron, Windus painted it in 1864 near the River Duddon in Cumberland, where he spent his summers with the painter Daniel Alexander Williamson.[5] The lamb, which gives the picture its title, stands on a rock in the left foreground and is tiny in proportion to the picture area as a whole. As in *The Outlaw*, there is no sky; our view consists entirely of rocks and trees with a bit of the water of the stream. The foreground rocks are carefully drawn; those in the background and the foliage are less precise. The colouring is straightforward: grey rocks, green foliage. The banks of the stream in the background are slightly purplish, but not obtrusively so, and the handling has an air of timid delicacy which seems appropriate to the subject.

The Liverpool artist most admired by the Pre-Raphaelites after Windus was the landscape painter William Davis. Davis was born in Dublin in 1812, which makes him considerably older than any of the London Pre-Raphaelites. His artistic education took place in Dublin, and he began his professional career as a portrait painter in his native city. Failing to find patronage there, he soon migrated to Liverpool. He became an associate member of the Liverpool Academy in 1851 and a full member in 1854. He first exhibited landscapes in 1853. The change of subject was made under the influence of another Liverpool artist, Robert Tonge, a gifted painter who had an unfortunately short career. Tonge went to Egypt because of ill health in 1853, at the age of thirty-one, and he died there two years later. Thus, he left Liverpool before he had much opportunity to fall under Pre-Raphaelite influence. His few known works generally show vast landscapes under cloudy skies, painted in a limited range of brown tones (Pl. 74a). Davis and Windus are said to have frequently painted the figures in his pictures.

Davis's earliest landscapes are often close to those of Tonge. An example is *Bidston Marsh at Wallasey* (Pl. 74b), dated 1853. Both Tonge's and Davis's pictures show a debt to John Linnell, and the loose, oily sky of Davis's landscape suggests that he had also looked at pictures by Mark Anthony, who exhibited regularly at the Liverpool Academy from 1851 onwards and was to win its prize in 1854. There is nothing in Davis's picture that gives any hint of an affinity with Pre-Raphaelitism.

Things had apparently changed by 1855, when Davis first exhibited a landscape at the Royal Academy. This painting, *Early Spring Evening – Cheshire*, was badly hung, but Rossetti spotted it and described it, along with Inchbold's pictures, as one of the best landscapes in the exhibition.[6] Rossetti also made Ruskin, who had not noticed the picture at the Academy, mention it anyway in *Academy Notes*:

[4]Reproduced in John Nicoll, *The Pre-Raphaelites* (London, 1970) p. 143, pl. 108.
[5]Smith, n.d., p. 18.

[6]George Birkbeck Hill, ed., *Letters of Dante Gabriel Rossetti to William Allingham, 1854–1870* (New York, 1897) p. 123.

Absence from London prevents, for the present, my seeing a picture, of which a friend in whose judgement I have great confidence, speaks with unusual enthusiasm – no. 514, *Early Spring Evening* (W. Davis). My friend says it contains the 'unity of perfect truth with invention'. I cannot answer for its doing this, which would place it in the first rank of works of art; but, as it is hung in a place where it is not easily caught sight of, I have little doubt it must be a work of merit.

Ruskin did have a chance to examine the picture before the third edition of the *Notes* was published. He added a supplement mentioning it again, less favourably:

In the work commended to me by my friend – Mr. Davis's *Spring Evening* (514) – I am disappointed. It is unfair to judge of it in its present position, but it seems to me merely good Pre-Raphaelite work, certainly showing no evidence whatever of inventive power, and perhaps less tact than usual in choice of subject; but it is assuredly superior to any of the landscapes hung on the line.[7]

This picture was also mentioned in the *Art Journal* where it was described as a grassy bank flanked on the left by a screen of leafless trees. The *Art Journal*'s reviewer more or less repeated Ruskin's criticism, but drew the opposite conclusion: 'The choice of such a subject, which has not one picturesque quality, argues considerable self-reliance, and the result justifies the confidence'.[8]

In 1856 Davis sent two further landscapes to the Royal Academy. One of them, *Wallasey Mill, Cheshire*, elicited an ecstatic response from Ford Madox Brown, who wrote in his diary after seeing the Academy exhibition: 'There is a little landscape by Davis, of Liverpool, of some leafless trees and some ducks, which is perfection. I do not remember ever having seen such an English landscape; it is far too good to be understood, and is on the floor'.[9] A few months later Brown was in Liverpool, and he met Davis at the home of John Miller, the collector. Brown's diary gives a touching description of the artist:

I met Davis, who brought a little sketch from nature, very beautiful. Miller asked me as a favour to purchase it, which I could not refuse him, though it put me in the awkward position of patronising a man I think far too well of to attempt the like with. This Davis, who has been one of the most unlucky artists in England (now about forty, with a wife and family), is a man with a fine-shaped head and well-cut features, and his manners are not without a certain modest dignity, but as it were all crushed by disappointment and conscious dependency of Miller who has entirely kept him for years – and the only man in the world who buys his pictures. Very sad; we must hope his turn will come.[10]

By 1857 Rossetti's and Brown's admiration had brought Davis into the sphere of Pre-Raphaelite activities. He exhibited six pictures at the exhibition in Russell Place, and he sent three works to the American exhibition in the same year. In 1858 he became a member of the Hogarth Club. However, inclusion in the Pre-Raphaelite group was no guarantee of success. From accounts other than Brown's we know that Davis had a neurotically touchy personality.[11] He refused to have anything to do with dealers, which, of course, increased the difficulty of selling his works. Although he did have consistent support from Miller, and eventually from a few other Liverpool collectors, he was fairly impoverished for most of his life.

Davis's output was large, and there are sizeable groups of his works in the Walker Art Gallery in Liverpool and in the Williamson Art Gallery in Birkenhead. He almost never dated his pictures, and it is usually impossible to identify his works from the titles under

[7]Ruskin, 1903–12, XIV, 30, 32.
[8]*Art Journal*, 1855, p. 179.
[9]Hueffer, 1896, p. 125.
[10]From the part of Brown's diary now in the Pierpont Morgan Library, New York, entry for 26 Sept. 1856. Quoted with omissions in Hueffer, 1896, p. 138.
[11]Marillier, 1904, 107–08; Stephens, 1884, 326–8.

which they were exhibited. Neither the *Early Spring Evening*, admired by Rossetti in 1855, nor the *Wallasey Mill*, praised by Brown in 1856, is now known. A picture of a mill with ducks in the foreground, *Old Mill and Pool at Ditton, Lancashire*, is in Liverpool (Pl. 75). This painting is not dated, but it is probably from approximately the same period as the lost *Wallasey Mill*. Its colours are brighter than those in *Bidston Marsh* of 1853; breadth has been superseded by a much smaller touch; and the spaciousness of the prospect in the earlier picture has given way to a more circumscribed view. These changes are in the direction of Pre-Raphaelitism, and we can assume that similar qualities in the works which Rossetti and Madox Brown saw were what drew their initial attention to Davis. In another undated picture in Liverpool, *At Hale, Lancashire* (Pl. 76a), there are also ducks in the foreground, and Davis's careful drawing of the branches and leaves on the trees to the left is more obviously Pre-Raphaelite.

Both paintings reflect Davis's affection for humble foreground detail. The duck ponds are not compositional foils for distant views, but are in themselves the objects of loving attention. Davis seems to have had little interest in grander scenery, and a number of stories are recorded of his turning his back on extensive views in order to sketch a duck pond or the opening of a drain.[12] In this respect, his landscapes are like those of Ford Madox Brown, who was also criticized by Ruskin for his choice of subject. In Brown's case, Ruskin's comment about the 'ugly subject' of *An English Autumn Afternoon* was made to the artist,[13] and Ruskin never mentioned Brown's work in print. Ruskin did not comment publicly on Davis's art again after expressing his disappointment in 1855, but in 1857, when Davis sent his pictures to the Russell Place exhibition, Rossetti solicited Ruskin's opinion. Ruskin wrote a letter to Davis which was found in a stamped envelope among Rossetti's papers. Apparently Ruskin had submitted it to Rossetti, who decided against sending it on. The main burden of the letter was a more specific repetition of Ruskin's earlier comments about lack of tact in choice of subject:

My Dear Sir,—I had much pleasure in examining the pictures of yours which Mr. Rossetti showed me this afternoon: they show an exquisite sense of colour, and much tender feeling of the expression of the scenes. Rossetti is himself so much delighted with them that I do not doubt their possessing qualities of peculiar interest to an artist, in the conquering of various technical difficulties. Your work, however, cannot become popular unless you choose subjects of greater interest, nor can I in the least direct you how to choose them – for there seems to me hardly a single point of communion or understanding between you and me as to the meaning of the word, 'Subject'. It seems to *me* that you might have sought over most landscapes for miles together, and not stumbled over anything so *little* rewarding your pains and skills as that 'ditch and wheatfield.'[14]

As we have seen in Ruskin's treatment of Inchbold and Brett, proper choice of subject was central in his consideration of landscape. The artists who followed his advice soon found themselves in the Alps, and Brett's *Val d'Aosta*, whatever its shortcomings, was at least a picture in which the artist's industry had not been wasted on scenes 'of no majesty or enduring interest'. On the other hand, intimate details of the English countryside were unworthy objects of an artist's labour. Ruskin made his feelings about this known not only in criticism of specific pictures in *Academy Notes*, but also in more general comments about the Pre-Raphaelites which he included in the later volumes of *Modern Painters*. In the fourth volume, published in 1856, he declared that a proper subject should be both pleasurable and instructive to the general public:

I should particularly insist at present on this careful choice of subject, because the Pre-Raphaelites,

[12]Marillier, 1904, 104–05.
[13]See above, p. 36.
[14]Rossetti, 1899, 168–9.

taken as a body have been culpably negligent in this respect, not in humble respect to Nature, but in morbid indulgence of their own impressions. They happen to find their fancies caught by a bit of an oak hedge, or the weeds at the side of a duck-pond, because, perhaps, they remind them of a stanza of Tennyson; and forthwith they sit down to sacrifice the most consummate skill, two or three months of the best summer time available for outdoor work (equivalent to some seventieth or sixtieth of all their lives), and nearly all their credit with the public, to this duck-pond delineation. Now it is indeed quite right that they should see much to be loved in the hedge, nor less in the ditch; but it is utterly and inexcusably wrong that they should neglect the nobler scenery which is full of majestic interest, or enchanted by historical association.[15]

In 1856 this discussion of choice of subject was still good-natured scolding, and Ruskin followed his criticism of Pre-Raphaelite subjects by saying what artists ought to paint:

views of our abbeys and cathedrals; distant views of cities, if possible chosen from some spot in itself notable by association; perfect studies of the battle-fields of Europe, of all houses of celebrated men, and places they loved, and, of course, of the most lovely natural scenery.

In 1860, when Ruskin returned to the subject in the final volume of *Modern Painters*, he spoke of the Pre-Raphaelites in the past rather than present tense, and he described their lack of feeling for grand subjects not as something to be corrected, but as a fatal flaw which had undermined the movement:

I saw with increasing wonder, that they [the Pre-Raphaelites] were almost destitute of the power of feeling vastness, or enjoying the forms which expressed it. A mountain or great building only appeared to them as a piece of colour of a certain shape. The powers it represented, or included, were invisible to them. In general they avoided subjects expressing space or mass, and fastened on confined, broken, and sharp forms; liking furze, fern, reeds, straw, stubble, dead leaves, and such like, better than strong stones, broad flowing leaves, or rounded hills; in all such greater things, when forced to paint them, they missed the main and mighty lines; and this no less in what they loved than in what they disliked; for though fond of foliage, their trees always had a tendency to congeal into little acicular thorn-hedges, and never tossed free. Which modes of choice proceed naturally from a petulant sympathy with local and immediately visible interests or sorrows, not regarding their large consequences, nor capable of understanding more massive view or more deeply deliberate mercifulness; – but peevish and horror-struck, and often incapable of self-control, though not of self sacrifice. There are more people who can forget themselves than govern themselves.[16]

Ruskin's choice in 1856 of 'duck-pond delineation' as his example of misplaced skill suggests that he was thinking of Davis, for whom ducks were almost a signature. The later comments reflect that disillusionment of Ruskin's hopes for Pre-Raphaelitism which contributed to his abandoning *Academy Notes*. Since Ruskin wrote about the artists' failure when painting mountains, his criticism applies to Brett and Inchbold as much as to Davis or Brown. But the 'sympathy with local and immediately visible interests' is most evident in Brown's and Davis's landscapes. Their inability to share Ruskin's feeling for 'greater things' is an indication of the Pre-Raphaelite generation's abandonment of the Romantic attitudes which were still basic for Ruskin. The painters were no longer attracted by what previous generations called 'the sublime', and Ruskin was unwilling to accept a feeling for 'a piece of colour of a certain shape' as its replacement.

Davis was not only criticized by Ruskin for his inability to choose subjects. He was also criticized by the generally sympathetic writers, F. G. Stephens and H. C. Marillier, for errors of perspective and proportion.[17] This was a widespread 'failing' in the middle of the nineteenth century. We can see it in different forms in artists as diverse as Dante

[15]Ruskin, 1903–12, VI, 30–31. [17]Stephens, 1884, p. 328; Marillier, 1904, pp. 103–4.
[16]*Ibid.*, VII, 233.

Gabriel Rossetti and Gustave Courbet.[18] In Davis's case, as in Rossetti's and Courbet's, the inability to master perspective seems less a weakness than a reflection of other interests. What need did a landscape painter who turned his back on traditional views have of traditional, illusionistic, three-dimensional space? Davis's lack of technical mastery in creating space goes hand-in-hand with the abandonment of conventional space-creating compositional devices that was a central element of the Pre-Raphaelite creed since Holman Hunt's attack on brown foliage and dark corners in February 1848.

The result of Davis's 'total disregard of composition' (in Marillier's words) and neglect of the 'requirements of art' (in Stephens's) is that his compositions often stay on the surface of the canvas.[19] His *Old Mill and Pool at Ditton* is a brightly coloured, two-dimensional pattern. The mill is of less interest for its picturesque dilapidation than as a coloured silhouette which is reflected in the water below. The foliage of the shrubbery around the mill is not drawn with botanic accuracy, but treated as small points of colour, which are also reflected in the water. There is no space; mill, plants, and pool all exist on one vertical plane. Other compositions recall Ford Madox Brown's landscapes. The *Field of Green Corn* (Pl. 76b), which could well be the 'ditch and wheatfield' criticized by Ruskin in 1857 (but could equally well be either the *Green Corn* or the *Cornfield* which Davis exhibited in Liverpool in 1860 and 1861 respectively), is like Brown's *Carrying Corn* (Pl. 14), but Davis has gone further in concentrating upon the foreground while minimizing the landscape beyond. It is also more freely painted than Brown's picture. Even more remarkable in its simplicity is the undated *Grass Field* (Pl. 77a). In composition and ease of handling this small picture seems to point straight to Impressionism. While the flattening of many Pre-Raphaelite pictures appears as an accidental result of filling the picture with foreground detail in a kind of *horror vacui*, that is not the case with Davis. *A Grass Field* does not have a closely studied foreground, and the view is extensive, yet the result is essentially two-dimensional. Marillier probably would have considered such a picture an example of Davis's disregard of composition, but the disregard now looks like a precocious and sophisticated feeling for the picture surface. The anonymity of the figure, who is neither more nor less important than everything else but simply part of the visual whole, also helps to make *A Grass Field* look like a curious anticipation of Monet, but we can see a precedent for this anonymity in the foreground figure in Brown's *Carrying Corn*.

Davis was not always so precocious. *At Hale, Lancashire* (Pl. 76a), for example, has more conventional space, and the child in the foreground has a personality apart from the setting. Davis's larger pictures frequently have subjects from rural life, which F. G. Stephens compared to those of Jean-François Millet.[20] *Harrowing* (Pl. 77b), which Davis exhibited in Liverpool in 1859, shows a boy with a team of horses working at twilight. A church tower is silhouetted on the horizon. This picture was rejected by the Royal Academy, possibly because of the faults of perspective which are evident in the different vanishing-points of the furrows. It was included in the International Exhibition of 1862, where William Michael Rossetti cited the differences between it and the *Val d'Aosta* as evidence of the width of range and aim within the Pre-Raphaelite movement.[21]

Later and larger ploughing subjects, one of which Davis exhibited at the Royal Academy in 1870, are in Birkenhead and Liverpool. They show less feeling for mood and an in-

[18]Rossetti's difficulties in this respect were notorious and are reflected in the quasi-two-dimensional compositions of all his finished works. For Courbet, see Linda Nochlin, 'Gustave Courbet's *Toilette de la Mariée*', *Art Quarterly*, XXXIV, 1971, pp. 46–50.

[19]Marillier, 1904, p. 103; F. G. Stephens, 'The Private Collections of England, no. XVIII – Mr. George Rae's, Birkenhead', *Athenaeum*, 9 Oct. 1875, p. 482.
[20]Stephens, 1884, p. 326.
[21]Rossetti, 1867, p. 160.

creased sense of two-dimensional pattern. In 1870 Davis moved to London, where, according to Stephens, he changed his style to a broader, more effective one. He died in 1873, supposedly of an attack of *angina pectoris* brought about by the bad hanging of one of his pictures in the International Exhibition of 1873.[22] A group of artists led by Madox Brown organized an exhibition and sale of his work to provide for his wife and ten children. Brown tried to get Gladstone to put Davis's widow on the civil list, but failed because of the family's Catholicism. He also helped one of Davis's sons work up a number of unfinished pictures that had been left in the studio, and ultimately did succeed in raising some two thousand pounds.

Davis was certainly a failure in terms of recognition. Living in the provinces, however, and supported by a few loyal patrons, he was relatively free to go his own way, and he did follow a more adventurous path than most of his more established contemporaries. However, Davis does not seem to have had the self-assurance to follow his independent path very far. There is no consistency in his development. At one moment he is suprisingly modern; at the next he is pedestrian. Davis's best work justifies Madox Brown's enthusiasm, but his output as a whole is disappointing. It may be that if he had worked in a more sympathetic atmosphere, he might have become an artist of greater stature. However, it seems more likely that his isolation allowed him the adventurous aspects of his art, and if he had flourished materially, as in the case of so many other Victorians, it would not have been to the benefit of his painting.

Among the Liverpool artists, as in the Pre-Raphaelite movement as a whole, we can discern a polarity. At one extreme is William Davis. At the other is Alfred William Hunt. While Davis was the object of Ruskin's disapproval, Hunt not only drew Ruskin's praise in *Academy Notes*, but also his lasting friendship. Hunt visited Brantwood in Ruskin's old age, and Ruskin was the godfather of one of Hunt's daughters. Like Ruskin, Hunt studied at Oxford, where, again like Ruskin, he won the Newdigate prize for poetry.

Hunt was born in Liverpool in 1830, the son of a landscape painter, Andrew Hunt, and he was active as an artist well before his graduation from Oxford in 1852. His early work is mainly in watercolour and is dependent on the example of David Cox, who was a friend of his father. As late as 1855, Hunt was still making watercolours of Welsh scenery which show no appreciable Pre-Raphaelite influence, but between 1855 and 1856 his style apparently changed. In the latter year he exhibited at the Royal Academy another Welsh subject, *The Stream from Llyn Idwal, Carnarvonshire*, which Ruskin praised lavishly: 'The best landscape I have seen in the exhibition for many a day – uniting most subtle finish and watchfulness of nature, with real and rare power of composition.' In 1857, Hunt exhibited a picture titled *When the Leaves Begin to Turn*, which again drew Ruskin's superlatives: 'Consummate in easy execution and blended colour; there is nothing else like it this year'.[23] Ruskin did qualify his praise of both pictures, but it is clear that in these years he considered Alfred Hunt the most promising landscape painter exhibiting. Inchbold had held first place in 1855, but in 1856 his *Mid-Spring* was 'not a satisfactory picture'. John Brett did not draw Ruskin's public praise until 1858.

Hunt had been offered a fellowship at Oxford and in 1856 was still vacillating between an academic and an artistic career. Ruskin's praise decided him in favour of the latter. In 1857, with three pictures accepted by the Academy and more praise from Ruskin, Hunt

[22]Davis's death provoked a letter from Inchbold in the *Athenaeum* of 3 May 1873, p. 573, proposing that the Royal Academy create a class of non-member painters such as Davis who would be entitled to exhibit one picture a year at the Academy without fear of rejection.

[23]Ruskin, 1903–12, XIV, 50–51, 116.

must have felt that he had made the right decision. Despite Ruskin's admiration, he does not seem to have been a close associate of the Pre-Raphaelites at this time. He did not have works in the exhibition in Russell Place, nor in the 1857 American exhibition, although other Liverpool artists, including Davis and Windus, participated in both. He was a member of the Liverpool Academy, and in 1858 he became a non-resident member of the Hogarth Club.[24]

Hunt may have thrown his lot in with the Pre-Raphaelites because his successes of the previous years were reversed by the rejection in 1858 of all his entries at the Royal Academy. One of the rejected pictures, *Gwm Trifaen – The Track of an Ancient Glacier*, is now in the Tate Gallery (Pl. 78a). This painting still retains reminiscences of David Cox in its exaggerated perspective and in the stormy sky, which, obscuring the outer parts of the painting, allows the centre to stand out dramatically. However, the freer handling of Hunt's earlier work has been replaced by much more precisely drawn detail in which lichens, striations, and pebbles are all carefully recorded. The subject, like that of Brett's *Glacier of Rosenlaui* of a year earlier, was probably inspired by the geological parts of the fourth volume of *Modern Painters*, and even the title was taken from Ruskin.[25] Hunt, like Brett, seems to have wanted to provide a quasi-geological demonstration, but, in comparison with Brett's work, Hunt's seems less scientifically detached. His picture is more obviously composed, and his use of light, with one sunbeam illuminating an isolated rock in the middle distance, is melodramatic. Nor did Hunt share Brett's powers as a draftsman. His rocks lack both the linear precision and the three-dimensional solidity of Brett's, and the painting as a whole, despite its rockiness, seems insubstantial. Hunt's sketchbooks are preserved in the Ashmolean Museum, and the number of careful studies of rocks and lichens which they contain demonstrates with what systematic care he prepared his pictures. His habit in later life was to sketch from nature in the summer, and in the winter to paint pictures in the studio from his sketches.[26] This was probably his procedure with *Gwm Trifaen*, which seems artificially composed when compared with the pictures that Brett and other Pre-Raphaelites painted from nature.

More appealing are a number of watercolours from the same period, which Hunt apparently did paint directly out of doors. A good example is a study of a rocky precipice in Wales, which is signed and dated 1858 (Pl. 78b). Atmospheric effect is unimportant, and although the view appears extensive, most of the watercolour consists of lichenous rocks in the immediate foreground. These watercolours from the 1850s are Hunt's freshest and strongest works. Their compositions seem to be the result of a direct confrontation with nature, whereas in his more pretentious pictures three-dimensional space and atmospheric effect seem to have been grafted on to the subjects to make them more conventionally pictorial.

After being excluded from the Royal Academy in 1858, Hunt had three works in the exhibition of 1859, one Welsh subject and two from the River Greta in Yorkshire. An oil painting in Liverpool of Brignal Banks, which overlook the Greta (Pl. 79a), is either one of these pictures or closely related. This justly celebrated scenery had been depicted in numerous earlier paintings, including some of John Sell Cotman's most beautiful watercolours. In taking it as a subject, as in painting in Wales, Hunt was following established patterns, and being more old-fashioned than any of his Pre-Raphaelite contemporaries.

[24] Where Dante Gabriel Rossetti described his landscapes sent to the exhibition of December 1858 as 'very second-rate'. Rossetti, 1899, p. 215.
[25] Ruskin, 1903–12, VI, 211.

[26] Violet Hunt, 'Alfred W. Hunt, R.W.S. (1830–1896)', *The Old Water-Colour Society's Club: Second Annual Volume: 1924–1925* (London, 1925) p. 37. Violet Hunt was the artist's daughter.

The picture in Liverpool is a fairly conventional landscape view, treated throughout with laborious care. The foreground leaves are microscopic, and the rest of the landscape, which is extensive, is painted in a tiny stipple.

Ruskin did not give Hunt's pictures of 1859 the same enthusiastic praise that he had devoted to those of 1856 and 1857; in fact, he only mentioned Hunt in passing while discussing a drawing by Henry Clarence Whaite:

Compare with it the interesting study opposite, by Mr. A. W. Hunt (997. *On the Greta*), entirely well meant, but suffering under the same oppression of plethoric labour. I do not often, in the present state of the English school, think it advisable to recommend 'breadth'; but assuredly both Mr. Whaite and Mr. Hunt, if they wish to do themselves justice, ought to give up colour for a little while, and work with nothing but very ill-made charcoal which will not cut to a point.

Ruskin wrote at some length about Whaite, whose *Barley Harvest* he declared the most covetable bit of landscape of the year. However, he criticized Whaite's execution, and this criticism, couched in general terms, provides an elaboration of what he wrote about Hunt:

The execution of the whole by minute and similar touches is a mistake. Certain textures need to be so produced and certain complexities of form; but the work is never good unless it varies with every part of the subject, and is different in method, according to the sort of surface or form required. Nothing finished can be done without labour; but a picture can hardly be more injured than by the quantity of labour in it which is lost. Uncontributive toil is one of the forms of ruin. . . .

Many other studies of great interest may be found scattered on the walls, in which, while there is much to be admired, this is generally to be regretted, that the painters, not being able to do their work entirely well, think to make progress by doing a great quantity of work moderately well, which will by no means answer the purpose. We cannot learn to paint leaves by painting trees-full, nor grass by painting fields-full. Learning to paint one leaf rightly is better than constructing a whole forest of leaf definitions.[27]

This is consistent with what Ruskin had written earlier about Pre-Raphaelite detail. In his discussion of the foliage in *The Light of the World* in 1854, he had drawn a distinction between true Pre-Raphaelite work and spurious imitations which represented 'the most minute leaves and other objects with sharp outlines, but with no variety of colour, and with none of the concealment, none of the infinity of nature'. His criticism in 1859 was not of Pre-Raphaelite detail, but of insensitive elaboration. Yet, his conclusion that artists should make careful studies of individual leaves rather than paint trees-full seems to deny the Pre-Raphaelite practice of painting entire pictures directly from nature and to anticipate his later criticism of Brett's painting 'large studies by way of pictures'.[28] The excess of labour which he lamented in 1859 was an outgrowth of the Pre-Raphaelite care and finish which Ruskin had earlier championed. Something had gone wrong, and Ruskin's criticism here is a reflection of the disappointment of his hopes for the movement as much as is his criticism of the *Val d'Aosta* in the same year.

After 1860, Hunt worked chiefly in watercolour. He became a member of the Old Water-Colour Society in 1862, and he was reasonably successful, although his failure to be elected a member of the Royal Academy was the cause of bitter recriminations.[29] All his later watercolours are painted with the same exhausting stipple that we have seen in *Brignal Banks*. Many of them show spectacular and unusual effects of light. The best-known example is *A November Rainbow – Dolwyddelane Valley, 1865* (Pl. 79b), a large and elaborate watercolour which combines geology, comparable to that in *Gwm Trifaen*, with meteoro-

[27]Ruskin, 1903–12, XIV, 229–30.
[28]See above, pp. 61 and 133.

[29]Rossetti, 1903, pp. 232–3. See also Gosse, 1884, pp. 6–7.

logy. According to H. C. Marillier, it was 'one of the few instances (if not the solitary one) of a rainbow painted according to nature'.[30] The result is so melodramatic that the scientific pretensions seem spurious, but for Hunt's admirers works such as this were products of the highest skill of an artist who combined 'poetical instincts and scientific knowledge'. For Edmund Gosse, Hunt was the one Victorian heir of Turner, and for the young Roger Fry in 1887, his watercolours were 'very magnificent.'[31]

The Liverpool group included several other more-or-less Pre-Raphaelite artists, including two interesting genre painters, James Campbell and John J. Lee. Another Liverpool Pre-Raphaelite, John Edward Newton, painted still lifes, genre subjects and landscapes in microscopic detail. H. C. Marillier described Newton's landscapes as 'little more than handmade photographic transcripts, . . . pathetic for the immense care and labour they exhibit, and the extraordinary fidelity of detail, without any corresponding charm.'[32] However, the one thing which Newton's *Gresford Mill* (Pl. 80a) does possess as a result of the painstaking detail is a naive, primitive charm. More sophisticated were W. J. J. C. Bond and J. W. Oakes, two landscape painters who came passingly under Pre-Raphaelite influence. Bond was an eclectic artist, who never gained a reputation outside Liverpool. Much of his work is weak imitation of Turner. Oakes moved to London in 1859. In 1874 he was elected an associate member of the Royal Academy. His later pictures are not at all Pre-Raphaelite; however, he was a member of the Hogarth Club, and in 1862 William Michael Rossetti included him along with Inchbold, Boyce, Brett, and Davis in a list of Pre-Raphaelite landscape painters.[33] His work of the 1850s seems to have consisted mainly of close foreground studies, which drew some praise from Ruskin.[34]

One other landscape painter should be included in the context of the Liverpool group, although he stands rather apart from the others. This is Daniel Alexander Williamson, who was born in Liverpool in 1823, the son of one Liverpool artist and nephew of another. He went to London in 1847 and remained there until 1860. From 1848 to 1851, he exhibited portraits at the Liverpool Academy, and he exhibited at the Royal Academy every year from 1853 to 1858. Although Williamson continued to exhibit portraits through 1856, the majority of his works from the 1850s are of either sheep or cattle. The main influence upon them seems to have been that of the Barbizon animal painter, Constant Troyon. A watercolour, *Peckham Common – Milking Time* (Pl. 80b), for example, recalls Troyon's *Oxen Going to Work: Morning* (Louvre), which was exhibited in the Salon of 1855.[35] None of Williamson's work of the 1850s suggests any awareness of Pre-Raphaelitism.

In 1861 Williamson left London to settle in the village of Warton-in-Carnforth in northern Lancashire. In 1864 he moved nearby to Broughton-in-Furness, where he remained for the rest of his life. He seems to have had no personal connections with the London Pre-Raphaelites. He did not exhibit at the Royal Academy after 1858, but he did exhibit in Liverpool, although he was not a member of the Liverpool Academy. He was friendly with Windus, and the two painted together in the summers during the early 1860s, when Windus also was living in northern Lancashire, near Preston. Windus and Williamson shared the devoted admiration of one collector, James Smith of Blundell-

[30]H. C. Marillier, 'Modern Pictures at Red Heath, Croxley Green', *Art Journal*, 1903, p. 225.
[31]See *ibid.*, p. 229; Gosse, 1884, p. 3; and Virginia Woolf, *Roger Fry: A Biography*, New York, 1940, p. 53.
[32]Marillier, 1904, p. 179.

[33]Rossetti, 1867, p. 160.
[34]Ruskin, 1903–12, XIV, 115, 154n., 169, 230.
[35]Troyon's works were visible in London in the 'French Exhibitions' held annually at 121 Pall Mall beginning in 1854.

sands, and it is due to Smith that Williamson is remembered at all today. All the pictures by Williamson in the museums of Liverpool and Birkenhead, with only insignificant exceptions, were once in Smith's collection. In 1912 the Manchester City Art Gallery held an exhibition of four northern artists including Williamson. All the Williamsons were lent by Smith, who also wrote the appropriate catalogue notes.[36] Smith also privately and anonymously published a small memorial pamphlet about Williamson and Windus which is the chief source of information about the former.[37] Other collectors did own pictures by Williamson, but Smith was far and away his most important patron.

Two small pictures by Williamson in Liverpool justify Smith's attention. Both were painted while Williamson was living at Warton-in-Carnforth. One, *Morecambe Bay from Warton Crag* (Pl. 81a), bears a label on its back with Williamson's monogram and the date 1862, the year it was exhibited at the Liverpool Academy. The other, *Spring: Arnside Knot and Coniston Range of Hills from Warton Crag* (Pl. 81b and Col. Pl. 7), has a label with the date 1863, but apparently was not exhibited.

There can be no doubt about the Pre-Raphaelite influence on these works. *Morecambe Bay from Warton Crag* is a pastiche of Holman's Hunt's *Strayed Sheep* of a decade earlier. The subject is similar and the prismatic green and violet of the sea are based on Hunt's colours. The luminosity even surpasses *Strayed Sheep*, but, while Hunt's colour seems to be the result of attempting to gain greater naturalism, Williamson's appears to have brightness for brightness's sake. Compared to *Strayed Sheep*, Williamson's painting is relatively abstract. The trees in the distance are a vivid purple that can not be explained naturalistically, and the other colours are heightened correspondingly. Similarly, Williamson's touch is Pre-Raphaelite in origin, but it is employed to embroider a decorative filigree out of natural materials rather than to describe the natural world with minute precision. Drawing is relatively unimportant; the foreground rocks lack both linear detail and three-dimensional volume.

Spring: Arnside Knot and Coniston Range of Hills is more individual and more remarkable. While the colour of *Morecambe Bay* is borrowed from Hunt, in the later picture the colour no longer seems derivative. The foreground is made up of bright green grass, orange bracken, and yellow gorse. The group of trees before the rock outcrop are deep purplish red, and Arnside Knot in the distance is vibrantly blue. Throughout the picture the colours are so heightened that the landscape seems to glow. In both pictures there are flocks of birds in the sky, but all else is still. The sheep in the foreground of *Morecambe Bay* seem as immobile as the rocks, and in the foreground of *Arnside Knot* a rabbit crouches motionless. The world is seen frozen for a moment, and with hyper-clarity.

Although inspired by Pre-Raphaelitism, these two small paintings also recall the overtly visionary works of Samuel Palmer. We do not know if Williamson was aware of Palmer; it seems unlikely. As far as we know, Williamson did paint out of doors directly from nature, and he did intend the pictures as naturalistic studies. These pictures, painted in the early 1860s, represent a late flowering of Pre-Raphaelite naturalism in which the detail, the clarity, and the bright colours have all become the elements of visionary stylization.

Two other pictures by Williamson from the same period are in Birkenhead. One, *The Startled Rabbit, Warton Crag*, is close in handling to the Liverpool paintings, but it has a genre subject. A girl and a man carrying a bundle of faggots frighten a rabbit, which

[36]*Paintings and Drawings by James Charles, George Sheffield, William Stott, and D. A. Williamson* (City Art Gallery, Manchester, 1912).
[37]Smith, n.d., pp. 4–9.

bounds away. This picture is not dated. The other, *Near the Duddon* (Pl. 82a), is signed and dated 1864 and is of considerable interest because it seems to contain two different and conflicting styles. On the right, in the immediate foreground, foliage is painted with leaf-by-leaf Pre-Raphaelite detail. In the background, the distant hills are comparable to the outcrop in *Arnside Knot* of the previous year. They are precisely outlined and strongly coloured in rusty autumnal purples. The rest of the painting is vague. It shows a stream with ducks in the foreground, but the stream and its surroundings are painted in a thin washy blur of greens and oranges. There is no detail except in the foliage on the right, and it is impossible to tell where the water ends and the shore begins. There is some similarity to the foreground of water and ducks in Davis's *Old Mill and Pool at Ditton*, in which the reflections have a painterly imprecision, but Williamson treats the shore as well as its reflection with greater vagueness. The effect is not quite successful; clarity and ambiguity seem too closely juxtaposed. The picture is a transitional work, and the departure from Pre-Raphaelite elaboration in a substantial part of it heralds the redirection of Williamson's art.

After 1864 Williamson gave up painting in oil for some twenty years. His later oils are totally unlike those of the early 1860s, all tending to be misty visions. Although for an admirer like Smith they constituted Williamson's best work, they are nebulous to the point of being vacuous. In the intervening years Williamson worked entirely in water-colour. A large number of these are in Liverpool, and several are dated 1865. None of them has any similarity to his paintings of the previous few years. Those from the 1860s are reminiscent of David Cox, while the later ones become increasingly indistinct. Without Pre-Raphaelite discipline, Williamson's later work bogged down in a hazy dream world, which seems slack and empty compared to the taut richness of his best pictures. The Pre-Raphaelite influence alone does not explain the high quality of Williamson's work of the early 1860s. But, whatever it was that made Williamson a poetic artist during the years he lived at Warton-in-Carnforth, as soon as he abandoned Pre-Raphaelitism his art rapidly deteriorated.

XII

Some Friends and Followers

IN NOVEMBER 1849, William Michael Rossetti recorded in *The P.R.B. Journal*, his intermittent diary of the Pre-Raphaelite movement, that John Everett Millais's older brother, William Millais, had begun painting from still lifes, and that Millais intended to get him to paint landscapes. On 29 December 1849, William Michael mentioned William Millais again; by now he was determined to become a professional artist, and 'John is to bully him into doing nothing all summer but paint in the fields'. In the summer of 1850 William Millais did paint landscapes in Jersey; according to the *P.R.B. Journal* some of them were 'excellent and most promising' and probably would be exhibited.[1]

William Millais did not exhibit any of his landscapes from Jersey, but his activity in the summer of 1850 makes him the first artist who set out to be a Pre-Raphaelite landscape painter. He did not become a professional artist, but during the 1850s he produced a substantial body of works which show the application of Pre-Raphaelite care and precision to landscape subjects. In the summer of 1851 he joined his brother and Holman Hunt at Worcester Park Farm, at Ewell in Surrey, where they were working on *The Hireling Shepherd* and *Ophelia*, and in 1852 he exhibited his first work at the Royal Academy, *The Rookery, Worcester Park Farm, Surrey*. William Michael Rossetti discussed it in the *Spectator*, together with Collins's *May in Regent's Park* and Inchbold's *Study*, and announced that it promised 'first-rate things when practice shall have developed the artist's powers, and among them that of representing solidity of form'.[2]

In the following summers, 1852 and 1853, William Millais again accompanied his brother: in the former year to Hayes, south-east of London, where Millais was painting *The Proscribed Royalist*, and in the latter on the trip to the Trossachs with John and Effie Ruskin. *Hayes Common*, signed and dated 1853 (Pl. 83a), shows the same oak tree as *The Proscribed Royalist* and is painted in comparable Pre-Raphaelite detail. But the view is more spacious and the composition and imagery are more like older artists such as Richard Redgrave or W. H. Witherington than John Everett Millais of the 1850s. *Glenfinlas* (Pl. 83b) shows the same stream from a different spot as John Everett Millais's *Waterfall* (Pl. 21a) and *Portrait of Ruskin* (Pl. 20). A fisherman, traditionally said to have been painted by J. E. Millais, is in the middle distance. Like *Hayes Common*, the painting stays within the conventions of early Victorian landscape. Although the rocks in the foreground appear to reflect the same obsessive concern with geological detail as those in the *Portrait of Ruskin*, they are much less meticulously painted. William spent a considerably shorter time in Scotland than his brother (they arrived at Brig o'Turk on 1 July; William left on 18 August; John stayed until the end of October), so it is understandable that his picture shows less painstaking accuracy.

William continued to paint for the rest of his life, but most of his later work is in watercolour. *Hayes Common* and *Glenfinlas* are the largest and most ambitious of his works

---

[1]Rossetti, 1900, pp. 232, 277–8. [2]*Spectator*, 19 June 1852, p. 593.

which are now known. He never stepped out of the shadow of his more gifted brother; in later years, according to Mary Lutyens, when John Everett Millais showed his works in the studio of his palatial home in Palace Gate, William would hang his works in the hall and catch his brother's visitors as they came and went.[3]

Several other relatives and friends on the amateur fringes of the Pre-Raphaelite movement also painted landscapes. Among them were John Brett's sister, Rosa Brett, who exhibited at the Royal Academy both under her name and under the name Rosarius, and William Bell Scott's friend Alice Boyd. Michael Halliday, a friend of Millais and Holman Hunt, was taught by Millais and exhibited landscapes at the Pre-Raphaelite exhibition in Russell Place in 1857. He also was a 'Resident Artistic' member of the Hogarth Club, and he exhibited at the Royal Academy from 1853 to 1866. Works by Rosa Brett belong to descendants of John Brett; watercolours by Miss Boyd are occasionally seen; most of Halliday's works seem to have disappeared.[4] None of these figures can be considered of more than peripheral interest, but another amateur friend of the Pre-Raphaelites is of considerably more importance. That is Ruskin. During the 1850s Ruskin became more and more ambitious in his own drawings. Although he did not participate in the Russell Place exhibition, he was represented by a watercolour in the American exhibition of the same year, and he was a 'Resident Artistic' member of the Hogarth Club. In 1859 he sent a drawing to the exhibition of the Royal Scottish Academy in Edinburgh.[5] The one oil painting listed in the 'Catalogue of Drawings' in the *Library Edition* of Ruskin's works is there dated 1859. However, as the subject was *Glen Tilt*, which is in Scotland, the origins of the picture must date from Ruskin's Scottish trip of 1857.[6] This painting, which was surprisingly large (fifty-four by thirty-six inches) was given away in 1860. In 1861 George Price Boyce reported in his diary, after dining with Ruskin, that Ruskin intended to give up writing and lecturing to devote himself to painting.[7] Ruskin, of course, did not give up writing and lecturing, and his painting remained secondary. Nonetheless, his artistic activity during the second half of the 1850s was more than amateur dabbling. In 1854 he began to plan a history of Switzerland, for which he would provide the illustrations, and in subsequent years he made a large number of careful topographical drawings of Swiss towns for this project. In 1854 he also began to teach drawing at the Working Men's College along with Rossetti and Lowes Dickinson, and he wrote two books based on his teaching, *The Elements of Drawing*, published in 1857 and *The Elements of Perspective*, published in 1859.

Many of Ruskin's own drawings from the later 1850s are not unlike the works of the artists whom he admired and encouraged. The *Study of a Block of Gneiss, Valley of Chamouni*, drawn probably in 1856 (Pl. 68b),[8] was the work which Ruskin sent to the American exhibition of 1857. Like some of the watercolours Ruskin made in Scotland in 1857,

[3]Lutyens, 1967, p. 36n.
[4]A watercolour by Miss Boyd is in the British Museum. Halliday's best-known picture, *The Measure for the Wedding Ring*, exhibited at the Royal Academy in 1856, was sold at Sotheby's Belgravia, London, 19 Oct. 1971, no. 54, and is illustrated in the catalogue. He painted the background of this picture under Millais's supervision at Winchelsea in 1854 (see Hunt, 1905, I, 334).
[5]See *Art Journal*, 1859, pp. 110–11, for a lengthy criticism.
[6]Ruskin, 1903–12, XXXVIII, p. 255, no. 783. See also James Dearden, *Facets of Ruskin* (London, 1970) pp.

100–01.
[7]Boyce, 1941, p. 39.
[8]This drawing is reproduced by Ruskin's editors as *Study of Rocks and Trees near Chamouni;* they date it 1858 (Ruskin, 1903–12, XXXVI, pl. XVII, and XXXVIII, p. 241, no. 422); however, it was in America in time for the exhibition of 1857. Charles Eliot Norton kept it after the exhibition closed in Boston (*ibid.*, XXXVI, pp. 277 and 294). Ruskin did not visit the Alps in 1857, but he was at Chamonix for a long stay in 1856, part of it in the company of Norton. More recently this drawing has been known as *Fragment of the Alps*.

notably *The Pass of Killiecrankie* in the Fitzwilliam Museum, it is as strongly coloured as an oil painting. The precise geological detail was anticipated in many of Ruskin's earlier studies and cannot be considered a result of Pre-Raphaelite influence, but most of his earlier studies of detail remained studies, whereas in the watercolours of 1856 and 1857 the detailed observation is incorporated into a pictorial whole. Although comparable in subject to the *Gneiss Rock in Glenfinlas* of 1853 (Pl. 21b), these slightly later watercolours show considerably more ambition in the use of colour and in the treatment of space. But they represent the height of Ruskin's pictorial ambitions. In the 1860s, when he complained that John Brett painted 'large studies by way of pictures', Ruskin was again generally content to leave his own studies as studies, instead of working them up into completed compositions.

Among the professional landscape painters whose work was affected by Pre-Raphaelitism, the most unlikely was Edward Lear. Born in 1812, Lear had been active as a topographical landscape draughtsman since the late 1830s. Between 1841 and 1852 he published five volumes containing illustrations based on his views in Italy, Greece, and Albania. These were sufficiently successful for him to be summoned in 1846 to give drawing lessons to Queen Victoria. Lear himself was self-taught as a draughtsman. The distinctive style which he developed during the 1840s was readily translatable into the lithographic illustrations of his books, but when he attempted to paint pictures in oil on the basis of his sketches his lack of training became a major handicap. He had painted occasionally in oils through the 1840s, but he first exhibited a picture at the Royal Academy in 1850. He continued to send works there in each of the following six years (after which he did not exhibit at the Academy again until 1870). His increase in ambition meant an increase in frustration. Consequently, in 1850, at the age of thirty eight, he sat 'with 51 little boys' for the examination to enter the Royal Academy schools.[9] He was accepted, but the Academy schools were of no help for Lear's immediate problem in painting landscapes in oil from his sketches. So in the summer of 1852 he sought Holman Hunt's advice.

Holman Hunt was fifteen years younger than Lear, and in 1852 was only twenty-five years old. His pictures were still considered aberrations by most of the critical press, and none of his exhibited works had been landscapes. That Lear should have turned to Hunt, rather than to an established landscape painter like David Roberts or Clarkson Stanfield, is surprising and testifies to the impact which the landscape parts of *The Hireling Shepherd* must have made when it was exhibited in May 1852. Hunt was taken to Lear's studio by Robert Braithwaite Martineau, whose *Kit's Writing Lesson*, exhibited at the Royal Academy in 1852 (Tate Gallery), had been painted under Hunt's direction. Lear showed Hunt his sketches and explained the difficulty he had in painting pictures from them. Hunt's reply to this was that he would not paint pictures in the studio from such sketches, but he did not tell Lear to go back to Italy and paint his pictures directly from the subjects they were supposed to show. He took a drawing by Lear of *The Quarries of Syracuse* (Pl. 84a) and suggested that all the different elements in it, limestone cliffs, fig trees, and the rest, could be found in England. As a result, when Hunt went to Fairlight, near Hastings, a few weeks later to paint *Strayed Sheep* (Pl. 28a), Lear went with him and set to work on a painting of *The Quarries of Syracuse* under Hunt's direction. The two shared a house, and in return for Hunt's tutelage Lear gave him lessons in Italian. During their evenings together Lear recorded Hunt's advice in a book he called 'Ye Booke of Hunte.'[10]

At Fairlight Lear worked on several other pictures as well as *The Quarries of Syracuse*.

[9]Noakes, 1968, p. 105.   [10]Hunt, 1905, I, 328–34.

After Hunt had returned to London, Lear wrote to him on 19 December:

I really cannot help again expressing my thanks again for the progress I have made this Autumn. The *Reggio* & the *Venosa* are both done & in frame, – except that the latter will have to benefit by some of your remarx when we meet – and I hardly believe I did them. I am now beginning to have perfect faith in the means employed & if the *Thermopylae* turns out right I am a P.R.B. for ever. Indeed, in no case shall I ever return to the old style. The *Venosa* is wonderfully true and brilliant. Of course painting out of doors has been out of the question – but I have sloshed as little as possible...[11]

Lear exhibited *Thermopylae* at the British Institution in February. Meanwhile he stayed on at Fairlight through the winter working on *The Quarries of Syracuse*, which he completed in time to send to the Royal Academy in April. There it was won as an Art Union prize by the Earl Beauchamp. It now belongs to the present Earl.

On receipt of Lear's letter of 19 December, Hunt wrote back that he was delighted to hear of the pictures' completion, adding that he was sure 'they must be very brilliant and charming'.[12] Brilliant they are – in a way that is purely Pre-Raphaelite. The foreground of *Reggio* (Tate Gallery) is filled with cacti which are as brightly green as the foreground grass in *The Hireling Shepherd*.[13] In the foreground of *Venosa* (Pl. 84b) there is a tangle of foliage which is so like the foreground foliage of *Strayed Sheep* that it is tempting to think that it was painted either in direct emulation or as an exercise set by Hunt.

Reggio and *Venosa* were both based on sketches which Lear made on a trip to Sicily and Calabria in 1847. The sketch of *The Quarries of Syracuse*, made on the same trip, is typical of Lear's vignette style of picturesque sketching. The chief object of topographic interest, the city, is near the top of the sheet and seen from a distance of several miles. The large forms in the foreground provide a dramatic foil, but they are treated with less precise detail, and a substantial part of the foreground, including both corners, is empty. The compositions of *Reggio* and *Venosa* suggest that both began as such conventionally organized views, which are about as un-Pre-Raphaelite as landscape can be. In the finished paintings leaves and cacti fill the lower corners which were originally empty. Particularly in *Venosa*, the foliage, which is disproportionate in scale, appears as a display of Pre-Raphaelite observation and labour applied to a picture which otherwise remains fairly conventional.

Hunt and Lear remained friends until Lear's death in 1888. They painted together again at Fairlight in 1858. Lear always referred to Hunt as 'Pa' or 'Daddy' (he could not be a Pre-Raphaelite brother, but he considered himself a Pre-Raphaelite son; Millais was his Pre-Raphaelite uncle). But Lear's Pre-Raphaelitism was short-lived. The finished *Quarries of Syracuse*, which he completed in the winter of 1853 away from Hunt, is less obviously Pre-Raphaelite than the two pictures he completed in the autumn of 1852. As he mentioned in the letter to Hunt quoted above, working out of doors in the winter in England was impossible, so even the *Venosa* was finished in the studio. In the following July he discovered that there were difficulties in working out of doors in the summer as well. In a letter to Hunt written from Windsor, where he was painting a picture for the Earl of Derby, he complained about the unco-operative weather and concluded:

It is therefore utterly impossible to do the view on a strictly P.R.B. principle – for supposing a tree is black one minute – the next it's yellow, & the 3rd green: so that were I to finish any one part the whole would be all spots – a sort of Leopard Landscape. I must therefore – if ever there is sun again (toward evening) mark out the shadows properly & work away as I can...[14]

[11]Formerly collection of Mrs. Elizabeth Burt; partly quoted in Sotheby, 1970, no. 894, and in Noakes, 1968, p. 114.

[12]John Rylands Library, Manchester, Rylands Eng.

MS. 1214, f. 4.

[13]Reproduced in Noakes, 1968, p. 114.

[14]Formerly collection of Mrs. Elizabeth Burt; quoted in Noakes, 1968, pp. 118–19.

In December 1853 Lear went to Egypt. He was together with Thomas Seddon in Cairo for a while, but he set off for a trip up the Nile before Hunt arrived. He apparently left Cairo intending to paint directly from nature in Pre-Raphaelite fashion, but he soon reverted to drawing. On 15 March Seddon wrote to his fiancée, 'Lear returned to-day. He gave up oil painting, and has brought back an enormous number of sketches, which are exceedingly interesting'.[15] Hunt was in Egypt by then, but Lear returned to England rather than accompanying Hunt and Seddon on to Palestine. He did visit Jerusalem in 1858. A painting of the city from the Mount of Olives, which he completed in 1859 from sketches made on his visit (private collection), still shows vestiges of Pre-Raphaelite foliage in the foreground,[16] but this is about the last trace of Lear's Pre-Raphaelitism. His stay with Hunt at Fairlight was an interlude, not a lasting influence.

Another artist older than the members of the Pre-Raphaelite Brotherhood who developed a short-lived passion for detailed naturalism was James Smetham. Smetham was born in 1821 in Yorkshire, the son of a Methodist preacher. He studied in London in the 1840s at Cary's Academy and at the Royal Academy schools. In the early 1850s he was supporting himself by teaching drawing at the Wesleyan Normal School in Westminster when he fell under the spell of Ruskin's writing. He was one of the first three pupils to enroll under Ruskin's instruction when the Working Men's College opened in the autumn of 1854. Ruskin was impressed by 'the talent and industry and thoughtfulness' of Smetham's drawings,[17] and in February 1855 Smetham was invited to dine with Ruskin and his parents at Denmark Hill. A rapturous letter to a friend describing the visit shows that Smetham was more than ready to become a disciple: 'I was in a sort of soft dream all the way home; nor has the fragrance, which, like the June sunset, "Dwells in heaven half the night," left my spirit yet'.[18]

In 1868 Smetham wrote that he had read Ruskin in 1849 and 'determined to put it to the proof, painting several pictures in the severely imitational style'.[19] If Smetham had put Ruskin to the test as early as 1849, he was still ready to throw himself at Ruskin's feet five years later, and in 1856, when the third volume of *Modern Painters* appeared, Smetham immediately bought a copy and declared that he would read it, 'with the slowness, iteration, and thought it deserves' ... 'I have glanced at the chapter on "Finish," and see the exquisite definition of it: "added fact". How clear, how true! Finish, from first to last – added fact. How this leads to the great principle, *study nature*'.[20] Smetham's attempts at the 'severely imitational style' can be seen in his tiny *Naboth's Vineyard* of 1856 (Pl. 85a), in which the leaves of the vines across the upper part of the picture are painted in Pre-Raphaelite detail. But close study of nature is only part of the picture; Naboth reclines in the foreground enjoying the fruits of his vines while Ahab looks on covetously from the upper left corner. The contradictions in scale within the picture and the strange prominence of the leaves are disturbing, and they apparently do reflect something wrong in Smetham's mental balance. In February 1857 he sent Ruskin a drawing which prompted Ruskin to warn him, 'it is unsafe for you, with your peculiar temperament, to set yourself subjects of this pathetic and exciting kind for some time to come'.[21] This warning was prophetic; Smetham had a breakdown in the autumn of 1857. He soon recovered, but another collapse in 1877 plunged him into insanity for the last twelve years of his life.

[15]Seddon, 1858, p. 60.
[16]Reproduced in *Edward Lear: 1812–1888*, exhibition catalogue (Gooden and Fox Ltd., London, 1968) pl. XIV.
[17]Ruskin, 1903–12, XIV, 460.
[18]Smetham and Davies, 1891, pp. 52–7; reprinted in Ruskin, 1903–12, V, pp. xlvii–xlviii.
[19]Smetham and Davies, 1891, p. 169.
[20]*Ibid.*, p. 68.
[21]Ruskin, 1903–12, XIV, 461.

In the 1860s Smetham remained a friend of Dante Gabriel Rossetti; in fact, they were closer than they had been in the previous decade. According to the *Memoir* of Smetham by William Davies, he spent every Wednesday from 1863 to 1868 at Rossetti's studio. However, his devotion to Pre-Raphaelite naturalism was over. Already, when looking at the Turner sketches which Ruskin had put on exhibition at Marlborough House in 1856, he had decided that it was best not to paint finished things from nature, 'but to make slight, often symbolic records, in abundance of facts'.[22] In 1863, despite the generally small scale of his works, he proclaimed himself a 'Monumentalist', whose speciality would be 'Idylls in Oil'.[23] In the letter in which he described putting Ruskin 'to the proof', he declared that he soon found the severely imitational style impossible. The true basis of painting was 'the expression of the feeling of an individual man about nature'. His correspondence from the 1860s and 1870s shows not only the redefinition of his own goals, but also a critical recon- sideration of Pre-Raphaelitism. In one letter he compared Thomas Seddon's *Jerusalem and the Valley of Jehoshaphat* (Pl. 51b) with William Collins's *Seaford, Sussex* of 1844 (Victoria and Albert Museum), both of which were then hanging at South Kensington, and he decided that Collins's scheme of light and shade in relation to the picture as a whole was as true as Seddon's 'flat accuracy'. Although he found Seddon's lighting quite correct, and much feeling in Seddon's details, he preferred the Collins.[24] In another letter, written in 1870 praising Rembrandt's landscapes, he declared, 'The pre-Raffaelite dicta of ten years ago would have laid these landscapes dead. The "awe of observation" peeping and botanizing, and putting the screw on square inches, would slay all such art, and it is the grandest of all.'[25]

Among living landscape painters, Smetham had greatest respect for John Linnell and Samuel Palmer, both of whom were well along in years by the 1860s and represented a con- tinuation of pre-Pre-Raphaelite attitudes towards landscape. Specifically, Linnell and Palmer were a link with Blake, for whom Smetham, like Rossetti, had the profoundest admiration. In a long review of the first edition of Gilchrist's *Life of Blake* (which was printed in the second edition) Smetham praised Linnell for 'that grandeur and sense of awe and power of landscape', the germ of which had been contained in Blake's illustrations for Thornton's *Virgil*.[26] In turn, Rossetti, in a note which also appeared in the second edition of Gilchrist's *Life of Blake*, wrote that Smetham was more closely akin to Blake than any other living artist and that he was 'often nearly allied by landscape intensity to Samuel Palmer'.[27] This connection with Palmer and also with Linnell is more evident in most of Smetham's land- scapes than any Pre-Raphaelite influence. *Going Home*, a watercolour painted just before Smetham's final breakdown (Pl. 85b), is so close to some of Palmer's etchings, *The Weary Ploughman* for example, that there can be no doubt that Palmer had become the chief in- fluence on the *quondam* disciple of Ruskin. We have seen affinities between both Ford Madox Brown and Daniel Alexander Williamson and Palmer, but these seem to have been the result of approaching nature in similar ways, not of imitating Palmer. In Brown's and Williamson's *oeuvres* the affinity with Palmer is most evident in their most Pre-Raphaelite landscapes. In Smetham's case the affinity with Palmer replaced Pre-Raphaelitism, and a work such as *Going Home* owes more to looking at Palmer than to looking at nature.

Ruskin had a number of other students at the Working Men's College who spent the rest of their lives in his shadow. One of them, William Ward, became a drawing master for people who applied to Ruskin for assistance; he was later employed by Ruskin to make

[22]Smetham and Davies, 1891, pp. 70–71.
[23]*Ibid.*, p. 129.
[24]*Ibid.*, pp. 309–310.
[25]*Ibid.*, p. 206.

[26]William Davies, ed., *The Literary Works of James Smetham* (London, 1893), p. 130.
[27]Rossetti, 1911, p. 594.

copies of Turner's watercolours. Another, George Allen, engraved many of the illustrations in Ruskin's books and eventually became Ruskin's publisher. More important as an artist in his own right was John Wharlton Bunney. Born in 1828, Bunney was a clerk with Smith, Elder and Co. (Ruskin's publishers until George Allen replaced them), when he became a pupil at the Working Men's College. In 1857 he exhibited a painting and a watercolour in the American Exhibition of British Art and was described by William Michael Rossetti as a pupil of both Ruskin and Dante Gabriel Rossetti.[28] Like other painters who were willing to listen to Ruskin he was soon in the Alps. In 1864 he exhibited at the Royal Academy *Autumn Snow in the Bonneville Valley, Savoie*. His address listed in the catalogue of the 1864 exhibition, however, was Florence, and he continued to reside primarily in Florence for the rest of the decade. He was a friend there of Holman Hunt, who was in Florence intermittently from 1866 to 1869. A *Landscape from Fiesole*, which is dated 1867 (Pl. 86a), once belonged to Hunt. It shows a view comparable to those in Hunt's watercolours *Festa at Fiesole* (Pl. 34b) and *Sunset in the Val d'Arno* (Pl. 35b), but in a drier, more linear and more literal style, without the lurid sunset colour which is such a prominent feature of Hunt's watercolours.

In 1869 Ruskin spent the summer, from May to August, in Verona making studies for what seems to have been intended as a *Stones of Verona*. Bunney worked as his assistant, making large coloured drawings of the buildings. Ruskin drew the detail, 'requiring (though I say it) my advanced judgement to render accurately'.[29] No *Stones of Verona* resulted, but Ruskin did give a lecture, 'Verona and Its Rivers', in February 1870 and accompanied it with an exhibition of drawings and photographs. In the catalogue Ruskin did not make much distinction between his own drawings, those by Bunney and another assistant, Arthur Burgess, and photographs. His comment on one of Bunney's drawings, the *North Porch of the Church of St. Fermo* (now in the Ashmolean Museum, along with several other Verona drawings by Bunney), began with the remark that the drawing was 'so faithful and careful as almost to enable the spectator to imagine himself on the spot'.[30] This repeats, almost *verbatim*, part of Ruskin's criticism of John Brett's *Val d'Aosta*, but whereas Ruskin eventually found Brett's impersonal accuracy disappointing, in Bunney's case he seems to have expected nothing higher. Indeed, Ruskin was soon to commission from Bunney a picture which is among the supreme examples of selfless labour in the entire history of art.

For the last twelve years of his life, from 1870 until 1882, Bunney worked almost entirely at Venice, and the last six of those years he devoted to one picture, *The West Front of St. Mark's* (Pl. 86b). From September 1876 to May 1877 Ruskin paid his last visit to Venice, where he worked on a new edition of *The Stones of Venice* and wrote a guide to the Academy and a fragmentary history of the city, *St. Mark's Rest*. He also became involved in a campaign to prevent the re-building of the west front of St. Mark's, and, fearing the worst, he set several artists to work recording what was in danger of being destroyed. Of these records Bunney's picture is the most monumental. According to Ruskin's editors Bunney spent six hundred days of 'constant labour' upon it, with the intention of making a strictly accurate architectural record.[31] It is the ultimate example of what Ruskin had defined as 'historic landscape art', being of a subject which artist and patron expected to be swept away by 'modern progress and improvement', and coming as close as humanly possible to showing that subject 'wholly unmodified by the artist's execution'.[32] What

[28]MS. letter, Yale University Library.
[29]Ruskin, 1903–12, XIX, p. li.
[30]*Ibid.*, p. 451.

[31]*Ibid.*, X, p. lxiii.
[32]See above, p. 104.

Bunney achieved was the not inconsiderable feat of making a painting look remarkably like a large (fifty-seven by eighty-nine inches), tinted photograph.

One day in 1879 or 1880, while Bunney was at work in the Piazza San Marco, Whistler managed to sneak up and attach a card to his back saying 'I am totally blind'.[33] In Whistler's estimation this must have seemed not only funny, but at least symbolically true. The thought of artists as disparate as Bunney and Whistler working in Venice at the same time is pleasantly ironic, as is the fact that both were doing it because of Ruskin. Whistler had had to flee to Venice because of his bankruptcy caused by his libel suit against Ruskin in 1878. He was commissioned to go to Venice by the Fine Art Society, a gallery with which Ruskin had the closest of associations, and following his return he exhibited his Venetian works in a series of exhibitions at the Fine Art Society. A memorial exhibition of Bunney's works was held in the same premises in 1882.

Following Bunney's death, Ruskin instituted a memorial fund for the benefit of his children. In 1883 he sent the money raised to the artist's widow, accompanying it with a letter in which he stated:

... Mr. Bunney's name will remain ineffaceably connected with the history of all efforts recently made in Italy for preservation of true record of her national monuments; nor less with the general movement in which he so ardently and faithfully shared, for the closer accuracy and nobler probity of pictorial – more especially of landscape – art; a movement which was initiated about the time when he first took up residence in Venice, and of which he remained, to the day of his death, the most clearly recognized exponent and representative to the foreign schools, both of Italy and America.[34]

The 'movement' to which Ruskin referred was largely one of his creation, and the artists involved in it were mostly in his employ. The 'foreign schools, both of Italy and America', can be identified as one Italian painter, Angelo Alessandri, and one American, Henry Newman, both of whom worked extensively for the organization that gave the 'movement' its focus: the Guild of St. George. This was a utopian scheme for the reform of agricultural life in England, which Ruskin began to plan during the 1870s. The Guild of St. George did eventually own several tracts of land around England, but soon the better part of Ruskin's energies were devoted to St. George's Museum, which was opened in a cottage at Walkley, near Sheffield, in 1876. The museum's first curator, Henry Swan, had been another pupil of Ruskin's at the Working Men's College, and the museum's collections – natural history as well as art – were a reflection of Ruskin's didactic interests. Bunney's *West Front of St. Mark's* was commissioned for the museum and was its largest single possession, for which a gallery had to be built out behind the original cottage. Most of Ruskin's initial commissions for the museum, beginning in 1876, were of Venetian subjects. In 1879 he started a special fund for 'Memorial Studies of St. Mark's' to pay for them. Soon, however, this activity took other directions, and Ruskin had artists working under his orders in France and Switzerland as well as in Italy. What began as a program of making antiquarian records evolved into one of actively training, encouraging, and patronizing a group of young artists – an echo of Ruskin's relations some twenty years previously with the Pre-Raphaelite landscape painters Inchbold and Brett. None of this later group was allowed to take as independent a stance as the earlier painters, and the results, consequently, may have been on a lower level, but relations between patron and artists proceeded without the conflicts which marked Ruskin's earlier attempts at patronage.[35]

---

[33]E. R. and J. Pennell, *The Life of James McNeill Whistler* (London, 1908) I, 270.
[34]Ruskin, 1903–12, XXXIII, 564.

[35]For this activity see *ibid.*, XXX, pp. xxi–lxxv. The collections of the Guild of St. George are now housed at the University of Reading.

One of the artists Ruskin set to work in Venice was Burne-Jones's studio assistant, Thomas Matthews Rooke. During the 1870s, in addition to working for Burne-Jones, Rooke had painted and exhibited a series of Old-Testament subjects which had considerable success. In 1875 he won a Royal Academy competition for a historical picture, and his *Story of Ruth* (Tate Gallery), a triptych exhibited at the Royal Academy in 1877, was one of the first purchases under the Chantrey Bequest. Nonetheless, Rooke was apparently happy to play second fiddle to Burne-Jones, whom he continued to assist for the rest of Burne-Jones's life. In the 1890s he spent 'day after day' painting foreground flowers in Burne-Jones's huge *Sleep of King Arthur in Avalon* (Museo de Arte de Ponce, Puerto Rico).[36] For Ruskin, Rooke first made copies of the mosaics in St. Mark's during the summer and autumn of 1879. In 1884 Ruskin sent Rooke to Venice again, then to Ravenna, where he stayed two months, to Brig in the Valais, and, in October, to Sallanches, near Chamonix. In 1885 Rooke worked at Chartres from June to December, and in 1886 Ruskin sent him to Laon, Auxerre, Avallon, and on to Italy for the winter. He was still in Florence in March 1887, but by June he was back in Sallanches. His watercolours made on these trips are conscientious, accurate records, and Ruskin loved them: 'Let me congratulate you in the most solemn way on these glorious drawings. Nothing has given me so much pleasure, and the pleasure these drawings give me will be shared by all the good world'.[37]

Rooke's watercolours made at Chartres and the other cathedral cities show architectural subjects, though they often contain extensive landscapes as well (Pl. 87c). Those made in Switzerland and near Chamonix are generally of cottages or villages, with the mountains as backdrops rather than subject (Pl. 88a). These humbler aspects of mountain scenery had long appealed to Ruskin. In 1856 and 1857 he commissioned drawings of Alpine cottages from Inchbold. In 1880, when he lent Brett's *Val d'Aosta* to an exhibition and lamented in the catalogue that Brett had sympathized insufficiently with Swiss and Italian life, he went on, 'How lovely an old-fashioned Swiss or Italian village would have been, painted like this single cottage, some future disciple of the school may consider and hope to show'.[38] Four years later, Ruskin apparently designated Rooke as that future disciple. Although Rooke's drawings of ramshackle Swiss cottages have little of Brett's fine precision, they satisfied Ruskin, which cannot be said of the work of either Brett or Inchbold.

Of the other artists who worked for the Guild of St. George, the busiest was Frank Randal. He was younger than Rooke, and his employment by Ruskin was intended as an education. He first worked for Ruskin in 1881 at Amiens, where, as Ruskin wrote to the artist, Randal's practice was more important than what he was actually producing. From Ruskin he received a steady barrage of letters full of instruction, advice, and encouragement.[39] In 1882 Ruskin had him back in England, making studies of vegetation, then in France, where Randal worked again in 1883, after a period of sketching animals in the London Zoo. In 1884 Ruskin sent him to Ravenna and Verona, and to the Italian Lakes.

In Randal's case, Ruskin's methods seem to have worked. We can follow the artist's progress from timid pencil drawings made at Amiens in 1881 to elaborate watercolours made in Verona in 1884. A large watercolour of the *Piazza delle Erbe Looking South* (Pl. 87a) dated August and September 1884, shows the exact rather dry clarity of Bunney with greater genre animation and spatial complexity. As Randal had never met Bunney, who died in 1882, works like this do justify Ruskin's talking about a 'movement', but the founder of the movement was Ruskin, not Bunney. Randal's watercolour is like one of Ruskin's

---

[36]Burne-Jones, 1904, II, 344.
[37]Ruskin, 1903–12, XXX, p. lxiii.

[38]*Ibid.*, XIV, p. 238n. 1.
[39]*Ibid.*, XXX, pp. lxv–lxix and p. 72.

architectural studies in Verona, such as the *Palazzo Miniscalchi* of 1851–2 (versions in the Education Trust, Bembridge School, Isle of Wight, and the Royal Institute of British Architects),[40] carried to a degree of detailed completeness which even Ruskin never attempted. A view of *Verona from the Garden of the Palazzo Giusti* (Pl. 87b) is a beautifully careful view over the roofs of the city. A work like this from a high vantage-point still seems fully Pre-Raphaelite and is distinctly reminiscent of John Brett's *Florence from Bellosguardo* (Pl. 71a), painted twenty-one years earlier. But in comparison with Brett's painting, Randal's watercolour is more modest in both ambition and attainment. These works were done in exact accordance with Ruskin's instructions, and Ruskin was lavish in their praise: 'Yours of the town from Giusti is extremely marvellous and delicious. You can do *anything* now in realization, and this is beyond all I've seen of the kind.' Ruskin also gave tangible evidence of his approval of Randal's views of Verona by proposing to raise the artist's salary from £160 to £240 per year.[41]

Alas, Randal was not allowed to enjoy his higher pay for very long. Ruskin was laid low by attacks of insanity in 1885 and 1886, and his patronage was brought to an abrupt end. Randal drifted into complete obscurity. Rooke became the object of the semi-charitable patronage of 'The Subscribers of the Society for the Preservation of Pictorial Records of Ancient Works of Art'. This 'Society' consisted of Sydney Cockerell and whoever he could get to contribute. It existed solely to commission each year from 1894 to 1920 a drawing or drawings from Rooke, which it then presented to the Birmingham City Art Gallery. Rooke lived on until 1942, dying at the ripe age of one hundred.

It is perhaps hardly necessary to add that the rapid demise of this movement was inevitable once Ruskin ceased giving it his active support. In the 1880s this quasi-photographic art, whose goal was exact documentation, represented one of the last gasps of a dying tradition of topographical reportage. Unlike the original Pre-Raphaelites, who were the most progressive force in English painting in the 1850s, Ruskin's followers in the 1880s were a tiny backward-looking minority, whose activities were carried on in the teeth of changing artistic standards. In the same year – 1881 – that Frank Randal began to work under Ruskin, Walter Sickert began to work under Whistler. In May 1886, to publicize the group in the hope of gaining public support, Ruskin presented an exhibition of drawings made for the Guild of St. George at the Fine Art Society. In the previous month the first exhibition of the New English Art Club had opened. At exactly the same time in France, Seurat and Signac were exhibiting their Neo-Impressionist works in the eighth and last Impressionist exhibition.

Ruskin's artists shared their exhibition in 1886 with Albert Goodwin, a painter who was not of their group though he was patronized by Ruskin. In the introduction to the catalogue Ruskin worried that the elaborately finished drawings of his artists would look too literal next to Goodwin's sketchier drawings. He decided that the 'resolutely complete works' made for the Guild could not be too highly esteemed for their antiquarian value, but 'for pure artistic delight, an untouched sketch of Albert Goodwin's on the spot is better than any finished drawing'.[42] Thus, even Ruskin was ready to see values other than those of Pre-Raphaelite completeness. The artist about whom he made this judgement was one of a number of young artists who were first attracted to Pre-Raphaelitism in the early 1860s and then moved away from it.

Goodwin was not only attracted to Pre-Raphaelitism, he also had the encouragement

[40]See *Ruskin a Verona*, exhibition catalogue (Museo di Castelvecchio, Verona, 1966) no. 9 and fig. 16.

[41]Ruskin, 1903–12, XXX, pp. lxxi, 81, and 206.
[42]*Ibid.*, p. 178.

of several of the movement's leading figures. Born in 1845, he was found as a boy of fifteen or sixteen attempting to paint from nature by Arthur Hughes, who invited him to come see his work. In the 1860s Goodwin was instructed by both Hughes and Ford Madox Brown, and he was taken up by their patron James Leathart. One of Goodwin's watercolours, which he sold to Leathart, was a view of Leathart's lead factory, *St. Anthony's Works, Newcastle upon Tyne*, made on a visit to Newcastle in September 1864 (Pl. 88b). This same factory appears in the background of Brown's *Portrait of James Leathart* (Leathart Family), painted a year earlier.[43] On his trip to Newcastle Goodwin visited William Bell Scott, and his watercolour, like Scott's *Newcastle Quayside* (Pl. 46a), is among the few even peripherally Pre-Raphaelite images of the modern industrial world. Stylistically, this view of factories is not particularly Pre-Raphaelite; it is more spacious, more overtly romantic, and is without foreground detail. Its sunset effect is comparable to those in William Bell Scott's landscapes of the early 1860s.

Around 1870 Goodwin met Ruskin. Ruskin asked Goodwin to give him a lesson in watercolour painting, but, as Goodwin later realized, this was Ruskin's flattering way of asking the artist to come and be instructed by Ruskin.[44] In 1871 Goodwin worked at Abingdon and Hinksey near Oxford for Ruskin, and in 1872 he accompanied Ruskin to Italy. He subsequently followed a more independent path, but Ruskin remained friendly and continued to proffer advice. His disapproval of Goodwin's painting in oil has been quoted.[45] Most of the works which Goodwin produced during his long life (he died in 1932) are in watercolour. They show only traces of lingering Pre-Raphaelite influence and are usually easily recognizable because of Goodwin's use of a pen line to define form.

Though Goodwin did not remain a Pre-Raphaelite, Pre-Raphaelitism remained a part of his conscience. In 1918 he completed two pictures for the Royal Academy in less than two weeks and then wrote in his diary, 'How ashamed the Pre-Raphaelites would be of work done is so short a time'.[46] In practice, he not only worked faster, he also found it was better not to work from nature – 'I can paint Switzerland better when it is a somewhat far-away memory . . . the reality would put me out, partly because nature is so changeful' – and he lamented the Pre-Raphaelite liking for bright colours, from which he had not been able to shake himself free – 'I think I have suffered all my artistic life from having started under Pre-Raphaelite superlatives in colours.'[47] As late as 1918, seventy years after the formation of the Pre-Raphaelite Brotherhood, he was still struggling with this heritage: 'I owe so much to Arthur Hughes and to Ruskin, that it has been difficult and hard to unlearn that which I got also from them'.[48]

In the North of England, where Pre-Raphaelitism found its earliest and most consistent patronage, it also attracted disciples. The movement's impact in Liverpool has been discussed in a separate chapter. The second most important provincial centre was probably Newcastle, where William Bell Scott was master of the School of Art, and James Leathart formed a major Pre-Raphaelite collection under Scott's guidance. Henry H. Emmerson (1831–95) was a local artist instructed by Scott, patronized by Leathart, and mentioned by Ruskin in *Academy Notes* in 1858 for 'a promising average example of the kind of study from nature which fills the rooms.'[49] Charles Napier Hemy, another native of Newcastle ten years younger than Emmerson, also studied under Scott. He left Newcastle around

[43]Reproduced in *The Leathart Collection*, exhibition catalogue (Laing Art Gallery, Newcastle upon Tyne, 1968), pl. 7. For Goodwin, see *ibid.*, p. 19, nos. 40–42.
[44]Goodwin, 1934, p. 105.
[45]See above, p. 134.
[46]Goodwin, 1934, p. 389.
[47]*Ibid.*, p. 105.
[48]*Ibid.*, p. 448.
[49]Ruskin, 1903–12, XIV, 161.

1860 to enter a Dominican monastery, but returned three years later and began to paint under the combined influence of *Modern Painters*, Scott's teaching, and exposure to Leathart's collection. *Among the Shingle at Clovelly* (Pl. 89a), dated 1864 and shown at the Royal Academy in 1865, the first year Hemy exhibited, contains an impressive display of Pre-Raphaelite industry in the one-by-one delineation of the foreground stones. Hemy soon decided that he wanted to return to the Dominicans, and to prepare himself he went to work for Morris and Company. However, marriage put an end to his monastic ambitions, and he returned to painting. He went to Antwerp to study under the Belgian historical painter Baron Henri Leys, then settled down to a successful career of painting rivers, coast scenes, and seascapes, which show no lingering Pre-Raphaelite influence.

Leeds, where the Pre-Raphaelites were patronized by Thomas Plint, was the home of Inchbold, but, as Inchbold went to London to study, his adoption of Pre-Raphaelitism was not the result of local influences. A younger Leeds artist, John Atkinson Grimshaw, who remained in the North for most of his life, also fell temporarily under the sway of the movement. Grimshaw's early paintings were bought by Inchbold's father, the proprietor of the *Leeds Intelligencer*, so the younger artist probably did have a tenuous personal connection with the London Pre-Raphaelites.[50] All his pictures from the 1860s show closely studied foreground detail, which was obviously painted in emulation of Pre-Raphaelite pictures. A particularly elaborate example is *The Old Mill: Audby* of 1869 (Pl. 89b), which recalls Holman Hunt's *Haunted Manor* (Pl. 19b). In the 1870s Grimshaw began to specialize in moonlit landscapes and nocturnal city views in which Pre-Raphaelite influence is less evident. It is worth remembering, however, that Inchbold started to paint nocturnal subjects in the 1860s. In 1871 Inchbold was in Yorkshire, and he painted at least one moonlit watercolour at Scarborough (City Art Gallery, Leeds), where Grimshaw worked regularly. A group of later pictures by Grimshaw of autumn foliage over suburban lanes (Pl. 17b) are remarkably similar to the small *Platt Lane* which Ford Madox Brown painted in Manchester in October 1884 (Pl. 17a). In this case, Grimshaw's pictures came first, and Brown could easily have seen them in Northern collections during his stay in Manchester from 1881 to 1887.

[50]Guy Phillips, 'Atkinson Grimshaw', in *Grimshaw*, exhibition catalogue (Ferrers Gallery, London, 1964), p. 8.

XIII

William Dyce

WILLIAM DYCE has already been mentioned as an artist of the 1840s who anticipated the interest of the Pre-Raphaelites not only in early Italian art, but also in outdoor light and colour.[1] Born in 1806, he was considerably older than any of the Brotherhood, and by 1848 he had an established reputation. He never became an intimate associate of the group, as did Ford Madox Brown, and his art kept a strong character of its own. In the 1850s Dyce's chief occupation was the fresco decoration of the Queen's Robing Room in the Palace of Westminster. This was a project of monumental proportions and one which he left unfinished at his death in 1864. He did, however, also paint a number of easel pictures during the later 1850s and early 1860s, which reveal an interest in minute natural detail that certainly was influenced by the Pre-Raphaelite painting of the 1850s. These pictures are today his best known and most admired works, partly because we tend to look at him in terms of Pre-Raphaelitism, but it should be emphasized that Dyce was not primarily a landscape painter. These paintings were a peripheral activity, undertaken as a diversion from the work in fresco which forms his most significant achievement.

Dyce did paint occasional landscapes throughout his career. His earliest known painting is a re-arranged view of Aberdeen in which several local landmarks, including Westburn House, the home of his mother's family, are recognizable (Aberdeen Art Gallery). The style reflects that of the Scottish landscape painters Alexander and Patrick Nasmyth, but on a rather unaccomplished level. The painting is undated, but it was probably done before 1825, when Dyce paid his first visit to Italy.[2] Following his two trips to Italy, Dyce exhibited a number of landscapes in Edinburgh between 1829 and 1832. Some of these were of views in Italy and France; others had titles such as *Coast Scene: Composition*. None can be surely identified, but a picture of *Fisherfolk near a Wreck*, which is signed and dated 1830 (Pl. 90a), must be similar to the exhibited pictures and might well be one of them. This painting is a pastiche of Bonington, and shows no hint of the influence of Dyce's German Nazarene friends. It parallels Dyce's portraits from the 1830s, which also show no reflection of his Italian experience, but recall Raeburn and Lawrence. Some of Dyce's watercolours are so like Bonington that they could easily be attributed to that artist, and as most of Dyce's works are unsigned, it is possible that some do bear the wrong label.

In 1832 Dyce visited Southern France and Venice, where David Scott made a drawing of him sketching from a gondola (Scottish National Portrait Gallery, Edinburgh). A large number of drawings from this trip were included in the Dyce sale of 1865. One, inscribed 'Rhône at Avignon / 1832' is in the British Museum (Pl. 90b). The low horizon, empty, washy sky, and sketchy picturesque details are again reminiscent of Bonington, but the drawing reveals Dyce as less concerned with colour. It is almost in monochrome, the luminous distance and boldly cast shadows giving a sense of Mediterranean light so strong that it destroys colour. The architecturally structured composition of large simple forms

---

[1]See above, pp. 6–7. [2]Reproduced in Staley, 1963, pl. 2.

bears no resemblance to the delicate linear style of the landscape drawings of the German Nazarenes.

From 1837 to 1843 Dyce painted little because of his teaching duties, and after 1843 he was engaged in decorating the new Houses of Parliament with frescoes. He also received Royal commissions for frescoes at Buckingham Palace and at Osborne House. In 1845 he travelled to Italy to study early frescoes, and there, as we have seen, he took a keen interest in the effects of outdoor light which he found in Pinturicchio. His main easel pictures of the 1840s are close in style to his frescoes. The *Madonna* painted for Prince Albert in 1845 (Pl. 92a), for example, combines reminiscences of the *Madonnas* of Raphael with Quattrocento profile portraits and is more Italianate than any later Pre-Raphaelite picture. The *Madonna* and a pendant *Saint Joseph* have landscape backgrounds, but the backgrounds are of minor importance in the compositions. They are thinly painted on a white ground, which occasionally shows through the brush marks. The outlines are precise, but there is little detail. The background of the *Madonna* consists of generalized mountains, which could be anywhere. In the *Saint Joseph* there is some vaguely Mediterranean architecture.

A small painting of *The Flight into Egypt* (Pl. 91a) may date from about the same time. It has relatively free brushwork, comparable to that of the two pictures in the Royal Collection, and the landscape consists of large, rounded shapes, broadly composed in light and dark. A small cactus in the foreground indicates the Holy Land, but otherwise there is little feeling of exact location. The Holy Family is small, but the figures dominate the composition. The dark clump of trees behind repeats their shape, and their robes provide the picture's strongest accents of light and colour. Nothing distracts from their quiet movement, and the picture has a tenderness and harmony of mood which increasing literalness seems to have made impossible in Dyce's later paintings. A similar feeling also pervades the small *Gethsemane* (Pl. 93a). This painting is undated, and has generally been thought to have been painted in the 1850s. However, there is still no hint of Pre-Raphaelite influence. The twilight glow over the landscape, in which Christ is proportionately smaller than the figures in *The Flight into Egypt*, gives the picture an aura of mystical stillness quite unlike the mood of Dyce's later religious paintings.

Of approximately the same size and probably of the same period as these two paintings is a landscape in the National Gallery of Scotland, which has been exhibited under the various titles of *Welsh Landscape, A Loch in Arran,* and *Shirrapburn Loch.*[3] This is in the style of the 1840s, not unlike the painting of an academician like Thomas Creswick. It is more detailed than the background of *The Flight into Egypt,* but that should be expected, as the landscape is the subject of the picture, not just a setting for the figures.

In 1855, the first year of Ruskin's *Academy Notes,* Dyce exhibited a painting of *Christabel,* 'praying at the old oak tree' (Pl. 92b). This bust-length picture of a girl, in an oval frame, is of the traditional Victorian 'Keepsake' type. It is no more archaizing than Dyce's *Madonna* of 1845, but the *Art Journal* declared that it had more in common with the *Madonnas* of Nuremburg or the early Italian school than with the mystic conception of Coleridge.[4] Ruskin was also displeased:

An example of one of the false branches of Pre-Raphaelitism, consisting in imitation of the old religious masters. This head is founded chiefly on reminiscence of Sandro Botticelli. The ivy

---

[3]Reproduced in *National Gallery of Scotland: Illustrations,* (Edinburgh, 1965) pl. 32c. See also *Centenary Exhibition of the Work of William Dyce, R.A. (1806–1864),* exhibition catalogue (Aberdeen Art Gallery, and Thos. Agnew & Sons Ltd., London, 1964) p. 39, no. 33. These three pictures are all approximately twelve by sixteen inches.

[4]*Art Journal,* 1855, p. 173.

leaves at the side are as elaborate as in the true school, but are quite false both in colour and shade. There is some sweet expression in the face.[5]

Ruskin's argument in defence of Pre-Raphaelitism ever since 1851 had been that the movement had nothing to do with archaism. His criticism of Dyce seems like an attempt to differentiate between the naturalism of the Pre-Raphaelites and revivalism, and to discredit the latter. But as Dyce had been initially responsible for arousing Ruskin's interest in the younger artists, the attack must have seemed ungracious, to say the least.

In 1856 Dyce exhibited a picture of *The Good Shepherd* at the Royal Academy. According to his son, it was only a study, and it went unnoticed by Ruskin.[6] Then, in 1857 he exhibited *Titian Preparing to Make his First Essay in Colouring* (Pl. 93b). This picture, which shows the young Titian surrounded by carefully drawn and brightly coloured flowers and foliage, appears to be the product of an effort to paint the sort of Pre-Raphaelite picture which Ruskin had criticized Dyce for failing to paint two years before. It immediately drew a complimentary letter from Ruskin: 'I have not the least idea whether you and I are friends or not – but I can't help *writing* to congratulate you on your wonderful picture. . . . I don't think the colour of the face is right – but you have beat everybody this time in thoroughness'.[7] Ruskin was even more laudatory in print. In *Academy Notes* he devoted a long review to the painting, which began,

Well done! Mr. Dyce, and many times well done! though it is of little use for any of us to say so to you; for when a man has gone through such a piece of work as this he knows he is right, and knows it so calmly that it does not matter much to him whether people see it or not. This is a notable picture in several ways, being, in the first place, the only one quite up to the high-water mark of Pre-Raphaelitism in the exhibition this year . . . Mr. Dyce has encountered all discoverable difficulties at once, and chosen a subject involving an amount of toil only endurable by the boundless love and patience which are first among the Pre-Raphaelite characteristics.

He then went on to discuss the picture's particular qualities. He praised its 'sculpturesque sense of grace in form', but he was critical of the accompanying deficiency in colouring: 'We cannot part so lightly with the blood of Titian; no boy could ever have coloured a Madonna's face who had so little colour in his own.' He was also critical of Dyce's visualization of the subject, which did not agree with his own conception (in which, of course, the young Titian spent his boyhood in the Alps), but, except for declaring that Dyce would never 'colour like a Venetian', he made no comment about the vast disparity between Dyce's style and that of his subject. He concluded that no one need hope to do much better in painting dress, flowers, grass, and leafage, and warned his readers, 'It will take about an hour to see this picture properly'.[8]

As seen through this criticism, between 1855 and 1857 Dyce changed from a pernicious influence undermining Pre-Raphaelitism into one of the movement's most admirable proponents. A major change certainly did take place, and, if it can not be measured in such black-and-white terms, it was enough to place Dyce's later works among the leading examples of Pre-Raphaelite naturalism. There is certainly no doubt of Pre-Raphaelite influence on the *Titian*, and all of Dyce's later pictures follow its example of an elaborately detailed and minutely finished natural setting, which generally dominates the figural content of the painting. His *George Herbert at Bemerton* (Pl. 91b), for example, which appeared at the Royal Academy in 1861, the last year in which Dyce exhibited, also shows a historical figure in a landscape setting. The figure is smaller than the Titian, and the foliate detail is still more elaborate, but this only continues the trend begun in 1857.

[5]Ruskin, 1903–12, XIV, 19.
[6]Dyce MSS., ch. XXXIII.

[7]Dated 8 May 1857; *ibid.*, ch. XXXVII.
[8]Ruskin, 1903–12, XIV, 98–100.

In the later 1850s Dyce also painted a group of religious paintings which show a similar relationship between figure and landscape. The earliest seems to have been a second *Good Shepherd*, which he exhibited at the Royal Academy in 1859. The *Art Journal* described it as a literal presentation of Christ as the Shepherd tending a flock in 'a landscape with a sheep fold paled in, trees and a cultivated country, such as might be seen in any rural district round London'.[9] Two pictures of biblical subjects with Highland settings probably date from the summer of 1859, when we know that Dyce was painting in Scotland. They are *David in the Wilderness* and *The Man of Sorrows* (Pl. 94). The former was not exhibited during Dyce's lifetime; the latter was shown at the Royal Academy in 1860 accompanied in the catalogue by a quotation from Keble which is also inscribed upon the frame.[10]

If we compare these two paintings with Dyce's earlier *Flight into Egypt*, we can see substantial differences. The figures are about the same in scale and are not radically different in style, but in the landscapes we need only look at the foreground rocks to see the greater elaboration of detail in the later pictures. Primary importance is given to the accumulation of minutely realized detail of rocks and blades of grass, and for this a more uniform range of tone replaces the broad contrast of light and dark in *The Flight into Egypt*. The focus has shifted from the ostensible subjects of the pictures to the landscapes surrounding them. There is some correspondence between the figures and their barren settings, but the pictures could stand almost as well without the figures, simply as clearly seen and precisely detailed Scottish landscapes. They are views of Highland scenery into which biblical figures seem to have strayed accidentally, and the contrast between figures and settings gives them an anachronistic appeal. The *Art Journal*, describing *The Good Shepherd* of 1859, decided that Dyce was following 'the simple conceptions of early Florentine painters,'[11] but for some critics the contrast was disturbing. In 1860 F. G. Stephens, writing in the *Athenaeum* (and remembering, no doubt, that the exhibition of Holman Hunt's *Finding of Christ in the Temple* had opened the month before), criticized *The Man of Sorrows*: 'It is true that the omnipresence of the typical idea may be well conveyed by thus treating it, but the individuality of the Saviour is lost thereby . . . the picture is completely realistic in all respects . . . but why – with all this literalness – not be completely loyal, and paint Christ himself in the land where he really lived?' Elsewhere in the same review, Stephens wrote that Dyce's pictures at the Royal Academy indicated 'a transitional state of mind', and he suggested again that Dyce should go further: 'Mr. Dyce is rapidly becoming a realistic artist – such a one, indeed, that the growing strength of his conviction will soon lead him, when painting a scriptural subject again, to go to the East, and to do so under all possible advantage'.[12]

The Man of Sorrows and *David in the Wilderness* are two of a group of related pictures. All are painted on millboard, and all have the same measurements – approximately fourteen by twenty inches. They include *The Woman of Samaria* (City Art Gallery, Birmingham), *Henry VI during the Battle of Towton* (Guildhall Art Gallery, London), *A Scene in Arran* (Pl.

[9]*Art Journal*, 1859, p. 164.

[10]   'As, when upon His drooping head
      His Father's light was pour'd from heaven,
      What time, unsheltered and unfed,
      Far in the wild His steps were driven,
      High thoughts were with Him, in that hour,
      Untold, unspeakable on earth.'
Dyce exhibited this picture at the Liverpool Academy in 1861 under the title *And Jesus was Led by the Spirit into the Wilderness*. The *David* was sold at Christie's in 1933 as *Christ in the Wilderness*, and it bears an inscription with this title on the back of the frame. However, the figure is obviously David, not Christ, and on the back of the panel itself there is another old inscription: *David when a Shepherd and Skillful Harpist*. It is possible that Dyce temporarily switched frames in 1861 to exhibit *The Man of Sorrows* at Liverpool without the Keble quotation. .

[11]*Art Journal*, 1859, p. 164.

[12]*Athenaeum*, 11 May 1860, p. 653.

95a), and *Welsh Landscape with Figures* (Pl. 95b), The former two are related to Dyce's other pictures of biblical and historical subjects. Both have rising ground and stone walls immediately behind the figures, so, although they contain detailed backgrounds, they do not show extensive views. Neither is dated, nor were they exhibited, but they must have been painted in the late 1850s.

The latter two pictures can be ascribed to holiday trips taken by the artist. A reference in a letter from Dyce to his brother-in-law written in October 1860, when he had just returned from Wales, accounts for both of them: 'These trips for change of air always pay. I made £400 by my trip to Ramsgate two years ago, and £620 by my last year's trip to Arran, and I hope to make an equally good thing out of the Welsh excursion'.[13] The *Scene in Arran* bears an inscription on the back: 'painted by William Dyce RA for his father-in-law, James Brand, of Bedford Hill House, Balham in the year 1858 or 1859'. So it must date from Dyce's trip to Arran in the latter year. The *Welsh Landscape* is almost certainly from the trip of 1860. An unfinished watercolour, *Goat Fell, Isle of Arran* (Victoria and Albert Museum), may also date from the 1859 trip, and a watercolour of Welsh mountains (Ashmolean Museum, Oxford) seems related to the 1860 picture. In the letter just quoted, Dyce stated that he had made sketches which he hoped to turn to account. But as the *Scene in Arran* and the *Welsh Landscape* are small and on prepared millboard, which the painter could easily have carried with him, it seems probable that Dyce at least began them on his travels.

We also learn from Dyce's letter that the Welsh mountains were more rugged, 'more awful and terrific looking than anything I know of in Scotland.' He ascribed the beauty of the Welsh mountains to their geological formation, and he analysed the reasons for the differences between Welsh and Scottish scenery:

In Scotland, the granite mountains by the process of disintegration become rounded and their asperities smoothed down – but in Wales, the material being slate rock, it does not crumble like granite into dust or sand, but splits and tumbles down in huge flakes which leave the peaks from which they have fallen as sharp and angular as if they had never been acted upon by the atmosphere at all.[14]

If we compare the *Welsh Landscape* with *The Man of Sorrows*, we see angular rocks in the foreground of one and rounded rocks in the other, and corresponding differences in the configurations of the terrain.

Unlike most of Dyce's earlier paintings, the *Scene in Arran* and *Welsh Landscape* do not have biblical or historical, but genre subjects. Dyce apparently began to take an interest in these subjects only during the 1850s. The first date we can associate with this development is 1858, when he exhibited a picture entitled *The Highland Ferryman* (Aberdeen Art Gallery) at the Royal Scottish Academy. He exhibited the same painting at the Royal Academy in London in 1859 as *Contentment*. When it appeared there, the *Art Journal* described it as 'a subject in humble life – the only one we remember to have seen by this artist'.[15]

The Highland Ferryman does not show a particularly contemporary figure, but a rural character who stands apart from the modern world. The figures in the *Welsh Landscape* wear traditional Welsh peasant costume and seem, like the ferryman, to be relics of another age. Dyce's other genre pictures, however, do not show such concern for indigenous traditions. A small undated picture entitled *The Manse* or *Entrance to the Vicarage* (collection

[13]Dyce MSS., ch. XXXIX.
[14]*Ibid.*

[15]*Art Journal*, 1859, p. 168.

of Mrs. Margaret Rose) shows a boy, probably Dyce's son, with a wheelbarrow. *A Scene in Arran* has a group of children splashing in a stream, and Dyce's masterpiece, *Pegwell Bay* (Pl. 96a, and Col. Pl. 8b), shows his own family collecting shells while on a seaside holiday. This picture appeared at the Royal Academy in 1860 under the title *Pegwell Bay, Kent – a Recollection of October 5th, 1858*. It is a product of that trip to Ramsgate which Dyce mentioned in his letter to his brother-in-law two years later. Donati's comet, which was visible in 1858, appears in the sky. The foreground figures are Dyce's son, his wife, and his wife's two sisters. The picture was bought by the artist's father-in-law, James Brand, who owned several of his works.

Among Dyce's other pictures, the one most closely related to *Pegwell Bay* is the *Scene in Arran* of 1859. It was also the product of a holiday trip, and also bought by James Brand. It shows green, grass-covered hills rather than grey chalk cliffs, and, as it is on a smaller scale, the detail seems less obsessively elaborate. Otherwise, the two pictures have much in common: a great deal of litter lying about, small background figures who seem accidentally included in the view, children staring fixedly out of the picture, and frozen main figures who are curiously aloof from one another. Both pictures contain figures caught in acts which seem to be simple movements observed unawares, and which have no real narrative interest. In *Pegwell Bay* a man in the background stares at the sky, and in *A Scene in Arran* the small girl on the right unselfconsciously holds up her skirt. These details could be considered photographic – the result of the camera's indiscriminate inclusion of everything within its focus – and *Pegwell Bay* has repeatedly attracted comparison with photographs and suggestions that it was influenced by photography. The *Art Journal*, reviewing the Royal Academy Exhibition in 1860, wrote that the picture's foreground was painted 'with a truth equal to that of photography'.[16] In 1917 Charles Aitken wrote that it showed 'daguerreotype vision', and in 1964 William Gaunt suggested that it 'perhaps indicates some desire to emulate photography.'[17]

Dyce was a friend of his fellow Scottish painter David Octavius Hill, and he was interested enough in Hill's photographic activity to suggest in 1846 that Hill make a trip to Rome with his 'Kalotype machinery'. In 1858, painting a portrait commissioned by Gladstone, Dyce wrote a letter proposing to make photographs of the model.[18] So he was aware of photography and its possible use in connection with at least some aspects of painting. On the other hand, in 1860, the same year that *Pegwell Bay* was exhibited, James Dafforne wrote a biographical article about Dyce in the *Art Journal* in which he acknowledged that some critics believed *Pegwell Bay* had been painted from a photograph. Dafforne categorically denied it: 'Its wonderful elaborated detail favoured the supposition; but we happen to know it was done from memory, aided by a slight and hasty sketch, in pencil, of the locality.'[19] Without evidence to the contrary, this denial should probably be accepted, although Dyce may still have adopted stylistic suggestions from photographs by Hill and others. If we compare *Pegwell Bay* with a contemporary photograph of the same locality[20] we can see that Dyce not only equalled, but outdid the camera in clarity and thoroughness. Furthermore, the documented occasions of the use of photographs by Dyce's contemporaries, Frith for example, led to such different results, that even if Dyce's use of photographs were established, the look of his pictures could hardly be considered its in-

[16]*Ibid.*, 1860, p. 160.
[17]Charles Aitken, 'English Nineteenth-Century Art at the National Gallery', *Burlington Magazine*, XXI, 1917, p. 9; and William Gaunt, *A Concise History of English Painting* (London, 1964) p. 180.

[18]Dyce MSS., chs. XXIII and XXXIX.
[19]Dafforne, 1860, p. 296.
[20]Helmut Gernsheim, *Masterpieces of Victorian Photography* (London, 1951) pl. 21.

evitable result. Perhaps as important an explanation for the personal and unhackneyed quality of these pictures is the fact that they were painted primarily as a diversion and were apparently guaranteed a purchaser within Dyce's own family. He was thus free to indulge his remarkably clear vision and imagination without the need of consulting conventional taste and forcing his pictures into a mould of smiling prettiness.

The pencil sketch mentioned by Dafforne has not come to light, but a watercolour of *Pegwell Bay* is known (Pl. 96b). It shows the same view as the picture, and was apparently used in painting it. The watercolour is broader in effect than the painting, or than Dyce's watercolours of Welsh and Scottish mountains. It shows the seacoast at sunset, with a purplish sky, and without the foreground figures. By adding the figures in the painting, Dyce turned a pure landscape into a contemporary genre scene of the type of Frith's *Life at the Seaside*, the successful exhibition of which in 1854 had started the mid-century vogue for paintings of the seaside. However, in Frith's picture the landscape setting is incidental; the figures dominate the composition and the main interest is anecdotal. Dyce's figures seem stuck on to what is still essentially a landscape. They are in the immediate foreground, and the colours of their garments stand out from the almost monochrome greys of their setting. They are before the landscape rather than in it, and their positions seem dictated by the painter's interest in repetition and balance rather than by narrative interests comparable to those of Frith. If we look from the watercolour to the painting, we see Dyce consistently modifying the sketch towards greater clarity of structure and geometrical order. The sketch has an atmospheric freshness and a looseness of organization which have disappeared in the painting. The foreground figures, the pilings added behind them, and the lines of rock reaching into the sea provide precise punctuation in a manner that seems arbitrary. Yet the painting seems, if anything, more natural than the watercolour. It does have the look and the feel of the seashore, and it has attracted perhaps as many testimonials to its truth as any nineteenth-century painting.

The subject of heavily clothed figures by the edge of the sea gives *Pegwell Bay* a superficial similarity to the many slightly later seashore paintings by the French artist Eugène Boudin. However, Dyce's tight organization and elaboration of detail seem the antithesis of Boudin's breezy freshness. Dyce obviously spent an amount of time on one painting that the French artist could have used to paint several. Although he sacrificed spontaneity, he entered into the subject in a way that makes almost all Impressionist paintings seem superficial. The picture does not share the general sunny pleasantness of Impressionism, and even of much of Pre-Raphaelitism. The landscape is bleak, the figures collect their shells with a seriousness that verges on gloom, and the mood is distinctly melancholy.

Pegwell Bay does not look like a Pre-Raphaelite picture mainly because it does not have the brilliant colours of Pre-Raphaelitism. We have seen that Ruskin, while praising *Titian Preparing to Make His First Essay in Colouring*, criticized Dyce's colour. It also came in for criticism from other sources. The *Art Journal* declared his *Highland Ferryman* 'too grey in the foreground and too blue in the distance',[21] and F. G. Stephens thought that *Pegwell Bay* should have deeper tone.[22] When Dyce was in Italy, he had admired the richly coloured flesh tones of Perugino and speculated about theories of prismatic flesh painting, but his own painting of flesh was far from prismatic.[23] Ruskin criticized the lack of colour in the face of his *Titian*, and Dyce's later pictures tend more and more to lack colour in the flesh tones. The extreme example is *George Herbert at Bemerton*, in which the face is not even

[21]*Art Journal*, 1859, p. 168.
[22]*Athenaeum*, 12 May 1860, p. 653.

[23]Dyce MSS., ch. XXI. See also Staley, 1963, pp. 473, 475.

modelled in light and shade, but here Dyce may have been imitating an Elizabethan artist such as Nicholas Hilliard in a slightly quixotic attempt to match style to subject. In Italy, Dyce also praised the general effect of outdoor colour in Pinturicchio's frescoes, and he went on to emphasize the value of study in the open air. However, what he saw in Pinturicchio was consistency of local colour through both light and shade.[24] This is what we see in Dyce's painting; the colour is local colour, occasionally strong, but never interfering with the linear and structural clarity of the paintings, and never complicated by reflected lights and colours. In 1846 Dyce inveighed against the unnaturalness of conventional studio shadowing. Ten years later he probably found the reflected blues and purples of Holman Hunt and Ford Madox Brown equally unnatural, although he himself had encouraged the study of outdoor light which led to them.

In other respects also, Dyce was more conservative than any of the Pre-Raphaelite group. Even when at his most Pre-Raphaelite, he never provoked the hostile reactions that greeted many Pre-Raphaelite paintings. The *Art Journal* called *Titian Preparing to Make His First Essay in Colouring* 'Pre-Raphaelite', but without 'the inconsistencies and extravagancies presented in the works so called'.[25] Dyce's painting is always clear and controlled, and it lacks the excitement of innovation of the best Pre-Raphaelite pictures. Nonetheless, the minute detail and increasing literalness of Dyce's painting at the end of the 1850s clearly depends upon the Pre-Raphaelite example. His work is not central to the movement, but with sobriety and discipline he built upon Pre-Raphaelitism to paint a handful of the most memorable pictures of the Victorian era.

[24]See above, p. 7.   [25]*Art Journal*, 1857, p. 167.

XIV

Pre-Raphaelitism and Nineteenth-Century Landscape Painting

PRE-RAPHAELITISM as a movement marked an almost complete break in the continuity of the English landscape tradition. This was in part because the original members of the Pre-Raphaelite Brotherhood did not start out as landscape painters. The background of their art lay in the developments in figural painting during the 1840s which were mentioned in the first chapter. They had little interest in the landscape painters of the preceding generation, and when a Pre-Raphaelite school of landscape emerged, it had few roots in the immediate past.

English landscape painting of the 1840s did not provide much of a basis for new developments. The great period of English landscape painting was drawing to a close. Bonington had worked and died in the 1820s. Constable died in the year that Queen Victoria came to the throne. Turner was painting some of his greatest pictures in the 1840s, but they were far too personal to have had any influence, and by the second half of the decade he was thought to be slipping. In the words of Holman Hunt 'Turner was rapidly sinking like a glorious sun in clouds of night that could not yet obscure his brightness, but rather increased his magnificence. The works of his meridian day were then shut up in their possessors' galleries, unknown to us younger men.'[1] A few artists, notably David Cox and John Linnell, carried some of the breadth of earlier English landscape into the 1850s, and, in Linnell's case, beyond. Cox, during the last years of his life, was admired as the grand old man of English landscape, and he had an early influence on George Price Boyce and Alfred William Hunt, both of whom later fell under the Pre-Raphaelite spell. The Pre-Raphaelites elected Cox an honorary member of the Hogarth Club, and Ruskin regularly praised his work in *Academy Notes*, although he noted that 'Mr. Cox's work is every year broader in handling, and therefore further, as mere work, from the completeness I would generally advocate'.[2] The completeness advocated by Ruskin and practised by the Pre-Raphaelites had nothing to do with Cox, and Cox's popularity, not only with the Pre-Raphaelite group, but in Victorian England in general, is remarkable because, whatever the qualities of his art, prevailing taste was moving in another direction.

Landscape painting in the 1840s like earlier English landscape painting can be divided into two main classes: topographical and pastoral. Among painters, the chief topographers were David Roberts and Clarkson Stanfield. There were also large numbers of watercolourists, of whom Samuel Prout, who died in 1852, was the most popular and James Duffield Harding had the highest pretensions. These artists reflect the taste of the mid-century by the ever greater importance given in their works to accurate reporting of places of interest. David Roberts spent 1838 and 1839 in Egypt and Palestine, and the resulting three-volume *Views in the Holy Land, Syria, Idumea, Egypt, and Nubia*, published between 1841

[1]Hunt, 1905, I, 50–51.　　　　　　　　[2]Ruskin, 1903–12, XIV, 195.

170

and 1849, was a monumental precursor of Pre-Raphaelite attempts to make accurate records of the East. This group of painters received an amount of attention in the first volume of *Modern Painters* which today seems disproportionate, but Ruskin's interest in them is easily understood. Their subjects were the subjects that attracted him and that he would urge younger artists to paint. He had learned to draw by imitating first Samuel Prout, then David Roberts, and he travelled in Italy in 1845 with Harding, while preparing the second volume of *Modern Painters*. However, by the 1850s Ruskin was generally critical of these artists' reliance upon artifice and convention rather than fresh observation, and both Harding and Roberts came in for attacks in *Academy Notes*.[3] William Michael Rossetti, describing the international exhibition of 1855 in Paris, wrote that the works of Stanfield, Roberts, *et al.*, looked 'flimsy and artificial'.[4] This was probably representative of the general Pre-Raphaelite attitude.

The other class of landscape was represented by a number of Academicians – Thomas Creswick, William Frederick Witherington, Frederick Richard Lee, and Richard Redgrave who was also a figural painter. Their pictures of a rural, pastoral England carried on the tradition of the Norwich school or Constable, but, stylistically, they replaced the breadth of earlier English landscape with a small, dry touch and thinness of paint. Their more careful handling, accompanied by brighter colours, was part of the general redirection of English painting in the 1840s leading to Pre-Raphaelitism. However, tighter detail was not necessarily accompanied by fresh observation. The pictures seem both artificial and repetitive. As the Redgraves wrote about Creswick, 'He had a true feeling for the elegance of foliage and for graceful passages of interest in a landscape, but his touch is inclined to mannerism, and there is a good deal of sameness in his work'.[5] Ruskin did not take this painting very seriously. He only mentioned Creswick twice in *Academy Notes*, although he was generally considered the most important landscape painter in the Royal Academy. Here is the first mention:

This, like most other of the landscapes hung on the line, is one of those works so characteristic of the English school, and so little creditable to them, in which everything is carelessly or ill-painted – because it is in a landscape. Nothing is really *done*. The cows have imperfect horns and hides; the girl has an imperfect face and imperfect hands; the trees have imperfect leaves; the sky imperfect clouds; the water imperfect waves.

This was written in 1855. In the same year Ruskin's comments on Witherington and Redgrave complemented what he had said about Creswick:

We have here two interesting examples of another fallacious condition of landscape – that which pretends to Pre-Raphaelite distinctness of detail; but is in all detail industriously wrong. In Creswick's work the touches represent nothing; here they represent perpetual error, assuming that all leaves of trees may be represented by oval, sharp-pointed touches of yellow or green – as if leaves had not their perspectives, shadows, and changes of hue like everything else! There is great appearance of fidelity to nature in these works, but there is none in reality; they are mere mechanical accumulations of similar touches, as a sempstress mechanically accumulates similar stitches.[6]

The Pre-Raphaelites had little use for any of these artists, except Creswick, and for him they had a special antipathy. In *Pre-Raphaelitism and the Pre-Raphaelite Brotherhood*, Holman Hunt describes an unpleasant incident with an Academician who gave Hunt a commission for his *Claudio and Isabella*, then denied it after Hunt had prepared the designs.

[3]*Ibid.*, pp. 28, 67, 126, 220–21.
[4]Rossetti, 1867, p. 125.
[5]Richard and Samuel Redgrave, *A Century of Painters*, ed. Ruthven Todd (London, 1947) p. 387. As Creswick was still alive in 1866, he was not mentioned in the first edition, but first appeared in the edition of 1890.
[6]Ruskin, 1903–12, XIV, 13, 20.

The Academician was Creswick.[7] Creswick managed to dominate landscape painting in the Royal Academy for some twenty years. His influence was probably a major reason why Pre-Raphaelite landscapes were generally treated badly at the Academy exhibitions, and he was bitterly hated by artists such as Alfred Hunt who had Academic ambitions.[8]

Of course, the Pre-Raphaelites did have substantial support within the Academy. When Creswick repudiated his commission for *Claudio and Isabella*, it was taken up by Augustus Egg. William Dyce encouraged Holman Hunt, and several other older artists welcomed the advent of the new movement. Of these artists, the most interesting is William Mulready. In the 1840s, Mulready exhibited several landscapes which he had painted about 1810, showing views around the Mall and Gravel Pits in Kensington (Pl. 97a). These are delicately drawn, but composed in contrasts of light and dark, with a limited range of brownish colours. During most of his career Mulready painted figural subjects, in which landscape backgrounds, if they appeared at all, were summarily treated. However, in 1852, he exhibited a view of *Blackheath Park* at the Royal Academy in which he replaced the tonal breadth of his early landscapes by over-all brightness of colour and precise leaf-by-leaf detail (Pl. 97b). Mulready's figural paintings of the 1830s and 1840s (Pl. 3b) had anticipated and probably influenced Pre-Raphaelite detail and brilliance of colour.[9] *Blackheath Park* carried the qualities of these paintings to another class of subject, but the result differed enough from Mulready's previous work to outrage the *Art Journal*, which called the picture 'a Pre-Raffaellesque eccentricity'. It described the painting as a minute transcription of a locality of no pictorial value, and it criticized the 'lively' green colour; yet, it went on, 'in the whole there is an attractive softness and sweetness of execution, which we presume is proposed as a lesson to those youths who "babble of green fields".'[10]

It is doubtful whether Mulready was as conscious of the Pre-Raphaelites when painting *Blackheath Park* as the *Art Journal* suggested, since before 1852 there was not yet any real Pre-Raphaelite landscape painting. But the picture does indicate the basis of Mulready's sympathy for the movement, which he shared with a number of artists of his generation. Geoffrey Grigson has pointed out the kinship between the Pre-Raphaelites and the group of painters who had studied with the watercolourist John Varley at the beginning of the century.[11] Mulready was the most influential of the group; indeed, he seems to have been more admired by the other students than Varley himself. The others included John Linnell and William Henry Hunt. All these artists painted with a concern for careful detail and a crispness of colour that explains much of the admiration which the Pre-Raphaelites had for them. They were more humbly pious in their approach to nature than a Constable, more willing to accept nature as it is than to synthesize. Their pictures have more observation of detail and less concern with atmospheric effect as a whole, and it is noteworthy that Constable had a low opinion of both Linnell and Mulready.[12] The motto of the group was 'Go to nature for everything', but their work is more than dryly realistic. It reflects a belief that spiritual value lies in natural detail. The attitude is perhaps best reflected in a statement made by William Henry Hunt: 'I feel really frightened when I sit down to paint a flower', which, as F. G. Stephens admiringly remarked, 'was going to nature with a vengeance'.[13]

[7]Hunt, 1905, I, 211–12, and Troxell, 1937, p. 34.
[8]Gosse, 1884, pp. 5–7.
[9]See above, pp. 5 and 22; Frederick George Stephens, *Masterpieces of Mulready* (London, 1867), p. 5; and Stephens, 1860, p. 11.
[10]*Art Journal*, 1852, p. 167.

[11]Grigson, 1948, pp. 24–5.
[12]R. B. Beckett, ed., *John Constable's Correspondence*, III (Ipswich, 1965), pp. 85 and 143; *ibid.*, IV (1966), pp. 287–96.
[13]F. G. Stephens, 'John Linnell', *Portfolio*, III, 1872, p. 46. For Hunt see also Ruskin, 1903–12, XIV, 373–84.

The importance of Mulready and William Henry Hunt for the Pre-Raphaelites was mentioned in the first chapter. Linnell painted highly detailed landscapes in the second decade of the century, some of which have been confused with his later landscapes and have been said to reflect Pre-Raphaelite influence.[14] This painting is, on the one hand, related to the scientific orientation of the late eighteenth-century painters George Stubbs and Joseph Wright of Derby, and, on the other, to the mystical identification with nature of Samuel Palmer. Palmer became Linnell's son-in-law, and he was encouraged to a close, niggling study of nature by Linnell and Mulready. Linnell also encouraged Palmer to study Dürer and Lucas Van Leyden as a means of gaining greater natural truth and escaping the 'effects' of 'the moderns'.[15] This concern with 'archaic honesty' in approaching nature anticipated that of the Pre-Raphaelites. We have seen that Ford Madox Brown and Daniel Alexander Williamson occasionally recall Palmer's work in their own pictures. There seems to have been no direct influence from Palmer, but the later artists did approach nature with an outlook much like that urged upon Palmer by Linnell and Mulready, and these two older artists were sympathetic and encouraging to the young Pre-Raphaelites in the midst of Academic hostility.

To these painters should be added John Frederick Lewis. Ruskin always called Lewis a Pre-Raphaelite, but Lewis was neither an intimate of the Pre-Raphaelites nor an influence upon them, at least not until well into the 1850s, when he may have had some influence upon Thomas Seddon and John Brett.[16] As Lewis spent the entire decade of the 1840s in the East, without exhibiting in London, his art was almost unknown in England at the time the Pre-Raphaelite Brotherhood was being formed, and he developed his brightly coloured, almost miniaturist style independently of Pre-Raphaelitism. In comparison to Lewis, much Pre-Raphaelite painting seems broad. His pictures reflect similar interests, including a concern for outdoor sunlight, but most of them were painted in the studio after his return from the East, and they have a dainty Victorian prettiness which allowed him to gain popular success and academic distinctions almost as soon as he returned.

For the Pre-Raphaelites themselves, success was slow in coming, and their best work of the 1850s never became really popular. Conservative periodicals such as the *Art Journal* and the *Athenaeum* (until 1860 when F. G. Stephens became its art critic) were always critical of the movement. Although the early Pre-Raphaelite pictures were well hung at the Royal Academy and Millais was elected an associate member of the Royal Academy in 1853, the Academy was generally unsympathetic to Pre-Raphaelite landscape painting, and there were annual complaints from the artists and from friendly critics, such as William Michael Rossetti and Ruskin, about rejections and bad hanging. As a result, Ford Madox Brown stopped exhibiting at the Academy entirely, and Holman Hunt exhibited there rarely after 1856. In 1857, the Pre-Raphaelites organized their own exhibition in Russell Place, and in 1858 they formed their own exhibiting society, the short-lived Hogarth Club, in order to be independent of the Academy.

From a conservative point of view, and in terms of official success, Pre-Raphaelite naturalism was an abortive movement of little importance; and painters like Brown, Inchbold, or Brett were notoriously unsuccessful in terms of recognition during their best years. On the other hand, if we read Ruskin, we get a different picture. Ruskin was, of course, partisan, and in his reviews he assigned a degree of importance to his favourites,

[14]Grigson, 1948, p. 24.
[15]A. H. Palmer, *The Life and Letters of Samuel Palmer* (London, 1892) p. 15 *et passim*.

[16]For Brett and Lewis, see above, p. 128; for Seddon, see pp. 98 and 103. See also Hunt, 1905, I, 270–1.

such as Brett, with which few of his contemporaries would have concurred. Nonetheless, Ruskin was an observer as well as a proselytizer. From his annual reviews, we can see that each year more and more young artists were attempting to paint from nature in emulation of the Pre-Raphaelites. In figural painting the influence of Frith's genre scenes, commencing in 1854, and of the continentally trained Leighton, who created a sensation at the Royal Academy in 1855, counteracted that of Pre-Raphaelitism, but in landscape painting there was no such opposing force. Older artists, such as Creswick, continued their opposition, but otherwise, as Ruskin claimed, and as William Michael Rossetti wrote in 1862, landscape came almost entirely into the domain of Pre-Raphaelitism.

An illustration of the influence of Ruskin and the Pre-Raphaelites on younger painters is provided by Philip Gilbert Hamerton. Around 1860, Hamerton set out to paint landscapes in the Scottish Highlands, living in a tent and painting directly from nature. While there, he wrote an essay, entitled 'Painting from Nature', in which he declared:

The practice of painting from nature, in the modern sense, is of very recent adoption. It is probable that before our own time no landscape painter ever began and finished an oil *picture* out of doors and from nature itself. . . . At the present day, however, many painters – especially our younger ones – are devoting immense labour to the finishing of pictures out of doors; a costly and inconvenient proceeding, and one which ought to reward its votaries very richly for all the trouble and fatigue it inevitably entails.[17]

He then proceeded to discuss the pros and cons of painting from nature and to give advice about some of its difficulties. The essay is long-winded and rather pointless, but it does make clear that Pre-Raphaelitism set the standards, and the only two pictures mentioned by name are Seddon's *Jerusalem and the Valley of Jehoshaphat* and Brett's *Val d'Aosta*. More interesting than the essay itself is a note appended by Hamerton in 1873, when his outlook had changed considerably. The note asserts that the younger English painters were misdirected into painting detailed pictures direct from nature, rather than sketches, by the example of the Pre-Raphaelites and by the recommendations of Ruskin. Ruskin's influence was especially harmful:

He had two very strong and catching enthusiasms, the enthusiasm for natural magnificence and the enthusiasm for novelty and discovery in the Fine Arts. Many of us were fully prepared to be partakers of these enthusiasms, by the same influence of literature and science which had excited them in Mr. Ruskin himself. . . . But our ardour was not really and fundamentally artistic, though we believed it to be so. It came much more from a scientific motive than from any purely artistic feeling, and was a part – though we were not ourselves aware of it – of that great scientific exploration of the realms of nature which this age has carried so much farther than any of its predecessors. While botanists and geologists were occupied in investigating the construction of landscape, we investigated its aspect. . . . We went in the search for rigorously accurate truth, which is an entirely scientific state of mind. Our pictorial work was as much a scientific exposition as the chapters on the structure of the Alps in the fourth volume of *Modern Painters*. And I perceive now, having learned to distinguish between the scientific and artistic spirits, that the proper expression for what I learned in the Highlands . . . would have been, not pictures, but a book with coloured illustrations.[18]

In 1873, Hamerton was living primarily in France, and he felt that the proper practice was that of the French artists who sketched from nature in broad masses and tones but did not concern themselves with detail. According to Hamerton, the mania for scientific detail which dominated English painting in the 1850s was a mistake, and the artists who had attempted to paint pictures directly from nature later learned to change their ways:

The most experienced landscape painters of the generation immediately preceding ours were

[17]Hamerton, 1874, p. 10.   [18]*Ibid.*, p. 32.

agreed in the conviction that it was useless to paint pictures from nature, because effects would not stay to be painted. For some years the younger English artists hoped otherwise, but now these men (no longer young men) have also come to recognize the necessity for painting *pictures* in the studio.[19]

Most of the artists discussed in this book who had any success as landscape painters after the 1850s did change, as Hamerton claimed was generally the case, and in their later careers did paint their finished pictures in the studio. In the 1850s, however, they provided the lead for an army of younger artists who attempted to work carefully from nature. How pervasive the influence was can best be realized by reading through Ruskin's *Academy Notes*. Edward C. Booth, Charles Frederick Williams, Henry Anelay, Miss Anna Blunden, and John Samuel Raven can be little more than unfamiliar names to most modern readers, but they form the beginning of a long list of names of artists who came in for commendation for their faithful studies from nature.[20] In only a few cases did artists initially praised by Ruskin have any subsequent contact with the Pre-Raphaelite group or achieve any reputation beyond the pages of *Academy Notes*. John Mulcaster Carrick, who first exhibited at the Royal Academy in 1854 and was praised by Ruskin for his 'immense labour' in 1856,[21] became a member of the Hogarth Club. Later landscapes by Carrick, still highly laboured, are occasionally seen.[22] Henry Moore, whose *Swiss Meadow in June* Ruskin called 'very perfect' in 1857, was the older brother of Albert Moore.[23] After a brief Pre-Raphaelite beginning, he started to paint seascapes in 1858, and in the 1880s and 1890s he was the successful rival of John Brett, his exact contemporary.

Albert Moore also exhibited careful studies from nature at the Royal Academy, but they went unnoticed by Ruskin. Moore's watercolour *Study of an Ash Trunk* of 1857, which he exhibited in 1858 (Pl. 100a), is a study of foliage as microscopically close as anything done in the Pre-Raphaelite sphere. In the 1860s Albert Moore began to paint pictures of women in classical robes which have nothing to do with Pre-Raphaelite naturalism, but during the later 1850s, when both Moores were students at the Royal Academy schools, the Pre-Raphaelite influence was inescapable. Turner in his will had left money for a gold medal and scholarship to be awarded biennially to an Academy student. After Turner's estate was settled in 1856, the first competition for the medal was held in 1857, the prize to go to the best English landscape. According to Henry Holiday, who was one of the contestants, all the works but one had been studied from nature. Holiday thought that Henry Moore should have won, but the medal went to the one picture not painted from nature, by a student of Witherington. The next time the competition was held, the Academicians made sure the pictures were not painted from nature by setting as subject 'The Palatine Hill before the Building of Rome'.[24] Despite this opposition, almost every young student at the Royal Academy in the later 1850s, Holiday included, did have a short Pre-Raphaelite period before going on to a career of doing something entirely different.

Almost all the chief artists considered in this study also moved away from the detailed Pre-Raphaelite style after the 1850s or 1860s. Nonetheless, despite the short life of the movement, and despite the continuing opposition to it from established landscape painters such as Creswick or Witherington or Harding, it did permanently deflect the course of English landscape painting. The change from a popular older artist like Creswick to a

[19]*Ibid.*, p. 33.
[20]Ruskin, 1903–12, XIV, 49, 171, 230, 231.
[21]*Ibid.*, p.58.
[22]For example, *Siesta*, signed and dated 1874; reproduced in *Aspects of Victorian Art*, exhibition catalogue

(Fine Art Society, London, 1971) pl. 16.
[23]Ruskin, 1903–12, XIV, 104.
[24]Henry Holiday, *Reminiscences of My Life* (London, 1914) pp. 45–6.

popular younger one like Benjamin Williams Leader is partly due to the intervention of Pre-Raphaelitism. Leader, born in 1831, began by making careful studies from nature, some of which are not unlike pictures by William Millais, and the outgrowth was the illusion of exact verisimilitude which brought Leader's later works their immense popular success. The watercolours which Myles Birket Foster began to paint around 1859 owe more to older artists such as Creswick or Clarkson Stanfield than to the Pre-Raphaelites, but their bright colours and minute finish distinguish them from the works of the earlier painters. The tiny stipple of Foster's *Milk-maid* of 1860 (Pl. 98a) is comparable to that in Alfred Hunt's watercolours and is a later example of the plethora of labour about which Ruskin had complained in 1859.[25] Another heir of Pre-Raphaelitism was the Scottish painter William McTaggart. At the end of the 1850s his pictures showed the influence of Pre-Raphaelitism both in colour and detail. As McTaggart grew older he abandoned careful detail, but he retained an interest in outdoor light and colour. Ultimately, he created an insular equivalent of Impressionism, which no longer looked even remotely Pre-Raphaelite. However, McTaggart was a solitary figure working in a provincial centre. When Impressionism came to England, it came late and as an import from France.

When English artists began to realize that painting highly finished pictures directly from nature was an impractical way of working, they did not stop painting highly finished pictures, but stopped painting directly from nature. In the 1860s and 1870s the most talented younger landscape painters turned away from the naturalism of Pre-Raphaelitism to return to a more pictorially disciplined and subjective art. The chief impulse in this redirection came from abroad, and the most important single figure was an Italian painter who paid only a few brief visits to the British Isles: Giovanni Costa. Costa, in turn, owed a considerable debt to French painting, particularly that of Corot. In the 1850s Costa became friendly with two English artists living in Rome, George Hemming Mason and Frederic Leighton, and it was through them that he first had an impact in England. Later, in the 1860s, he attracted numerous other English disciples, including William Blake Richmond and the amateur George Howard, who in 1889 became the ninth Earl of Carlisle. These followers formed a little group calling itself the 'Etruscan School'; their bible consisted of Costa's maxims, which Howard recorded:

The whole of the Etruscan School consists in this – to draw your subject by drawing the spaces of the background.

The Etruscan School consists in seeing the direction of the lines and in drawing them with strength.

. . .

A picture should not be painted from nature. The study which contains the sentiment, the divine inspiration, should be done from nature. And from this study the picture should be painted at home, and, if necessary, supplementary studies be made elsewhere.

Sentiment before everything.[26]

Point by point, this teaching is the antithesis of the Pre-Raphaelite belief in painting pictures directly from nature in scrupulously objective detail.

During the 1850s, Leighton, while he was in Italy, made a large number of pencil drawings of plant forms. These minutely careful drawings were at least partly inspired by *Modern Painters*. In the spring of 1852 Leighton wrote to his mother that he was looking

---

[25]See above, p. 146.

[26]Olivia Rossetti Agresti, *Giovanni Costa: His Life, Work, and Times* (London, 1904) pp. 212–13.

forward to making studies outside Rome during the coming summer: 'I long to find myself again face to face with Nature, to follow it, to watch it, and to copy it, closely, faithfully, ingenuously – as Ruskin suggests, "choosing nothing, and rejecting nothing".'[27] However, these drawings owe nothing to the English Pre-Raphaelite painters. Leighton's education took place on the continent, not in England. From 1850 to 1852 he studied in Frankfurt under Edward von Steinle, a follower of the German Nazarenes. Leighton was probably influenced by Nazarene drawings such as the studies of withered leaves made by Friedrich Olivier and Julius Schnorr von Carolsfeld. In 1859, after Leighton had come into contact with the English painters (he was a member of the Hogarth Club), he made a large and careful drawing of a lemon tree purposely to outdo the Pre-Raphaelites at their own game (Pl. 100b).[28] But the contest was a false one. The Pre-Raphaelites painted nature; they did not draw it, and except in the work of a later follower such as Sandys there are no comparable Pre-Raphaelite drawings at all. After the 1850s Leighton stopped making such drawings, but he did paint remarkably beautiful oil sketches on his various travels. These reveal his debt to Costa, and ultimately, via Costa, to Corot.

George Hemming Mason was born in 1818 and lived in Italy from 1843 until 1858. In 1857 he sent a picture of *Ploughing in the Campagna* to the Royal Academy from Rome. After his return to England he exhibited regularly until his death in 1872, and although he was older than most of the Pre-Raphaelite group, he had probably the greatest single influence on landscape in the period when the Pre-Raphaelite influence was beginning to wane. *The Gander*, which he exhibited at the Royal Academy in 1865 (Pl. 99a), is typical of the pictures he painted in England. They are not pure landscapes, but rustic idylls, and they exemplify Giovanni Costa's principles put into effect. They are studio compositions, based on careful spacing and strong linear axes, and they have 'Sentiment before everything'. Most of them show twilight. Mason's pictures also recall contemporary French paintings of rural subjects by Jean-François Millet and Jules Breton, of whom he was probably well aware.[29] Mason visited Paris in 1855 and again in 1863 in the company of Costa. In the following year, when Frederick Walker, an artist whose name is often associated with Mason's, visited Paris, Jules Breton was the only living artist whose work attracted him.[30]

Mason at the time of his death was one of a small group of artists painting similar rustic subjects. Of the others – Frederick Walker, George Pinwell, and John William North – Walker is the most interesting in terms of Pre-Raphaelitism. He was a student at the Royal Academy schools in the late 1850s and learned to paint by working directly from nature. In the 1860s he continued to paint out of doors on large pictures even in January and February. He worked on *The Plough* (Pl. 99b) in the winter of 1869–70 wearing thick gloves, and on windy days he laid the canvas flat on the ground with stones and lumps of wood on its corners to keep it steady. After painting in detail directly from nature, Walker erased much of what he had done. According to his close friend North, 'His knowledge of nature was sufficient to disgust him with the ordinary conventions which do duty for grass, leaves, and boughs', but, on the other hand,

Certainly he was not content with his work unless it had suggestiveness, finish, and an appear-

[27]Mrs. Russell Barrington, *The Life, Letters and Work of Frederic Leighton* (London, 1906) I, 180, and illustrations facing pp. 69, 116, 200, 202, 205, 206, and 207.
[28]*Ibid.*, p. 202. For a drawing by Friedrich Olivier see Andrews, 1964, pl. 39b.
[29]The similarity of Mason's works to Breton's was noted by critics during Mason's lifetime. See Sidney Colvin, 'English Artists of the Present Day. XXVIII – George Mason, A.R.A.', *Portfolio* II, 1871, pp. 115–16.
[30]John George Marks, *Life and Letters of Frederick Walker A.R.A.* (London, 1896) p. 36.

ance of ease; and to the latter I sorrowfully feel that he gave rather too much weight, destroying many a lovely piece of earnest, sweetest work, because it did not appear to have been done without labour. Probably this excessive sensitiveness (to what is after all of minor importance) may have been due to a reaction from the somewhat unnatural clearness of definition in the early pictures of the Pre-Raphaelite Brotherhood.[31]

To an already uneasy mix of naturalism and suggestiveness, Walker added sentiment and grace, inspired partly by Jules Breton, partly by Mason, and partly by classical sculpture. *The Plough* shows even more clearly than Mason's pictures a concern with linear design. There are echoes of Verrocchio's *Colleoni* monument in the small horse and rider in the left middle-distance, and of the Parthenon frieze (of which Walker had casts in his studio) in the team of horses pulling the plough. Despite Walker's arduous work out of doors, the picture appears to be the product of a highly conscious attempt to create a two-dimensional frieze-like composition in which the lines of the landscape flow across the canvas, repeating the lines of the ploughman and team.

Walker died in 1875, three years after Mason. Their deaths, along with that of Pinwell, also in 1875, snuffed out what some later nineteenth-century critics considered the most promising development in English painting since Pre-Raphaelitism. However, in Walker's case in particular, although the ambitions were high, they were full of unresolved contradictions, which remained only too evident in the finished pictures. Following Walker's death, Ruskin was asked to express an opinion about his art. Ruskin was not very enthusiastic, and among the things he found to criticize was Walker's refusal to learn anything from the artists who had gone before him, with the result that his art remained 'perpetual experiment instead of achievement'.[32]

If Ruskin had wished, he could have made the same criticism of much earlier nineteenth-century painting, including that of the Pre-Raphaelites. He had, indeed, criticized Constable in similar terms.[33] Most of the best art of the nineteenth century was based upon perpetual experiment, but by the 1860s and 1870s the most adventurous experiments were no longer in quest of greater naturalism. Mason's and Walker's painting, like Whistler's and Burne-Jones's, was part of a larger development in English painting which can be called Aestheticism. In 1877, the year after his comments about Walker, Ruskin praised Burne-Jones's pictures in the opening exhibition of the Grosvenor Gallery as 'the best things the mid-nineteenth century in England could do', but to other pictures of 'the modern schools' in the same exhibition Ruskin did not extend his admiration: 'their eccentricities are almost always in some degree forced; and their imperfections gratuitously, if not impertinently, indulged'. And in the following sentences, the former champion of Turner, and of the Pre-Raphaelites, proceeded to attack 'the ill-educated conceit' of James Abbott McNeill Whistler.[34]

Whistler had been a close friend of Dante Gabriel Rossetti during the 1860s, and he had earlier admired Millais. The influence of Millais and Rossetti on several of Whistler's most important pictures – *The White Girl* (1863; National Gallery, Washington), *The Little White Girl* (1864; Tate Gallery), *The Lange Lijzen of the Six Marks* (1864; John G. Johnson Collection, Philadelphia) – is evident.[35] There are also affinities between Whistler's Nocturnes and earlier pictures by Inchbold and Boyce.[36] However, it was not the naturalistic aspect of Pre-Raphaelitism which attracted Whistler, but more abstract or suggestive

[31]*Ibid.*, p. 168.
[32]Ruskin, 1903–12, XIV, 340.
[33]*Ibid.*, III, pp. 45n., 191.
[34]*Ibid.*, XXIX, pp. 159–60.
[35]See *From Realism to Symbolism: Whistler and His*

World, exhibition catalogue (Department of Art History, Columbia University, New York, and Philadelphia Museum of Art, 1971) pp. 12–14 and 39–42.
[36]See above, pp. 110 and 120.

elements. During the later 1860s he struggled to escape from the heritage of Courbet's Realism, which he had brought from France to England. The Nocturnes which he painted in the 1870s, and which were the objects of Ruskin's attack, were the most original fruits of his attempt to create a severely disciplined, quasi-abstract art in which all vestiges of naturalistic detail had been eliminated. The trial for libel which Whistler brought following Ruskin's criticism was a disgraceful affair, reflecting credit upon neither of the adversaries; it mainly demonstrated that what was *avant-garde* in the early 1850s had become old-fashioned a quarter of a century later. Whistler's 'Ten O'Clock Lecture' of 1885 was a more considered attack on the aesthetics of Ruskin. Whistler's assertions of the differences between art and nature, such as 'To say to the painter, that Nature is to be taken as she is, is to say to the player, that he may sit on the piano', provided ammunition for countless subsequent attacks on Ruskinian standards of naturalism. But the critics who quoted Whistler were flogging a dying horse. By 1885 new influences were beginning to flow across the Channel, which would soon bury the lingering traces of Pre-Raphaelite naturalism under a succession of imitations of Bastien-Lepage, Impressionism, and Post-Impressionism.

The quarrel between Whistler and Ruskin was a quarrel between generations, but it has often been made to sound like a conflict between Victorian insularity and progressive French painting. In fact, Pre-Raphaelitism was an insular movement. In the formation of the Brotherhood in 1848 there was some awareness of the German Nazarenes, but as the movement developed in the 1850s and in later years, it turned its back on contemporary art on the continent. However, if the English artists were uninfluenced by French painting, they were not unexposed to it. Ford Madox Brown lived in France during the early 1840s and among his close friends were Charles Lucy and Mark Anthony. Lucy, who was a historical painter seven years older than Brown, had studied in Paris at the Ecole des Beaux Arts. In 1857 or 1858 he returned to France, and he lived at Barbizon for the rest of his life. In England he was at different times the landlord of both Brown and John Brett, and he was the first instructor of Thomas Seddon.

Anthony lived in France from around 1834 to 1841. He spent some time at Barbizon and was a friend of Corot and Dupré. In F. G. Stephens's words, 'technically speaking, he was the only one of our landscape painters who could fairly be compared with Jules Dupré, whose art his resembled in many respects.'[37] This resemblance is most evident in paintings of forest scenes such as *Thinking of the Future: an Irish Sketch*, which Anthony exhibited at the Royal Academy in 1845 (Pl. 98b), but all of Anthony's landscapes from the 1840s and early 1850s show affinities with contemporary French painting. They are looser in handling and heavier in colour than Pre-Raphaelite pictures. Nonetheless, Anthony was constantly lauded in William Michael Rossetti's exhibition reviews as the outstanding landscape painter in England. He won the prize of the Liverpool Academy in 1854, and his pictures were bought by the Pre-Raphaelite collectors J. Hamilton Trist, James Leathart, and George Rae. Ford Madox Brown's diary is full of praise for Anthony – 'like Constable, only better by far' – and we have seen similarities between Brown's landscapes of 1848 and 1849 and Anthony's pictures.[38] William Davis was also probably influenced by Anthony. In turn, in the 1850s Anthony began to be affected by Pre-Raphaelitism, but the result was a rather unsatisfactory compromise. In 1855 Brown wrote in his diary that Anthony's pictures were all unfinished and could only be finished if Anthony took them back to the places where he had painted them.[39] This suggests that Anthony did try to paint directly

[37]*Athenaeum*, 11 Dec. 1886, p. 790.
[38]Rossetti, 1900, p. 176, and see above, pp. 31 and 32.
[39]Rossetti, 1900, p. 156. See also Rossetti, 1906, II, pp. 140–41.

out of doors. However, his pictures were too large to have been painted comfortably in the open air or with the consistent care of Pre-Raphaelitism. He seems to have attempted to give his pictures a feeling of detailed observation without sacrificing breadth, but he did so at the expense of solidity, and most of his later pictures seem theatrically insubstantial. Examples are in the museums of Wolverhampton and Liverpool.

Of the immediate Pre-Raphaelite circle, Thomas Seddon painted at Barbizon. Boyce also painted in France, and he owned pictures by Diaz, Daubigny, and Corot. Yet if either artist was ever influenced by the Barbizon painters, he soon changed; none of the known works by either Seddon or Boyce betrays any interest in French painting. Pre-Raphaelite opinions about the Barbizon painters were mixed. Ruskin was always scornful of French landscape painting,[40] but it is never clear exactly what artists he was talking about. Holman Hunt's dislike of French art, expressed in *Pre-Raphaelitism and the Pre-Raphaelite Brotherhood* seems almost pathological; however a letter which he wrote to F. G. Stephens in 1876 gives a reasonably lucid explanation for his dislike of Daubigny: 'I am perfectly unable to see his merit: square flat touches, all equally chopping, whether to represent cloud, distance, vegetation or cattle soon lose their interest.'[41] On the other hand, William Michael Rossetti writing in 1855 was sympathetic to French landscape painting: 'the school is, on the whole, a noble one; which Englishmen, addicted to an opposite principle are far too chary of admitting'.[42] And Dante Gabriel Rossetti, in 1851, was well enough disposed to Théodore Rousseau's painting to suggest that it resembled John Linnell's.[43]

The French artist most admired by the Pre-Raphaelite group was Delacroix. They elected him an honorary member of the Hogarth Club (the only other foreigner so honoured was Ralph Waldo Emerson), and in 1863 Fantin-Latour planned to include Rossetti in his *Hommage à Delacroix*, but Rossetti was unable to go to Paris for sittings. Courbet did not fare so well in English estimation. When Holman Hunt and Rossetti visited Paris in 1849, they saw 'certain paintings of the new Realistic School', which Hunt described as 'coarse and ugly'. This probably referred to Courbet, as did Hunt's ensuing comment, 'naturalism was, in fact, a repudiation, rather than a purgation of art'.[44] Dante Gabriel Rossetti was also critical of Courbet in 1864. However, when William Michael Rossetti visited the *Exposition Universelle* of 1855 in Paris, he wrote that Courbet held in France 'as the apostle of "Realism" a position somewhat analogous to that of the Pre-Raphaelites in England'. William Michael seems to have genuinely admired Courbet; he declared that Courbet 'commands wonder and merits honour', and he praised *La Roche de Dix-heures* (Louvre) as 'a glorious snatch of landscape, as real as stone and grass, of which Anthony might be proud'.[45] Nonetheless, William Michael was aware of enough differences between Courbet and the Pre-Raphaelites to make any analogy between them false. One difference was in method: 'the Frenchman is the roughest of the rough, the Englishmen the most exquisite of the elaborated'. While French and English artists were both concerned with naturalism, the English alone sought 'the realization of the effect through its minutest details'.[46] There was more of a gap between French and English naturalism, however, than

[40]For example, see Ruskin, 1903-12, IV, 212n.
[41]Grylls, 1957, II, 232.
[42]Rossetti, 1867, p. 116.
[43]Rossetti, 1911, p. 578.
[44]Hunt, 1905, I, 189, Hunt, unlike Rossetti, also disliked Delacroix (*ibid.*, p. 188).
[45]Rossetti, 1867, pp. 112-13. William Michael's

catalogue of the 1855 *Exposition* is in the Yale University Library. In his marginal notes he described Courbet's *Ruisseau du Puits-Noir, Vallée de la Loue* as 'Creswicky done broad', which seems less complimentary.
[46]Rossetti, 1867, p. 100.

could be explained by technique alone. William Michael thought Courbet had only a 'half-grasp' of realism. He was capable, but not thoughtful: 'He sees as far into a millstone as another man – and no further; and is honest enough to paint with a rough and ready freedom, exactly what he sees'. For William Michael this was not enough. The artist's purpose should be to translate the sentiment of things as well as their appearance. The Pre-Raphaelites had vitality because they had love and reverence, rather than just the 'hail-fellow-well-met' attitude towards nature of Courbet.[47] Hence, after surveying the art of the world, William Michael concluded his review: 'To English Praeraphaelitism – after admiring foreign excellence with no stinted or un-catholic homage – we return in the deliberate conviction that it embodies the highest, truest, and most vitally essential, among the fresh and direct movements of the aera.'[48]

That the Pre-Raphaelites did not paint like Courbet, or like the Barbizon artists, was not because they were unaware of French art, but because they were convinced that their own path was superior. They may have failed to grasp what was significant about Courbet, and why Courbet's art provided a more substantial basis for future developments than their own, but they were so convinced of their own revolutionary significance that it is understandable that they would not be entirely receptive to the claims of Courbet. To a sympathetically inclined viewer the English paintings could well have looked the most progressive of any works included in the exhibition of 1855. Delacroix's excitement about the Pre-Raphaelite pictures, and particularly about Holman Hunt's *Strayed Sheep*, has already been mentioned.[49] While the landscapes of the Barbizon painters and of Courbet were painted in the studio, *Strayed Sheep* was painted out of doors. Its colours do not have the old-masterly depth of contemporary French painting, but are light and bright, and the shadows are of blues and purples. Its composition is fresher and freer than the usual compositions of mid-century French pictures, and it presents a less traditional view of nature. The Barbizon painters and Courbet were still painting the forest primeval, dark grottoes, and a countryside inhabited by weathered trees and timeless peasants; but Hunt's picture is remarkably free of Romantic imagery. And his colleague Ford Madox Brown had progressed even further in the direction of the modern world by painting landscapes showing the view from his own middle-class suburban window.

In important ways, the Pre-Raphaelite landscape paintings have more in common with Impressionism than with French Realism of the 1850s. However, they do not seem to have had any actual influence upon the Impressionists. There is no evidence that the Impressionists were conscious of the outdoor painting done in England in the 1850s, and there are, of course, as many conspicuous differences as similarities between the English and French paintings. The most obvious difference is the amount of detail in the Pre-Raphaelite pictures, and the explanation for this difference lies in the amount of time spent on each individual Pre-Raphaelite picture. When Henry James wrote a review of the Impressionist exhibition of 1876 at Durand-Ruel, he tried to explain the Impressionists' purpose:

The painter's proper field [they say] is simply the actual, and to give a vivid impression of how a thing happens to look, at a particular moment, is the essence of his mission. This attitude has something in common with that of the English Pre-Raphaelites, twenty years ago, but this little band [of Impressionists] is on all grounds less interesting than the group out of which Millais and Holman Hunt rose into fame.

James declared that none of the Impressionists showed signs of possessing talent, and that,

[47] *Ibid.*, p. 113.
[48] *Ibid.*, p. 124.

[49] See above, p. 63.

indeed, the Impressionist doctrine seemed incompatible with the existence of talent. He then proceeded to a discussion of the differences between the Impressionists and Pre-Raphaelites:

But the divergence in method between the English Pre-Raphaelites and this little group is especially striking, and very characteristic of the moral differences of the French and English races. When the English realists 'went in', as the phrase is, for hard truth and stern fact, an irresistible instinct of righteousness caused them to try and purchase forgiveness for their infidelity to the old more or less moral proprieties and conventionalities, by an exquisite, patient, virtuous manipulation – by being above all things laborious. But the Impressionists, who, I think, are more consistent, abjure virtue altogether, and declare that a subject which has been crudely chosen shall be loosely treated . . . the Englishmen, in a word, were pedants, and the Frenchmen are cynics.[50]

This is as good an explanation as any of what makes the Pre-Raphaelites seem to us more dated than the Impressionists. It is not the fact that their paintings are detailed, but it is the moral attitude behind the details, the attempt to make a picture significant in a manner about which the Impressionists no longer cared. There is a compromise, in the theory and in the pictures themselves, between what seems precociously modern and what James called 'an instinct of righteousness'. Ford Madox Brown's explanations of his pictures are the Pre-Raphaelite statements of purpose which seem most advanced, because they are least weighed down by this righteousness. Brown's colleagues are more complicated. Hunt, for example, at times seems as precocious as Brown, but at other times he hedges in a way that often makes reading his memoirs embarrassing. His declaration that the Pre-Raphael-ites were not 'realists' is an example of the compromise:

I think art would have ceased to have the slightest interest for any of us had the object been only to make a representation, elaborate or unelaborate, of a fact in nature. Independently of the conviction that such a system would put out of operation the faculty making man 'like a God', it was apparent that a mere imitator gradually comes to see nature claylike and finite, as it seems when illness brings a cloud before the eyes. Art dominated by this spirit makes us esteem the world as without design or finish, unbalanced, unfitting, and unlovely, not interpreted into beauty as true art makes it.[51]

Hunt wrote this; yet he spent months on end painting directly from nature with the most scrupulous care. Another example of the compromise is Ruskin's apparent belief that Brett could combine photographic fidelity with the emotional content of a Turner. The Pre-Raphaelites, in a way, wanted too much. They refused to accept the possibility of incompatibilities. William Michael Rossetti, in fact, in 1862, wrote an explanation of Pre-Raphaelitism in which the movement's essence became the reconciliation of seeming opposites:

Praeraphaelitism has arisen to assert that there is no necessary antagonism between the most pictorial conception of a thing and the thing itself; that it is open to the painter, however imaginative, to follow nature in all respects, not only in some, in detail and in all details, not only in generals and in hints for after adaptation; that entire freedom of invention, and every possible latitude of artistic aim and point of view, are compatible with, and may in the main be even aided by, entire adherence to visible matter of fact. This is the gist of Praeraphaelitism, and not the crude notion, so often attributed to it, that mere matter of fact, subserving no artistic purpose, is the be-all and end-all of art.[52]

The most successful Pre-Raphaelite landscapes are probably those in which 'mere matter of fact', treated with sensitivity, does seem to be the be-all and end-all. However, for most members of the Pre-Raphaelite circle, interest in the look of things was not enough, and to

[50]Henry James, *The Painter's Eye: Notes and Essays on the Pictorial Arts*, ed. John L. Sweeney (London, 1956) pp. 114–15.

[51]Hunt, 1905, I, 150.

[52]Rossetti, 1867, p. 147.

the extent that they tempered naturalism with other values, their pictures seem more old-fashioned than those of the Impressionists.

The most important of these other values was James's 'irresistible instinct of righteousness'. James cited the fact that the Pre-Raphaelites were laborious. To painting they brought the Victorian exaltation of hard work. An artist like Hunt demanded and received credit for the sheer labour which he put into his pictures. Along with work came other Victorian virtues: thoroughness, precision, honesty, even chastity. As F. G. Stephens wrote in *The Germ*, the 'simple chastity of nature' was to provide the artist's sole model: 'Let the artist be content to study nature alone, and not dream of elevating any of her works which are alone worthy of representation'.[53]

The Pre-Raphaelites were critical of the frivolity of the preceding generation. For them, art had to have a high moral purpose:

Believe that there is that in the fact of truth, though it be only in the character of a leaf earnestly studied, which may do its share in the great labour of the world: remember that it is by truth alone that the Arts can ever hold the position for which they were intended, as the most powerful instruments, the most gentle guides.[54]

Occasionally, particularly in pictures by Holman Hunt, the high moral purpose of art becomes only too obvious. But relatively few Pre-Raphaelite pictures are such out-and-out sermons as *The Awakening Conscience* or *The Light of the World*. In most cases of Pre-Raphaelite landscape painting, the pictures were to be a means of conveying important knowledge. This is, for example, what Ruskin saw as the chief value of Brett's *Val d' Aosta*, and Ruskin's criticism in general was directed to making landscape painting more scientifically informative. As we have seen, Hamerton thought that Ruskin had succeeded too well in making art the hand-maiden of science. But science also became the hand-maiden of art. There was a flurry of publications in the 1850s which discussed the application of scientific knowledge to art,[55] and Stephens urged that the artist follow the scientist's example:

The sciences have become almost exact within the present century. Geology and chemistry are almost reinstituted. The first has been nearly created; the second expanded so widely that it now searches and measures the creation. And how has this been done but by bringing greater knowledge to bear upon a wider range of experiment; by being precise in the search after truth? If this adherence to fact, to experiment and not theory . . . has added so much to the knowledge of man in science; why may it not greatly assist the moral purposes of the arts?[56]

Ford Madox Brown is the most attractive figure in this study because he remained somewhat detached from this high-minded seriousness. His art does not generally claim to be useful, and it has little of the scientific pretension demanded by Ruskin. However, in Brown's pictures we still feel the urge to exact observation, and in his catalogue of 1865

[53]Stephens, 1850, p. 62.

[54]*Ibid.*, p. 64. To this might be added Holman Hunt's statement: 'One scarcely expressed purpose in our reform, left unsaid by reason of its fundamental necessity, was to make art a hand maid in the cause of justice and truth.' (Hunt, 1905, I, 172). See also, of course, *Modern Painters, passim*.

[55]For example, D. T. Ansted, *Scenery, Science, and Art: Being Extracts from the Note-Book of a Geologist and Mining Engineer* (London, 1854). Ansted also gave lectures at the Society of British Artists, which Ford Madox Brown attended and described in his diary: 'Went to Suffolk Street, to hear Professor Ansted tell us that the colour of the air is blue, and that of mist grey, etc.; this they call geology!' (31 Jan. 1848;

Rossetti, 1900, p. 82). The *Art Journal* published several series devoted to the application of science to art. One was 'The Natural Philosophy of Art,' by John Sweetlove, the purpose of which was to explain 'the laws of those phenomena in nature which have an immediate connexion with art, especially painting, and with which the artist must be acquainted in order to produce a truthful representation of nature.' The writer began by declaring, 'A moment's consideration of the objects and means of art will show how much it resembles the more strictly experimental sciences in relation to both nature and the human mind.' *Art Journal*, 1852, p. 6.

[56]Stephens, 1850, p. 62.

he gave semi-scientific explanations of certain effects. Brown, like his colleagues, was studious, industrious, and self-effacing. The artists' values were those of the scientist and the scholar. Henry James was right when he called them pedants.

The subjects of Pre-Raphaelite landscape painting remained more or less within the traditional gamut. The two main classes were still topographical views of places of interest, and pastoral landscapes, and for most of the variations of these basic categories there was some precedent in earlier English landscape painting. The one new development was the increased importance given by an artist like Brown to his own immediate surroundings, to showing nature as it was experienced by the modern city-dweller. The fact that Brown's views lay outside his back window was not of incidental but of primary significance in his conception; he was not painting the 'Nature' of the Romantics, but his own environment. The artist's immediate experience became part of the subject of the picture. Brown and Dyce showed themselves or their families on their holidays, without additional comment. In other Pre-Raphaelite works, if the subject of the picture was not brought into the personal sphere of the artist, we feel the personal experience of the artist projected into the picture as a result of the painter's almost morbidly high degree of involvement. We cannot look at *The Scapegoat*, for example, without thinking of Hunt's heroic labours of painting on the shores of the Dead Sea. The Pre-Raphaelites tried to replace personal expression and invention by scientific accuracy, but the amount of labour given by Hunt or Brett to a picture makes us as aware of the artist's act of creation as if the pictures had been painted by Cézanne. Today, we admire Brett less for the accuracy of his observation than for the virtuosity of his painting and for the sheer effort made manifest in his pictures.

That there can be no such thing as an absolutely literal view of nature, 'wholly unmodified by the artist's execution',[57] is to us a truism that was not so evident to the Victorians. It is impossible for us not to feel the presence of Brett or Hunt in their pictures; not only, paradoxically, are we the more aware of them because of their very efforts at being self-effacing, but now, as we look at their pictures over a century later, we can also see how their vision of nature was tempered by the tastes of their day. Their bright colours and crowded compositions are fundamentally Victorian. They share these qualities with Victorian architecture and Victorian interiors. As the pictures were intended to be hung in the midst of cluttered Victorian houses, the artist had to scream to be heard in the din. Thus, although the Pre-Raphaelites wanted to be absolutely literal, to most modern viewers their pictures, compared to Constable, Corot, or Monet, look relatively unnatural and artificial. This is, in part, a result of our greater familiarity with Constable and the French artists; we automatically take them as the standard of naturalistic representation, and any divergence appears correspondingly unnatural. But even if we were capable of approaching nineteenth-century paintings without preconceptions, it is doubtful that the palm of naturalism would go to the Pre-Raphaelites. They were keen and industrious observers and recorders, and in their pictures there is an amount of naturalistic observation which we should not discount. Yet in looking at Ford Madox Brown's landscapes, we have seen that, despite his attempts to record exactly what he saw, his pictures are characterized by bold surface patterns of closely knit details and bright colours. In this one respect, Brown's pictures are similar to those of Rossetti, who shared none of Brown's naturalistic orientation but intended his works to be fanciful and decorative; and almost all Pre-Raphaelite pictures show some tendency toward a richly articulated two-dimensional pattern. In

[57]Ruskin re. Seddon, see above, p. 104.

many cases, they seem to anticipate not the naturalism of the Impressionists but the stylization of *fin-de-siècle* art.

The reasons for this relatively abstract aspect of Pre-Raphaelite painting have been discussed: essentially it results from the abandonment of most of the traditional space-creating devices of landscape painting, and, particularly, from the insistence upon bright local colours at the expense of tonal modulation. The Pre-Raphaelites were against 'brown foliage, smoky clouds and dark corners' because they considered them artificial. They felt that in avoiding such conventions they were not on the road to abstraction but to realizing in paint the exact look of nature.[58] That their pictures should become flat in effect because of the bright colours, and visually confusing because of the weight of detail was not what they intended; it does, however, provide a demonstration of the limits of naturalism in painting. Ernst Gombrich in *Art and Illusion* has discussed at length the conflict between traditional schemata of painting and direct observation of nature. He contends that there is no natural vision, no 'innocent eye', but that we learn to see, and that the naturalistic advances of a painter like Constable were made by the progressive modification of inherited schemata. Progress could only be made in the context of respect for tradition. The Pre-Raphaelites, however, had little respect for tradition, and they did believe in the innocent eye.[59] Thus, while they seem by their direct confrontation with nature more radically naturalistic than a Constable, they did not succeed in making their pictures look more natural. They sacrificed too much of what makes a picture work. Constable and the Impressionists approached nature with greater respect for pictorial values than the Pre-Raphaelites, and they succeeded where the Victorian artists failed. In some respects, the Pre-Raphaelites seem too conservative, too held back by their 'instinct of righteousness', but, stylistically, they were, if anything, too revolutionary. The general objection to Pre-Raphaelitism is not to the timidity of the revolution, but rather to its extremity, to the movement's too complete abandonment of its artistic heritage. While the French could, and did, build on Constable, the Pre-Raphaelites turned their backs and went their own precarious ways. As Gombrich says, illusionist art grew out of a long tradition, and 'it collapsed as soon as this tradition was questioned by those who relied on the innocent eye'.[60] In Pre-Raphaelite landscapes, painted in as immediate a confrontation with nature as was perhaps possible to an educated artist, we see the beginning of the collapse.

The Pre-Raphaelites did not lay 'the foundations of a school of art nobler than the world has seen for three hundred years', as Ruskin had promised in 1851, but they did form a movement which for a few years had immense vitality, and they did paint a number of remarkably ambitious and beautiful pictures. If they failed in terms of what they set out to do, they are yet failures who have a considerable historical significance. They anticipated the collapse of the illusionist tradition, which has established the terms of twentieth-century art, and, in attempting to rely on their own resources without the aid of sustaining tradition, they seem extremely modern. Having turned their backs on the past, Holman Hunt and Ford Madox Brown tried almost literally to re-invent the whole art of painting in each picture, and in their pictures we can see them tentatively feeling their way. Whether they succeeded in finding it or not is perhaps still an undecided critical question, but, historically, it is less important than the fact that they looked.

[58]See also Ruskin's arguments against aerial perspective, cited above, p. 47.
[59]Cf. Hunt's 'child-like reversion from existing schools to Nature herself' (Hunt, 1905, I, 125). The concept of the 'innocent eye' was basic to Ruskin (see Ruskin, 1903–12, III, 140–48, and XV, 27n.), and Ruskin's arguments are Gombrich's point of departure (Gombrich, 1960, pp. 14, 296–7).
[60]Gombrich, 1960, p. 313.

Index

Acland, Henry, 49
Aestheticism, 95, 178
Aitken, Charles, 167
Albert, Prince, 2, 3, 6, 163
Alessandri, Angelo, 157
Allen, George, 156
Allingham, William, 30, 85
Alma-Tadema, Lawrence, 87
Alpine Club, 125
American Exhibition of British Art (1857–8), 41,
   85, 109, 138, 140, 144–5, 151, 156
Anelay, Henry, 175
Angelico, Fra, 2, 9
Ansted, D. T., 183n
Anthony, Mark, 26, 31–3, 138–9, 179–80;
   Killarney: the Lower Lake, Pl. 10c, 32–3; *Severn
   Valley*, Pl. 7b, 31; *Thinking of the Future*, Pl. 98b,
   179
Armstrong, Thomas, 63, 134
Art Journal, 3n, 64, 173, 183n; criticism of Pre-
   Raphaelitism in general, 2, 12, 173; criticism of
   individual artists: Brett, 135; Brown, 27;
   Collins, 83; Davis, 140; Dyce, 3, 163, 165–9;
   Hopley, 82; Hughes, 85n; Holman Hunt, 2, 63,
   65, 69, 76–7; Inchbold, 113, 115, 118; Millais, 2,
   13–14, 47, 53; Mulready, 172; D. G. Rossetti, 2
Art Union, see Art Journal
Athenaeum, 110, 173; criticism of individual
   artists: Collins, 83; Holman Hunt, 21, 26;
   Millais, 24–6, 47; *see also* Stephens, Frederick
   George
Athenaem Français, 64

Barbizon School, 29, 97, 179–81
Bastien-Lepage, Jules, 179
Bate, Percy, 89
Beauchamp, Earl, 153
Bell, Lowthian, 110
Bellini, Giovanni, 9
Bellotto, Bernardo, 135
Bennett, Mary, 45n, 138
Besnard, Albert, 64
Blackwood's Magazine, 7
Blagden, Isa, 134
Blake, William, 29, 155
Blunden, Anna, 175
Boase, T. S. R., 130
Bond, W. J. J. C., 147
Bonington, Richard Parkes, 162, 170
Booth, Edward C., 175
Botticelli, Sandro, 163
Boucher, François, 22
Boudin, Eugène, 43, 168
Boyce, George Price, 82, 96, 107–110, 180; *At

Binsey*, Pl. 55b, 109; *Edward the Confessor's
Chapel*, 108n; *From a Window at Ludlow*, Pl. 57b,
109–110; *Landscape: Wootton, Autumn*, Pl. 56b,
109; *Llyn Hilsi*, 107n; *Mill on the Thames at
Mapledurham*, Pl. 55a, Col. Pl. 8a, 109; *Near the
Public Gardens, Venice*, Pl. 54a, 108; *Red Barn at
Whitchurch*, Pl. 56a, 109–110; *Streatley Mill*, 109;
Thames by Night from the Adelphi, Pl. 57a, 110;
Tomb of Cangrande della Scala, Pl. 54b, 108;
Windmill Hills, Gateshead-on-Tyne, 109;
diary, 107, 110;
references to: Holman Hunt, 59; Millais, 49;
D. G. Rossetti, 107, 110; Ruskin, 107–8, 151;
relations with: Inchbold, 110; D. G. Rossetti, 82,
107, 110; Ruskin, 107–8; Seddon, 99n, 107, 110;
107, 110; Whistler, 110, 120
Boyd, Alice, 151
Brand, James, 166–8
Breton, Jules, 177–8
Brett, John, 36, 88, 96, 106, 124–37, 151, 173, 184;
Britannia's Realm, 136–7; *British Channel Seen
from the Dorsetshire Cliffs*, Pl. 73b, 135–6; *Etna
from the Heights of Taormina*, Pl. 73a, 135–6;
Faces in the Fire, 124; *February in the Isle of Wight*,
135; *Florence from Bellosguardo*, Pl. 71a, 134–5,
159; *Glacier of Rosenlaui*, Pl. 68a, 124–7, 145;
Grass, 126; *Hedger*, Pl. 72b, 133; *Lady with a
Dove*, 124; *Landscape (1852)*, Pl. 69a, 124;
Massa, Bay of Naples, Pl. 71b, 135–6; *Morants
Court in May*, Pl. 72a, 135; *Moss and Gentians
from the Engels Hörner*, 126; *Near Goring-on-
Thames*, Pl. 72c, 135; *Near Sorrento*, 136;
North-west Squall in the Mediterranean, 136;
Ponte Vecchio, Florence, 133; *Stonebreaker*, Pl. 69b,
Col. Pl. 2d, 126–30, 135; *Val d'Aosta*, Pl. 70,
Col. Pl. 6b, 105, 128–35, 158, 174; *Warwick
Castle*, 133; *Wetterhorn, Well Horn and Eiger*, 126;
Yarmouth, 135;
Three Months on the Scottish Coast (exhibition),
136;
references to: Constable, 136n; Lewis, 128;
relations with: Inchbold, 121, 124–6;
D. G. Rossetti, 126; Ruskin, 51, 105, 125–6,
128–9, 132–4
Brett, Rosa, 128, 151
British Quarterly Review, 21, 83
Brown, Emma, 26, 35, 42
Brown, Ford Madox, 4–6, 26–44, 96–7, 138, 155,
173, 179, 181–5; *Body of Harold Brought before
William the Conqueror*, 4, 36; *Brent at Hendon*,
Pl. 12b, 33, 38–40; *Byron's Dream*, Pl. 16b, 44;
Carrying Corn, Pl. 14, 33, 38, 40–1, 43, 109, 143;
Chaucer at the Court of Edward III, Pl. 6, 4–6, 14,
31, 34, 36, 38, 44, 96–7; *Christ Washing Peter's*

187

1a. William Holman Hunt, *Rienzi Vowing to Obtain Justice for the Death of His Younger Brother Slain in a Skirmish between the Colonna and Orsini Factions*, 1848–9. Oil on canvas, 32½ × 47½ in. Collection of Mrs. E. M. Clarke

1b. William Holman Hunt, *Valentine Rescuing Sylvia from Proteus*, 1850–1. Oil on canvas, 38¾ × 52½ in. City Museum and Art Gallery, Birmingham

2b. John Everett Millais, *The Woodman's Daughter*, 1850–1. Oil on canvas, 35 × 25½ in. Guildhall Art Gallery, London

2a. John Everett Millais, *Ferdinand Lured by Ariel*, 1849–50. Oil on panel, 25½ × 20 in. Collection of Lord Sherfield

3b. William Mulready, *Open Your Mouth and Shut Your Eyes*, exhibited 1839. Oil on panel, 12¼ × 12 in. Victoria and Albert Museum, London

3c. Unknown Spanish Artist, *The Meeting of Jacob and Rachel*, seventeenth century. Oil on canvas, 36⅞ × 58¼ in. Dulwich College Picture Gallery, London

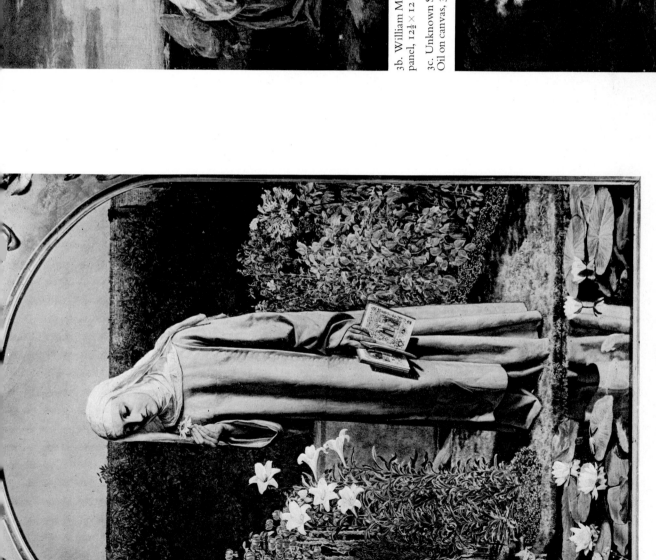

3a. Charles Allston Collins, *Convent Thoughts*, dated 1851. Oil on canvas, 33 × 23¼ in. Ashmolean Museum, Oxford

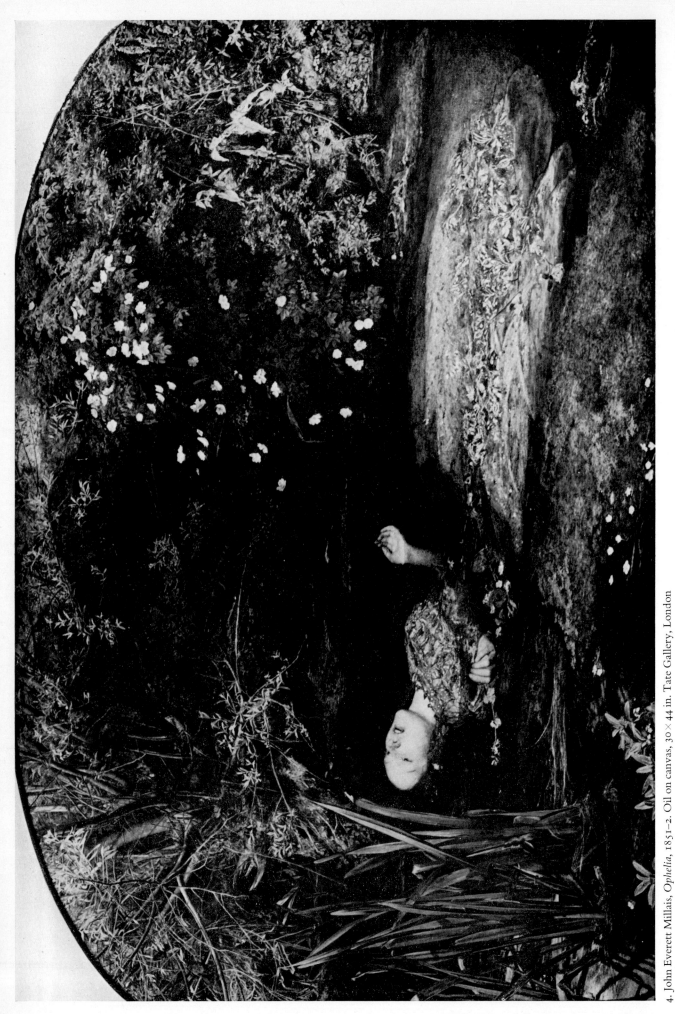

4. John Everett Millais, *Ophelia*, 1851–2. Oil on canvas, 30 × 44 in. Tate Gallery, London

5 (*below*). William Holman Hunt, *The Hireling Shepherd*, 1851–2. Oil on canvas, 30⅜ × 43⅛ in. City Art Gallery, Manchester

6. Ford Madox Brown, *Chaucer at the Court of Edward III*, 1845–51. Oil on canvas, 146½ × 116½ in. Art Gallery of New South Wales, Sydney

7a. Ford Madox Brown, *View from Shorn Ridgeway*, 1849–51. Oil on board, 8 × 12 in. Collection of Miss S. Crawshay

7b. Mark Anthony, *The Severn Valley*, c.1850. Oil on canvas, 12 × 18 in. Collection of Dr. Gilbert Leathart

8 (*above*). Ford Madox Brown, *The Pretty Baa-Lambs*, 1851–9. Oil on panel, 24 × 30 in. City Museum and Art Gallery, Birmingham

9. Ford Madox Brown, *An English Autumn Afternoon*, 1852–5. Oil on canvas, 28¼ × 53 in. City Museum and Art Gallery, Birmingham

10a. Ford Madox Brown, *Windermere*, 1848–55. Oil on canvas, $6\frac{7}{8} \times 18\frac{1}{2}$ in. Lady Lever Art Gallery, Port Sunlight

10b. Ford Madox Brown, *Winandermere*, 1859? Watercolour and bodycolour, $5\frac{1}{2} \times 11\frac{1}{2}$ in. William Morris Gallery, Walthamstow

10c. Mark Anthony, *Killarney: The Lower Lake*, exhibited 1845. Oil on canvas, $21\frac{3}{8} \times 48\frac{3}{8}$ in. Collection of Her Majesty Queen Elizabeth II

11a. Ford Madox Brown, *Work*, 1852–65. Oil on canvas, 54½ × 77⅛ in. City Art Gallery, Manchester

11b. Ford Madox Brown, *Study at Hampstead*, 1852–5. Oil on canvas, 9 × 12 in. City Art Gallery, Manchester

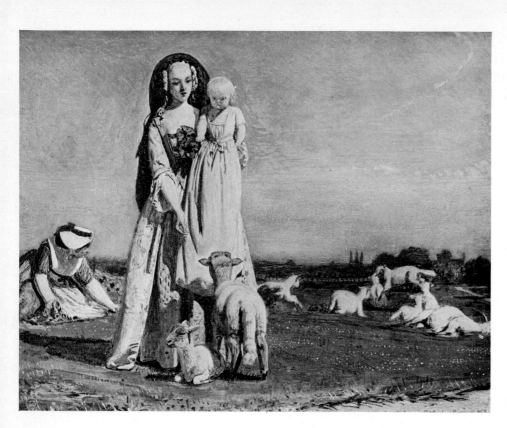

12a. Ford Madox Brown, *The Pretty Baa-Lambs* (copy), 1852. Oil on panel, 7¾ × 10 in. Ashmolean Museum, Oxford

12b. Ford Madox Brown, *The Brent at Hendon*, 1854. Oil on board, 8 × 9¾ in. Tate Gallery, London

13a. Ford Madox Brown, *Hampstead from My Window*, 1857. Watercolour, $5\frac{1}{2} \times 8\frac{1}{2}$ in. The Wilmington Society of the Fine Arts, Wilmington, Delaware

13b. Ford Madox Brown, *Walton-on-the-Naze*, dated 1860. Oil on canvas, $12\frac{1}{2} \times 16\frac{1}{2}$ in. City Museum and Art Gallery, Birmingham

14 Ford Madox Brown, *Carrying Corn*, 1854. Oil on canvas, $7\frac{3}{4} \times 10\frac{7}{8}$ in. Tate Gallery, London

15. Ford Madox Brown, *The Hayfield*, 1855. Oil on panel, 9 × 12½ in. Collection of John Gillum

16a. Ford Madox Brown, *The Coat of Many Colours*, dated 1866. Oil on canvas, 42½ × 40⅝ in. Walker Art Gallery, Liverpool

16b. Ford Madox Brown, *Byron's Dream*, dated 1874. Oil on canvas, 28¼ × 21¾ in. City Art Gallery, Manchester

17a. Ford Madox Brown, *Platt Lane*, 1884. Oil on canvas, $10\frac{1}{4} \times 15\frac{1}{2}$ in. Tate Gallery, London

17b. Atkinson Grimshaw, *Golden Autumn Glow*, 1881. Oil on board, 12×20 in. Collection of Mrs. Lytle Hull

18a. John Everett Millais, *The Gipsy*, 1846. Watercolour, $9\frac{3}{4} \times 13\frac{7}{16}$ in. City Museum and Art Gallery, Birmingham

18b. John Everett Millais, *Landscape, Hampstead*, c.1848? Oil on panel, $9\frac{1}{8} \times 13\frac{1}{4}$ in. Walker Art Gallery, Liverpool

19a. John Everett Millais, *The Kingfisher's Haunt*, 1849–54? Oil on panel, 9⅝ × 11½ in. Destroyed; formerly collection of Mrs. Arthur E. Street

19b. William Holman Hunt, *The Haunted Manor*, dated 1849. Oil on board, 9⅛ × 13¼ in. Tate Gallery, London

20. John Everett Millais, *John Ruskin*, 1853–4. Oil on canvas, 31 × 26¾ in. Private collection, Great Britain

21a. John Everett Millais, *The Waterfall*, 1853. Oil on board, 10½ × 12½ in.
The Wilmington Society of the Fine Arts, Wilmington, Delaware

21b. John Ruskin, *Gneiss Rock in Glenfinlas*, 1853. Pen and wash and
bodycolour, 18¾ × 12⅞ in. Ashmolean Museum, Oxford

22. John Everett Millais, *Waiting*, 1854. Oil on panel, 12 × 9 in. City Museum and Art Gallery, Birmingham

23 (*right*). John Everett Millais, *The Blind Girl*, 1854–6. Oil on canvas, 32 × 24½ in. City Museum and Art Gallery, Birmingham

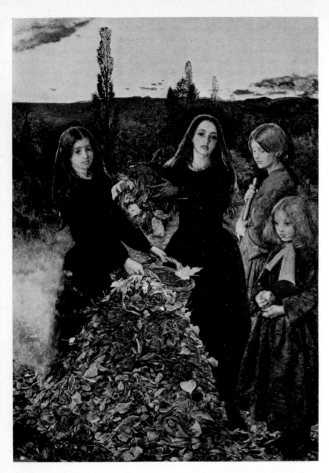

24a. John Everett Millais, *Autumn Leaves*, 1855–6. Oil on canvas, 41 × 29⅛ in. City Art Gallery, Manchester

24b. John Everett Millais, *A Dream of the Past: Sir Isumbras at the Ford*, 1856–7. Oil on canvas, 49 × 67 in. Lady Lever Art Gallery, Port Sunlight

25a. John Everett Millais, *Apple Blossoms* (*Spring*), 1856–9. Oil on canvas, $43\frac{1}{2} \times 68$ in. Collection of Viscount Leverhulme

25b. John Everett Millais, *Lingering Autumn*, 1890. Oil on canvas, 47×72 in. Lady Lever Art Gallery, Port Sunlight

26a. William Holman Hunt, *Love at First Sight*, 1848. Oil on canvas, 9 × 11¼ in. Collection of Mrs. E. M. S. C. Tompkin

26b. William Holman Hunt, *A Converted British Family Sheltering a Christian Priest from the Persecution of the Druids*, 1849–50. Oil on canvas, 43¾ × 52½ in. Ashmolean Museum, Oxford

27a. William Holman Hunt, *The Light of the World*, 1851–4.
Oil on canvas, 49⅜ × 23½ in. Keble College, Oxford

27b. William Holman Hunt, *View of the River Thames*, 1853.
Oil on panel, 5¾ × 7¾ in. Fitzwilliam Museum, Cambridge

28a (*left*). William Holman Hunt, *Strayed Sheep (Our English Coasts, 1852)*, 1852. Oil on canvas, 17 × 23 in. Tate Gallery, London

28b (*below left*). Edwin Landseer, *Peace*, exhibited 1846. Oil on canvas, 34 × 52 in. Destroyed; formerly Tate Gallery, London

29a. William Holman Hunt, *The Scapegoat*, 1854–5. Oil on canvas, 33¾ × 54½ in. Lady Lever Art Gallery, Port Sunlight

29b. Edwin Landseer, *Coming Events Cast Their Shadows Before (The Challenge)*, exhibited 1844. Oil on canvas, 38 × 82 in. Collection of the Duke of Northumberland

30a. William Holman Hunt, *Cairo: Sunset on the Gebel Mokattum*, 1854. Watercolour, 6½ × 14 in. Whitworth Art Gallery, University of Manchester

30b. William Holman Hunt, *The Dead Sea from Siloam*, 1854–5. Watercolour, 9¾ × 13¾ in. City Museum and Art Gallery, Birmingham

31a. William Holman Hunt, *Jerusalem during Ramazan*, 1854–5. Watercolour, 8¾ × 14 in. Whitworth Art Gallery, University of Manchester

31b. William Holman Hunt, *A Wadi in Palestine*, 1854. Watercolour, 13⅝ × 19½ in. Collection of Mrs. E. M. S. C. Tompkin

32a. William Holman Hunt, *The Plain of Rephaim from Mount Zion*, 1855–61. Watercolour, 14 × 20 in. Whitworth Art Gallery, University of Manchester

32b. William Holman Hunt, *Nazareth*, 1855–61. Watercolour, $13\frac{7}{8} \times 19\frac{5}{8}$ in. Whitworth Art Gallery, University of Manchester

33a. William Holman Hunt, *The Sea of Galilee*, 1855. Pencil, 14 × 19½ in. Collection of Mrs. E. M. S. C. Tompkin

33b. William Holman Hunt, *The Plain of Esdraelon from the Heights above Nazareth*, 1870–7. Oil on canvas, 16⅛ × 29½ in. Ashmolean Museum, Oxford

34a. William Holman Hunt, *Helston, Cornwall*, 1860. Watercolour, 7⅝ × 10⅛ in. Whitworth Art Gallery, University of Manchester

34b. William Holman Hunt, *Festa at Fiesole (True Merit Overlooked)*, 1868. Watercolour, 13¾ × 19⅞ in. Collection of Mrs. E. M. S. C. Tompkin

35a. William Holman Hunt, *Sunset at Chimalditi*, 1868. Watercolour, 14 × 20⅛ in. Private collection, Great Britain

35b. William Holman Hunt, *Sunset in the Val d'Arno*, 1868. Watercolour, 14 × 19¾ in. The Johannesburg Art Gallery

36a. William Holman Hunt, *The Ponte Vecchio, Florence*, between 1866 and 1869. Watercolour, 10 × 21½ in. Victoria and Albert Museum, London

36b. William Holman Hunt, *The Festival of St Swithin*, dated 1866–75. Oil on canvas, 28¾ × 35⅞ in. Ashmolean Museum, Oxford

37a. William Holman Hunt, *London Bridge on the Night of the Marriage of the Prince and Princess of Wales*, 1863. Oil on canvas, $25\frac{5}{8} \times 38\frac{5}{8}$ in. Ashmolean Museum, Oxford

37b. William Holman Hunt, *The Ship*, 1875. Oil on linen, $29\frac{1}{2} \times 38$ in. Tate Gallery, London

38a (*left*). James Collinson, *Mother and Daughter: Culver Cliff, Isle of Wight, in the Distance*, c.1855. Oil on panel, 20¾ × 16⅝ in. Collection of Mr. and Mrs. Paul Mellon

38b (*above*). Dante Gabriel Rossetti, *The Bower Meadow*, 1850–72. Oil on canvas, 33½ × 26½ in. City Art Gallery, Manchester

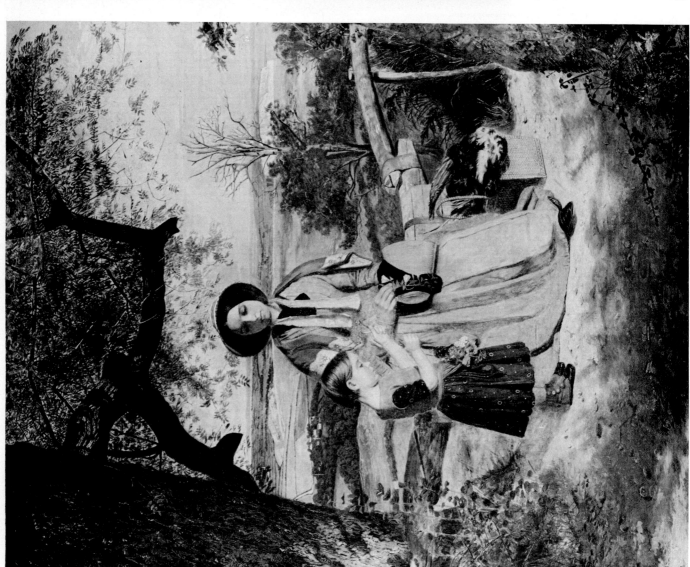

39a and b (*below*). Edward Hopley, *Puck and the Moth—two treatments*, exhibited 1853. Oil on board, each 10⅞ × 6¼ in. Collection of Lady Clark

40b. Charles Allston Collins, *The Good Harvest of 1854*, exhibited 1855. Oil on canvas, 17¼ × 13¾ in. Victoria and Albert Museum, London

40a. John Everett Millais, *A Huguenot, on St. Bartholomew's Day, Refusing to Shield Himself from Danger by Wearing the Roman Catholic Badge*, 1851–2. Oil on canvas, 36⅞ × 25⅝ in. Private collection, Great Britain

41c. Arthur Hughes, *The Long Engagement*, 1853–9. Oil on canvas, 41½ × 20½ in. City Museum and Art Gallery, Birmingham

41b (*left*). Arthur Hughes, *Ophelia*, exhibited 1852. Oil on canvas, 27 × 48¾ in. City Art Gallery, Manchester

41a. Arthur Hughes, *The Young Poet*, c.1849. Oil on canvas, 25 × 36 in. City Museum and Art Gallery, Birmingham

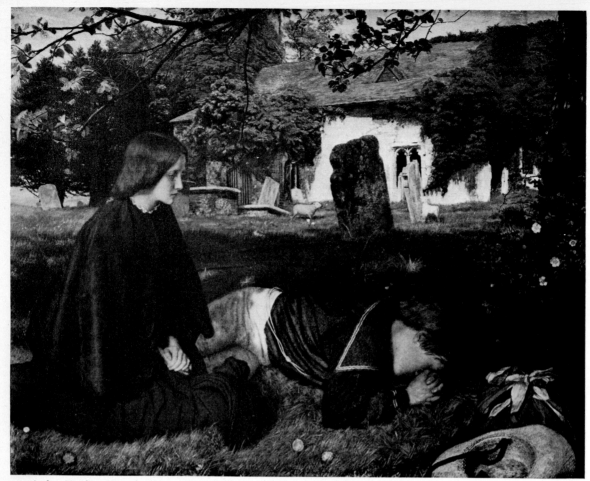

42a. Arthur Hughes, *Home from Sea*, 1856–63. Oil on panel, 20 × 25¾ in. Ashmolean Museum, Oxford

42b. Arthur Hughes, *The Knight of the Sun*, 1860. Oil on canvas, 40 × 52 3⁄16 in. Collection of the Hon. Neil Hogg

43a. Henry Wallis, *The Stonebreaker*, exhibited 1858. Oil on panel, 25¾ × 31 in. City Museum and Art Gallery, Birmingham

43b. William Shakespeare Burton, *The Cavalier and the Puritan*, exhibited 1856. Oil on canvas, 35 × 41 in. Guildhall Art Gallery, London

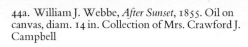

44a. William J. Webbe, *After Sunset*, 1855. Oil on canvas, diam. 14 in. Collection of Mrs. Crawford J. Campbell

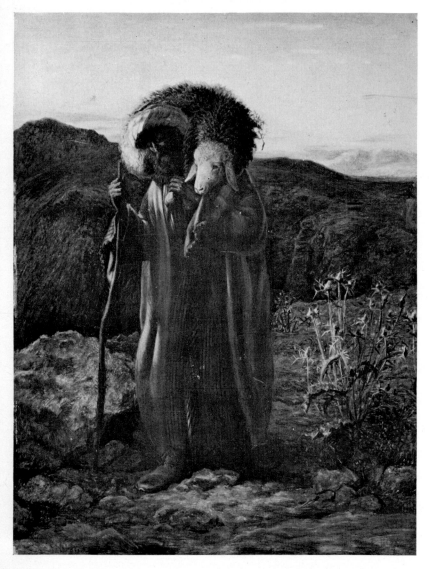

44b. William J. Webbe, *The Lost Sheep*, 1864. Oil on panel, 13 × 10 in. City Art Gallery, Manchester

45. Joseph Noel Paton, *The Bluidie Tryste*, 1855. Oil on canvas, $28\frac{3}{4} \times 25\frac{5}{8}$ in. Museum and Art Gallery, Glasgow

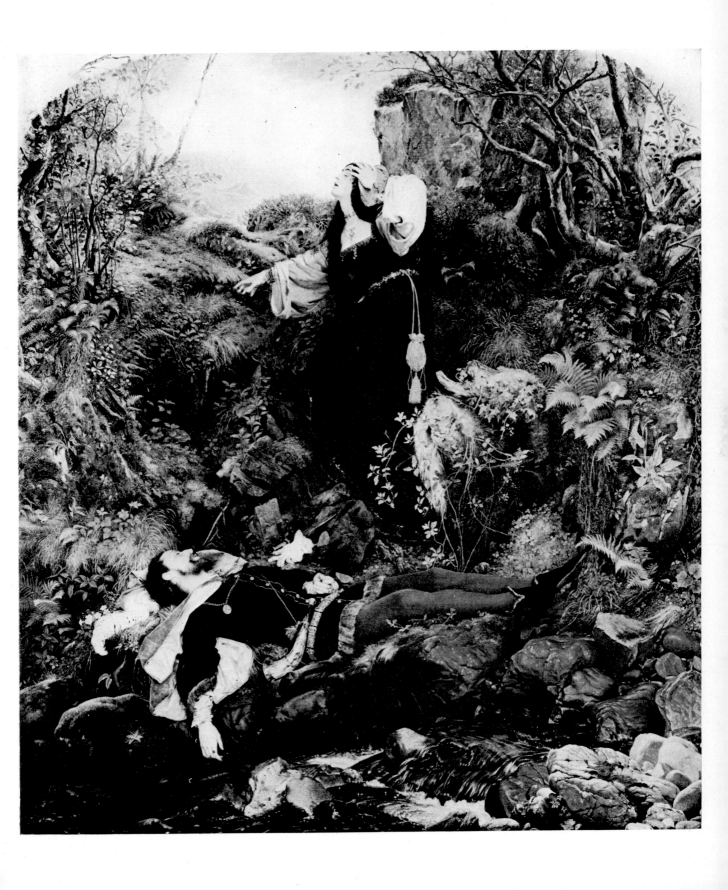

45. Joseph Noel Paton, *The Bluidie Tryste*, 1855. Oil on canvas, $28\frac{3}{4} \times 25\frac{5}{8}$ in. Museum and Art Gallery, Glasgow

46a. William Bell Scott, *Newcastle Quayside in 1861*, 1861. Oil on canvas, 74 × 74 in. The National Trust, Wallington Hall

46b. William Bell Scott, *Albrecht Dürer of Nuremburg*, 1854. Oil on canvas, $23\frac{1}{8} \times 28\frac{1}{4}$ in. National Gallery of Scotland, Edinburgh

47a. William Bell Scott, *The Gloaming: Manse Garden in Berwickshire*, 1863. Oil on canvas, 15½ × 24 in. Philadelphia Museum of Art

47b. William Bell Scott, *Ascending St. Gothard from Altdorf*, c.1862. Watercolour, 7 × 5 in. National Gallery of Scotland, Edinburgh

48a. (*above left*). Frederick Sandys, *Wild Arum and Grass*, c.1861–2. Pencil, $7\frac{5}{16} \times 6\frac{1}{8}$ in. City Museum and Art Gallery, Birmingham

48b (*above*). Frederick Sandys, *Study of Ivy*, c.1861–2. Watercolour, $6\frac{3}{4} \times 3\frac{3}{8}$ in. City Museum and Art Gallery, Birmingham

48c. Frederick Sandys, *The Old Chartist*, 1862. Wood engraving by Joseph Swain, $4\frac{3}{16} \times 5$ in. Published in *Once a Week*, VI, 1862

49a. Frederick Sandys, *The Reverend James Bulwer*, 1863. Oil on panel, 29¾ × 21¾ in. National Gallery of Canada, Ottawa

49b (*below*). Edward Burne-Jones, *The Briar Wood*, 1870–90. Oil on canvas, 49 × 98¼ in. The National Trust, Buscot Park

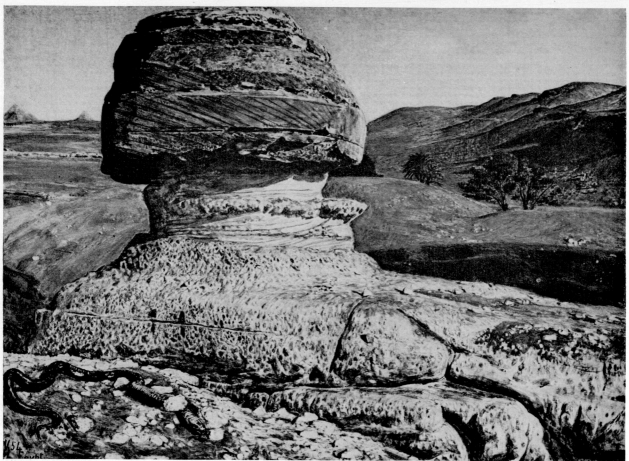

50a. William Holman Hunt, *The Sphinx, Giza, Looking towards the Pyramids of Saqqara*, 1854. Watercolour, 10 × 14 in. Harris Museum and Art Gallery, Preston

50b. Thomas Seddon, *The Great Sphinx at the Pyramids of Giza*, 1854. Watercolour, 9¾ × 13¾ in. Ashmolean Museum, Oxford

51a. Thomas Seddon, *Léhon, from Mont Parnasse, Brittany*, 1853. Oil on canvas, 23 × 30 in. Museo de Arte de Ponce, Puerto Rico

51b. Thomas Seddon, *Jerusalem and the Valley of Jehoshaphat from the Hill of Evil Counsel*, 1854–5. Oil on canvas, 26½ × 32¾ in. Tate Gallery, London

52a. Thomas Seddon, *The Well of Enrogel*, 1854. Watercolour, 9¾ × 13¾ in. Harris Museum and Art Gallery, Preston

52b. Thomas Seddon, *The Mountains of Moab*, 1854. Watercolour, 9¹⁵⁄₁₆ × 13⅞ in. Ashmolean Museum, Oxford

53a. Thomas Seddon, *Arabs at Prayer in the Desert*, begun 1855. Oil on canvas, 25⅜ × 44⅛ in. Private collection, U.S.A.

53b. Thomas Seddon, *View on the Nile*, dated 1855. Oil on canvas, 8 × 12 in. Ashmolean Museum, Oxford

54a. George Price Boyce, *Near the Public Gardens, Venice*, 1854.
Watercolour, 7⅜ × 10⅝ in. Collection of Mrs. John Gere

54b. George Price Boyce, *Tomb of Cangrande della Scala, S. Maria
Antica, Verona*, 1854. Watercolour, 15 × 11 in. J. S. Maas & Co. Ltd.,
London

55a. George Price Boyce, *The Mill on the Thames at Mapledurham*, 1860. Watercolour, 10½ × 22 in. Fitzwilliam Museum, Cambridge

55b. George Price Boyce, *At Binsey, near Oxford*, 1862. Watercolour, 12½ × 21⅛ in. Cecil Higgins Art Gallery, Bedford

56a. George Price Boyce, *Red Barn at Whitchurch*, 1863. Watercolour, 8 1/16 × 11 5/16 in. Ashmolean Museum, Oxford

56b. George Price Boyce, *Landscape: Wootton, Autumn*, 1864–5. Watercolour, 9 3/4 × 13 3/4 in. Tate Gallery, London

57a. George Price Boyce, *The Thames by Night from the Adelphi*, exhibited 1866. Watercolour, $8\frac{3}{4} \times 13\frac{1}{8}$ in. Tate Gallery, London

57b. George Price Boyce, *From a Window at Ludlow*, 1871. Watercolour, $5\frac{1}{2} \times 7\frac{7}{8}$ in. National Gallery of Scotland, Edinburgh

58a. John William Inchbold, *Flamborough Head*, 1849. Watercolour, 9½ × 12¼ in. Collection of M. Hailparn

58b. John William Inchbold, *Thames, Early Morning*, *c.*1849. Watercolour, 10 × 14 in. Collection of Mr. and Mrs. Paul Mellon

59a. John William Inchbold, *The Chapel, Bolton*, 1853. Oil on canvas, 25½ × 33 in. Northampton Art Gallery

59b. John William Inchbold, *The Moorland (Dewar-Stone, Dartmoor)*, 1854. Oil on canvas, 13¾ × 20½ in. Tate Gallery, London

60a (*left*). John William Inchbold, *At Bolton* (*The White Doe of Rylstone*), 1855. Oil on canvas, 27 × 20 in. City Art Gallery, Leeds

60b (*above*). John William Inchbold, *A Study in March* (*In Early Spring*), exhibited 1855? Oil on canvas, 20 × 13½ in. Ashmolean Museum, Oxford

61 (*below*). John William Inchbold, *Anstey's Cove, Devon*, 1853–4. Oil on canvas, 19⅞ × 26 13/16 in. Fitzwilliam Museum, Cambridge

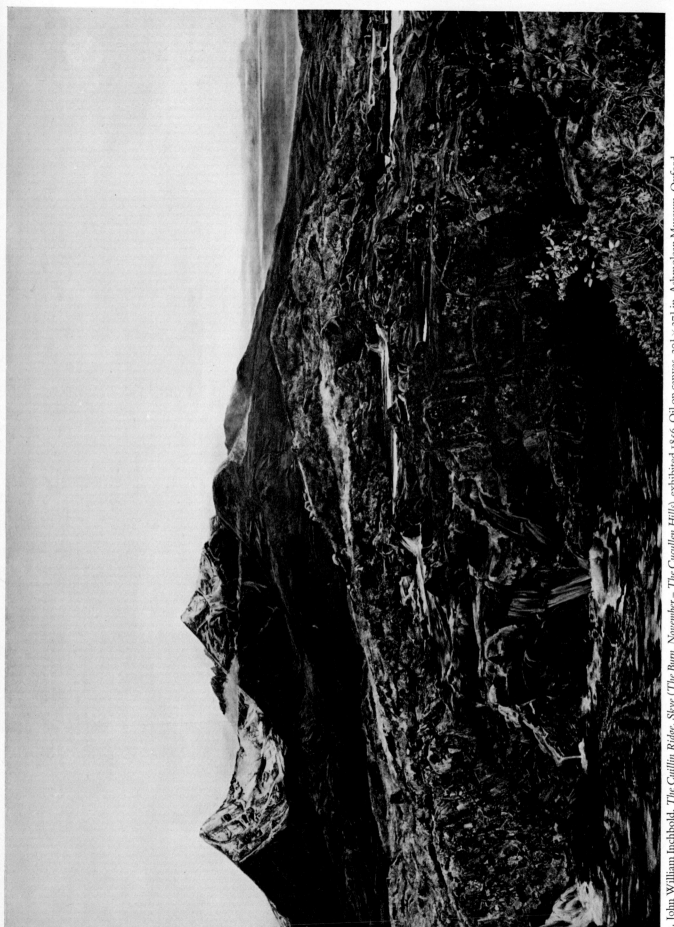

62. John William Inchbold, *The Cuillin Ridge, Skye (The Burn, November – The Cucullen Hills)*, exhibited 1856. Oil on canvas, 20⅝ × 27⅞ in. Ashmolean Museum, Oxford

63. John William Inchbold, *The Lake of Lucerne, Mont Pilatus in the Distance*, 1857. Oil on board, 14¼ × 18½ in. Victoria and Albert Museum, London

64a. John William Inchbold, *Vesuvius and the Bay of Naples, from Posillipo*, 1857. Watercolour, 9½ × 13½ in. Victoria and Albert Museum, London

64b. John William Inchbold, *The Certosa, Venice, from the Public Gardens*, 1860s. Oil on canvas, 15 × 28 in. City Art Gallery, Leeds

65a. John William Inchbold, *Venice from the Public Gardens*, 1860s. Oil on canvas, 13½ × 20½ in. Private collection, Great Britain

65b. John William Inchbold, *Cordelia, Valencia*, 1865. Oil on canvas, 12 × 18 in. Collection of Mr. and Mrs. Allen Staley

66a (*above left*). John William Inchbold, *Recollection – Barden Fells, 1866*. Oil on paper, $9\frac{3}{4} \times 6\frac{3}{4}$ in. Collection of Mr. D. L.T. Oppé

66b (*above*). John William Inchbold, *Peat Burning*, c.1866. Oil on paper, $6\frac{3}{4} \times 9\frac{3}{4}$ in. Collection of Mr. D. L. T. Oppé

66c (*left*). John William Inchbold, *Recollection – Strid, Barden Tower, 1866*. Oil on paper, $9\frac{3}{4} \times 6\frac{3}{4}$ in. Collection of Mr. D. L. T. Oppé

66d (*below*). John William Inchbold, *Stonehenge from the East*, exhibited 1869. Oil on canvas, $33\frac{1}{2} \times 71\frac{1}{2}$ in. Society of Antiquaries, London

67a. John William Inchbold, *The Under-cliffe – Spring Time*, 1869–70. Oil on panel, 22½ × 33½ in. Collection of David Daniels

67b. John William Inchbold, *View above Montreux*, 1880. Watercolour, 12⅛ × 19¹³⁄₁₆ in. Victoria and Albert Museum, London

68a. John Brett, *Glacier of Rosenlaui*, 1856. Oil on canvas, $17\frac{1}{2} \times 16\frac{1}{2}$ in. Tate Gallery, London

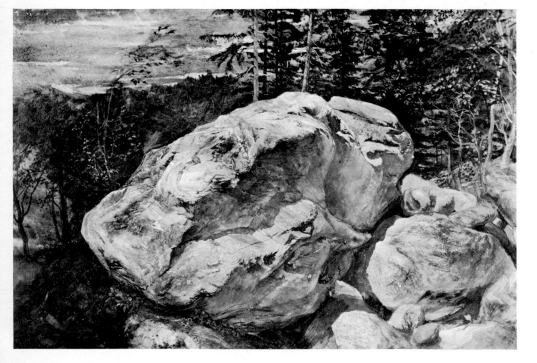

68b. John Ruskin, *Study of a Block of Gneiss, Valley of Chamouni, Switzerland*, 1856. Watercolour, $12 \times 18\frac{1}{4}$ in. Fogg Art Museum, Harvard University, Cambridge, Mass.

69a. John Brett, *Landscape*, 1852. Oil on board, 7 × 10 in. Fitzwilliam Museum, Cambridge

69b. John Brett, *The Stonebreaker*, 1857–8. Oil on canvas, 19½ × 26½ in. Walker Art Gallery, Liverpool

70. John Brett, *Val d'Aosta*, 1858. Oil on canvas, $34\frac{1}{2} \times 26\frac{7}{8}$ in. Collection of Sir Francis Cooper, Bt.

71a. John Brett, *Florence from Bellosguardo*, 1862–3. Oil on canvas, 23½ × 39½ in. Tate Gallery, London

71b. John Brett, *Massa, Bay of Naples*, 1864. Oil on canvas, 25¾ × 40¾ in. Herron Museum of Art, Indianapolis

72a. John Brett, *Morants Court in May*, 1864. Oil on canvas, 17½ × 27½ in. Collection of Mr. and Mrs. Allen Staley

72b. John Brett, study for *The Hedger*, c.1860. Monochrome wash and bodycolour, 9¾ × 7⅛ in. Private collection, Great Britain

72c John Brett, *Near Goring-on-Thames*, 1865. Watercolour, 12 × 16 in. Whitworth Art Gallery, University of Manchester

73a. John Brett, *Etna from the Heights of Taormina*, 1870–1. Oil on canvas, 33 × 48½ in. Mappin Art Gallery, Sheffield

73b. John Brett, *The British Channel Seen from the Dorsetshire Cliffs*, 1871. Oil on canvas, 41¾ × 83¾ in. Tate Gallery, London

74a. Robert Tonge, *Cheshire Landscape*, 1853. Oil on canvas, 20 × 34⅜ in. Walker Art Gallery, Liverpool

74b. William Davis, *Bidston Marsh at Wallasey*, 1853. Oil on board, 11⅞ × 17⅞ in. Walker Art Gallery, Liverpool

75 (*right*). William Davis, *Old Mill and Pool at Ditton, Lancashire*. Oil on canvas, 20⅞ × 14½ in. Walker Art Gallery, Liverpool

76a. William Davis, *At Hale, Lancashire*. Oil on canvas, 13 × 19¾ in. Walker Art Gallery, Liverpool

76b. William Davis, *A Field of Green Corn*. Oil on panel, 12 × 15 in. Collection of John Gillum

77a. William Davis, *A Grass Field*. Oil on canvas, 9 × 13 in. Collection of John Gillum

77b. William Davis, *Harrowing*, c.1859. Oil on canvas, 17¼ × 26 in. Private collection, Great Britain

78a. Alfred William Hunt, *Gwm Trifaen – The Track of an Ancient Glacier*, c.1858. Oil on canvas, $23\frac{3}{4} \times 35\frac{3}{4}$ in. Tate Gallery, London

78b. Alfred William Hunt, *Welsh Landscape*, 1858. Watercolour, $9\frac{7}{8} \times 14\frac{1}{4}$ in. Ashmolean Museum, Oxford

79a. Alfred William Hunt, *Brignal Banks*, c.1859. Oil on canvas, $11\frac{1}{4} \times 18\frac{1}{8}$ in. Walker Art Gallery, Liverpool

79b. Alfred William Hunt, *A November Rainbow – Dolwyddelan Valley*, 1865. Watercolour, $19\frac{1}{2} \times 29\frac{3}{4}$ in. Ashmolean Museum, Oxford

80a. John Edward Newton, *Gresford Mill*, c.1861.
Oil on canvas, $12 \times 14\frac{1}{2}$ in. Walker Art Gallery,
Liverpool

80b. Daniel Alexander Williamson, *Peckham
Common – Milking Time*, c.1855–60. Watercolour,
$11\frac{1}{2} \times 15\frac{1}{8}$ in. Walker Art Gallery, Liverpool

81a. Daniel Alexander Williamson, *Morecambe Bay from Warton Crag*, 1862. Oil on board, 9 $\frac{15}{16}$ × 13 $\frac{1}{4}$ in. Walker Art Gallery, Liverpool

81b. Daniel Alexander Williamson, *Spring: Arnside Knot and Coniston Range of Hills from Warton Crag*, 1863. Oil on canvas, 10 $\frac{5}{8}$ × 16 in. Walker Art Gallery, Liverpool

82a. Daniel Alexander Williamson, *Near the Duddon*, 1864. Oil on board, 8½ × 14 in. Williamson Art Gallery, Birkenhead

82b. William Lindsay Windus, *The Stray Lamb*, 1864. Oil on board, 8¾ × 12½ in. Walker Art Gallery, Liverpool

83a. William Millais, *Hayes Common*, 1852–3. Oil on canvas, $21\frac{1}{2} \times 33\frac{1}{2}$ in. Collection of Mr. and Mrs. Paul Mellon

83b. William Millais, *Glenfinlas*, 1853. Oil on canvas, $17\frac{1}{2} \times 25\frac{1}{2}$ in. Collection of Lord Sherfield

84a. Edward Lear, *The Quarries of Syracuse*, 1847. Pen and watercolour, 13⅞ × 19⅞ in. Walker Art Gallery, Liverpool
84b. Edward Lear, *Venosa*, 1852. Oil on canvas, 19¾ × 32⅜ in. Toledo Museum of Art, Toledo, Ohio

85a. James Smetham, *Naboth's Vineyard*, 1856. Oil on panel, 8¾ × 6¾ in. Tate Gallery, London

85b. James Smetham, *Going Home*, c.1877. Watercolour, 14½ × 20½ in. Walker Art Gallery, Liverpool

86a. John Bunney, *Landscape from Fiesole*, 1867. Watercolour, 19¼ × 29½ in. Collection of Mrs. E. M. S. C. Tompkin

86b. John Bunney, *The West Front of St. Mark's*, 1876–82. Oil on canvas, 57 × 89 in. Collection of the Guild of St. George, University of Reading

87a. Frank Randal, *Piazza delle Erbe Looking South*, 1884. Watercolour, $13\frac{7}{8} \times 9\frac{3}{4}$ in. Ashmolean Museum, Oxford

87b. Frank Randal, *Verona from the Garden of the Palazzo Giusti*, 1884. Watercolour, $8\frac{1}{2} \times 5\frac{1}{4}$ in. Collection of the Guild of St. George, University of Reading

87c. Thomas Matthews Rooke, *Laon: View of the Town and Cathedral from the Northeast*, 1886. Watercolour, $9 \times 11\frac{3}{4}$ in. Collection of the Guild of St. George, University of Reading

88a. Thomas Matthews Rooke, *Old Chalet at Sierre*, 1884. Watercolour, $13\frac{1}{4} \times 9\frac{5}{8}$ in. Collection of the Guild of St. George, University of Reading

88b. Albert Goodwin, *St. Anthony's Works, Newcastle upon Tyne*, 1864. Watercolour, $9\frac{1}{2} \times 13\frac{3}{4}$ in. Private collection, Great Britain

89a. Charles Napier Hemy, *Among the Shingle at Clovelly*, 1864. Oil on canvas, 17¼ × 28¼ in. Collection of Mrs. Charlotte Frank

89b. Atkinson Grimshaw, *The Old Mill: Audby*, 1869. Oil on panel, 24½ × 34½ in. City Art Gallery, Leeds

90a. William Dyce, *Fisherfolk near a Wreck*, 1830. Oil on canvas, 36 × 46 in. Collection of Henry J. Hurst

90b. William Dyce, *The Rhône at Avignon*, 1832. Watercolour, 7¼ × 12 in. British Museum, London

91a. William Dyce, *The Flight into Egypt*. Oil on board, $11\frac{1}{4} \times 15\frac{1}{2}$ in. Private collection, Great Britain

91b. William Dyce, *George Herbert at Bemerton*, exhibited 1861. Oil on canvas, 34×44 in. Guildhall Art Gallery, London

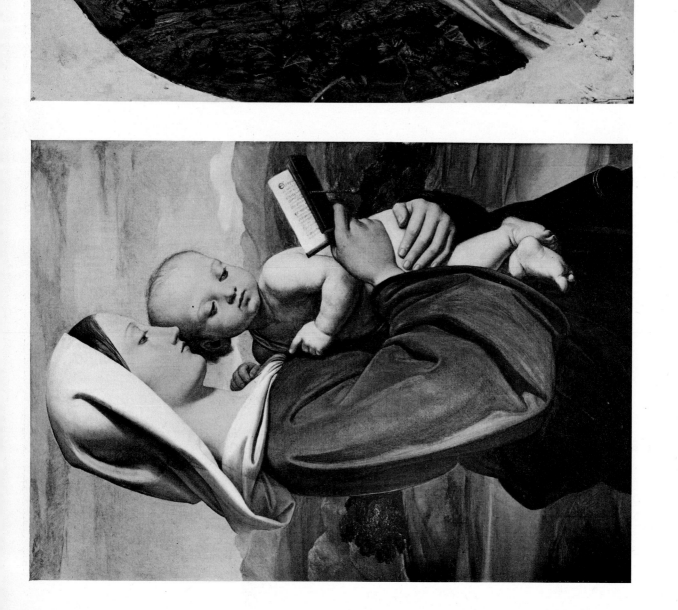

92b. William Dyce, *Christabel*, exhibited 1855. Oil on panel, 21¼ × 17⅞ in. Museum and Art Gallery, Glasgow

92a. William Dyce, *Madonna and Child*, 1845. Oil on canvas, 31½ × 25 in. Collection of Her Majesty Queen Elizabeth II

93b. William Dyce, *Titian Preparing to Make His First Essay in Colouring*, exhibited 1857. Oil on canvas, 36 × 26½ in. Art Gallery and Regional Museum, Aberdeen

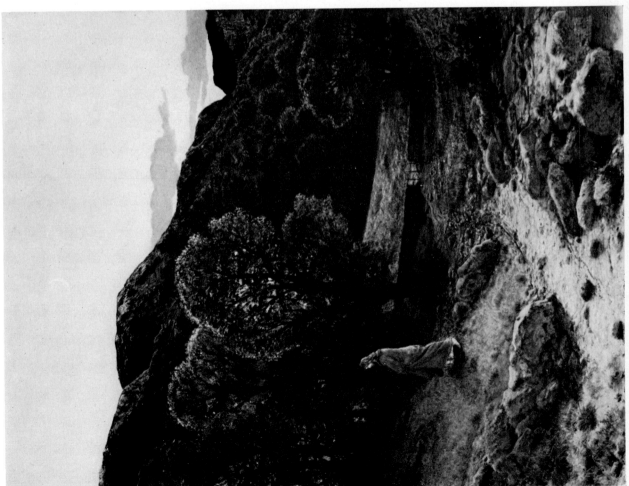

93a. William Dyce, *Gethsemane*. Oil on board, 16½ × 12⅞ in. Walker Art Gallery, Liverpool

94a. William Dyce, *David in the Wilderness*, c.1859. Oil on board, 13⅞ × 19 15/16 in. Private collection, Great Britain

94b. William Dyce, *The Man of Sorrows*, c.1859. Oil on board, 13⅞ × 19 15/16 in. Private collection, Great Britain

95a William Dyce, *A Scene in Arran*, 1859. Oil on board, 13¾ × 19¾ in. Art Gallery and Regional Museum, Aberdeen

95b. William Dyce, *Welsh Landscape with Figures*, 1860. Oil on board, 13⅞ × 19⅞ in. Collection of Sir David Scott

96a. William Dyce, *Pegwell Bay, Kent – a Recollection of October 5th, 1858*, exhibited 1860. Oil on canvas, 24½ × 34½ in. Tate Gallery, London

96b. William Dyce, *Pegwell Bay*, *c*.1858. Watercolour, 9¾ × 13¾ in. Private collection, Great Britain

97a. William Mulready, *The Mall, Kensington Gravel Pits*, c.1811. Oil on canvas, 14 × 19¼ in. Victoria and Albert Museum, London

97b. William Mulready, *Blackheath Park*, exhibited 1852. Oil on panel, 13½ × 24 in. Victoria and Albert Museum, London

98a. Myles Birket Foster, *The Milk-maid*, 1860. Watercolour, 11¾ × 17½ in. Victoria and Albert Museum, London

98b. Mark Anthony, *Thinking of the Future: an Irish Sketch*, exhibited 1845. Oil on canvas, 21 × 32½ in. Location unknown

99a. George Hemming Mason, *The Gander*, exhibited 1865. Oil on canvas, 18 × 32 in. Lady Lever Art Gallery, Port Sunlight

99b. Frederick Walker, *The Plough*, 1869–70. Oil on canvas, 56½ × 83¾ in. Tate Gallery, London

100a. Albert Moore, *Study of an Ash Trunk*, 1857. Watercolour, 12 × 9 in. Ashmolean Museum, Oxford

100b. Frederic Leighton, *The Lemon Tree*, 1859. Pencil, 21 × 15½ in. Collection of E. W. Huddart